CANINE LIBRARY

PEDIGREE DOGS IN COLOUR

Official Standards and Colour Illustrations

OTHER TITLES AVAILABLE OR IN PREPARATION

20th Century Bulldog — by Marjorie Barnard
The Kennelgarth Scottish Terrier Book — by Betty Penn-Bull
The Bulldog — A Monograph by Edgar Farman
Keeshond of the World — by Margo Emerson
Staffordshire Bull Terrier in History and Sport — by Mike Homan
The Bullmastiff — by Clifford L.B. Hubbard
The Butterfly Dog — by Clarice Waud and Pat Chalice (limp)
The German Shepherd Dog — by Joyce Ixer
The Dalmation — by Clifford L.B. Hubbard
Toy Dogs — A Comprehensive Guide to Toy Dogs (HB) C. Waud and Mark Hutchings
Concise Guide to Dog Showing — by Paddy Petch (limp)
The Dog Book — by Betty Penn-Bull (limp)
Small Dog Obedience Training — by Mrs. R.A. Foreman (limp)
Bird Dogs of the World — Stanley W.C. Smith

PEDIGREE DOGS IN COLOUR

Roy Hodrien

Official Standards

Colour Illustrations by the Author

NIMROD PRESS LTD

Dedicated to the memory of
Nan and Charlie

First Published in 1990

Pedigree Dogs in Colour	ISBN 1 85259 094 7
Book One – Hounds	ISBN 1 85259 205 2
Book Two – Gundogs	ISBN 1 85259 206 0
Book Three – Terriers	ISBN 1 85259 207 9
Book Four – Utility Group	ISBN 1 85259 208 7
Book Five – Working Group	ISBN 1 85259 209 5
Book Six – Toy Group	ISBN 1 85259 210 9

NIMROD PRESS LTD
15 The Maltings
Turk Street
Alton, Hants, GU34 1DL

Produced by Jamesway Graphics
Middleton, Manchester

Printed in England

CONTENTS

BOOK THREE – **TERRIERS**

BOOK FOUR – **UTILITY GROUP**

BOOK FIVE – **WORKING GROUP**

BOOK SIX – **TOY GROUP**

ACKNOWLEDGEMENTS

My thanks are offered to all those who assisted with this book. In particular I acknowledge the role of the British Kennel Club who gave permission for the *Official Standards* to be reproduced. The American Club also kindly allowed me to quote from their *Standards* showing the main variations from the British Standards.

ROY HODRIEN

PEDIGREE DOGS IN COLOUR

BOOK ONE

HOUNDS

This is Book One in a volume consisting of six books each dealing with a main group of dogs. The page numbering follows that used in the main volume.

Afghan Hound

Basenji

AFGHAN HOUND

It is not difficult to see why this breed has so many devotees. An Afghan in full show condition is often breathtaking.

The history of the breed is fogged in conflicting reports and ideas, which perhaps contributes to it's obvious romance. The Afghan people are still to this day largely a tribal, nomadic race which makes documentation of their activities, dog breeding included, very difficult.

It was towards the end of the 19th century that the Afghan Hound had his beginnings in Britain. Two types of dog were imported from Afghanistan, one being of Saluki type, rangy, with a short silky coat, and a stockier dog with a thick woolly coat. The former was the dog of the plains and the latter was of the mountain regions. Today's Afghan is perhaps closer to the mountain variety although these early specimens bore little resemblance to the present ones.

He is a dog of great speed and agility and, although, not quite as quick as the likes of the Greyhound, there are still some Afghan Hound races to be found.

Their aloof, arrogant air can make these dogs quite difficult to train, much strong willed application being required. The coat, of course, requires an immense amount of attention.

KEY TO CHARACTER	
INTELLIGENCE	***
TEMPERAMENT	***
EASE OF COAT CARE	*
SUITABILITY FOR SMALL DWELLING	*
***** (5) = VERY GOOD	

BRITISH KENNEL CLUB STANDARD

AFGHAN HOUND

CHARACTERISTICS. — The Afghan Hound should be dignified and aloof with a certain keen fierceness. The Eastern or Oriental expression is typical of the breed. The Afghan looks at and through one.

GENERAL APPEARANCE. — The gait of the Afghan Hound should be smooth and springy with a style of high order. The whole appearance of the dog should give the impression of strength and dignity combining speed and power. The head must be held proudly.

Head and Skull. — Skull long, not too narrow with prominent occiput. Foreface long with punishing jaws and slight stop. The skull well balanced and surmounted by a long "top-knot". Nose preferably black but liver is no fault in light coloured dogs.

Eyes. — Should be dark for preference but golden colour is not debarred. Nearly triangular, slanting slightly upwards from the inner corner to the outer.

Ears. — Set low and well back, carried close to the head. Covered with long silky hair.

Mouth. — Level.

Neck. — Long, strong with proud carriage of the head.

Forequarters. — Shoulders long and sloping, well set back, well muscled and strong without being loaded. Forelegs straight and well boned, straight with shoulder, elbows held in.

Body. — Back level, moderate length, well muscled, the back falling slightly away to the stern. Loin straight, broad and rather short. Hip-bones rather prominent and wide apart. A fair spring of ribs and good depth of chest.

Hindquarters. — Powerful, well bent and well turned stifles. Great length between hip and hock with a comparatively short distance between hock and foot. The dew claws may be removed or remain at the discretion of the breeder.

Feet. — Forefeet strong and very large both in length and breadth and covered with long thick hair, toes arched. Pasterns long and springy, especially in front and pads well down on the ground. Hindfeet long, but not quite so broad as forefeet, covered with long thick hair.

Tail. — Not too short. Set on low with ring at the end. Raised when in action. Sparsely feathered.

Coat.— Long and very fine texture on ribs, fore and hind-quarters and flanks. From the shoulder backwards and along the saddle the hair should be short and close in mature dogs. Hair long from the forehead backward, with a distinct silky "top-knot". On the foreface the hair is short as on the back. Ears and legs well coated. Pasterns can be bare. Coat must be allowed to develop naturally.

Colour. — All colours are acceptable.

Weight and Size. — Ideal height: Dogs 68-74cm (27″-29″). Bitches 5-8cm (2″-3″) smaller.

Faults. — Any appearance of courseness. Skull too wide and foreface too short. Weak underjaw. Large round or full eyes. Neck should never be too short or thick. Back too long or too short.

Note. — Male animals should have two apparently normal testicles fully descended into the scrotum.

MAIN AMERICAN KENNEL CLUB VARIATION TO STANDARD FOR THE AFGHAN HOUND —

Height. — Dogs, 27 inches, plus or minus one inch; bitches, 25 inches, plus or minus one inch.

Weight. — Dogs, about 60 pounds; bitches about 50 pounds.

AFGHAN HOUND REGISTRATIONS 1981 — 87 INCLUSIVE

1981 — 1187
1982 — 933
1983 — 763
1984 — 911
1985 — 643
1986 — 665
1987 — 645

CRUFTS BEST-IN-SHOW WINNER — 1983 — CH. MONTRAVIA KASKARAK HITARI MRS. P. GIBBS.

BASENJI

This interesting breed was depicted in a similar form in Egyptian tomb paintings dating back to 3600 B.C. Little was known of the progress of these dogs until explorers rediscovered specimens in the Congo and Sudan around 1860. The Africans who kept them valued their hunting ability very highly, using them in packs to flush game into strategically placed nets. Although of only moderate size, the Basenji had the necessary courage and tenacity for this work and some believe he has passed on these traits as a progenitor of modern terriers.

The Basenji is famous as the dog who never barks, instead he emits his own unique sound which is accurately described in the breed standard as a type of yodel. This fascinating characteristic and the extreme cleanliness of the Basenji have helped contribute to a fair size following for the breed in Britain. He is known to be an excellent dog for showing, having a sensible temperament and attractive sleek coat.

In the home he behaves well and his comparitive silence and lack of odour will appeal to many people. He mixes well with children and despite his apparently semi-wild past, he is in fact a thoroughly domesticated dog.

With the Basenji's active history, exercise must be liberal and this will prove to be enjoyable for dog and owner alike, as the Basenji makes a lively companion.

KEY TO CHARACTER	
INTELLIGENCE	***
TEMPERAMENT	****
EASE OF COAT CARE	*****
SUITABILITY FOR SMALL DWELLING	****
***** (5) = VERY GOOD	

BRITISH KENNEL CLUB STANDARD

BASENJI

CHARACTERISTICS. — The Basenji does not bark but is not mute, its own special noise is a mixture of a chortle and a yodel. It is remarkable for its cleanliness in every way. The wrinkled forehead, tightly curled tail, and legs carried straight foreward with a swift, long, tireless, swinging stride, are typical of the breed.

GENERAL APPEARANCE. — The Basenji should be a lightly built, finely boned aristocratic looking animal, high on the leg compared with its length, always poised, alert and intelligent. The wrinkled head, with pricked ears, should be proudly carried on a well-arched neck. The deep brisket should run up into a definite waist and the tail be tightly curled, presenting a picture of a well-balanced dog of gazelle-like grace.

Head and Skull. — The skull should be flat, well-chiselled and of medium width, tapering towards the nose, with only a slight stop. The distance from the top of the head to the stop is slightly more than from the stop to the tip of the nose. The side lines of the skull taper gradually towards the mouth, giving a clean-cheeked appearance. Fine and profuse wrinkles should appear on the forehead when the ears are pricked, side wrinkles are desirable but should not be exaggerated into dewlap. Wrinkles are more noticeable in puppies, but, because of lack of shadowing, are not as noticeable in tri-colours. A black nose is greatly desired.

Eyes. — Dark, almond shaped, obliquely set, far-seeing and rather inscrutable in expression.

Ears. — Small, pointed, erect and slightly hooded, of fine texture, set well forward on top of the head, the tip of the ear should be nearer the centre of the skull than the outside base.

Mouth. — The mouth should be level, with scissors bite, the upper teeth slightly overlapping and touching the lower teeth.

Neck. — Strong and of good length, without thickness, well-crested and slightly full at the base of the throat with a graceful curve accentuating the crest. It should be well-set into laid back shoulders so as to give the head a "lofty" carriage.

Forequarters. — The shoulders must be well laid back, muscular but not loaded. The points of the scapulae should be fairly close at the withers. The elbows should be firmly tucked in against the brisket. When viewed form in front the elbows should be in line with the ribs and the legs should continue in a straight line to the ground giving a narrow front. The forelegs should be straight with fine bone and very long fore-arms. Pasterns should be of good length, straight but flexible.

Body. — Balanced with short, level back. Ribs well sprung, deep and oval. The join short-coupled and the deep brisket running up into a definite waist.

Hindquarters. — Strong and muscular, with hocks well let down, turned neither in nor out, with long second thighs and moderately bent stifles.

Feet. — Small, narrow and compact, with deep pads, well-arched toes and short nails.

Tail. — The tail should be high set with the posterior curve of the buttock extending beyond the root of the tail giving a reachy appearance to the hindquarters. The tail curls tightly over the spine and lies closely to the thigh with a single or double curl.

Coat. — Short, sleek and close, very fine. Skin very pliant.

Colour. — Pure bright red, or pure black, or black and tan, all with white feet, chest and tail tips. White legs, white blaze and white collar optional.

Size and Weight. — Ideal heights. Dogs 43cm (17″) at shoulder; Bitches 40cm (16″); a few cm (an inch) either way should not penalize an otherwise well-balanced specimen. Ideal weights: Dogs 11Kg (24lbs), Bitches 9½Kg (21lbs).

Faults. — Coarse, domed or peaked skull. Muzzle too long or too broad. Cheekiness. Mouth over-shot or under-shot. Round or light eyes. Ears too low-set or too large. Wide chest, barrel ribs, shelly brisket. Short in the leg, out at elbows, toeing in. Heavy bone, cow hocks, low-set or straight tail, thin flat open feet. Long or heavy coat. Creams, sables, or any other colours than those defined in the Colour paragraph above should be heavily penalised. Poor temperament.

Note. — Male animals should have two apparently normal testicles fully descended into the scrotum.

BASENJI REGISTRATIONS 1981 — 87 INCLUSIVE

1981 — 67
1981 — 83
1983 — 132
1984 — 91
1985 — 66
1986 — 93
1987 — 121

YET TO WIN CRUFTS BEST-IN-SHOW.

BASSET HOUND

The Basset Hound is one of the most instantly recognisable breeds in Britain. It's unique form and various advertising appearances have ensured a growing popularity in recent years.

He is a direct descendant of the St. Hubert Hound of France. This truly ancient breed was developed in the Ardennes region by the man who lent his name to it, Hubert, who was an abbot. Although a man of the cloth, he had a great passion for hunting, and wanted a hound who was capable of following a scent in the dense undergrowth of the area. This was a difficult task for long-legged hounds who had to stoop continuously. So the short-legged Basset type dog was developed the words "Bas set" meaning low set in French. These hounds eventually spread throughout France and various forms of the breed began to appear, but all were of the shorter-legged variety. Several of these dogs were imported by the English, and after careful cross-breeding, the Basset Hound was registered in 1883.

Although he is the slowest of the hounds, in the field he is one of the most thorough and consistent workers. He is fundamentally a gentle, easy going character, rarely attacking game when he has located it.

In the home he fits well into any family environment, being faithful and affectionate. Despite his apparently sluggish disposition, he does require a fair amount of exercise to avoid laziness and obesity.

Bassett Hound

Beagle

Bloodhound

Borzoi

KEY TO CHARACTER	
INTELLIGENCE	***
TEMPERAMENT	*****
EASE OF COAT CARE	*****
SUITABILITY FOR SMALL DWELLING	**
***** (5) = VERY GOOD	

BRITISH KENNEL CLUB STANDARD

BASSET HOUND

GENERAL CHARACTERISTICS. — A short-legged hound of considerable substance, well-balanced and full of quality. Action is most important. A smooth free action with forelegs reaching well forward and hind legs showing powerful thrust and the hound moving true both front and rear. Hocks and stifles must not be stiff in movement nor must any toes be dragged.

Head and Skull. — Domes, with some stop and the occipital bone prominent; of medium width at the brow and tapering slightly to the muzzle; the general appearance of the foreface is lean but not snipy. The top of the muzzle nearly parallel with the line from stop to occiput and not much longer than the head from stop to occiput. There may be a moderate amount of wrinkle at the brows and beside the eyes and in any event the skin of the head should be so loose as to wrinkle noticeably when drawn forward or when the head is lowered. The flews of the upper lip overlap the lower substantially.

Nose. — Entirely black, except in light-coloured hounds, when it may be brown or liver. Large with well opened nostrils and may protrude a little beyond the lips.

Eyes. — Brown, but may shade to hazel in light-coloured hounds, neither prominent nor too deep set. The expression is calm and serious and the red of the lower lid appears, though not exceedingly.

Ears. — Set on low but not excessively so and never above the line of the eye, very long, reaching at least to the end of a muzzle of correct length, narrow throughout their length and curling well inwards; very supple, fine and velvety in texture.

Mouth. — The teeth level with a scissors bite although if they meet edge to edge it is not a fault.

Neck. — Muscular and fairly long with pronounced dewlap but not exaggerated.

Forequarters. — Shoulder-blades well laid back and shoulders not heavy. Forelegs short, powerful and with great bone, the elbows turned neither out nor in but fitting easily against the side. The knees at least slightly crooked inwards but not to so great an extent as to prevent free action or to result in legs touching each other when standing or in action. Knuckling-over is a bad fault. There may be wrinkles of skin between knee and foot.

Body. — The breast bone slightly prominent but the chest not narow or unduly deep; the ribs well-rounded and sprung and carried well back. The back rather broad, level, and with withers and quarters of approximately the same height, though the loins may arch slightly. The back from withers to the inset of the quarters not unduly long.

Hindquarters. — Full of muscle and standing out well, giving an almost spherical effect when viewing the hound from the rear. Stifles well bent. The hocks as low to the ground as possible and lightly bent under the hound but not turned in or out. They should be placed just under the body when standing naturally. One or two wrinkles of skin may appear between hock and foot and at the rear of the joint a slight pouch resulting from the looseness of the skin.

Feet. — Massive well knuckled-up and padded. Thre forefeet may point straight ahead or be turned slighly outwards but in every case the hound must stand perfectly true, the weight being borne equally by toes with pads together so that the feet would leave the imprint of a large hound and no unpadded areas in contact with the ground.

Tail. — Well set-on, rather long, strong at the base and tapering with a moderate amount of coarse hair underneath. When the hound is moving the stern is carried well up and curves gently sabre-fashion over the back but is never curling or gay.

Coat. — Smooth short and close without being too fine. The whole outline should be clean and free from feathering. The presence of a long-haired soft coat, with feathering, is very undesirable.

Colour. — Generally black, white and tan or lemon and white, but any recognised hound colour is acceptable.

Height. — Height 33-38cm (13″-15″).

Faults. — Any departure from the foregoing points should be considered a fault and the seriousness with which the fault should be regarded should be in exact proportion to its degree.

Note. — Male animals should have two apparently normal testicles full descended into the scrotum.

MAIN AMERICAN KENNEL CLUB VARIATION TO STANDARD FOR THE BASSET HOUND —

Size. — The height should not exceed 14 inches. Height over 15 inches at the highest point of the shoulder blades is a disqualification.

BASSET HOUND REGISTRATONS 1981 — 87 INCLUSIVE

1981 — 713
1982 — 659
1983 — 626
1984 — 609
1985 — 737
1986 — 641
1987 — 657

YET TO WIN CRUFTS BEST-IN-SHOW.

Long-Haired Dachshund

BEAGLE

First mention of the Beagle was in the fifteenth century and it is widely believed that he goes back a great deal further than that, some saying that a similar dog existed in the third century.

He is a hound of beautiful proportions, having the Basset's advantage of being close to the ground, whilst being very speedy over any terrain. He is chunky and tireless, showing great exuberance when hunting. They are one of the most esteemed scent hounds among huntsmen as they have very few faults in their makeup.

There used to be a liking amongst some breeders for packs of miniature Beagles, even royalty have bred such packs. But these dwarf dogs have become increasingly rare, and in fact the last century has seen an overall increase in the size of the breed.

The hound used for the hunt tends to differ from the show dog, the latter being more compact with a larger skull.

The Beagle makes a marvellous family dog, with no malice or untrustworthiness. His often striking markings and expressive face make him very popular with children and adults alike. Exercise should be frequent and he will especially appreciate running with other dogs.

KEY TO CHARACTER	
INTELLIGENCE	***
TEMPERAMENT	*****
EASE OF COAT CARE	*****
SUITABILITY FOR SMALL DWELLING	***
***** (5) = VERY GOOD	

BRITISH KENNEL CLUB STANDARD

BEAGLE

CHARACTERISTICS. — A merry hound whose essential function is to hunt, primarily hare, by following a scent. Bold with great activity, stamina and detrmination. Alert, intelligent and of even temperament.

GENERAL APPEARANCE. — A sturdy and compactly-built hound, conveying the impression of quality without coarseness.

Head and Skull. — Head fair length, powerful in the dog without being coarse, but finer in the bitch; free from frown and excessive wrinkle. Skull slightly domed, moderately wide, with indication of peak. Stop well defined and dividing length between occiput and top of nose as equally as possible. Muzzle not snipy, lips reasonably well flewed. Nose broad and nostrils well expanded; preferably black, but less pigmentation permissible in the lighter coloured hounds.

Eyes. — Dark brown or hazel, fairly large, not deep set or bulgy, set well apart and with a mild appealing expression.

Ears. — Long with round tip, reaching nearly to end of nose when drawn out. Set on low, fine in texture and hanging gracefully close to cheek.

Mouth. — Teeth strongly developed. Upper incisors just overlapping and touching outer surface of lower incisors to form scissor bite.

Neck. — Sufficiently long to enable hound to come down easily to scent, slightly arched and showing a little dewlap.

Forequarters. — Shoulder clean and sloping. Forelegs straight and upright, well under the hound, of good substance, strong, hard and round in bone. Not tapering off to feet. Pasterns short. Elbows firm, turning neither in nor out. Height to elbow about half the hound's height to withers.

Body. — Topline straight and level. Chest well let down to below elbow. Ribs well sprung and extending well back. Short between the couplings. Loins powerful and supple, without excessive tuck-up.

Hindquarters. — Very muscular about the thighs. Stifles well bent. Hocks firm, well let down and parallel to each other.

Feet. — Tight and firm. Well knuckled up and strongly padded. Not hare-footed. Nails short.

Gait. — Back level and no roll. Stride free, long-reaching and straight without high action. Hind legs showing drive. Should not move close behind or paddle or plait in front.

Tail. — Sturdy and moderate length. Set on high and carried gaily but not curled over back or inclined forward from the root. Well covered with hair, especially on underside.

Coat. — Short, dense and weatherproof.

Colour. — Any recognised hound colour other than liver. Tip of stern white.

Weight and Size. — It is desirable that height from ground to withers should neither exceed 40cm (16") nor fall below 33cm (13").

Note. — Male animals should have two apparently normal testicles fully descended into the scrotum.

MAIN AMERICAN KENNEL CLUB VARIATION TO STANDARD FOR THE BEAGLE —

Two size varieties. — Thirteen Inch — which shall be for hounds not exceeding 13 inches in height. Fifteen inch — which shall be for hounds over 13 but not exceeding 15 inches in height.

BEAGLE REGISTRATONS 1981 — 1987 INCLUSIVE

1981 — 1134
1982 — 943
1983 — 915
1984 — 947
1985 — 1012
1986 — 940
1987 — 780

YET TO WIN CRUFTS BEST-IN-SHOW.

BLOODHOUND

This is one of the very ancient breeds and he can be linked directly to a dog of some 1300 years ago. This was the St. Hubert hound of France, an excellent scent hound which was later introduced to England by William the Conqueror. This breed was then developed into the Talbot Hound. It is the Talbot Hound which lends it's name to so many inns throughout Britain and early descriptions of the breed suggest a fair resemblance to the modern Bloodhound.

The Bloodhound was one of the 40 breeds that were entered in the first Kennel Club stud book of 1874 and although he has become an instantly recognisable and well-liked breed, he is not kept in great numbers as a pet.

His great forte, of course, is his amazing scenting power in open countryside. No other dog can follow an old, weak scent as efficiently as the Bloodhound and in particularly difficult cases of criminal detection, the police often turn to his expertise.

Despite his rather gruesome sounding name, the Bloodhound is one of the gentlest dogs imaginable. Children are totally safe in his company, as he is patient and affectionate. Anyone with sufficient space and the inclination for long exercise spells in the country will find him a model companion.

KEY TO CHARACTER	
INTELLIGENCE	****
TEMPERAMENT	*****
EASE OF COAT CARE	*****
SUITABILITY FOR SMALL DWELLING	*
***** (5) = VERY GOOD	

BRITISH KENNEL CLUB STANDARD

BLOODHOUND

CHARACTERISTICS. — The Bloodhound possesses in a most marked degree every point and characteristic of those dogs which hunt together by scent (Sagaces). He is very powerful and stands over more ground than is usual with hounds of other breeds. The skin is thin and extremely loose, this being especially noticeable about the head and neck, where it hangs in deep folds. In temperament he is affectionate, neither quarrelsome with companions nor with other dogs. His nature is somewhat reserved and sensitive.

GENERAL APPEARANCE. — The expression is noble and dignified and characterized by solemnity, wisdom and power. The gait is elastic, swinging and free; the stern being carried high scimitar fashion.

Head and Skull. — The head is narrow in proportion to its length and long in proportion to the body, tapering but slightly from the temples to the muzzle, thus (when viewed from above and in front) having the appearance of being flattened at the sides and of being nearly equal in width throughout its entire length. In profile the upper outline of the skull is nearly in the same plane as that of the foreface. The length from the end of the nose to stop (midway between the eyes) should not be less than that from stop to back or occipital protuberance (peak). The entire length of head from the posterior part of the occipital protuberance to the end of the muzzle should be 30cm (12″) or more in dogs and 28cm (11″) or more in bitches. The skull is long and narrow, with the occipital peak very pronounced. The brows are not prominent although owing to the deep-set eyes they may have that appearance. The foreface is long, deep and of even width throughout, with square outlines when seen in profile. The head is furnished with an amount of loose skin, which in nearly every position appears superabundant, but more particularly so when the head is carried low; the skin then falls into loose pendulous ridges and folds, especially over the forehead and sides of the face. The nostrils are large and open. In front the lips fall squarely making a right angle with the upper line of the foreface; whilst behind they form deep hanging flews, and, being continued into the pendant folds of loose skin about the neck, constitute the dewlap, which is very pronounced.

Mouth. — A scissor bite with the inner faces of the upper incisors touching the outer faces of the lower incisors.

Eyes. — The eyes are deeply sunk in the orbits, the lids assuming a lozenge or diamond shape, in consequence of the lower lids being dragged down and everted by the heavy flews. The eyes correspond with the general colour of the animal varying from deep hazel to yellow. The hazel colour is however to be preferred, although very seldom seen in liver and tan (red and tan) hounds. The eye should be free from any interference from the eyelashes.

Ears. — The ears are thin and soft to the touch, extremely long, set on very low and fall in graceful folds, the lower parts curling inwards and backwards.

Neck. — Should be long.

Forequarters. — The shoulders muscular and well sloped backwards. The forelegs are straight, large and round in bone with elbows squarely set. The pasterns should be strong.

Hindquarters. — The thighs and second thighs (gaskins) are very muscular, the hocks well bent and let down and squarely set.

Feet. — Should be strong and well knuckled up.

Body. — The ribs are well sprung and the chest well let down between the forelegs forming a deep keel. The back and loins are strong, the latter deep and slightly arched.

Tail. — The stern is long and thick tapering to a point, set on high with a moderate amount of hair underneath. It should be carried scimitar fashion, but not curled over the back or corkscrew at any time.

Colour. — The colours are balck and tan, liver and tan (red and tan) and red. The darker colours being sometimes interspersed with lighter or badger-coloured hair and sometimes flecked with white. A small amount of white is permissible on chest, feet and tip of stern.

Weight and Size. — The mean average height of adult dogs is 66cm (26″) and of bitches 61cm (24″). Dogs usually vary from 63-69cm (25″-27″) and bitches from 58-63cm (23″-25″). The mean average weight of adult dogs in fair condition is 41Kg (90lbs) and of adult bitches 36Kg (80lbs). Dogs attain the weight of 50Kg (110lbs) and bitches 45Kg (100lbs). Hounds of the maximum height and weight are to be preferred providing always that quality, proportion and balance combine.

Note. — Male animals should have two apparently normal testicles fully descended into the scrotum.

BLOODHOUND REGISTRATONS 1981 — 1987 INCLUSIVE

1981 — 90
1982 — 113
1983 — 90
1984 — 83
1985 — 140
1986 — 91
1987 — 114

YET TO WIN CRUFTS BEST-IN-SHOW.

BORZOI

The Borzoi has all the classic features of the Greyhound group, taut muscular limbs, long narrow skull and a high arched back, the trademark of the speediest dogs.

The breed is of Russian origin and very ancient. Although there are other theories, it seems very possible that today's Borzoi came from the crossing of one of several coursing hounds used in Russia in the 17th and 18th centuries, with a massive breed called a Liptok. The longer coated of the dogs resulting from this cross were called Psovi Borzois, which is the type we are now familiar with.

Borzois were rarely taken as pets by the Russian people of the time as they were mainly employed, very effectively, as wolf coursing dogs. This was an enormously popular pursuit with well heeled noblemen and was performed with great ceremony and spectacle. The Revolution of 1917 naturally saw the last of these hunts and the Borzoi entered a serious decline, so serious in fact, that extinction threatened. But dedicated enthusiasts rallied to the problem and gradually bolstered the numbers.

The first Borzois seen in England came in the latter half of the 19th century and were then called Russian Wolfhounds, the Borzoi club proper being formed in 1892

It would be wrong to suggest to a prospective owner that the Borzoi is the easiest dog to train but with perseverance he can become a rewarding member of the household. People with little space or time for exercise, however, should never consider this breed.

KEY TO CHARACTER	
INTELLIGENCE	***
TEMPERAMENT	**
EASE OF COAT CARE	**
SUITABILITY FOR SMALL DWELLING	*
***** (5) = VERY GOOD	

BRITISH KENNEL CLUB STANDARD

BORZOI

GENERAL APPEARANCE. — A very graceful, aristocratic and elegant dog possessing courage, muscular power and great speed.

Head and Skull. — Head, long and lean. Well filled in below the eyes. Measurement equal from the occiput to the inner corner of the eye and from the inner corner of the eye to tip of nose. Skull very slightly domed and narrow, stop not perceptible, inclining to Roman nose. Head fine so that the direction of the bones and principal veins can be clearly seen. Bitches heads should be finer than the dogs. Jaws long, deep and powerful; nose large and black, not pink or brown, nicely rounded, neither cornered nor sharp. Viewed from above the skull should look narrow, converging very gradually to top of nose.

Eyes. — Dark, intelligent, alert and keen. Almond shaped, set obliquely, placed well back but not too far apart, Eye rims dark, Eyes should not be light, round or staring.

Ears. — Small and fine in quality; not too far apart. They should be active and responsive; when alert can be erect; when in repose nearly touching at the occiput.

Mouth. — The jaws should be strong, with a perfect, regular and complete scissor bite, i.e. the upper teeth closely overlappi ng the lower teeth and set square to the jaws.

Neck. — Clean, slightly arched; reasonably long. Well set on, free from throatiness. Flat at the sides, not round.

Forequarters. — Shoulders clean, sloping well back, fine at withers, free from lumpiness. Forelegs, lean and straight. Seen from the front, narrow like blades; from the side, wide at shoulder narrowing down to foot; elbows neither turned in nor out, pasterns strong, flexible and springy.

Body. — Chest, great depth of brisket, rather narrow. Ribs well sprung and flexible; neither flat sided nor barrel-shaped; very deep giving heart room and lung play, especially in the case of mature males. (It is from depth of chest rather than breadth that the Borzoi derives its heart room and lung play). Back, rising in a graceful arch from as near the shoulder as possible with a well balanced fall-away. The arch to be more marked in dogs than bitches. Rather bony, muscular and free from any cavity. Muscles, highly developed and well distributed.

Hindquarters. — Loins, broad and very powerful, with plenty of muscular development. Quarters should be wider than shoulders, ensuring stability of stance. Thighs long, well developed with good second thigh. Hind-legs, long, muscular, stifles well bent, hocks broad, clean and well let down.

Feet. — Front feet rather long, toes close together; well arched, never flat, neither turning in nor out. Hind feet hare-like, i.e., longer and less arched.

Tail. — Long, rather low set. Well feathered, carried low, not gaily. In action may be used as rudder but not rising above level of back. From the level of the hocks may be sickle shaped but not ringed.

Coat. — Long and silky (never woolly), or flat, or wavy, or rather curly. Short and smooth on head, ears and front legs; on the neck the frill profuse and rather curly; forelegs and chest well feathered; on hind-quarters and tail, long and profuse feathering.

Weight and Size. — Height at shoulder; Dogs from 74cm (29″) upwards. Bitches from 68cm (27″) upwards.

Note. — Male animals should have two apparently normal testicles fully descended into the scrotum.

MAIN AMERICAN KENNEL CLUB VARIATION TO THE STANDARD FOR BORZOI —

Size. — Mature males should be at least 28 inches at the withers and mature bitches at least 26 inches at the withers. Range in weight for males from 75 to 105 pounds and for bitches from 15 to 20 pounds less.

BORZOI REGISTRATIONS 1981 — 87 INCLUSIVE

1981 — 206
1982 — 158
1983 — 269
1984 — 246
1985 — 180
1986 — 240
1987 — 244

YET TO WIN CRUFTS BEST-IN-SHOW.

DACHSHUND

The first specimens of this breed to appear were almost certainly the Smooth-haired type. Developed in Germany where it was first called the 'Teckel', the Dachshund was first and foremost a burrowing dog used for the hunting of badgers and foxes. It is thought that similar dogs have been used in this way for over four centuries and it is not difficult to see why. The shape of the Dachshund is unique, having very short strong legs and a long muscular body, with which he can writhe and dig with great effectiveness in a confined space.

The German people well and truly took the Dachshund to their hearts, to the point in fact where he became their national dog. This, unfortunately, worked against the breed when, during and just after World War I, anything remotely Teutonic in origin was despised by the rest of Europe, so the poor Dachshund was reviled for some time. But that ridiculous situation is mere history now, and he is a much loved breed all over the world.

There are two other types of coat in the Dachshund family, the Long-haired and the Wire-haired. The former is thought to have resulted from the introduction of Spaniel blood and possibly some outcrossing with an ancient German breed called the Stöberhund. The Wire-haired variety comes from the crossing of Smooth-haired Dachshunds with Dandie Dinmont and Scottish Terriers.

In the home he is normally well-behaved, affectionate and loyal. Small children, though should be discouraged from teasing him as he can have a fairly aggressive streak. He barks with great vigour and makes a forceful guard despite his size. Great care should be taken not to overfeed, as overweight Dachshunds are often known to suffer with spinal problems. A moderate amount of daily exercise should always be given.

KEY TO CHARACTER	
INTELLIGENCE	***
TEMPERAMENT	****
EASE OF COAT CARE	
Smooth-haired	*****
Long-haired	***
Wire-haired	****
SUITABILITY FOR SMALL DWELLING	*****
***** (5) = VERY GOOD	

BRITISH KENNEL CLUB STANDARD

DACHSHUND (Long-Haired)

CHARACTERISTICS. — The long-haired Dachshund is an old, fixed sub-variety of the "Teckel", and its history extends back to the beginning of Teckel breeding. The breed is full of character, quick in attack and defence, faithful when properly brough up and very obedient. All the senses are well developed. It has the reputation of being extraordinarily intelligent and easy to train. Its build and temperament fit it to hunt quarry both above and below ground; its eagerness, keen sight and hearing and its sonorous bark make it especially suitable for tracking. In these respects it compares very favourably with any other variety. The thick, soft hair protects it against thorns, enables it to endure both cold and heat and is rain-proof. It is especially suited to water work. In following a trail to retrieve. The long-haired Dachshund can therefore be used in many different ways by the sportsman.

GENERAL APPEARANCE. — Form, colour, size and character similar in all respects to those of the smooth Dachshund, except for the long, soft hair. The form is compact, short-legged and long, but sinewy and well muscled, with bold and defiant head carriage, and intelligent expression. In spite of the shortness of the legs the body should be neither too plump nor so slender as to have weasel-like appearance. Height at shoulder should be half the length of the body measured from breast bone to the set-on of the tail, and the girth of the chest double the height at the shoulder. The length from the tip of the nose to the eyes should be equal to the length from the eyes to the base of the skull. The tail should not touch the ground when at rest, neither should the ears (i.e., the leather) extend beyond the nose when pulled to the front.

Head and Skull. — Long and conical when seen from above, and in profile, sharp and finely modelled. Skull neither too broad nor too narrow, only slightly arched, without prominent stop. Foreface long and narrow, finely modelled. Lips should be tightly drawn, well covering the lower jaw, neither too heavy nor too sharply cut away, the corners of the mouth slightly marked.

Eyes. — Medium in size, oval, set obliquely, clear, expressive and dark in colour.

Ears. — Broad and placed, relatively well back, high and well set on lying close to the cheeks, broad and long, nicley feathered and very mobile.

Mouth. — Wide, extending back to behind the eyes, furnished with strong teeth which should fit into one another exactly, the inner side of the upper incisors closing on the outer side of the under ones.

Neck. — Sufficiently long, muscular, showing no dewlap, slightly arched at the nape, running gracefully into the shoulders, carried well up and forward.

Forequarters. — Muscular, with deep chest. Shoulders long and broad, set obliquely, lying firmly on well developed ribs. Muscles hard and plastic. Breast bone prominent, extending so far forward as to show depressions on both sides. Upper arm the same length as the shoulder blade, jointed at right angles to the shoulder, well boned and muscled, set on close to the ribs but moving freely as far as the shoulder blade. Lower arm comparatively short, inclined slightly inwards, solid and well muscled.

Body. — Long and well muscled, the back showing oblique shoulders and short and strong pelvic region. Ribs very oval, deep between the fore-legs and extending far back. Loin short, strong and broad. The line of the back only slightly depressed over the shoulders and slightly arched over the loin, with the ouline of the belly moderately tucked up.

Hindquarters. — Rump round, full broad, with muscles well modelled and plastic. Pelvis bone not too short, broad, strongly developed and set obliquely. Thigh bone strong, of good length and jointed to the pelvis at right angles. Second thigh short, set at right angles to the upper thigh, well muscled. Hocks set wide apart, strongly bent and, seen from behind, the legs should be straight.

Feet. — Broad and large, straight or turned slightly outwards; the hind feet smaller and narrower than the fore. Toes close together and with a distinct arch to each toe. Nails strong. The dog must stand equally on all parts of the foot.

Tail. — Set on fairly high, not too long, tapering and without too marked a curve. Not carried too high. Fully feathered.

Coat. — Soft and straight or slightly waved, of shining colour. Longer under the neck, the underparts of the body and, particularly, on the ears, behind the legs, where it should develop into abundant feathering, and reach the greatest length on the tail, where it should form a flag. The feathering should extend to the outsides of the ears, where short hair is not desired. Too heavy a coat gives an appearance of undue plumpness and hides the outline. The coat should resemble that of an Irish Setter, giving the dog an appearance of elegance. Too much hair on the feet is ugly and useless.

Colour. — Black and tan, dark brown with lighter shadings, dark red, light red, dappled, tiger-marked or brindle. In Black and tan, red and dappled dogs the nose and nails should be black, in chocolate they are often brown.

Weight and Size. — As a rule Long-Haired Dachshunds are classified as follows:- Middle weight up to 7.7Kg (17 lbs) for bitches and 8.2Kg (18 lbs) for dogs. Heavy weight over 7.7Kg (17 lbs) for bitches and over 8.2Kg (18 lbs) for dogs. The Middle-weights are best suited for badger and fox drawing and the Heavy-weights for tracking, hunting larger animals and for water work. The last named are also very useful for retrieving rabbits and water fowl.

Note. — Male animals should have two apparently normal testicles fully descended into the scrotum.

DACHSHUND (Smooth-Haired)

CHARACTERISTICS. — First and foremost a sporting dog, the Smooth Dachshund is remarkably versatile, being equally adaptable as a house pet; his smooth, close coat is impervious to rain and mud. His temperament and acute intelligence make him the ideal companion for town or country. In the field of sport he is unequalled, combining the scenting powers of a Foxhound with unflinching courage, and will go to ground to fox, otter or badger.

GENERAL APPEARANCE. — Long and low, but with compact and well-muscled body, not crippled, cloddy, or clumsy, with bold defiant carriage of head and intelligent expression.

Head and Skull. — Long and appearing conical when seen from above, and, from a side view tapering to the point of the muzzle. Stop not pronounced, skull should be slightly arched in profile, appearing neither too broad nor too narrow. Jaw neigher too square nor snipy but strong, the lips lightly stretched fairly covering the lower jaw.

Eyes. — Medium in size, oval, and set obliquely. Dark in colour, except in the case of Chocolates, in which they may be lighter; in Dapples one or both wall eyes are permissible.

Ears. — Broad, of moderate length, and well rounded (not narrow, pointed or folded), relatively well back, high and well set on, lying close to the cheek, very mobile as in all intelligent dogs; when at attention the back of the ear directed forward and outward.

Mouth. — Teeth must be strongly developed. The powerful canine teeth must fit closely. The correct bite is a scissors bite, any deviation being a fault.

Neck. — Sufficiently long, muscular, clean, no dewlap, slightly arched in the nape, running in graceful lines into the shoulders, carried well up and forward.

Forequarters. — Shoulder blades long, broad and set on sloping, lying firmly on fully-developed ribs, muscles hard and plastic. Chest very oval, with ample room for the heart and lungs, deep and with ribs well sprung out towards the loins, breast-bone very prominent. The front legs should, when viewed from one side, cover the lowest point of the breastline. Forelegs very short andin proportion to size strong in bone. Upper arm of equal length with, and at right angles to, the shoulder blade; elbows lying close to ribs, but moving freely up to shoulder blades. Lower arm short as compared with other animals, slightly inclined inwards (crook), seen in profile moderately straight; not bending forward or knuckling over (which indicates unsoundness).

Body. — Long and muscular, the line of back slighly depressed at shoulders and slightly arched over the loin, which should be short and strong; outline of belly moderately tucked up. What is required is a general levelness of the back, the hindquarters (the rump) not being higher than the shoulders.

Hindquarters. — Rump round, full, broad; muscles hard and plastic; hip bone or pelvic bone not too short, broad and strongly developed, set moderately sloping, thigh bones strong, of good length, and joined to pelvis at right-angles; lower thighs short in comparison with other animals; hocks well developed and seen from behind the legs should be straight (not cow-hocked). The dog should not appear higher at the quarters than at shoulders.

Feet. — The front feet should be full, broad and close-knit, and straight or very slightly turned outwards, the hind feet smaller and narrower. The toes must be close together with a decided arch to each toe, with strong regularly placed nails and firm pads. The dog must stand true, i.e., equally on all parts of the foot.

Tail. — Set on fairly high, strong and tapering, but not too long and not too curved or carried too high.

Coat. — Short, dense and smooth, but strong. The hair on the underside of the tail course in texture; skin loose and supply, but fitting the dog closely all over, without much wrinkle.

Colour. — Any colour other than white (except a white spot on breast). Nose and nails should be black. In red dogs a red nose is permissible but not desirable. In Chocolate and Dapples the nose may be brown or flesh-coloured. In Dapples large spots of colour are undesirable, and the dog should be evenly dappled all over.

Weight and Size. — Dogs should not exceed 11.3Kg (25 lbs). Bitches should not exceed 10.4Kg (23 lbs).

Faults. — In general appearance weak or deformed, too high or too low to the ground; ears set on too high or too low, eyes too prominent; muzzle too short or pinched, either undershot or overshot; forelegs too crooked; hare or terrier feet, or flat spread toes (flat-footed); out at elbows; body too much dip behind the shoulders; loins weak or too arched; chest too flat or too short; hindquarters weak or cow-hocked, quarters higher than the shoulders.

Note. — Male animals should have two apparently normal testicles fully descended into the scrotum.

DACHSHUND (Wire-Haired)

CHARACTERISTICS. — The Dachshund should be clever, lively, courageous to the point of rashness, sagacious and obedient. He is especially suited for going to ground because of his low build, very strong forequarters and forelegs, long, strong jaw, and the immense power of his bite and hold. His loose skin enables him to manoeuvre with ease for attack or defence. His deep, loud bay indicates his position to those working him. He is also well equipped for field work on account of his good nose and sound construction. He can force his way through cover so dense that it would stop even the smallest gundog. Because of his nose, voice, good sight and perseverence he makes a good tracking dog.

GENERAL APPEARANCE. — Low to ground, short legged, the body long but compact and well muscled. The head should be carried boldly and the expression be very intelligent. Despite his short legs, compared with the length of this body, he must not be awkward, cramped, crippled or lacking in substance.

Head and Skull. — Looked at from above or from the side, the head should taper uniformly to the tip of the nose and be clean cut. The skull is only slightly arched, being neither too broad nor too narrow and slopes gradually, without marked stop, to a finely formed, slightly arched muzzle, the nasal bones and cartilage (Septum) being long and narrow. The ridges of the frontal bones are well developed giving prominence to the nerve bosses over the eyes. Jaw has extremely strong bones, is very long and opens very wide. It should not be too square nor yet snipy. The lips are lightly stretched, the corners just marked and the upper lip covers the lower jaw neatly.

Eyes. — Oval, medium size, set obliquely, lustrous and expressive. The colour should be dark except in the case of Chocolates, when they may be lighter, and of Dapples, when one or both wall eyes are allowed.

Ears. — Broad and rounded, the front edge touching the cheek. They are relatively well back and high and are well set on. The length is such at when the ears are pulled forward they reach a point approximately half-way between the eyes and the tip of the nose.

Mouth. — The powerful canine teeth fit closely. The correct bite is a scissor bite, any deviation being a fault.

Neck. — Sufficiently long, muscular, clean cut, not showing any dewlap, slightly arched in the nape, extending in a graceful line into the shoulders and carried erect.

Forequarters. — The shoulder blades are long, broad and placed firmly and obliquely upon a very robust rib cage. The upper arm is the same length as the shoulder blade, set at right angles to it and, like the shoulder blade, is very strong and covered with hard but supple muscles. The upper arm lies close to the ribs and is able to move freely. The forearm is comparatively short, inclined slightly inwards to form the crook, when seen in profile is moderately straight and must not bend forward or knuckle over, a state which indicates unsoundness. A correctly placed front leg covers the lowest point of the breast bone.

Body. — The breast bone is strong and prominent enough to show a dimple at each side. Looked at from the front the thorax should be very oval allowing ample room for the heart and lungs; seen from the side it should intersect the forearm just above the wrist. The top line, very slightly depressed at the shoulders and slightly arched over the loin, is parallel to the ground. The whole trunk should be long, well ribbed up and underneath should merge gradually into the line of a moderately tucked up belly. The rump is full, round and wide with strong and pliant muscles.

Hindquarters. — The pelvis is strong, set obliquely and not too short. The upper thigh, set at right angles to the pelvis, is strong and of good length, the lower this is short, set at right angles to the upper thigh and is well muscled. The hocks are well developed. The legs when seen from behind, are set well apart, straight and parallel to one another.

Feet. — The front feet are full, broad in front, straight or turned just a trifle outwards. The four toes forming the foot are compact, well arched and have tough pads. The fifth toe (dewclaw) is usually left on. The nails are strong and short. The dog must stand true and equally on all parts of the foot. The hind feet are smaller and narrower than the fore feet and placed straight. There should be no dewclaw. In all other respects the hind feed and toe are similar to the fore feet and toes.

Tail. — Continues line of the spine; is but slightly curved, must not be carried too gaily or reach the ground when at rest.

Coat. — With the exception of the jaw, eyebrows and ears, the whole body is covered with a completely even, short, harsh coat and an undercoat. There should be a beard on the chin. The eyebrows are bushy. The hair on the ears is almost smooth.

Colour. — All colours are allowed but a white patch on the chest, though not a fault, is not desirable. Except in the case of Chocolates, when it may be brown or flesh-coloured, the nose should be black.

Weight and Size. — It is recommended that dogs should weigh from 9 to 10Kg (20 to 22 lbs) and bitches from 8.2Kg — 9Kg (18 to 20 lbs).

Faults. — PRIMARY FAULTS. — An overshot or undershot jaw. Out at elbow. Knuckling over. Toes turned inwards. Splayed feet. Cow hocks. A bad coat. SECONDARY FAULTS. — Very light eyes. A narrow chest. Breast bone insufficiently prominent. A dip behind the shoulders. A hollow back. A roach back. Rump higher than withers. Weak loins. Excessively drawn up flanks. Bad angulation of forequarters or hindquarters. Legs too long, too close in front, or behind. Toes turned too much outwards. Bowed hind legs. A sluggish, clumsy or waddling gait. Poor muscle. Too long a tail. MINOR FAULTS. — Ears too high, too low, sticking out, folded or narrow. Too marked a stop. Head too wide, too narrow or too short. Too pointed or too weak a jaw. Short neck or swan neck. Dewlaps. Goggle eyes. Too short a tail.

Note. — Male animals should have two apparently normal testicles full descended into the scrotum.

DACHSHUND REGISTRATIONS 1981 — 87 INCLUSIVE

	LONG-HAIRED	SMOOTH-HAIRED	WIRE-HAIRED
1981 —	490	444	284
1982 —	466	362	160
1983 —	509	395	240
1984 —	437	372	249
1985 —	462	303	217
1986 —	375	333	265
1987 —	352	304	224

NO DACHSHUND HAS YET WON CRUFTS BEST-IN-SHOW.

MINIATURE DACHSHUND

The Dachshund was always used primarily for the hunting of badger and fox and his German breeders always kept this thought uppermost in their minds. He was developed into the ideal burrowing dog and there was no reason to alter his basic shape and character. But a certain group of hunting men decided that they would like to introduce a scaled-down version of this successful breed for the pursuit of smaller game, mainly rabbits. There were some attempts to outcross with other breeds to produce the desired size but this did not prove as satisfactory as selective breeding from small Dachshund specimens.

Modern Miniature Dachshunds are virtually exact replicas of their larger relatives and so share all their commendable points. All three coat types of this breed make fine show dogs as they all display great confidence and charisma and if presented well can often hold their own against larger hounds.

The obvious advantages that go with such a small dog make him an excellent companion for an elderly or infirm owner or for anyone with limited space. Although he is not a breed who takes easily to strangers, he is normally a good-natured and playful dog. He is very loyal and protective and can produce a surprisingly loud bark when required to guard.

Although the Miniature Dachshund does not require a huge amount of exercise, a daily walk should always be provided as this will appease his lively disposition. Care should always be taken not to overfeed as an overweight Miniature Dachshund can sometimes suffer with spinal trouble.

KEY TO CHARACTER	
INTELLIGENCE	***
TEMPERAMENT	****
EASE OF COAT CARE	
Smooth-haired	*****
Long-haired	***
Wire-haired	****
SUITABILITY FOR SMALL DWELLING	*****
***** (5) = VERY GOOD	

BRITISH KENNEL CLUB STANDARD

DACHSHUND (Miniature Long-Haired)

CHARACTERISTICS. — The Miniature Dachshund should be gay, alert, bold and highly intelligent. Despite its small size it should be strong, extremely active, hardy and game. Movement should be free and gay. Both fore and hind feet should move straight forward without plaiting or crossing in front and free from any tendency to throw out the hind feet sideways.

GENERAL APPEARANCE. — In conformation the Miniature Dachshund should be in all respects similar to the Dachshund of standard size. It should be compact, short-legged and long in body, well muscled and strong, with bold and intelligent expression. The body should be neither so plump as to give an impression of cobbiness, nor so slender as to impart a weasel-like appearance. Height at shoulder should be half the length of the body measured from the breast bone to the base of the tail, and the girth of the chest double the height at the shoulder. The length of from the tip of the nose to the eyes should be equal the length from eyes to base of skull.

Head and Skull. — Long and conical when seen from above, sharp in profile and finely modelled. Skull neither too broad nor too narrow, only slightly arched and without prominent stop. Foreface long and narrow, finely modelled. The lips should be tightly drawn but well covering the lower jaw, neither heavy nor too sharply cut away. The corners of the mouth slightly marked.

Eyes. — Of medium size, neither prominent not too deeply set, oval in shape placed obliquely. They should be clear and expressive and dark in colour except in Dapples and Chocolates, in which wall or light eyes are permissible.

Ears. — Broad and placed relatively well back, high and well set on, lying close to the cheeks and very mobile. The leather of the ears when pulled to the front should not extend beyond the tip of the nose.

Mouth. — Wide, extending back to behind the eyes. Teeth sound and strong, the inner side of the upper incisors closing on the outer side of the under ones.

Smooth-Haired Dachshund

Wire-Haired Dachshund

Miniature Long-Haired Dachshund

Miniature Smooth-Haired Dachshund

Neck. — Long and muscular, showing do dewlap, slightly arched at the nape, running cleanly into the shoulders, carried well up, giving the dog an alert, defiant appearance.

Forequarters. — Muscular, with deep chest. Shoulder blades should be long and broad, set obliquely and lying firmly on well-developed ribs. The breast bone should be prominent, extending so far forward as to show depressions on both sides. Upper arm equal in length to the shoulder blade, which it should join at an angle of 90 degrees, well boned and muscled, set on close to the ribs but moving freely. Lower arm short, inclined slightly inwards, well boned and free from wrinkle.

Body. — Long and well muscled with oblique shoulders and short strong pelvic region. Ribs well-sprung and extending far back. Chest oval, well let down between the forelegs, with the deepest point of the keel level with the wrist-joints. The line of the back level or only slightly depressed over the shoulders and slightly arched over the loin, with the belly moderately tucked up.

Hindquarters. — Rump full, round and broad. Pelvis bone not too short, broad, strong and set obliquely. Thigh bone strong, of good length and jointed to the pelvis at an angle of 90 degrees. Second thighs short, set at right angles to the upper thigh and well muscled. Hocks well let down, set wide apart, strongly bent. Seen from behind the legs should be straight, with no tendency for the hocks to turn inwards or outwards.

Feet. — Broad and large in proportion to the size of the dog, straight or turned only slightly outwards. The hind feet smaller than the fore. Toes close together and with each toe well arched. Nails strong. The dog must stand equally on all parts of the foot.

Tail. — Set on fairly high, not too long, tapering and without too makred a curve. It should not be carried too high and never curled over the back.

Coat. — The coat should be soft and straight or only slightly waved. It is longest under the neck, on the under-parts of the body and behind the legs, where it should form abundant feathering and on the tail where it should form a flag. The outside of the ears should also be well feathered. The coat should be flat, resembling that of an Irish Setter, and should not obscure the outline. Too much hair on the feet is not desired.

Colour. — Any colour. No white is permissible except for a small spot on the breast and even this is undesirable. The nose should be black except in Dapples and Chocolates in which it may be flesh coloured or brown. In all cases the coat colour should be bright and clearly defined. In black and tans the tan should be rich and sharp. Dapples should be free from large unbroken patches, the dappling being evenly distributed over the whole body.

Weight and Size. — The ideal weight is 4.5Kg (10 lbs) and it is of the utmost importance that judges should not award a prize to any dog exceeding 5Kg (11 lbs) in weight. Other points being equal the smaller the better, but mere diminutiveness must never take precedence over general type and soundness. Any appearance of weediness or toyishness is to be avoided at all costs.

Faults. — Round skull. Round or protruding eyes. Short ears. Shallow chest. Narrowness in front or behind. Short body. Long legs. Splayed feet. Cow hocks. Mouth under or overshot. Nervous or cringing demeanour.

Note. — Male animals should have two apparently normal testicles fully descended into the scrotum.

MAIN AMERICAN KENNEL CLUB VARIATION TO THE STANDARD FOR MINIATURE LONG-HAIRED DACHSHUND —

Miniature Dachshunds have not been given separate classification but are a division of the Open Class for "under 10 pounds, and 12 months old or over".

DACHSHUND (Miniature Smooth-Haired)

The Standard of the Dachshund (Miniature Smooth-Haired) is identical with the Standard of the Dachshund (Miniature Long-Haired) with the following exceptions:-

Coat. — In Smooths, short, dense and smooth, adequately covering all the parts of the body; coarsest on the under-side of the tail.

Weight and Size. — The ideal weight is 4.5Kg (10 lbs) and it is of the utmost importance that judges should not award a prize to any dog exceeding 5Kg (11 lbs) in weight. Other points being equal the smaller the better, but mere diminutiveness must never take precedence over general type and soundness. Any appearance of weediness or toyishness is to be avoided at all costs.

Faults. — Wooly or curly coat.

MAIN AMERICAN KENNEL CLUB VARIATION TO THE STANDARD FOR MINIATURE SMOOTH-HAIRED DACHSHUND —

Miniature Dachshunds have not been given separate classification but are a division of the Open Class for "under 10 pounds, and 12 months old or over".

DACHSHUND (Miniature Wire-Haired)

The Standard of the Dachshund (Miniature Wire-Haired) is identical with the Standard of the Dachshund (Miniature Long-Haired) with the following exceptions:-

Coat. — With the exception of the jaw, eyebrows and ears, the whole body is covered with a completely even, short, harsh coat and undercoat. There should be a beard on the chin. The eyebrows are bushy. The hair on the ears is almost smooth.

Weight and Size. — The ideal weight is 4.5Kg (10 lbs) and it is of the utmost importance that judges should not award a prize to any dog exceeding 5Kg (11 lbs) in weight. Other points being equal the smaller the better, but mere diminutiveness must never take precedence over general type and soundness. Any appearance of weediness or toyishness is to be avoided at all costs.

MAIN AMERICAN KENNEL CLUB VARIATION TO THE STANDARD FOR MINIATURE WIRE-HAIRED DACHSHUND —

Miniature Dachshunds have not been given separate classification but are a division of the Open Class for "under 10 pounds, and 12 months old or over".

Miniature Wire-Haired Dachshund

Deerhound

Elkhound

Finnish Spitz

MINIATURE DACHSHUND REGISTRATIONS 1981 — 87 INCLUSIVE

	LONG-HAIRED	SMOOTH-HAIRED	WIRE-HAIRED
1981 —	1837	1010	602
1982 —	1618	909	556
1983 —	1670	839	593
1984 —	1568	851	557
1985 —	1616	915	614
1986 —	1417	819	595
1987 —	1372	760	598

NO MINIATURE DACHSHUND HAS YET WON CRUFTS BEST-IN-SHOW.

DEERHOUND

This, one of the speediest of breeds, was developed in Scotland for one particular purpose, namely hunting deer. Having obvious physical characteristics similar to a Greyhound, the Deerhound was ideally suited to the task. He covers the ground in enormous athletic strides and even the fleet-footed red deer can barely match his pace.

As well as having Greyhound ancestry, he is also related to the Irish Wolfhound, as is clearly seen in the similarity of coat.

He has been a dog much favoured by Scottish aristocracy, being very much at home on huge, rolling highland estates. When out hunting, the Deerhound would show great single minded agression toward his prey, but this behaviour was seen to vanish once in his master's home. In fact his manners are excellent and if well treated he will repay with extreme devotion and affection.

Although the breed naturally declined with the reduction in deer hunting, he is still highly prized by his loyal, if not huge, band of followers in Britain. The Deerhound has that rare combination of speed, strength and grace and to be seen at his best a good deal of his life should be spent outdoors running free.

If an owner's home is large and he can spare sufficient time for exercise, the Deerhound makes an impressive pet. He is sensitive without being neurotic and a strong attachment between dog and owner usually develops.

Greyhound

Ibizan Hound

Irish Wolfhound

Otterhound

KEY TO CHARACTER	
INTELLIGENCE	***
TEMPERAMENT	****
EASE OF COAT CARE	****
SUITABILITY FOR SMALL DWELLING	*
***** (5) = VERY GOOD	

BRITISH KENNEL CLUB STANDARD

DEERHOUND

Head and Skull. — The head should be broadest at the ears, tapering slightly to the eyes, with the muzzle tapering more decidedly to the nose. The muzzle should be pointed but the lips level. The head should be long, the skull rather flat than round, with a very slight rise over the eyes, but with nothing approaching a stop. The skull should be coated with moderately long hair, which is softer than the rest of the coat. The nose should be black (though in some blue-fawns the colour is blue) and slightly aquiline. In the lighter coloured dogs a black muzzle is preferred. There should be a good moustache or rather silky hair, and a fair beard.

Eyes. — The eyes should be dark; generally they are dark-brown or hazel. A very light eye is not liked. The eye is moderately full, with a soft look in repose, but a keen, far-away look when the dog is roused. The rims of the eyelids should be black.

Ears. — The ears should be set on high, and, in repose, folded back like the Greyhound's, though raised above the head in excitement without losing the fold, and even in some cases semi-erect. A prick ear is bad. A big thick ear hanging flat to the head, or heavily coated with long hair, is the worst of faults. The ear should be soft, glossy, and like a mouse's coat to the touch, and the smaller it is the better. It should have no long coat or long fringe, but there is often a silky silvery coat on the body of the ear and the tip. Whatever the general colour, the ears should be black or dark-coloured.

Mouth. — Teeth level.

Neck. — The neck should be long; that is, of the length that befits the Greyhound character of the dog. An over-long neck is not necessary or desirable, for the dog is not required to stoop to his work like a Greyhound, and it must be remembered that the mane, which every good specimen should have, detracts from the apparent length of neck. Moreover, a Deerhound requires a very strong neck to hold a stag. The nape of the neck should be very prominent where the head is set on, and the throat should be clean cut at the angle and prominent.

Forequarters. — The shoulders should be well sloped, the blades well back and not too much width between them. Loaded and straight shoulders are very bad faults. The forelegs should be straight, broad and flat, a good broad forearm and elbow being desirable.

Body. — The body and general formation is that of a Greyhound of larger size and bone. Chest deep rather than broad, but not too narrow and flat-sided. The loin well arched and dropping to the tail. A straight back is not desirable, this formation being unsuitable for going uphill, and very unsightly.

Hindquarters. — Drooping, and as broad and powerful as possible, the hips being set wide apart. The hind legs should be well bent at the stifle, with great length from the hip to the hock, which should be broad and flat.

Feet. — Should be close and compact, with well arranged toes. Nails strong.

Tail. — Should be long, thick at the root, tapering, and reaching to within about 1½ inches of the ground. When the dog is still, dropped perfectly straight down, or curved. When in motion, it should be curved when excited, in no case to be lifted out of the line of the back. It should be well-covered with hair; on the inside, thick and wiry; on the underside longer, and towards the end a slight fringe is not objectionable. A curl or ring tail is very undesirable.

Coat. — The hair on the body, neck and quarters should be harsh and wiry, and about three to four inches long; that on the head, breast and belly is much softer. There should be a slight hairy fringe on the inside of the fore and hind legs, but nothing approaching the "feather" of a Collie. The Deerhound should be a shaggy dog, but not over-coated. A woolly coat is bad. Some good strains have a mixture of silky coat with the hard, which is preferable to a woolly coat; but the proper coat is a thick, close-lying, ragged coat, harsh or crisp to the touch.

Colour. — Colour is much a matter of fancy. But there is no manner of doubt that the dark blue-grey is the most preferred because quality tends to follow this colour. Next comes the darker and lighter greys or brindles, the darkest being generally preferred. Yellow and sandy-red or red-fawn, especially with black points, i.e., ears and muzzles, are also in equal estimation, this being the colour of the oldest-known strains, the McNeil and Cheethill Menzies. White is condemned by all the old authorities, but a white chest and white toes, occurring as they do in a great many of the darkest-coloured dogs, are not so greatly objected to, but the less the better, as the Deerhound is a self-coloured dog. A white blaze on the head, or a white collar should be heavily penalised. In other cases, though passable, yet an attempt should be made to get rid of white markings. The less white the better, but a slight white tip to the stern occurs in the best strains.

Weight and Size. — Should be from 38.6Kg to 47.7Kg (85 to 105 lbs) in dogs and from 29.5 to 36.3Kg (65 to 80 lbs) in bitches. Height of dogs should not be less than 76cm (30″) and bitches 71cm (28″) at the shoulder, respectively.

Faults. — Thick ear hanging flat to the head, or heavily coated with long hair. Curl or ring tail. Light eye. Straight back. Cow hocks, weak pasterns, straight stifles, splay feet, woolly coat, loaded and straight shoulders, white markings.

Note. — Male animals should have two apparently normal testicles fully descended into the scrotum.

Pharaoh Hound

Rhodesian Ridgeback

Saluki

Whippet

MAIN AMERICAN KENNEL CLUB VARIATION TO THE STANDARD FOR DEERHOUND —

Known as the Scottish Deerhound in the U.S.A.

Height. — Height of Dogs — from 30 to 32 inches. Height of Bitches — from 28 inches upwards.

Weight. — From 85 to 110 pounds in dogs, and from 75 to 95 pounds in bitches.

DEERHOUND REGISTRATIONS 1981 — 87

1981 — 161
1982 — 193
1983 — 176
1984 — 185
1985 — 216
1986 — 205
1987 — 298

YET TO WIN CRUFTS BEST-IN-SHOW.

ELKHOUND

The Elkhound was once extensively used in packs for hunting in his native Norway. His principal prey was, as his name indicates, the huge Scandanavian Elk. These hunts were a perilous pursuit that required dogs of great strength and positive character. The Elkhounds would risk severe injury or death from the massive antlers of the Elk whilst cornering it for their masters to kill. Often the prevailing conditions during a hunt would be appalling, driving snow, bitter cold and dense forest all had to be dealt with. A Spitz-type dog with his roots in the Arctic Circle was the obvious choice for such work and the Elkhound is a Spitz family member.

The breed is now quite well known in the U.S.A., and Europe and has figured to a fair degree in the show world, where he exhibits great self-confidence and even temper.

Although the modern Elkhounds have less hunting aggression than their forefathers, they still retain their rugged physical characteristics. They have endless stamina, are solidly built, being neither leggy not squat and they never feel the cold. The fairly fierce appearance might discourage some people but if the Elkhound puppy is sensibly trained from the outset, he can be as reliable as any breed. He guards his owners home well and although he will happily sleep outdoors, he enjoys the family environment. He possesses great energy and alertness and will be happiest with an owner of a similarly active disposition who could exercise his dog extensively.

KEY TO CHARACTER	
INTELLIGENCE	****
TEMPERAMENT	****
EASE OF COAT CARE	****
SUITABILITY FOR SMALL DWELLING	*
***** (5) = VERY GOOD	

BRITISH KENNEL CLUB STANDARD

ELKHOUND

CHARACTERISTICS. — The Elkhound is a hardy sporting dog of Nordic type of a bold and virile nature, and has good scenting power. Its disposition should be friendly and intelligent, with great energy and independence of character, and without any sign of undue nervousness.

GENERAL APPEARANCE. — It has a compact and proportionately short body, a coat thick and abundant but not bristling, and prick ears; tail tightly curled over back.

Head and Skull. — Broad between the ears; the forehead and back of the head are slightly arched with a clearly marked but not large stop. Muzzle moderately long, broader at the base and gradually tapering — whether seen from above or from the side — but not pointed; bridge of the nose straight, jaw strong with lips tightly closed.

Eyes. — Not prominent, in colour brown and as dark as possible, giving a frank, fearless and friendly expression.

Ears. — Set high, firm and upstanding, height slightly greater than their width at the base, pointed and very mobile.

Mouth. — Jaw strong with lips tightly closed, teeth meeting in a scissor bite.

Gait. — Demonstrates agility and endurance; stride at the trot even and effortless, back remaining level; as the speed of the trot increases, front and rear legs converge equally in straight lines towards a centre line beneath the body.

Neck. — Of medium length, firm, muscular and well set up.

Forequarters. — Legs firm straight and powerful with good bone; elbows closely set on.

Body. — Short in the couplings; back, wide and straight from neck to stern; chest, wide and deep with well-rounded ribs; loins, muscular; stomach, very little drawn up.

Hindquarters. — Hind legs firm strong and powerful, a little but definite bend at stifle and hock, and straight when viewed from behind.

Feet. — Compact, oval in shape and not turned outwards; toes, tightly closed; toe nails, firm and strong.

Tail. — Set high, tightly curled over the back but not carried on either side; hair, thick and coarse.

Coat. — Thick, abundant, course and weather-resisting; short on the head and on the front of the legs; longest on the chest, neck, buttocks, behind the forelegs and on the underside of the tail. It is composed of a longish and coarse top coat, dark at the tips with a light-coloured, soft and woolly undercoat. About the neck and front of the chest the longer coat forms a sort of ruff which, with the pricked ears, the energetic eyes and the curled tail, gives the animal its unique and alert appearance.

Colour. — Grey, of various shades with black tips to the long outer coat; lighter on the chest, stomach, legs, and the underside of the tail. Any distinctive variation from the grey colour is most undesirable and too dark or too light colouring should be avoided. Pronounced markings on legs and feet are also not desirable.

Weight and Size. — For dogs, the ideal height at the shoulder should be 52cm (20½″) and for bitches 49cm (19½″). Weight approximately 23Kg (50 lbs) and 20Kg (43 lbs) respectively.

Note. — Male animals should have two apparently normal testicles fully descended into the scrotum.

MAIN AMERICAN KENNEL CLUB VARIATION TO THE STANDARD FOR ELKHOUND —

Known as the Norwegian Elkhound in the U.S.A.

Size. — Weight for dogs about 55 pounds; for bitches about 48 pounds.

ELKHOUND REGISTRATIONS 1981 — 87 INCLUSIVE

1981 — 151
1982 — 161
1983 — 142
1984 — 199
1985 — 178
1986 — 175
1987 — 146

YET TO WIN CRUFTS BEST-IN-SHOW.

FINNISH SPITZ

Like most countries at the top of the northern hemisphere, Finland has it's own particular Spitz — type dog. Although the Finnish Spitz has only been recognised for about a hundred years, it seems probable that similar dogs have existed in Finland for centuries. He has been used as an efficient hunting dog, being particularly suited to bird work. This is not surprising, as closely related breeds from Russia and Norway are fine hunters, too. Although one of the lighter Spitz breeds, he is well capable of the often horrendous weather of Finland. His dense coat provides perfect insulation and he is of a fearless, positive disposition.

He is not a dog that figures very greatly outside his homeland, although in Britain a following is growing steadily, many now being seen at larger dog shows. He is a particularly striking show dog, mainly due to his fabulous bright red colour.

Despite his rugged past, the Finnish Spitz is a marvellous dog for the home. He is might what be called a very well-rounded breed, being clean, attractive, intelligent and friendly. He guards with great vigour and enjoys the company of children. Plenty of exercise is essential for this tireless breed and although not absolutely vital, a rural life might be preferred.

KEY TO CHARACTER	
INTELLIGENCE	****
TEMPERAMENT	*****
EASE OF COAT CARE	****
SUITABILITY FOR SMALL DWELLING	***
***** (5) = VERY GOOD	

BRITISH KENNEL CLUB STANDARD

FINNISH SPITZ

CHARACTERISTICS. — The Finnish Spitz characteristics are eagerness to hunt, courage, tempered with caution, fidelity and intelligence.

GENERAL APPEARANCE. — The dog is considerably larger and carries more coat than the bitch. Bearing bold. The whole appearance, particularly eyes, ears and tail indicates liveliness.

Head. — Medium sized and clean cut. Longer than it is broad in the ratio of 7:4. Forehead slightly arched, stop pronounced. Muzzle narrow, seen from above and from the sides evenly tapering. Nose pitch black. Lips tightly closed and thin. Scissor bite.

Eyes. — Medium sized, lively, preferably dark. Almond shaped, with black rims, set slightly aslant, with outer corners tilted upwards.

Ears. — Small, cocked, sharply pointed. Fine in texture and mobile.

Neck. — Muscular, of medium length — in males it may appear to be shorter due to a dense ruff.

Forequarters. — Stong and straight.

Body. — Almost square in outline. Back straight and strong. Chest deep. Belly slightly drawn up.

Hindquarters. — Strong. Only moderate turn of stifle.

Feet. — Preferably round. Hind dewclaws are always removed. Removal of front dewclaws optional.

Tail. — Plumed, curves vigorously from its root in an arch, forward, downward and backward, then pressing down against the thigh, with its tip extending to the middle part of the thigh. Extended, the bone of the tail usually reaches to the hock joint.

Coat. — On head and front legs short and close, on the body and back of legs longish, semi-erect or erect, stiffer on the neck and back. Outer coat on shoulders considerably longer and coarser, particularly in males. On back of thighs and on tail hair should be longer and denser. No trimming is allowed, not even of whiskers. Undercoat short, soft and dense.

Colour. — On the back reddish-brown or red-gold, preferably bright. The hairs on inner sides of ears, cheeks, under the muzzle, on the breast, abdomen, behind the shoulders, inside the legs, back of thighs, underside of tail, of lighter shades. Undercoat is also a lighter colour, making the whole coat glow. White markings on toes and a narrow white stripe, not exceeding two centimetres in width, on the breast permitted. Black hairs on lips and sparse separate black-pointed hairs on back and tail are permitted, even desirable. Puppies may have a good many black hairs which decrease with age, black on the tail persisting longer.

Gait. — Light and springy, quick and graceful.

Weight and Size. — Height at withers and length of body in males 44 to 50cm (17″ to 20″), in females 39 to 45cm (15½″ to 18″). Approximate weight in males 14 to 16Kg (31 to 36 lbs), in females 10 to 13Kg (23 to 29 lbs).

Faults. — Any departure from the foregoing points should be considered a fault and the seriousness of the fault should be in exact proportion to its degree.

Note. — Male animals should have two apparently normal testicles fully descended into the scrotum.

FINNISH SPITZ REGISTRATIONS 1981 — 87 INCLUSIVE

1981 — 55
1982 — 65
1983 — 75
1984 — 74
1985 — 63
1986 — 71
1987 — 67

YET TO WIN CRUFTS BEST-IN-SHOW.

GREYHOUND

The Greyhound is one of the oldest known breeds. In a similar form he existed in the Middle East some 4,000 years ago. These dogs were highly prized by the Arab people of the time and were used for the hunting of gazelle and other speedy prey which no other domesticated animal could pursue. These very early specimens of the Greyhound family were thought to have had fairly long, wispy coats, perhaps resembling a Saluki. As these dogs spread throughout other countries, their coat gradually evolved to suit different climatic conditions. The coat of the Afghan Hound, a member of the Greyhound family, developed it's coat in this way.

Today's smooth coated Greyhound has been in Britain for many hundreds of years and has been much favoured by royalty for hunting and for it's dignified air as a companion.

With his deep chest, arched loins and immense muscular quarters, the Greyhound is ideally built for speed. Indeed, it has been with this constant thought in mind that breeders have developed the near perfect running machine of today. Greyhound racing is as popular as ever and no other dog can sustain such speed for so long a distance.

Although happier to be racing or engaged in similar demanding work, the Greyhound can make a friendly companion. If treated well, he will respond with affection but he must never be teased as he can be a little impatient. Due to his extensive exercise needs, he should not be taken as a pet without careful thought.

KEY TO CHARACTER	
INTELLIGENCE	***
TEMPERAMENT	***
EASE OF COAT CARE	*****
SUITABILITY FOR SMALL DWELLING	*
***** (5) = VERY GOOD	

BRITISH KENNEL CLUB STANDARD

GREYHOUND

CHARACTERISTICS. — They Greyhound possesses remarkable stamina and endurance, its straight through, long reaching movement enables it to cover ground at great speed.

GENERAL APPEARANCE. — The general appearance of the typical Greyhound is that of a strongly built, upstanding dog of generous proportions, muscular power and symmetrical formation, with a long head and neck, clean well-laid shoulders, deep chest, capacious body, arched loin, powerful quarters, sound legs and feet, and a suppleness of limb, which emphasize in a marked degree its distinctive type and quality.

Head and Skull. — Long, moderate width, flat skull, slight stop. Jaws, powerful and well chiselled.

Eyes. — Bright and intelligent — oval — set obliquely.

Ears. — Small, rose-shape of fine texture.

Mouth. — Teeth white and strong. The incisors of the upper jaw clipping those of the lower jaw.

Neck. — Long and muscular, elegantly arched, well let into the shoulders.

Forequarters. — Shoulders, oblique, well set back, muscular without being loaded, narrow and cleanly defined at the top. Forelegs, long and straight, bone of good substance and quality. Elbows, free and well set under the shoulders. Pasterns, moderate length, slightly sprung. Elbows, pasterns and toes should incline neither outwards nor inwards.

Body. — Chest, deep and capacious, providing adequate heart room. Ribs, deep, well sprung, and carried well back. Flanks well cut up. Back, rather long, broad and square. Loin, powerful, slightly arched.

Hindquarters. — Thighs and second thighs, wide and muscular, showing great propelling power. Stifles, well bent. Hocks, well let down, inclining neither outwards nor inwards. Body and hindquarters features should be of ample proportions and well coupled, enabling adequate ground to be covered when standing.

Feet. — Moderate length, with compact well-knuckled toes, strong pads.

Gait. — Straight, low reaching free stride enabling it to cover ground at great speed. Hind legs should come well under body giving great propulsion.

Tail. — Long, set on rather low, strong at the root, tapering to the point, carried low, slightly curved.

Coat. — Fine and close.

Colour. — Black, white, red, blue, fawn, fallow, brindle, or any of the colours broken with white.

Height. — Ideal height: Dogs, 71 to 76cm (28″ to 30″); Bitches, 68 to 71cm (27″ to 28″).

Note. — Male animals should have two apparently normal testicles fully descended into the scrotum.

MAIN AMERICAN KENNEL CLUB VARIATION TO THE STANDARD FOR GREYHOUND —

Weight. — Dogs, 65 to 70 pounds; Bitches, 60 to 65 pounds.

GREYHOUND REGISTRATIONS 1981 — 87 INCLUSIVE

1981 — 57
1982 — 75
1983 — 40
1984 — 41
1985 — 83
1986 — 41
1987 — 68

CRUFTS BEST-IN-SHOW WINNER 3 TIMES.

1928 PRIMELEY SCEPTRE — H. WHITLEY
1934 SOUTHBALL MOONSTONE — B. HARTLAND WORDEN
1956 TREETOPS GOLDEN FALCON — MRS. W. DE CASEMBROOT and MISS H. GREENISH

IBIZAN HOUND

The Ibizan Hound can lay claim to being one of the oldest of all breeds. Paintings and carvings in the tombs of the Egyptian Pharoahs have shown dogs bearing an extreme likeness to the Ibizan Hound, some dating back over, 5,000 years.

Having enjoyed a place of great importance with the Egyptians, it was around the eighth century that traders took specimens of these dogs with them to the Mediterranean and the island which lends the breed it's name, Ibiza.

Due to it's isolation, food was not always easily obtainable on Ibiza and the islanders quickly realised the potential of these new dogs for hunting small game. They used the dog's great speed in the pursuit of rabbit, hare and civet cat, which doubtless improved the quality of their diet. On the Spanish mainland too, the Ibizan Hound became evident and there it was hunted in packs for game as large as deer.

This breed has remained virtually unchanged since his distant beginnings and it is of great credit to modern breeders that they have resisted any temptation to alter him. Although the best dogs are still to be found on Ibiza, there are many excellent specimens all over the world.

As a pet he does have one or two drawbacks but if correctly managed he makes an imposing companion of great intelligence. Being built for running and jumping, large amounts of exercise are essential. He can be a little aloof but once attached to a family he will show great loyalty and affection towards them.

KEY TO CHARACTER	
INTELLIGENCE	****
TEMPERAMENT	***
EASE OF COAT CARE	*****
SUITABILITY FOR SMALL DWELLING	*
***** (5) = VERY GOOD	

BRITISH KENNEL CLUB STANDARD

INTERIM STANDARD OF THE IBIZAN HOUND

CHARACTERISTICS. — A tireless controlled hunter. Retrieves to hand, very kind, rather cautious with strangers, has the ability to jump great heights without take-off run. An agile hound.

GENERAL APPEARANCE. — Tall, narrow, finely built, large erect ears.

Head and Skull. — Fine, long flat skull with prominent occipital bone. Stop not well defined, slightly convex muzzle, the length of which from the eyes to the tip of the nose should be equal to the length from the eyes to the occiput. Nose flesh coloured, should protrude beyond the teeth, jaw very strong and lean.

Eyes. — Clear amber, expressive. Almond shaped; not prominent, large or round.

Ears. — Large, thin, stiff, highly mobile, erect when dog is alert, in a continuous line with the arch of the neck when viewed in profile; base set on level with the eyes.

Mouth. — Perfectly even white teeth; scissor bite; thin lips with no dew-lap.

Neck. — Very lean, long, muscular and slightly arched.

Forequarters. — Rather steep short shoulder blade, long straight legs, erect pasterns of good length.

Body. — Level back sloping slightly from the pinbones to the rump. Long, flat ribcage. Short coupled with well tucked up waist, breast bone very prominent. Depth measured between the bottom of the ribcage and elbow 2½ inches to 3 inches.

Hindquarters. — Long, strong, straight and lean, no great angulation, long second thigh, turning neither in nor out.

Feet. — Well arched toes, thick pads, light coloured claws. Front feet may turn slightly outwards. Dew claws should not be removed in front. No hind dew claws.

Gait. — A suspended trot, which is a long far reaching stride, with a slight hover before placing the foot to the ground.

Tail. — Long, thin, low set, reaching well below the hock, when passed between the legs and round the flank should reach the spine; may be carried high when excited but not curled within itself or low over the back.

Coat. — Either smooth or rough always hard, close, dense. Longer under the tail and at the back of the legs. Hunting scars should not be penalised.

Colour. — White, Chestnut, or Lion solid colour, or any combination of these.

Weight and Size. — The Standard in the country of origin varies between 56 and 74cm (22″ to 29″), but balance is the overriding factor.

Faults. — Any departure from the foregoing, the degree of the departure stipulating the seriousness of the fault.

Note. — Male animals should have two apparently normal testicles fully descended into the scrotum.

MAIN AMERICAN KENNEL CLUB VARIATION TO THE STANDARD FOR IBIZAN HOUND —

Height. — Height of dogs at withers ranges from 23½ to 27½ inches; height of bitches at withers ranges from 22½ to 26 inches.

Weight. — Average weight of dogs, 50 pounds; Bitches, 42 to 49 pounds.

IBIZAN HOUND REGISTRATIONS 1981 — 87 INCLUSIVE

1981 — 15
1982 — 25
1983 — 16
1984 — 38
1985 — 14
1986 — 25
1987 — 37

YET TO WIN CRUFTS BEST-IN-SHOW.

IRISH WOLFHOUND

This is the true canine giant, the world's tallest dog. Despite his size he is neither lumbering nor clumsy, moving with grace and controlled power. His elegance and pleasing proportions can be largely attributed to the efforts of a certain Captain George Graham who spent over twenty years perfecting the standard, concluding his work in 1885.

As is plain to see, there is a good deal of Deerhound in the Irish Wolfhound's blood and some of the other breeds used by Captain Graham were of Great Dane descent.

The very early version of the breed was of lighter build and was referred to as the Irish Greyhound, being very similar to the Deerhound of today. They were used, in Ireland, to hunt deer, wolves and elk. When this type of prey diminished, so the breed declined. It was from here on that Captain Graham's efforts came to the rescue.

Today's Wolfhound has an excellent genial nature and makes a first class companion, if you have sufficient space for him. He is level headed and loyal, making an intimidating guard when roused.

KEY TO CHARACTER	
INTELLIGENCE	****
TEMPERAMENT	*****
EASE OF COAT CARE	***
SUITABILITY FOR SMALL DWELLING	*
***** (5) = VERY GOOD	

BRITISH KENNEL CLUB STANDARD

IRISH WOLFHOUND

GENERAL APPEARANCE. — The Irish Wolfhound should not be quite so heavy or massive as the Great Dane, but more so than the Deerhound, which in general type he should otherwise resemble. Of great size and commanding appearance, very muscular, strongly though gracefully built, movements easy and active; head and neck carried high; the tail carried with an upward sweep with a slight curve towards the extremity.

Head and Skull. — Long, the frontal bones of the forehead very slightly raised and very little indentaiton between the eyes. Skull, not too broad. Muzzle, long and moderately pointed.

Eyes. — Dark.

Ears. — Small and Greyhound-like in carriage.

Neck. — Rather long, very strong and muscular, well arched, without dewlap or loose skin about the throat.

Forequarters. — Shoulders muscular, giving breadth of chest, set sloping. Elbows well under, turned neither inwards nor outwards. Leg and forearm muscular, and the whole leg strong and quite straight.

Body. — Chest, very deep. Breast, wide. Back, rather long than short. Loins arched. Belly well drawn up.

Hindquarters. — Muscular thighs and second thighs; long and strong as in the Greyhound, and hocks well let down and turning neither in nor out.

Feet. — Moderately large and round, turned neither inwards nor outwards. Toes well arched and closed. Nails very strong and curved.

Tail. — Long and slightly curved, of moderate thickness, and well covered with hair.

Coat. — Rough and hardy on body, legs and head; especially wiry and long over eyes and under jaw.

Colour. — The recognised colours are grey, brindle, red, black, pure white, fawn, or any colour that appears in the Deerhound.

Weight and Size. — The minimum height and weight of dogs should be 79cm (31″) and 54.5Kg (120 lbs); of bitches, 71cm (28″) and 40.9Kg (90 lbs). *Anything below this should be heavily penalised.* Great size, including height at shoulder and proportionate length of body, is the desideratum to be aimed at, and it is desired to firmly establish a breed that shall average from 81 to 86cm (32″ to 34″) in dogs, showing the requisite power, activity, courage and symmetry.

Faults. — Too light or heavy a head, too highly arched frontal bone; large ears; ears hanging flat to the face; short neck; full dewlap; too narrow or too broad a chest; sunken, hollow or quite straight back; bent forelegs; overbent fetlocks; twisted feet; spreading toes; too curly a tail; weak hind-quarters and a general want of muscle; too short in body; pink or liver-coloured eyelids; lips and nose any colour other than black; very light eyes.

Note.— Male animals should have two apparently normal testicles fully descended into the scrotum.

MAIN AMERICAN KENNEL CLUB VARIATION TO THE STANDARD FOR IRISH WOLFHOUND —

General Appearance. — The minimum height and weight of dogs should be 32 inches and 120 pounds; of bitches, 30 inches and 105 pounds.

IRISH WOLFHOUND REGISTRATIONS 1981 — 87 INCLUSIVE

1981 — 623
1982 — 618
1983 — 686
1984 — 645
1985 — 700
1986 — 719
1987 — 646

CRUFTS BEST-IN-SHOW WINNER 1960

SULHAMSTEAD MERMAN — MRS NAGLE AND MISS CLARK

OTTERHOUND

This is a rare and ancient breed and one of the finest hunting dogs ever developed. Although he was undoubtedly perfected in Britain for the sole purpose of otter hunting, his early ancesty is open to question. Some believe his origins to be British and that his main ancestor was the Southern Hound, a long-extinct hunting dog. There is strong support, though, for the view that his roots are in France and that he comes from the same stock as the Basset Griffon Vendeen, a shaggy coated Basset Hound-type. There is also a resemblance to the Bloodhound in the Otterhound's bone structure, so this is another possibility.

For centuries the sport of otter hunting was widespread among the upper classes of Britain and they succeeded in developing the perfect dog for this demanding form of hunting. He has a waterproof coat and excellent swimming ability, partly due to his feet actually being webbed. He has a fine nose and is renowned for strength and stamina.

It is now illegal to hunt otters so the breed has been perpetuated purely by those who are interested in the undoubted beauty and character of these dogs. Although life in an average home would be difficult for the Otterhound, he does show great affection towards people and is excellent with children. Anyone contemplating owning an Otterhound will need plenty of space and must have the time to give his dog lengthy outings. A rural environment is virtually essential for this rugged breed.

KEY TO CHARACTER	
INTELLIGENCE	****
TEMPERAMENT	****
EASE OF COAT CARE	***
SUITABILITY FOR SMALL DWELLING	*
***** (5) = VERY GOOD	

BRITISH KENNEL CLUB STANDARD

INTERIM STANDARD FOR THE OTTERHOUND

CHARACTERISTICS. — An amiable, even tempered hound.

GENERAL APPEARANCE. — A big strongly built hound, straight limbed and sound, rough-coated with majestic head, strong body and loose long-striding action. Being primarily built for a long day's work in water, the rough double coat and large feet are essential. As the hound must be able to gallop on land, it must be free moving.

Head and Skull. — Clean and very imposing, deep rather than wide, clean cheekbones, skull nicely domed, not coarse nor overdone, rising from a distinct though not exaggerated stop to slight peak at the occiput. There should be no trace of scowl or bulge in forehead, the expression being open and amiable. Muzzle strong and deep with good wide nose ending in wide nostrils. Distance from nose-end to stop slightly shorter than from stop to occiput. Plenty of lip and flew, but not exaggerated. The whole head, except for nose should be well covered with rough hair, ending in slight moustaches and beard, both being part of the natural face hair.

Eyes. — An intelligent, moderately deepset eye, the haw showing only slightly. Eye colour and rim pigment variable according to coat colour, e.g. a blue and tan hound may have hazel eyes. Yellow eye undesirable.

Ears. — A unique feature of the breed. Should be long and pendulous, set on a level with the corner of the eye, easily reaching the nose when pulled forward, with the characteristic fold which denotes pure breeding. The leading edge should fold or roll inwards giving a curious, draped appearance. This is an essential point, which should not be lost. Well covered and fringed with hair.

Mouth. — Strong, very large, well placed teeth with scissor bite; viz. the jaws should be strong, with a perfect regular and complete scissor bite, i.e. the upper teeth closely overlapping the lower teeth and set square to the jaws. Level bite permissible.

Neck. — Neck long and powerful, set smoothly into well laid back, clean shoulders. Slight dew lap permissible.

Forequarters. — Forelegs strongly boned, straight from elbow to ground. Pasterns strong and slightly sprung.

Body. — Chest deep with well sprung oval ribcage which should be fairly long, with ribs carried well back allowing for plenty of heart and lung room; neither too wide nor too narrow. Body very strong with level top line and broad back. Loin short and strong. Angulation both at shoulder and elbow.

Hindquarters. — Very strong and well muscled when viewed from any angle, standing neigher too wide nor too narrow behind. The stifle fairly well bent; hocks well let down, turning neither in nor out. Thighs and second thighs heavily muscled. In natural stance, the hind legs from the hock to the ground should be perpendicular.

Feet. — Feet large, round, well knuckled, thick padded, turning neither in nor out. Compact when standing but capable of spreading, the hind feet only slightly smaller than the fore-feet. Web must be in evidence.

Gait. — Peculiar to the Otterhound, gait very loose and shambling at a walk, springing immediately into a loose and very long-striding sound, active trot. The gallop smooth and exceptionally long-striding.

Tail. — Set high and carried up when alert or on the move, it should never curl over the back and may droop when standing. Thick at the base, tapering to a point; bone should reach to the hock and be carried straight or in a slight curve. The hair under the tail (stern) rather longer and more profuse than that on the upper surface.

Coat. — Should be long (4 to 8cm; 1½″ to 3″) dense, rough, harsh and waterproof. An undercoat should be evident and there may be a slightly oily texture both in top and undercoat. The Otterhound requires no trimming for exhibition. Presentation should be natural.

Colour. — Recognised hound colours permissible:— Whole coloured, grizzle, sandy, red, wheaten, blue; these may have slight white markings on head, chest, feet and tail tip. White hounds may have slight lemon, blue or badger pied markings. Black and tan, blue and tan, black and cream, occasional liver, tan and liver, tan and white. Colours not permissible:— Liver and white, a white bodied hound with black and tan patches distincly separate. Pigment should harmonize though not necessarily blend with coat colour; for example a tan hound may have a brown nose and eye rims. A slight butterfly nose is permissible.

Size. — Dogs approximately 67cm (27″) at the shoulder. Bitches approximately 60cm (24″) at the shoulder.

Faults. — Any departure from the foregoing points should be considered a fault and the seriousness with which the fault should be regarded should be in exact proportion to its degree.

Note. — Male animals should have two apparently normal testicles fully descended into the scrotum.

MAIN AMERICAN KENNEL CLUB VARIATION TO THE STANDARD FOR OTTERHOUND —

Size. — Males range from 24 to 27 inches at the withers, and weigh from 75 to 115 pounds, depending on the height and condition of the hound. Bitches are 22 to 26 inches at the withers and 65 to 100 pounds.

OTTERHOUND REGISTRATIONS 1981 — 87 INCLUSIVE

1981 — 52
1982 — 44
1983 — 35
1984 — 43
1985 — 34
1986 — 64
1987 — 34

YET TO WIN CRUFTS BEST-IN-SHOW.

PHARAOH HOUND

Some contend that this is the oldest known domesticated dog, this argument being supported by the many drawings of similar dogs that have been found in and around Egyptian burial places. In fact there have been discoveries of mummified dogs that were also of comparable type to the Pharaoh Hound. But the most likely explanation seems to be that these dogs were the progenitors of all the Greyhound-type dogs of the world, the Pharaoh Hound certainly being one such breed.

The Egyptians had prized their dogs as great hunters, and eventually travellers from Europe also saw their potential and began to take specimens home with them. It was over 2,000 years ago when the Mediterranean regions began to see these dogs in any quantity. Some reached the Balearic Islands particularly Ibiza and Malta. The Ibizan Hound of today descends from this early stock and Malta became the place of the Pharaoh Hound's development. The Maltese used the great speed and surprisingly keen nose of the breed for the hunting of small game and he is known there as 'Kelb-tal-fenek' which translates to 'rabbit-dog'.

This is a fairly new breed to Britain but already he is to be seen in good numbers at the major dog shows. His glorious tan coat always creates a stir and he is usually steady and well-behaved in the ring.

The Pharaoh Hound would not be a good choice for every home, because there is still a lot of the hunter in his make-up. But he has an amiable disposition and will remain loyal and affectionate if given plenty of exercise every day.

KEY TO CHARACTER	
INTELLIGENCE	****
TEMPERAMENT	****
EASE OF COAT CARE	*****
SUITABILITY FOR SMALL DWELLING	*
***** (5) = VERY GOOD	

BRITISH KENNEL CLUB STANDARD

PHARAOH HOUND

CHARACTERISTICS. — An intelligent, friendly, affectionate, playful and alert breed. An alert keen hunter, the Pharaoh Hound hunts by scent and sight using its large ears to a marked degree when working close.

GENERAL APPEARANCE. — The Pharaoh Hound is medium sized, of noble bearing with clean-cut lines. Graceful yet powerful. Very fast with free easy movement and alert expression.

Head and Skull. — Skull long, lean and well-chiselled. Foreface slightly longer than the skull. Only slight stop. Top of skull parallel with the foreface, the whole head representing a blunt wedge when viewed in profile and from above.

Eyes. — Amber coloured, blending with the coat; oval, moderately deep set with keen, intelligent expression.

Ears. — Medium high set; carried erect when alert, but very mobile; broad at the base, fine and large.

Mouth. — Powerful jaws with strong teeth. Scissor bite.

Nose. — Flesh coloured only, blending with the coat.

Neck. — Long, lean, muscular and slightly arched. Clean throat line.

Forequaters. — *Shoulders* — Strong, long and well laid back. *Forelegs* — Straight and parallel. Elbows well tucked in. Pasterns strong.

Body. — Lithe with almost straight topline. Slight slope down from croup to root of tail. Deep brisket extending down to point of elbow. Ribs well sprung. Moderate cut up. Length of body from breast to haunch bone slightly longer than height at withers.

Hindquarters. — Strong and muscular. Moderate bend of stifle. Well developed second thigh. Limbs parallel when viewed from behind.

Feet. — Strong, well knuckled and firm, turning neither in nor out. Paws well padded. Dew claws may be removed.

Gait. — Free and flowing; the head should be held fairly high and the dog should cover the ground well without any apparent effort. The legs and feet should move in line with the body; any tendency to throw the feet sideways, or a high stepping "hackney" action is a definite fault.

Tail. — Medium set — fairly thick at the base and tapering (whip-like), reaching just below the point of hock in repose. Carried high and curved when the dog is in action. The tail should not be tucked between the legs. A screw tail is a fault.

Coat. — Short and glossy, ranging from fine and close to slightly harsh; no feathering.

Colour. — Tan or rich tan with white markings allowed as follows:-
White tip on tail strongly desired.
White on chest (called "The Star").
White on toes.
Slim white blaze on centre line of face permissible.
Flecking or white other than above undesirable.

Height. — Dogs; Ideally 56 to 63cm (22″ to 25″). Bitches; Ideally 53 to 61cm (21″ to 24″). Overall balance must be maintained.

Faults. — Any deviation from the foregoing is a fault, hunting blemishes excepted.

Note. — Male animals should have two apparently normal testicles fully descended into the scrotum.

MAIN AMERICAN KENNEL CLUB VARIATION TO THE STANDARD FOR PHARAOH HOUND —

Height. — Dogs 23 inches to 25 inches. Bitches 21 inches to 24 inches.

PHARAOH HOUND REGISTRATIONS 1981 — 87 INCLUSIVE

1981 — 36
1982 — 24
1983 — 23
1984 — 25
1985 — 35
1986 — 81
1987 — 121

YET TO WIN CRUFTS BEST-IN-SHOW.

RHODESIAN RIDGEBACK

A ridge-backed hunting dog has existed in South Africa for hundreds of years. The ridge on the back is a tapering strip of backward-growing hair and all the finest hunting dogs were seen to possess it. Amazing as it may seem, South African tribesmen would use these dogs for lion hunting. The technique seems to have been for a pack of the dogs to torment and entice the lion out into the open where he could be slain. The agility and courage of these dogs must have been phenomenal and although the dogs we know today have been slightly 'watered-down' by European canine blood, the Rhodesian Ridgeback still possesses great strength and self-confidence.

As well as his hunting prowess, the Rhodesian Ridgeback has a history of guarding his owner and his property with great ferocity. This side to his character only appears in the required situation and in the home he is gentle and affectionate with the whole family.

He is a dog of good intelligence, learning easily which is a definite asset when training such a powerful dog. Someone with a good size house and garden would be preferred as an owner and to keep the Rhodesian Ridgeback's taut muscularity, a large amount of regular exercise is needed.

It would be hoped that nobody would purchase one of these fine dogs on a whim, purely for the novelty of the unique coat.

KEY TO CHARACTER	
INTELLIGENCE	****
TEMPERAMENT	****
EASE OF COAT CARE	*****
SUITABILITY FOR SMALL DWELLING	*
***** (5) = VERY GOOD	

BRITISH KENNEL CLUB STANDARD

RHODESIAN RIDGEBACK

CHARACTERISTICS. — The peculiarity of the breed is the ridge on the back which is formed by the hair growing in the opposite direction to the rest of the coat; the ridge must be regarded as the escutcheon of the breed. The ridge must be clearly defined, tapering and symmetrical. It must start immediately behind the shoulders and continue up to the hip (haunch) bones, and must contain two identical crowns only opposite each other. The lower edges of the crowns must not extend further down the ridge than one-third of the length of the ridge. Up to two inches is a good average for the width of the ridge.

GENERAL APPEARANCE. — The Ridgeback should represent a strong, muscular and active dog, symmetrical in outline, and capable of great endurance with a fair amount of speed. Movement should be similar to the Foxhound's gait.

Head and Skull. — Should be of fair length, the skull flat and rather broad between the ears and should be free from wrinkles when in repose. The stop should be reasonably well defined, and not in one straight line from the nose to the occiput bone as required in a Bull Terrier. The nose should be black or brown, in keeping with the colour of the dog. No other coloured nose is permissible. A black nose should be accompanied by dark eyes; a brown nose by amber eyes.

Eyes. — Should be moderately well apart, and should be round, bright and sparkling, with intelligent expression, their colour harmonising with the colour of the dog.

Ears. — Should be set up rather high, of medium size, rather wide at base, and gradually tapering to a rounded point. They should be carried close to the head.

Mouth. — The muzzle should be long, deep and powerful, jaws level and strong, with well developed teeth, especially the canines or holders. The lips should be clean, closely fitting the jaws.

Neck. — Should be fairly long, strong and free from throatiness.

Forequarters. — The shoulders should be sloping, clean and muscular, denoting speed. The forelegs should be perfectly straight, strong and heavy in bone; elbows close to the body.

Body. — The chest should not be too wide but very deep and capacious; ribs moderately well sprung, never rounded like barrel-hoops (which would indicate want of speed). The back powerful, and loins strong, muscular and slightly arched.

Hindquarters. — In the hind legs the muscles should be clean, well defined and hocks well down.

Feet. — The feet should be compact with well arched toes, round, tough elastic pads, protected by hair between the toes and pads.

Gait. — Straight forward movement, free and active.

Tail. — Should be strong at the insertion and generally tapering towards the end, free from coarseness. It should not be inserted too high or too low, and should be carried with a slight curve upwards, never curled.

Coat. — Should be short and dense, sleek and glossy in appearance but neither woolly nor silky.

Colour. — Light wheaten to red wheaten. Head, body, legs and tail should be of a uniform colour. A litle white on the chest is permissible but excessive white hairs here, on belly, or above paws should be penalised. White toes are undesirable. Dark muzzle and ears are permissible.

Weight and Size. — The desirable weight is dogs 36.3Kg (80 lbs) and bitches 31.7Kg (70 lbs) with a permissible variation of 2.2Kg (5 lbs) above and below these weights. A mature Ridgeback should be a handsome upstanding dog; dogs should be of a height of 63 to 68cm (25″ to 27″) and bitches 61 to 66cm (24″ to 26″). Minimum bench standard; dogs 63cm (25″) and bitches 61cm (24″).

Note. — Male animals should have two apparently normal testicles fully descended into the scrotum.

MAIN AMERICAN KENNEL CLUB VARIATION TO THE STANDARD FOR RHODESIAN RIDGEBACK —

Weight. — (Desirable) dogs 75 pounds, bitches 65 pounds.

RHODESIAN RIDGEBACK REGISTRATIONS 1981 — 87 INCLUSIVE

1981 — 366
1982 — 351
1983 — 441
1984 — 507
1985 — 636
1986 — 623
1987 — 709

YET TO WIN CRUFTS BEST-IN-SHOW.

SALUKI

The elegant Saluki is a member of the most ancient family of dogs, the Greyhounds with an ancestry dating possibly from 8,000 B.C. Carvings and drawings from the age of the Egyptian Pharaohs have shown Greyhound-type dogs, some resembling Salukis and even mummified specimens have been unearthed in tombs.

Sometimes known as the Gazelle Hound, the Saluki has always been used for hunting in the Middle East. He is a sighthound, that is, he depends more on his eyes than on his nose to detect his prey which, as his name suggests, is normally gazelle. He was a natural choice for this kind of hunting as no other dog could match the gazelle for speed and he had the necessary strength to bring down his quarry. So great was the hunting prowess of the Saluki that he was held in almost God-like reverance by the people of the Middle East, particularly among nomadic tribesmen who depended on game hunting to survive. The Saluki is still used to hunt gazelle, although to a lesser extent and he is still much-loved in his homeland.

If a prospective owner is prepared to give his dog a great deal of vigorous exercise and has a good-sized home, the Saluki could be for him. He enjoys the company of children although such an aristocratic breed does not like too much teasing. He guards well and will become intensely loyal to his owner and wary of strangers.

KEY TO CHARACTER	
INTELLIGENCE	****
TEMPERAMENT	****
EASE OF COAT CARE	*****
SUITABILITY FOR SMALL DWELLING	*
***** (5) = VERY GOOD	

BRITISH KENNEL CLUB STANDARD

SALUKI OR GAZELLE HOUND

GENERAL APPEARANCE. — The whole appearance of this breed should give an impression of grace and symmetry and of great speed and endurance coupled with strength and activity to enable it to kill gazelle or other quarry over deep sand or rocky mountain. The expression should be dignified and gentle with deep, faithful, farseeing eyes.

Head and Skull. — Head long and narrow; skull moderately wide between ears, not domed, the stop not pronounced, the whole showing great quality. Nose black or liver.

Eyes. — Dark to hazel and bright, large and oval, but not prominent.

Ears. — Long and mobile, covered with long silky hair; hanging close to the skull.

Mouth. — Teeth strong and level.

Neck. — Long, supple and well muscled.

Forequarters. — Shoulders sloping and set well back, well muscled without being coarse. The chest deep and moderately narrow. The forelegs straight and long from the elbow to the knee.

Body. — Back fairly broad, muscles slightly arched over the loin.

Hindquarters. — Strong, hip bones set wide apart, and stifle moderately bent, hocks low to the ground, showing galloping and jumping power.

Feet. — Of moderate length, toes long, and well arched, not splayed out, but at the same time not cat footed; the whole being strong and supple and well feathered between the toes.

Tail. — Long, set on low and carried naturally in a curve, well feathered on the underside with long silky hair, not bushy.

Coat. — Smooth and of a soft silky texture; slight feather on the legs; feather at the back of the thighs; sometimes with slight woolly feather on thigh and shoulders. (In the Smooth variety the points should be the same with the exception of the coat which has no feathering).

Colour. — White, cream, fawn, golden, red, grizzle and tan, tricolour (white, black and tan), and black and tan, or variations of these colours.

Weight and Size. — Height should average 58 to 71cm (23″ to 28″), bitches proportionately smaller.

Note. — Male animals should have two apparently normal testicles fully descended into the scrotum.

SALUKI REGISTRATIONS 1981 — 87 INCLUSIVE

1981 — 272
1982 — 182
1983 — 184
1984 — 168
1985 — 213
1986 — 178
1987 — 118

YET TO WIN CRUFTS BEST-IN-SHOW.

WHIPPET

There is some controversy concerning the exact beginnings of the Whippet, although it seems indisputable that the Greyhound and/or the Italian Greyhound have played a major part in his origination.

For more than a century, Whippet racing has been a popular sport and in the early days it was more widespead than Greyhound racing. It is thought that some of these fanatical racing men of Englands northern counties crossed some of their dogs with various terriers. This was hoped to increase the dog's courage and hardiness but, most probably, decreased his pace. No Whippet litters of today ever throw up any terrier-like specimens which probably shows that these out crossings were few and far between. In fact, the Whippet has probably bred true to type for several centuries.

Obviously the most widely known attribute of this breed is his speed, which can exceed 40 m.p.h. Straight track racing and coursing take full advantage of this prodigious asset. But as a companion and house dog the Whippet has much to offer. He is exceptionally clean, inexpensive to feed and splendidly behaved with children. He is far hardier than he appears but in the winter care should be taken to protect him from extremes of cold. Exercise should be very frequent and lengthy but the Whippet will live happily in a small house or flat.

KEY TO CHARACTER	
INTELLIGENCE	***
TEMPERAMENT	***
EASE OF COAT CARE	*****
SUITABILITY FOR SMALL DWELLING	****
***** (5) = VERY GOOD	

BRITISH KENNEL CLUB STANDARD

WHIPPET

GENERAL APPEARANCE. — Should convey an impresson of beautifully balanced muscular power and strength, combined with great elegance and grace of outline. Symmetry of outline, muscular development and powerful gait are the main considerations; the dog being built for speed and work all forms of exaggeration should be avoided. The dog should possess great freedom of action, the forelegs should be thrown forward and low over the ground like a thoroughbred horse not in a Hackney-like action. Hind legs should come well under the body giving great propelling power, general movement not to look stilted, high stepping or in a short or mincing manner.

Head and Skull. — Long and lean, flat on top tapering to the muzzle, rather wide between the eyes, the jaws powerful and clean cut, nose black, in blues a bluish colour is permitted and in livers a nose of the same colour and in whites or parti-colour a butterfly nose is permissible.

Eyes. — Bright, expression very alert.

Ears. — Rose-shaped, small and fine in texture.

Mouth. — Level. The teeth in the top jaw fitted closely over the teeth in lower jaw.

Neck. — Long and muscular, elegantly arched.

Forequarters. — Shoulders oblique and muscular the blades carried up to the spine closely set together at the top. Forelegs straight and upright, front not too wide, pasterns strong with slight spring, elbows well set under the body.

Body. — Chest very deep with plenty of heart-room, brisket deep and well defined, brack back, firm, somewhat long and showing definite arch over the loin but not humped, loin giving the impression of strength and power, ribs well sprung; well muscled on back.

Hindquarters. — Strong and broad across thighs, stifles well bent, hocks well let down, second thighs strong, the dog then being able to stand over a lot of ground and show great driving power.

Feet. — Very neat, well split up between the toes, knuckles highly arched, pads thick and strong.

Tail. — No feathering. Long, tapering, when in action carried in a delicate curve upward but not over the back.

Coat. — Fine, short, as close as possible in texture.

Colour. — Any colour or mixture of colours.

Weight and Size. — The ideal height for dogs is 47cm (18½") and for bitches 44cm (17½"). Judges should use their discretion and not unduly penalise an otherwise good specimen.

Faults. — FRONT AND SHOULDERS — Weak, sloping or too straight pasterns, pigeon toes, tied elbows, loaded or bossy shoulders wide on top and straight shoulderblades, flat sides. An exaggerated narrow front not to be enouraged. HEAD AND SKULL — Appleskull, short fore face or down face. EARS — Pricked or tulip. MOUTH — Over or undershot. NECK — Throatiness at the join of neck and jaw, and at base of neck. BODY AND HINDQUARTERS — Short coupled or cramped stance, also an exaggerated arch, a Camel or Humped back (the arch started behind the shoulder-blades), a too short or overlong loin. Straight stifles, poor muscular development of thighs and second thighs. FEET — Splayed, flat or open. TAIL — Gay, ringed or twisted, short or docked. COAT — Wire or Broken coated; a coarse or wooly coat; coarse thick skin.

Note. — Male animals should have two apparently normal testicles fully descended into the scrotum.

MAIN AMERICAN KENNEL CLUB VARIATION TO THE STANDARD FOR WHIPPET —

Size. — Ideal height for dogs, 19 to 22 inches; for bitches, 18 to 21 inches.

WHIPPET REGISTRATIONS 1981 — 87 INCLUSIVE

1981 — 1417
1982 — 1247
1983 — 1295
1984 — 1124
1985 — 1293
1986 — 1172
1987 — 1221

YET TO WIN CRUFTS BEST-IN-SHOW.

PEDIGREE DOGS IN COLOUR

BOOK TWO

GUNDOGS

This is Book Two in a volume consisting of six books each dealing with a main group of dogs. The page numbering follows that used in the main volume.

ENGLISH SETTER

Of the three setters in Britain, the **English** is in the middle in the popularity stakes. Many would argue, though, that he is the most balanced dog of the three, being strong and efficient in the field and affectionate as a companion.

He descends from an ancient spaniel-type although accurate information on his exact beginnings does not exist. What is certain is that the excellent dogs we know today owe much of their refinement to a Mr. Edward Laverack who began expert selective breeding in the early nineteenth century. By the 1850's Laverack's work reached fruition and English Setters began to appear in the show ring. As well as now being a much esteemed gun dog and pet in Britain, he is also well established in the U.S.A.

The English Setter makes a marvellous house dog for someone with a reasonable amount of room and plenty of time to devote to him. With children his behaviour is impeccable and he loves to join in with whatever is going on around him. Obviously his working background demands that he has plenty of free running, varied exercise.

The attractive coat requires plenty of regular brushing and the Engish Setter always looks better if the feathering on the legs is kept free from matting or tangling.

KEY TO CHARACTER	
INTELLIGENCE	****
TEMPERAMENT	*****
EASE OF COAT CARE	**
SUITABILITY FOR SMALL DWELLING	*
***** (5) = VERY GOOD	

BRITISH KENNEL CLUB STANDARD

ENGLISH SETTER

CHARACTERISTICS. — An intensely friendly and quiet-natured dog with a keen game sense.

GENERAL APPEARANCE. — Of medium height, clean in outline, elegant in appearance and movement.

Head and Skull. — Head should be long and reasonably lean, with a well-defined stop. The skull oval from ear to ear, showing plenty of brain room, and with a well-defined occipital protuberance. The muzzle moderately deep and fairly square; from the stop to the point of the nose should equal the length of skull from occiput to eyes; the nostrils wide and the jaws of nearly equal length; flews not to be too pendulous; the colour of the nose should be black or liver, according to the colour of the coat.

Eyes. — The eyes should be bright, mild and intelligent, and of a dark haze colour, the darker the better.

Ears. — The ears of moderate length, set on low, and hanging in neat folds close to the cheek; the tip should be velvety, the upper part clothed in fine silky hair.

Mouth. — The jaws should be strong, with a perfect regular and complete scissor bite, i.e., the upper teeth closely overlapping the lower teeth and set square to the jaws.

Neck. — Neck should be rather long, muscular and lean, slightly arched at the crest, and clean cut where it joins the head; towards the shoulder it should be larger and very muscular, not throaty or pendulous below the throat, but elegant in appearance.

Forequarters. — The shoulders should be well set back or oblique; the chest should be deep in the brisket, and of good depth and width between the shoulder blades. The forearm big and very muscular, with rounded bone, and the elbow well let down, Pasterns short, muscular, round and straight.

Body. — The body should be of moderate length, the back short and level with good round widely-sprung ribs and deep in the back ribs, i.e., well ribbed up.

Hindquarters. — The loins should be wide, slightly arched, strong and muscular, with defined second thigh. Stifles well bent and rugged, thighs long from hip to hock.

Feet. — The feet should be set on almost in line with the back; medium length, not curly or ropy, to be slightly curved or scimitar-shaped but with no tendency to turn upwards; the flag or feather hanging in long pendant flakes. The feather should not commence at the root, but slightly below, and increase in length to the middle, then gradually taper off towards the end; the hair long, bright, soft and silky, wavy, but not curly.

Coat. — The coat from the back of the head in a line with the ears ought to be slightly wavy, long and silky, which should be the case with the coat generally; the breeches and forelegs, nearly down to the feet, should be well feathered.

Colour. — The colour may be either black and white, lemon and white, liver and white or tricolour — that is black, white and tan; those without heavy patches of colour on the body, but flecked all over, preferred.

Weight and Size. — Height: Dogs 65 to 68cm (25½″ to 27″). Bitches 61 to 65cm (24″ to 25½″). Weight: Dogs 27 to 30Kg (60 to 66 lbs). Bitches 25 to 28Kg (55 to 61½ lbs).

Faults. — Any departure from the foregoing points should be considered a fault and the seriousness with which the fault is regarded should be in exact proportion to its degree.

Note. — Male animals should have two apparently normal testicles fully descended into the scrotum.

MAIN AMERICAN KENNEL CLUB VARIATION TO STANDARD FOR THE ENGLISH SETTER —

Height. — Dogs about 25 inches; bitches about 24 inches.

ENGLISH SETTER REGISTRATIONS 1981 — 87 INCLUSIVE

1981 — 1246
1982 — 1013
1983 — 1248
1984 — 1205
1985 — 1166
1986 — 1019
1987 — 1027

CRUFTS BEST-IN-SHOW WINNER TWICE.

1964 SH.CH. SILBURY SOAMES OF MADAVALE — MRS. A. WILLIAMS
1977 BOURNEHOUSE DANCING MASTER — MR. G.F. WILLIAMS

English Setter

German Short-Haired Pointer

GERMAN SHORTHAIRED POINTER

This breed has been described as the ultimate gundog and it is difficult to dispute this statement.

Developed with typical German thoroughness from the Spanish Pointer, English Foxhound and German Pointer-types, he possesses all that a sporting dog could require. The early specimens were a little heavier and coarser than today's dogs and it was the use of English Pointers which added the finishing touch, increasing intelligence and athleticism.

In the field his pointing ability is held in the highest regard and he is totally at home in water or on land when retrieving. He is extremely obedient and has a fine nose. The length of a hunt is of no consequence to the German Shorthaired Pointer as he has boundless stamina.

In the showring he can be an impressive sight and his even temperament makes the handler's job a fairly simple one. His sleek good looks and often striking markings have ensured his place as a firm favourite in dog shows across the world.

Unlike some truly sporting breds, the German Shorthaired Pointer blends very easily into a family home. Provided that exercise is lengthy and frequent and that the house and garden are of a fair size, he can make a marvellous pet. He revels in the company of children and is an effective and forceful guard.

KEY TO CHARACTER	
INTELLIGENCE	****
TEMPERAMENT	*****
EASE OF COAT CARE	*****
SUITABILITY FOR SMALL DWELLING	*
***** (5) = VERY GOOD	

BRITISH KENNEL CLUB STANDARD

GERMAN SHORTHAIRED POINTER

CHARACTERISTICS. — The German Shorthaired Pointer is a dual-purpose Pointer-Retriever and this accounts for his excellence in the field, which requires a very keen nose, perseverance in searching, and enterprise. His style attracts attention; he is equally good on land and in water, is biddable, an extremely keen worker, and very loyal.

GENERAL APPEARANCE. — A noble, steady dog showing power, endurance and speed, giving the immediate impression of an alert and energetic (not nervous) dog whose movements are well co-ordinated. Neither unduly small nor conspicuously large, but of medium size, and like the hunter, "With a short back stand over plenty of ground". Grace of outline, clean cut head, sloping long shoulders, deep chest, short back and powerful hindquarters, good bone composition, adequate muscle, well carried tail and taut coat giving a thoroughbred appearance.

Head and skull. — Clean-cut, neither to light nor too heavy, but well proportioned to the body. The skull sufficiently broad and slightly rounded. The furrow between the eyes not so deep, and the occiput not so pronounced as in the English Pointer. The nasal bone rises gradually from nose to forehead (this is more pronounced in the male) and should never possess a definite stop as in the English Pointer, but when viewed from the side there is a well defined stop effect due to the position of the eyebrows. The lips fall away almost vertically from a somewhat protruding nose and continue in a slight curve to the corner of the mouth. Lips well developed but not over hung. Jaws powerful and sufficiently long to enable the dog to pick up and carry game. Dish-faced and snipy muzzle are not desirable. Nose solid brown, wide nostrils well opened and soft.

Eyes. — Medium size, soft and intelligent, not protruding nor too deep set. Varying in shades of brown to tone with coat. Light eye not desirable. Eyelids should close properly.

Ears. — Broad and set high; neither too fleshy nor too thin with a short soft coat; hung close to the head, no pronounced fold, rounded at the tip and should reach almost to the corner of the mouth when brought forward.

Gordon Setter

Hungarian Vizsla

Mouth. — Teeth sound and strong. Molar teeth meeting exactly and the eyeteeth should fit close in a true scissor bite. Neither overshot nor undershot.

Neck. — Moderately long, muscular and slightly arched, becoming larger towards the shoulders. Skin should not fit too closely.

Forequarters. — Shoulder sloping and very muscular with top of shoulder blades close; upper arm bones between shoulder and elbow long. Elbows well laid back, neither pointing outwards nor inwards. Forelegs straight and lean, sufficiently muscular and strong but not coarse-boned. Pasterns slightly sloping, almost straight but not quite.

Body. — Chest must appear deep rather than wide but not out of proportion to the rest of the body; ribs deep and well sprung, never barrel-shaped nor flat as in the hound; back ribs reaching well down to tucked up loins. Chest measurement immediately behind the elbows smaller than about a hands-breadth behind the elbows, so that the upper arm has freedom of movement. Firm, short back, not arched. The loin wide and slightly arched; the croup wide and sufficiently long, neither too heavy nor too sloping starting on a level with the back and sloping gradually towards the tail. Bones solid and strong not clumsy and porous.

Hindquarters. — The hips broad and wide falling slightly towards the tail. thighs strong and well muscled. Stifles well bent. Hocks square with the body and slightly bent, turning neither in nor out. Pasterns nearly upright.

Feet. — Compact, close-knit, round to spoon shaped, well padded, should turn neither in nor out. Toes well arched and heavily nailed.

Tail. — Starts high and thick growing gradually thinner. Docked to medium length by two-fifths to half its length. When quiet tail should be carried down and when moving horizontally, never held high over the back or bent.

Coat. — Skin should not fit loosely or fold. Coat short, flat and coarse to the touch, slightly longer under the tail.

Colour. — Solid liver, liver and white spotted, liver and white spotted and ticked, liver and white ticked, black and white.

Weight and Size. — Dogs 25 to 31.8Kg (55 to 70 lbs), bitches 20.4 to 27.2Kg (45 to 60 lbs). Size — dogs 58 to 64cm (23″ to 25″) and bitches 53 to 59cm (21″ to 23″) at the shoulder, Symmetry is most essential.

Faults. — Bone structure too clumsy, sway-back, head too large, deep wrinkles in forehead, cone-shaped skull or occiput too prominent. Ears too long or too closely set together, eye-lids not closing properly. Wrinkles in neck. Feet or elbows turned inwards or outwards. Soft, sunken or splayed toes; cowhocks, straight hindlegs, or down on pasterns. Tail starting too low, undocked, too thick, curled up or too furry. Tri-coloured.

Note. — Male animals should have two apparently normal testicles fully descended into the scrotum.

GERMAN SHORTHAIRED POINTER REGISTRATIONS 1981 — 87 INCLUSIVE

1981 — 850
1982 — 629
1983 — 829
1984 — 740
1985 — 780
1986 — 916
1987 — 710

YET TO WIN CRUFTS BEST-IN-SHOW.

Irish Setter

Pointer

Curly-Coated Retriever

Flat-Coated Retriever

GORDON SETTER

The Gordon Setter has his beginnings about two hundred years ago and is named after his founder, the fourth Duke of Gordon. The Kennels of Gordon Castle were known to have produced setters of varying colours, some black and tan, some black and white and some black, white and tan. Several other breeders of the time used the esteemed dogs of the Duke in their kennels with some slight variations resulting. Many people have varying views on exactly which breeds were introduced to the early Gordon Setter's blood to arrive at the standardised version. The Collie, Pointer, Field Spaniel, Bloodhound and Irish Setter have all been mentioned as possibilities. It seems likely that the Irish Setter, at least, is responsible for the superb, rich mahogony markings, with the occasional all red Gordon Setter still appearing. The black and tan coloured dogs were always the most popular and today no other colour is acceptable.

The Gordon Setter is the largest and hardiest setter with excellent stamina and recuperative powers, an immense asset in the eyes of the shooting enthusiast. Although he does not possess the speed of his lighter relatives, he is more stable and dependable.

He should not be taken on lightly as a pet, as he is a sporting dog first and foremost and will expect plenty of free running. This is not to say that he is difficult to get along with, quite the opposite being true, but an owner should never keep the Gordon Setter in "cooped up" conditions.

KEY TO CHARACTER	
INTELLIGENCE	****
TEMPERAMENT	****
EASE OF COAT CARE	**
SUITABILITY FOR SMALL DWELLING	*
***** (5) = VERY GOOD	

BRITISH KENNEL CLUB STANDARD

GORDON SETTER

GENERAL APPEARANCE. — A stylish dog, built on galloping lines, having a thoroughbred appearance consistent with its build which can be compared to a weight carrying hunter. Must have symmetrical conformation throughout, showing true balance. Strong, fairly short and level back. Shortish tail. Head fairly long, clearly lined and with intelligent expression, clear colours and long flat coat.

Head and Skull. — Head deep rather than broad, but definitely broader than the muzzle, showing brain room. Skull slightly rounded and broadest between the ears. The head should have a clearly indicated stop and length from occiput to stop should be slightly longer than from stop to nose. Below and above the eyes should be lean and the cheeks as narrow as the leanness of the head allows. The muzzle should be fairly long with almost parallel lines and not pointed, as seen from above or from the side. The flews not pendulous but with clearly indicated lips. Nose big and broad, with open nostrils and black in colour. The muzzle should not be quite as deep as its length.

Eyes. — Of fair size, not too deep not too prominent but sufficiently under the brows to show keen and intelligent expression. Dark brown and bright.

Ears. — Set low on the head and lying close to it, of medium size and thin.

Mouth. — Must be even and not under nor overshot.

Neck. — Long, lean and arched to the head and without any throatiness.

Forequarters. — Shoulders should be long and slope well back; with wide flat bone and fairly close at withers; should not be loaded, i.e., too thick, which interferes with liberty of movement. Elbows well let down and showing well under the body, which gives freedom of action. Forelegs big, flat-boned and straight, with strong upright pasterns, well feathered.

Body. — Of moderate length, deep in brisket, with ribs well sprung. Deep in back ribs, i.e., well-ribbed up. Loins wide and slightly arched. Chest not too broad.

Hindquarters. — Hind legs from hip to hock should be long, broad and muscular; hock to heel short and strong, stifles well bent; hocks straight, not inclined either in or out. Pelvis should tend to the horizontal, i.e., opposite of goose rump.

Feet. — Oval, with close knit, well-arched toes, with plenty of hair between. Full toe pads and deep heel cushions.

Tail. — Fairly short, straight or slightly scimitar shaped and should not reach below the hocks. Carried horizontal or below line of back. Thick at the root tapering to a fine point. The feather or flat which starts near the root should be long and straight, and growing shorter uniformly to the point.

Coat. — On the head and front of legs and tips of ears should be short and fine, but on the other parts of the body and legs it ought to be of moderate length, fairly flat and free as possible from curl or wave. The feather on the upper portion of the ears should be long and silky, on the back of the hind legs long and fine; a fair amount of hair on the belly forming a nice fringe which may extend on chest and throat. All feathering to be as flat and straight as possible.

Colour. — Deep shining coal-black, with no sign of rustiness, with tan markings of a rich chestnut red, i.e., colour of a ripe horse-chestnut as taken from shell. Tan should be lustrous. Black pencilling allowed on toes and also black streak under jaw. *Tan markings:* two clear spots over the eyes not over threequarters of an inch in diameter. On the sides of the muzzle, the tan should not reach above the base of nose, resembling a stripe around the end of the muzzle from one side to the other. On the throat. Two large clear spots on the chest. On the inside of the hind legs and inside the thighs showing down the front of the stifle and broadening out to the outside of the hind legs from the hock to the toes. It must, however, not completely eliminate the black on the back of the hind legs. On the forelegs, up to the elbows behind, and to the knees or a little above, in front. Around the vent. A white spot on chest is allowed but the smaller the better.

Weight and Size. — As a guide to size, shoulder height for males 66cm (26″) and weight about 29.5Kg (65 lbs). Females, 62cm (24½″) and weight about 25.4Kg (56 lbs). In show condition.

Faults. — General Impression: unintelligent appearance. The bloodhound type with heavy and big head and ears and clumsy body; the collie type with pointed muzzle and curved tail. The Head: pointed, snipy, down or upturned muzzle, too small or large mouth. The Eyes: too light in colour, too deep set or too prominent. The Ears: set too high, or unusually broad or heavy. The Neck: thick and short. Shoulders and Back: irregularly formed. The Chest: too broad. The Legs and Feet: crooked legs. Outturned elbows. The toes scattered, flat footed. The Tail: too long, badly carried or hooked at the end. The Coat: curly, like wool, not shining. The Colour: yellow, or straw-coloured tan, or without clearly defined lines between the different colours. White feet. Too much white on the chest. In the black there should be no tan hairs.

Note. — Male animals should have two apparently normal testicles fully descended into the scrotum.

MAIN AMERICAN KENNEL CLUB VARIATION TO STANDARD FOR THE GORDON SETTER —

Size. — Shoulder height for males, 24 to 27 inches. For females, 23 to 26 inches.

Weight. — Males, 55 to 80 pounds; females, 45 to 70 pounds.

GORDON SETTER REGISTRATIONS 1981 — 87 INCLUSIVE

1981 — 529
1982 — 501
1983 — 478
1984 — 575
1985 — 586
1986 — 528
1987 — 456

YET TO WIN CRUFTS BEST-IN-SHOW.

HUNGARIAN VIZSLA

Although it is not certain that the Vizsla was first bred in Hungary, there is little doubt that it is there that all the major refinements of this first class sporting dog have been developed.

During the prosperous days of the Austro-Hungarian empire, the Vizsla was used to hunt boar and deer amongst other prey. The well-to-do noblemen of the time wanted a fit, efficient dog that could be easily trained to all the sportsman's needs. The selective breeding pursued by these huntsmen was largely responsible for the form anc character of today's Vizsla. He has been kept as one of the purest of breeds which is not surprising as his ability in the field could scarcely have been improved upon by out-crossing.

As a family pet the Hungarian Vizsla is to be highly recommended. His temperament is unwavering with all age groups and his cleanliness and easy management make him a desirable member of any household.

Training is no problem and the beautiful russet gold coat requires only minimal attention.

Exercise should be lengthy and frequent, lovers of the outdoors being ideal owners.

KEY TO CHARACTER	
INTELLIGENCE	****
TEMPERAMENT	*****
EASE OF COAT CARE	*****
SUITABILITY FOR SMALL DWELLING	*
***** (5) = VERY GOOD	

BRITISH KENNEL CLUB STANDARD

HUNGARIAN VIZSLA

CHARACTERISTICS. — The Hungarian Vizsla should be lively and intelligent, obedient but sensitive, very affectionate and easily trained. It was bred for hunting for fur and feather on open ground or in thick cover, pointing and retrieving from both land and water.

GENERAL APPEARANCE. — A medium sized dog of distinguished appearance, robust and not too heavily boned.

Head and Skull. — The head should be gaunt and noble. The skull should be moderately wide between the ears with a median line down the forehead and a moderate stop. The muzzle should be a little longer than the skull and although tapering should be well squared at the end. The nostrils should be well developed, broad and wide. The jaws strong and powerful. The lips should cover the jaws completely and should be neither loose nor pendulous. The nose should be brown.

Eyes. — Neither deep nor prominent, of medium size, being a shade darker in colour than the coat. The shape of the eyes should be slightly oval and the eyelids should fit tightly. A yellow or black eye is objectionable.

Ears. — The ears should be moderately low set, proportionately long with a thin skin and hang down close to the cheeks, should be rounded 'V' shaped not fleshy.

Mouth. — Sound white teeth meeting in a scissor bite, full dentition is desirable.

Forequarters. — Shoulders should be well laid and muscular, elbow straight pointing neither in nor out, the forearm should be long.

Body. — Back should be level, short well muscled, withers high. The chest should be moderately broad and deep with prominent breast bone. The distance from the withers to the lowest part of the chest should be equal to the distance from the chest to the ground. The ribs should be well sprung and the belly should be tight with a slight tuck-up beneath the loin. The croup should be well muscled.

Hindquarters. — Should be straight when viewed from the rear, the thighs should be well developed with moderate angulation, the hocks well let down.

Feet. — Rounded with toes short, arched and well closed. A cat like foot is desirable, hare foot is objectionable. Nails short, strong and a shade darker in colour than coat, dew claws should be removed.

Gait. — Graceful and elegant with a lively trot and ground covering gallop.

Tail. — Should be of moderate thickness, rather low set, with one third docked off. Whilst moving should be held horizontally.

Coat. — Should be short and straight, dense and coarse and feel greasy to the touch.

Colour. — Russet gold. Small white marks on chest and feet, though acceptable, are not desirable.

Weight and Size. — Optimum Weight — 22 to 30Kg (48½ to 66 lbs). Height at withers — Dogs 57 to 64cm (22½″ to 25″) Bitches 53 to 60cm (21″ to 23½″).

Faults. — Any departure from the foregoing points should be considered a fault and the seriousness of the fault should be in exact proportion to its degree.

Note. — Male animals should have two apparently normal testicles fully descended into the scrotum.

MAIN AMERICAN KENNEL CLUB VARIATION TO STANDARD FOR THE HUNGARIAN VIZSLA —

Known in the U.S.A. as simply the Vizsla or the Hungarian Pointer.

Size. — The idal male is 22 to 24 inches at the highest point over the shoulder blades. The ideal female is 21 to 23 inches.

HUNGARIAN VIZSLA REGISTATIONS 1981 — 87 INCLUSIVE

1981 — 153
1982 — 173
1983 — 136
1984 — 226
1985 — 236
1986 — 225
1987 — 169

YET TO WIN CRUFTS BEST-IN-SHOW.

IRISH SETTER

This, the most popular of the Setters, was developed in Ireland in the mid-nineteenth century using Spaniels, Pointers and Setter-type dogs. Unfortunately it is impossible to ascertain exactly which combintions of breeds were used, but since the Irish Setter's official classification in 1876, he has remained a very pure-bred dog.

Surprising as it may seem to modern dog lovers who are familiar with the consistent solid red colour of these dogs, the earliest Irish Setters were mainly white with red patches. Being mainly a dog used for vigorous work in the field, appearance was secondary to physical durability and intelligence, therefore any coat colour was accepted. But eventually, as the breed began to make inroads into the show world, the fashion began to be for self-coloured red dogs. Although even to this day, some white is permissible, anything approaching a large area of white is undesirable.

As a gun dog he has a fine track record, showing great speed, agility and a keen nose. In recent years, the working side to his nature has somewhat taken a back seat to his need for beauty. Some would regard this as unfortunate, but it is also easy to see why the Irish Setter is in such demand as a show dog. When well presented he is a dog of great elegance and of course the coat always demands the onlooker's attention.

Training both for the gun and for the home can prove a little difficult at first, but with perseverance he will become responsive and loyal. He is a dog of very high spirits and natural friendliness so plenty of human attention and exercise are vital.

KEY TO CHARACTER	
INTELLIGENCE	****
TEMPERAMENT	****
EASE OF COAT CARE	**
SUITABILITY FOR SMALL DWELLING	*
***** (5) = VERY GOOD	

BRITISH KENNEL CLUB STANDARD

IRISH SETTER

GENERAL APPEARANCE. — Must be racey, full of quality, and kindly in expression.

Head and Skull. — The head should be long and lean, not narrow or snipy, and not coarse at the ears. The skull oval (from ear to ear), having plenty of brain room, and with well-defined occipital protuberance. Brows raised, showing stop. The muzzle moderately deep, and fairly square at end. From the stop to the point of the nose should be long, the nostrils wide, and the jaws of nearly equal length, flews not to be pendulous. The colour of the nose: dark mahogany, or dark walnut, or black.

Eyes. — Should be dark hazel or dark brown and ought not to be too large.

Ears. — The ears should be of moderate size, fine in texture, set on low, well back; and hanging in a neat fold close to the head.

Mouth. — Not over or undershot.

Neck. — Should be moderately long, very muscular, but not too thick, slightly arched, free from all tendency to throatiness.

Forequarters. — The shoulders to be fine at the points, deep and sloping well back. The chest as deep as possible, rather narrow in front. The fore legs should be straight and sinewy, having plenty of bone, with elbows free, well let down, not inclined either in or out.

Body. — Should be proportionate, the ribs well sprung, leaving plenty of lung room. Loins muscular, slightly arched.

Hindquarters. — Should be wide and powerful. The hind legs from hip to hock should be long and muscular; from hock to heel short and strong. The stifle and hock joints well bent, and not inclined either in or out.

Feet. — Should be small, very firm, toes strong, close together and arched.

Tail. — Should be of moderate length, proportionate to the size of the body, set on rather low, strong at root, and tapering to a fine point; to be carried as nearly as possible on a level with or below the back.

Coat and Feathering. — On the head, front of the legs, and tips of the ears, should be short and fine, but on all other parts of the body and legs it ought to be of moderate length, flat, and as free as possible from curl or wave. The feather on the upper portion of the ears should be long and silky; on the back of fore and hind legs should be long and fine; a fair amount of hair on the belly forming a nice fringe, which may extend on chest and throat. Feet to be well feathered between the toes. Tail to have a nice fringe of moderately long hair, decreasing in length as it approaches the point. All feathering to be as straight and as flat as possible.

Colour. — The colour should be rich chestnut, with no trace whatever of black; white on chest, throat, chin or toes, or a small star on the forehead, or a narrow streak or blaze on the nose or face not to disqualify.

Note. — Male animals should have two apparently normal testicles fully descended into the scrotum.

MAIN AMERICAN KENNEL CLUB VARIATION TO STANDARD FOR THE IRISH SETTER —

Size. — Twenty-seven inches at the withers and a show weight of about 70 pounds is considered ideal for a dog; the bitch 25 inches, 60 pounds.

IRISH SETTER REGISTRATIONS 1981 — 87 INCLUSIVE

1981 — 3122
1982 — 2675
1983 — 2450
1984 — 1997
1985 — 1938
1986 — 1790
1987 — 1529

CRUFTS BEST-IN-SHOW WINNER 1981.
CH. ASTLEY'S PORTIA OF RUA — MR. AND MISS TUITE.

POINTER

This lean, athletic gun dog breed has it's beginnings in Europe. It is thought that British soldiers returning from war in Spain in the early 18th century brought a strain of Spanish pointing dog home with them. The breed was very successful with the shooting fraternity of the time, but eventually the demanding English sportsmen felt they needed a faster breed. This was laboriously acheived through selective breeding, until the Pointer we know now was established in 1800. The idea of crossing the Pointer with the Foxhound was dabbled with, but it was thought that this lessened the ability to "point" out the game and that it made the breed a little unruly.

It should always be remembered by the Pointer owner that his dog was specifically bred for speed and stamina. Therefore, every effort should be made to provide plenty of running exercise, a walk "around the block" being inadequate. If allowed to use his boundless energy in this way, then his naturally sociable and even temperament will shine through.

A well cared for Pointer is a regal, graceful animal, and is to be highly recommended to a conscientious owner.

KEY TO CHARACTER	
INTELLIGENCE	****
TEMPERAMENT	*****
EASE OF COAT CARE	*****
SUITABILITY FOR SMALL DWELLING	*
***** (5) = VERY GOOD	

BRITISH KENNEL CLUB STANDARD

POINTER

CHARACTERISTICS. — The Pointer should be symmetrical and well built all over. Alert, with the appearance of strength, endurance and speed.

Head and Skull. — The skull should be medium breadth and in proportion to the length of fore-face; the stop well defined, pronounced occipital bone. Nose and eye-rims dark, but may be lighter in the case of a lemon and white-coloured dog. The nostrils wide, soft and moist. The muzzle somewhat concave, and ending on a level with the nostrils, giving a slightly dish-faced appearance. The cheek-bones should not be prominent. Well developed soft lip.

Eyes. — The same distance form the occiput as from the nostrils. A slight depression under the eyes, which should be bright and kindly in expression, not bold or staring, and not looking down the nose. The colour of the eyes either hazel or brown according to the colour of the coat.

Mouth. — Scissors bite, neither under nor overshot.

Neck. — Long, muscular, slightly arched, springing cleanly from the shoulders and free from throatiness.

Ears. — The ears should be set on fairly high, and lie close to the head, they should be of medium length, and inclined to be pointed at the tips.

Forequarters. — The shoulders long, sloping, and well laid back. The chest just wide enough for plenty of heart room. The brisket well let down, to a level with the elbows. The fore-legs straight and firm, of good oval bone, with the back sinews strong and visible. The knee joint should be flat with the front of the leg, and protrude very little on the inside. Pasterns lengthy, strong and resilient.

Body. — Well-sprung ribs, gradually falling away at the loin, which should be strong, muscular and slightly arched. The couplings short. The haunch bones well spaced and prominent, but not above the level of the back. The general outline from head to tail being a series of graceful curves, giving a strong but lissom appearance.

Hindquarters. — Well turned stifles. The hock should be well let down, and cose to the ground. A good expanse of thigh, which should be very muscular, as should also the second-thighs.

Feet. — The feet oval, with well-knit, arched toes, well cushioned underneath.

Gait. — Smooth, covering plenty of ground with each stride. Driving hind action, elbows neither turning in nor out. Definitely not a hackney action.

Tail. — The tail of medium length, thick at the root, growing gradually thinner to the point. It should be well covered with close hair, and carried on a level with the back, with no upward curl. With the dog in movement the tail should lash from side to side.

Coat. — The coat should be fine, short, hard and evenly distributed, perfectly smooth and straight, with a decided sheen.

Colour. — The usual colours are lemon and white, orange and white, liver and white, and black and white. Self colours and tricolours are also correct.

Size. — Desirable heights. Dogs 63 to 69cm (25″ to 27″). Bitches 61 to 66cm (24″ to 26″).

Note. — Male animals should have two apparently normnal testicles fully descended into the scrotum.

MAIN AMERICAN KENNEL CLUB VARIATION TO STANDARD FOR THE POINTER —

Size. — Dogs; height 25″ to 28″, weight 55 to 75 pounds. Bitches; height 23″ to 26″, weight 45 to 65 pounds.

POINTER REGISTRATIONS 1981 — 87 INCLUSIVE

1981 — 838
1982 — 737
1983 — 762
1984 — 737
1985 — 801
1986 — 626
1987 — 650

CRUFTS BEST-IN-SHOW WINNER TWICE.
1935 PENNINE PRIMA DONNA — A. EGGLESTON.
1958 CH. CHIMING BELLS — MRS. W. PARKINSON.

CURLY-COATED RETRIEVER

As can at once be seen in the coat of this fine breed, the Curly-Coated Retriever shares ancestry with the Poodle and the Irish Water Spaniel. All probably descend from the Water Dog which was common in Europe several centuries ago. Even when the Curly-Coated Retriever was established, it is believed that Poodle blood was re-introduced to the breed and this may have resulted in an even tighter curl to the coat.

This breed has always been highly regarded as a worker in the field and his great stamina and intelligence are well known. When working in water the dense curls of the coat are vitually water tight so cold conditions hold no fear for him. His coat also offers good protection when foraging in potentially hazardous undergrowth.

Although kept by relatively few people, the Curly-Coated Retriever has all the good points associated with retrievers. His temperament is very steady and all members of the family will receive his loyalty and affection. This devotion will be demonstrated when guarding the owner's house and his solid build makes him a force to be reckoned with.

A good deal of exercise is necessary for this essentially outdoor breed, with rural suroundings being preferred.

To maintain his striking appearance, the coat must never be brushed as this discourages the tight curling.

KEY TO CHARACTER	
INTELLIGENCE	****
TEMPERAMENT	*****
EASE OF COAT CARE	**
SUITABILITY FOR SMALL DWELLING	*
***** (5) = VERY GOOD	

BRITISH KENNEL CLUB STANDARD

RETRIEVER (CURLY-COATED)

GENERAL APPEARANCE. — A strong smart upstanding dog showing activity, endurance and intelligence.

Head and Skull. — Long, well proportioned flat skull, jaws strong and long but not inclined to snipiness. Nose black in the black-coated variety with wide nostrils, coarseness of head to be deprecated.

Eyes. — Black or brown but not "gooseberry" coloured, rather large but not too prominent.

Ears. — Rather small, set on low, lying close to the head and covered with short curls.

Mouth. — Teeth strong and level.

Neck. — Should be moderately long, free from throatiness.

Forequarters. — Shoulders should be very deep, muscular and well laid back.

Hindquarters. — Strong and muscular, hock low to the ground with good bend to stifle and hock.

Body. — Well sprung ribs, good depth of brisket, not too long in the loin, as little tucked-up in flank as possible.

Feet. — Round and compact with well-arched toes.

Gait. — Covering plenty of ground with drive.

Tail. — Moderately short, carried fairly straight and covered with curls, tapering towards the point, gay tail not desirable.

Coat. — Should be one mass of crisp small curls all over. This being the main characteristic of the breed should be given great consideration when making judging awards.

Colour. — Black or liver.

Size. — Desirable height at withers: Dogs 68.58cm (27″); Bitches 63.50cm (25″).

Faults. — Wide skull, light eyes, curled tail and bad movement.

Note. — Male animals should have two apparently normal testicles fully descended into the scrotum.

CURLY COATED RETRIEVER REGISTRATIONS 1981 — 87 INCLUSIVE

1981 — 90
1982 — 69
1983 — 100
1984 — 88
1985 — 114
1986 — 83
1987 — 135

YET TO WIN CRUFTS BEST-IN-SHOW.

FLAT-COATED RETRIEVER

The Flat-Coated Retriever has only been present in Britain since the late Nineteenth century and was originally known as the Wavy-Coated Retriever. The early dogs were rather unrefined and are though to have resulted from Labrador and Newfoundland crossings. Although evidence of these two breeds is still very visible in the Flat-Coated Retriever, modern specimens have been improved by the introduction of Collie and Setter blood. This helped to produce an agile dog with a flatter coat.

He is a highly-rated breed amongst the shooting fraternity having unsurpassed retrieving qualities and an ability to work well on land or in water, the latter skill no doubt reflecting his Newfoundland ancestry.

In the early part of this century, the Flat-Coated Retriever was a very popular breed in Britain and although his popularity is not at such a level today, he has a good size following and his future is assured.

He is a beautifully balanced dog in all respects. His physique is nicely proportional, strong but not heavy and his temperament is even and friendly. Like all retrievers he is of high intelligence and loves human company. A great deal of exercise is required by the Flat-Coated Retriever and an energetic owner who is keen on the outdoors would be ideal.

KEY TO CHARACTER	
INTELLIGENCE	****
TEMPERAMENT	*****
EASE OF COAT CARE	***
SUITABILITY FOR SMALL DWELLING	*
***** (5) = VERY GOOD	

BRITISH KENNEL CLUB STANDARD

RETRIEVER (FLAT-COATED)

GENERAL APPEARANCE. — A bright, active dog of medium size with an intelligent expression, showing power without lumber, and raciness without weediness.

Head and Skull. — The head should be long and nicely moulded. The skull flat and moderately broad. There should be a depression or stop between the eyes, slight and in no way accentuated, so as to avoid giving either a down or a dish-faced appearance. The nose of a good size, with open nostrils. The jaws should be long and strong, with a capacity of carrying a hare of pheasant.

Eyes. — Should be of medium size, dark-brown or hazel, with a very intelligent expression (a round, prominent eye is a disfigurement) and they should not be obliquely placed.

Ears. — Should be small and well set-on, close to the side of the head.

Neck. — the head should be well set in the neck, which latter should be long and free from throatiness, symmetrically set and obliquely placed in shoulders running well into the back to allow of easily seeking for the tail.

Forequarters. — The chest should be deep and fairly broad, with a well-defined brisket, on which the elbows should work cleanly and evenly. The legs are of the greatest importance, the forelegs should be perfectly straight, with bone of good quality carried right down to the feet and when the dog is in full coat the legs should be well feathered.

Body. — The fore-ribs should be fairly flat, showing a gradual spring and well-arched in the centre of the body, but rather lighter towards the quarters. Open couplings are to be ruthlessly condemned. The back should be short, square and well ribbed up.

Golden Retriever

Labrador Retriever

American Cocker Spaniel
Clumber Spaniel

Hindquarters. — Should be muscular. The stifle should not be too straight or too bent, and the dog must neither be cow-hocked nor move too widely behind; in fact he must stand and move true on legs and feet all round. The legs should be well feathered.

Feet. — Should be round and strong with toes close and well arched, the soles being thick and strong.

Gait. — Free and flowing, straight and true as seen from front and rear.

Tail. — Short, straight and well set on, carried gaily, but never much above the level of the back.

Coat. — Should be dense, of fine quality and texture, flat as possible.

Colour. — Black or liver.

Weight and Size. — Should be between 27.2 and 31.8Kg (60 to 70 lbs).

Note. — Male animals should have two apparently normal tesitcles fully descended into the scrotum.

MAIN AMERICAN KENNEL CLUB VARIATION TO STANDARD FOR THE FLAT-COATED RETRIEVER —

Size. — Preferred height is 23 to 24½ inches at the withers for dogs, 22 to 23½ for bitches.

FLAT-COATED RETRIEVER REGISTRATIONS 1981 — 87 INCLUSIVE

1981 — 667
1982 — 715
1983 — 818
1984 — 860
1985 — 992
1986 — 940
1987 — 971

CRUFTS BEST-IN-SHOW WINNER 1980.
CH. SHARGLEAM BLACKCAP — MISS P. CHAPMAN.

GOLDEN RETRIEVER

The origins of this magnificent breed are, as is so often the case, open to question. One popular theory has been that a certain Lord Tweedmouth developed the first Golden Retrievers from a group of yellow Russian circus dogs that were touring Britain in the mid-nineteenth century. Others believe he may have sprung from Flat-Coated Retriever stock with perhaps some out crossing with water spaniels.

However he came into being, there is no doubt that the Golden Retriever has been and still is one of the most complete dogs in the world. As a worker in the field his ability is beyond question. He learns very quickly and has the priceless asset of being able to use his own initiative. Stamina, strength and determination complete the picture of this true sportsman's dog.

Such is the intelligence and reliability of the Golden Retriever that he is one of the first choices as a guide dog for the blind, a task which we all see him perform so marvellously.

As a pet for a family with young children, he could not be recommended too highly. He seems incapable of any nastiness and will revel in human company and affection. But coupled with his placid nature is an ability to guard, something that is always appreciated in a family home.

A fair sized house and garden would suit a Golden Retriever best and lengthy and regular exercise sessions are very important.

Cocker Spaniel

English Springer Spaniel

Field Spaniel

KEY TO CHARACTER	
INTELLIGENCE	*****
TEMPERAMENT	*****
EASE OF COAT CARE	***
SUITABILITY FOR SMALL DWELLING	*
***** (5) = VERY GOOD	

BRITISH KENNEL CLUB STANDARD

RETRIEVER (GOLDEN)

GENERAL APPEARANCE. — Should be a symmetrical, active, powerful dog, a good level mover, sound and well put together, with a kindly expression, not clumsy nor long in the leg.

Head and Skull. — Broad skull, well set on a clean and muscular neck, muzzle powerful and wide, not weak-jawed, good stop.

Eyes. — Dark and set well apart, very kindly in expression, with dark rims.

Ears. — Well proportioned, of moderate size, and well set on.

Mouth. — Teeth should be sound and strong. Neither overshot nor undershot the lower teeth just behind but touching the upper.

Neck. The neck should be clean and muscular.

Forequarters. — The forelegs should be straight with good bone. Shoulders should be well laid back and long in the blade.

Body. — Well-balanced, short coupled, and deep through the heart. Ribs deep and well sprung.

Hindquarters. — The loins and legs should be strong and muscular, with good second thighs and well bent stifles. Hocks well let down, not cow-hocked.

Feet. — Round and cat-like, not open nor splay.

Tail. — Should not be carried too gay nor curled at the tip.

Coat. — Should be flat or wavy with good feathering, and dense, water-resisting undercoat.

Colour. — Any shade of gold or cream, but neither red nor mahogany. The presence of a few white hairs on chest permissible. White collar, feet, toes or blaze should be penalised. Nose should be black.

Weight and Size. — The average weight in good hard condition should be: Dogs, 32 to 37Kg (70 to 80 lbs); Bitches, 27 to 32Kg (60 to 70 lbs). Height at shoulder: Dogs 56 to 61cm (22″ to 24″); Bitches 51 to 56cm (20″ to 22″).

Note. — Male animals should have two apparently normal testicles fully descended into the scrotum.

MAIN AMERICAN KENNEL CLUB VARIATION TO STANDARD FOR THE GOLDEN RETRIEVER —

Size. — Males 23 to 24 inches in height at withers; Females 21½ to 22½ inches. Weight for dogs 65 to 75 pounds; bitches 55 to 65 pounds.

GOLDEN RETRIEVER REGISTRATIONS 1981 — 87 INCLUSIVE

1981 — 8837
1982 — 9702
1983 — 10270
1984 — 10448
1985 — 11451
1986 — 11948
1987 — 11290

YET TO WIN CRUFTS BEST-IN-SHOW.

Sussex Spaniel

Irish Water Spaniel

LABRADOR RETRIEVER

This excellent breed is now so numerous in this country that it is perhaps easy to forget that he has his origins thoudands of miles away in Newfoundland. These dogs were also to be found in Labrador but the first specimens to come to Britain were purchased from Newfoundland fishermen in the early nineteenth century. Their main function was to retrieve fish, a task they were perfectly suited to being strong, obedient and very much at home in the water.

There were two types of these dogs to be found in Newfoundland. One was very large with a thick, long coat and the other smaller with a smooth coat. They were both of similar conformation and when they first appeared in Britain they were both known as Newfoundlands. Later, though, the two were divided into the Labrador Retrievers and Newfoundlands we are now familiar with.

Ever since his standard was drawn up in 1916, the Labrador has been regarded as one of the finest gun dogs in the world. He is tireless and ultra efficient at all types of retrieving and still has a great affinity with water work.

The Labrador is blessed with extreme intelligence and this coupled with the most genial nature has made him a natural choice for that most complicated and important of tasks, guiding the blind.

If sufficient space is available then this breed is without fault as a pet. He has the patience and good humour to cope with teasing children and is a rewarding companion at all times. Plenty of exercise is very important and overfeeding must always be avoided.

KEY TO CHARACTER	
INTELLIGENCE	*****
TEMPERAMENT	*****
EASE OF COAT CARE	*****
SUITABILITY FOR SMALL DWELLING	*
***** (5) = VERY GOOD	

BRITISH KENNEL CLUB STANDARD

RETRIEVER (LABRADOR)

GENERAL APPEARANCE. — The general appearance of the Labrador should be that of a strongly-built, short-coupled, very active dog, broad in the skull, broad and deep through the chest and ribs, broad and strong over the loins and hindquarters. The coat close, short with dense undercoat and free from feather. The dog must move neither too wide nor too close in front or behind, he must stand and move true all round on legs and feet.

Head and Skull. — The skull should be broad with a pronounced stop so that the skull is not in a straight line with the nose. The head should be clean cut without fleshy cheeks. The jaws should be medium length and powerful and free from snipiness. The nose wide and the nostrils well developed.

Eyes. — The eyes of medium size expressing intelligence and good temper, should be brown or hazel.

Ears. — Should not be large and heavy and should hang close to the head, and set rather far back.

Mouth. — Teeth should be sound and strong. The lower teeth just behind but touching the upper.

Neck. — Should be clean, strong and powerful and set into well placed shoulders.

Forequarters. — The shoulders should be long and sloping. The forelegs well boned and straight from the shoulder to the ground when viewed from either the front or side. The dog must move neither too wide nor too close in front.

Body. — The chest must be of good width and depth with well-sprung ribs. The back should be short coupled.

Weimaraner

Welsh Springer Spaniel

Hindquarters. — The loins must be wide and strong with well-turned stifles; hindquarters well developed and not sloping to the tail. The hocks should be slightly bent and the dog must neither be cow-hocked nor move too wide or too close behind.

Feet. — Should be round and compact with well-arched toes and well-developed pads.

Tail. — The tail is a distinctive feature of the breed; it should be very thick towards the base, gradually tapering towards the tip, of medium length and practically free from any feathering, but clothed thickly all round with the Labrador's short, thick dense coat, thus giving that peculiar "rounded" appearance which has been described as the "Otter" tail. The tail may be carried gaily, but should not curl over the back.

Coat. — The coat is another distinctive feature of the breed, it should be short and dense and without wave with a weather-resisting undercoat and should give a fairly hard feeling to the hand.

Colour. — The colour is generally black or yellow — but other whole colours are permitted. The coat should be free from any white markings but a small white spot on the chest is allowable. The coat should be of a whole colour and not of a flecked appearance.

Weight and Size. — Desired height for Dogs, 56 to 57cm (22″ to 22½″); Bitches 54 to 56cm (21½″ to 22″).

Faults. — Under or overshot mouth; no undercoat; bad action; feathering; snipiness on the head; large or heavy ears; cow-hocked; tail curled over back.

Note. — Male animals should have two apparently normal testicles fully descended into the scrotum.

MAIN AMERICAN KENNEL CLUB VARIATION TO STANDARD FOR THE LABRADOR RETRIEVER —

Weight and Size. — Approximate weight of dogs and bitches in working condition: Dogs 60 to 70 pounds; Bitches 55 to 70 pounds. Height at shoulders: Dogs 22½ to 24½ inches; Bitches 21½ to 23½ inches.

LABRADOR RETRIEVER REGISTRATIONS 1981 — 87 INCLUSIVE

1981 — 12543
1982 — 13488
1983 — 14016
1984 — 13681
1985 — 15156

CRUFTS BEST-IN SHOW WINNER 3 TIMES.

1932 BRAMSHAW BOB — LORNA COUNTESS HOWE
1933 BRAMSHAW BOB — LORNA COUNTESS HOWE
1937 CH. CHEVERALLA BEN OF BANCHORY — LORNA COUNTESS HOWE

AMERICAN COCKER SPANIEL

The American and English Cocker Spaniels of today are both descended from the smallest of the original British Spaniels. It seems that the specimens that crossed the Atlantic developed differently purely as a result of American preferences.

In the U.S.A. breeders retained the hunting instinct of the breed but since their dogs were bred smaller, their prey was normally such things as small birds. The American Cocker excels at this work for although not as robust as his English cousin, he is blessed with good stamina and willingness to learn.

Since his registration in Britain in 1968 he has been well received here but mainly for the showring or as a pet, rather than for field work. The American Cocker is a dog that shows well, and the thick long coat is shown at it's glorious best when the dog is on the move. Apart from the coat, the main feature that distinguishes the American from the English Cocker is the shorter, squarer muzzle.

He has no faults as a dog for a family home and will prove to be well-liked by all age groups. He can be house-trained very simply and can reach a high standard of obedience if the owner puts in enough work with him.

The American Cocker Spaniel will revel in as much exercise both inside and outside the home as the owner's family can provide, so he is a breed more suited to active types.

KEY TO CHARACTER	
INTELLIGENCE	****
TEMPERAMENT	****
EASE OF COAT CARE	*
SUITABILITY FOR SMALL DWELLING	***
***** (5) = VERY GOOD	

BRITISH KENNEL CLUB STANDARD

SPANIEL (AMERICAN COCKER)

GENERAL APPEARANCE. — A serviceable-looking dog with a refinedly chiselled head; standing on straight legs and well up at the shoulders; of compact body and wide, muscular quarters. The American Cocker Spaniel's sturdy body, powerful quarters and strong, well-boned legs show him to be a dog capable of considerable speed combined with great endurance. Above all he must be free and merry, sound well balanced throughout, and in action show a keen inclination to work, equable in temperament with no suggestion of timidity.

Head and Skull. — Well developed and rounded with no tendency towards flatness, or pronounced roundness, of the crown (dome). The forehead smooth, i.e., free from wrinkles, the eyebrows and stop clearly defined, the median line distinctly marked and gradually dispappearing until lost rather more than halfway up to the crown. The bony structure surrounding the socket of the eye should be well chiselled; there should be no suggestion of fullness under the eyes nor prominence in the cheeks which, like the sides of the muzzle, should present a smooth, clean-cut appearance. To attain a well-proportioned head, which above all should be in balance with the rest of the dog, the distance from the tip of the nose to the stop at a line drawn across the top of the muzzle between the front corners of the eyes, should approximate one-half the distance from the stop at this point up over the crown to the base of the skull. The muzzle should be broad and deep, with square even jaws. The upper lid should be of sufficient depth to cover the lower jaw, presenting a square appearance. The nose of sufficient size to balance the muzzle and foreface, with well-developed nostrils and black in colour in the blacks and black-and-tans; in the reds, buffs, livers, and parti-colours and in the roans it may be black or brown, the darker colouring being preferable.

Mouth. — The teeth should be sound and regular and set at right angles to their respective jaws. The relation of the upper teeth to the lower should be that of scissors, with the inner surface of the upper in contact with the outer surface of the lower when the jaws are closed.

Eyes. — The eyeballs should be round and full and set in the surrounding tissue to look directly forward and give the eye a slightly almond-shape appearance. The eye should be neither weak nor goggled. The expression should be intelligent, alert, soft and appealing. The colour of the iris should be dark brown to black in the blacks, black and tans, buffs and creams, and in the darker shades of the parti-colours and roans. In the reds, dark hazel; in the livers, parti-colours, and roans of the lighter shades, not lighter than hazel, the darker the better.

Ears. — Lobular, set on a line no higher than the lower part of the eye, the leather fine and extending to the nostrils, well clothed with long, silky, straight or wavy hair.

Neck. — The neck sufficiently long to allow the nose to reach the ground easily, muscular and free from pendulous "throatiness". It should rise strongly from the shoulders and arch slightly as it tapers to join the head.

Forequarters. — The shoulders deep, clean-cut and sloping without protrusion and so set that the upper point of the withers are at an angle which permits a wide spring of rib. Forelegs straight, strongly boned and muscular and set close to the body well under the scapulae. The elbows well let down and turning neither in nor out. The pasterns short and strong.

Body. — Its height at the withers should approximate the length from the withers to the set-on of tail. The chest deep, its lowest point no higher than the elbows, its front sufficiently wide for adequate heart and lung space, yet not so wide as to interfere with straight forward movement of the forelegs. Ribs deep and well-sprung throughout. Body short in the couplings and flank, with its depth at the flank somewhat less than at the last rib. Back strong and sloping evenly and slightly downward from the withers to the set-on of tail. Hips wide with quarters well rounded and muscular. The body should appear short, compact and firmly knit together, giving the impression of strength.

Hindquarters. — The hind legs should be strongly boned and muscled with good angulation at the stifle and powerful, clearly defined thighs. The stifle joint should be strong and there should be no slippage in motion or when standing. The hocks should be strong, well let down and when viewed from behind, the hind legs should be parallel when in motion and at rest.

Feet. — Feet compact, not spreading, round and firm, with deep, strong, tough pads and hair between the toes; they should turn neither in nor out.

Gait. — The American Cocker Spaniel possesses a typical sporting dog gait. Prerequisite to good movement is balance between the fore and hind quarters. He drives with his strong powerful rear quarters and is properly constructed to the shoulder and forelegs so that he can reach forward without constriction in a full stride to counter balance the driving force of the rear. Above all, his gait is co-ordinated, smooth and effortless. The dog must cover ground with his action and excessive animation should never be mistaken for proper gait.

Tail. — The docked tail should be set on and carried on a line with the topline of the back, or slightly higher; never straight up like a terrier and never so low as to indicate timidity. When the dog is in motion the action should be merry.

Coat. — On the head, short and fine; on the body, medium length, with enough undercoating to give protection. The ears, chest, abdomen, and legs should be well feathered, but not so excessively as to hide the American Cocker Spaniel's true lines and movement or affect his appearance and function as a sporting dog. The texture is most important. The coat should be silky,flat or slightly wavy, and of a texture which permits easy care. Excessive or curly or cottony texture coat should be penalised.

Colour. — Black should be jet black; shadings of brown or liver in the sheen of the coat is not desirable. Black and Tan (classified under solid colours) should have definite tan markings on a jet black body. The tan markings should be distinct and plainly visible and the colour of the tan may be from the lightest cream to the darkest red colour. The amount of tan markings should be restricted to ten per cent or less of the colour of the specimen; tan markings in excess of ten per cent should be penalised. Tan markings which are not readily visible in the ring or the absence of tan markings in any of the specified locations should be penalised. The tan markings should be located as follows:-

1. A clear spot over each eye.
2. On the sides of the muzzle and on the cheeks.
3. On the underside of the ears.
4. On all feet and legs.
5. Under the tail.
6. On the chest, optional, presence or absence should not be penalised.

Tan on the muzzle which extends upwards over and joins should be penalised.

Any solid colour other than black should be of uniform shade. Lighter colouring of the feathering is permissible.

In all the above solid colours a small amount of white on chest and throat while not desirable, is allowed, but white in any other location should be penalised.

Parti-colours. Two or more definite colours appearing in clearly defined markings are essential. Primary colour which is ninety per cent or more should be penalised; secondary colour or colours which are limtied solely to one location should also be penalised. Roans are classified as parti-colours and may be of any of the usual roaning patterns. Tri-colours are any of the above colours combined with tan markings. It is preferable that the tan markings be located in the same pattern as for Black and Tan.

Size. — The ideal height at the withers for an adult dog is 38cm (15″) and for an adult bitch 35cm (14″). Height may vary 1.3cm (half an inch) above or below this ideal. A dog whose height exceeds 39cm (15½″) or a bitch whose height exceeds 37cm (14½″) should be penalised. An adult dog whose height is less than 37cm (14½″) or an adult bitch whose height is less than 34cm (13½″) should be penalised. Note: Height is determined by a line perpendicular to the ground from the top of the shoulder blades, the dog standing naturally with its forelegs and the lower hind legs parallel to the line of the measurement.

Note. — Male animals should have two apparently normal testicles fully descended into the scrotum.

AMERICAN COCKER SPANIEL REGISTRATIONS 1981 — 87 INCLUSIVE

1981 — 459
1982 — 462
1983 — 409
1984 — 405
1985 — 481
1986 — 367
1987 — 385

YET TO WIN CRUFTS BEST-IN-SHOW.

CLUMBER SPANIEL

The very early history of this heavyweight of the Spaniel family is very unclear, but it is known that the French Duc de Noailles presented several specimens of the Clumber Spaniel type to the Duke of Newcastle some 200 years ago. It is thought that the Duc de Noailles had probably possessed spaniels of the Cocker or Springer type and had crossed them with heavier breeds. When these dogs were received by the Duke of Newcastle, they were named after his home which was Clumber Park.

Since his introduction to Britain he has changed very little, having long been used as a successful shooting dog. The Clumber has an excellent nose and thorough appraoch to his work and although far from speedy he can move his bulk with surprising athleticism. His stamina is beyond question and he has been used as a good retriever and beater.

If taken as a pet, it should be remembered that like many heavy dogs the Clumber can tend towards laziness and obesity if not exercised sufficiently. He will prefer the country life, but will tolerate town living if he is given plenty of runs in parks or fields.

Providing an owner's home is of a fair size, he will make a fine family dog. He is no trouble to train and as his benign facial expression would suggest, has a commendable temperament.

KEY TO CHARACTER	
INTELLIGENCE	****
TEMPERAMENT	*****
EASE OF COAT CARE	***
SUITABILITY FOR SMALL DWELLING	*
***** (5) = VERY GOOD	

BRITISH KENNEL CLUB STANDARD

SPANIEL (CLUMBER)

GENERAL APPEARANCE. — That of a dog with a thoughtful expression, very massive but active, which moves with a rolling gait characteristic of the breed.

Head and Skull. — Head large, square and massive, of medium length, broad on top, with a decided occiput; heavy brows with a deep stop; heavy muzzle, with well-developed flew, and level jaw and mouth. Nose square and flesh-coloured.

Eyes. — Dark amber, slightly sunk with some haw showing.

Ears. — Large, vine-leaf shaped, and well covered with straight hair, and hanging slightly forward, the feather not to extend below the leather.

Mouth. — Should be level and neither over nor undershot.

Neck. — Fairly long, thick and powerful, and well feathered underneath.

Forequarters. — Shoulders strong, sloping and muscular; chest deep. Legs short, straight, thick and strong.

Body. — Long and heavy, and near the ground, with well-sprung ribs. Back straight, broad and long.

Hindquarters. — Very powerful and well developed. Loin powerful, well let down in flank. Hocks low, stifles well bent and set straight.

Feet. — Large and round, well covered with hair.

Tail. — Set low, well feathered, and carried about level with the back.

Coat. — Abundant, close, silky, and straight; legs well feathered.

Colour. — Plain white, with lemon markings, orange permissible; slight head markings and freckled muzzle, with white body preferred.

Weight and Size. — Dogs about 25 to 31.8Kg (55 to 70 lbs); Bitches about 20.4 to 27.2Kg (45 to 60 lbs).

Nots. — Male animals should have two apparently normal testicles fully descended into the scrotum.

MAIN AMERICAN KENNEL CLUB VARIATION TO STANDARD FOR THE CLUMBER SPANIEL —

Height and Weight. — Males weigh between 70 and 85 pounds, bitches between 55 and 70 pounds. Males are about 19 to 20 inches at the withers, bitches are about 17 to 19 inches at the withers.

CLUMBER SPANIEL REGISTRATIONS 1981 — 87 INCLUSIVE

1981 — 57
1982 — 113
1983 — 111
1984 — 156
1985 — 199
1986 — 143
1987 — 97

YET TO WIN CRUFTS BEST-IN-SHOW.

COCKER SPANIEL

The Cocker Spaniel is well established as one of Britain's most popular breeds. He is an ideal size for most households and his marvellous personality and doleful facial expressions have won over many thousands of owners.

In the distant past, all English Spaniels were grouped together with no distinct categories such as Springer, Cocker and Sussex etc. It was in the early 19th century that the Cocker first emerged in his own right but it was some 100 years later that he was registered officially. The name "Cocker" derives from his use in woodcock shooting, where his size gives him an advantage over his larger relatives, in that he can penetrate dense undergrowth with greater ease. Whether it be woodcock, pheasant or other game, the Cocker is a prized sporting dog. Although he does not have the speed of setters or larger spaniels, he does have excellent stamina and scenting ability. The dense, wavy coat of the Cocker gives him efficient protection from the cold and can even help prevent minor injury when hunting in thorny conditions.

This breed can not be recommended highly enough to anyone seeking a faithful companion and affectionate pet. He is compatible with all age groups and does not require a great deal of room. Exercise, however is essential, for mild natured as he is, he can become bad tempered if bored and neglected.

KEY TO CHARACTER	
INTELLIGENCE	****
TEMPERAMENT	*****
EASE OF COAT CARE	***
SUITABILITY FOR SMALL DWELLING	***
***** (5) = VERY GOOD	

BRITISH KENNEL CLUB STANDARD

SPANIEL (COCKER)

GENERAL APPEARANCE. — That of a merry sturdy sporting dog. The Cocker Spaniel should be well balanced and compact and should measure about the same from the withers to the ground as from the withers to the root of the tail.

Head and Skull. — There should be a good square muzzle with a distinct stop which should be mid way between the tip of the nose and the occiput. The skull should be well developed, cleanly chiselled, neither too fine nor too coarse. The cheek bones should not be prominent. The nose should be sufficiently wide to allow for the acute scenting power of this breed.

Eyes. — The eyes should be full but not prominent, brown or dark brown in colour but never light, with a general expression of intelligence and gentleness though decidely wide awake, bright and merry. The rims should be tight.

Ears. — Lobular, set on low, on a level with the eyes, with fine leathers which extend to but not beyond the top of the nose; well clothed with long silky hair which should be straight.

Mouth. — Jaws should be strong and teeth should have a scissor bite.

Neck. — Neck should be moderate in length, clean in throat, muscular and neatly set in fine sloping shoulders.

Forequarters. — The shoulders should be sloping and fine, the chest well developed and the brisket deep, neither too wide nor too narrow in front. The legs must be well boned, feathered and straight and should be sufficiently short for concentrated power but not too short to interfere with the tremendous exertions expected from this grand little sporting dog.

Body. — Body should be immensely strong and compact for the size and weight of the dog. The ribs should be well sprung behind the shoulder blades, the loin short wide and strong, with a firm topline gently sloping downwards to the tail.

Hindquarters. — Hindquarters should be wide, well rounded and very muscular. The legs must be well boned feathered above the hock with a good bend of stifle and short below the hock allowing for plenty of drive.

Feet. — Feet should be firm, thickly padded and catlike.

Tail. — Tail should be set on slightly lower than the line of the back; it must be merry, carried in line with the back and never cocked up. The tail should not be docked too long nor too short to interfere with its merry action.

Coat. — Flat and silky in texture, never wiry or wavy, with sufficient feather; not too profuse and never curly.

Colour. — Various. In self colours no white is allowed except on the chest.

Gait. — There should be true through action both for and aft, with great drive covering the ground well.

Weight and Size. — The weight should be about 12.7 to 14.5Kg (28 to 32 lbs). The height at the withers should be approximately 38 to 39cm (15″ to 15½″) for bitches and approximatly 39 to 41cm (15½″ to 16″) for dogs.

Faults. — Light bone; straight shoulder; flat ribs; unsound movement; weak hocks; weak pasterns; open or large feet; frown; small beady eyes; undershot or overshot mouth; uncertain or aggressive temperament.

Note. — Male animals should have two apparently normal testicles fully descended into the scrotum.

MAIN AMERICAN KENNEL CLUB VARIATION TO STANDARD FOR THE COCKER SPANIEL —

Known as the English Cocker Spaniel in the U.S.A.

Weight and Size. — Ideal heights at withers: Males, 16 to 17 inches; females 15 to 16 inches. The most desirable weights: Males, 28 to 34 pounds; females 26 to 32 pounds.

COCKER SPANIEL REGISTRATIONS 1981 — 87 INCLUSIVE

1981 — 8009
1982 — 7697
1983 — 8064
1984 — 7573
1985 — 7619

CRUFTS BEST-IN-SHOW WINNER 6 TIMES.

1930 LUCKYSTAR OF WARE — H. S. LLOYD
1931 LUCKYSTAR OF WARE — H. S. LLOYD
1938 EXQUISITE MODEL OF WARE — H. S. LLOYD
1939 EXQUISITE MODEL OF WARE — H. S. LLOYD
1948 TRACEY WITCH OF WARE — H. S. LLOYD
1950 TRACEY WITCH OF WARE — H. S. LLOYD

ENGLISH SPRINGER SPANIEL

The English Springer Spaniel has existed in similar form since the very birth of British sporting Spaniels. On a broad basis, the early shorter-legged Spaniels evolved into the Cocker and the taller dogs became Springers. But the latter were once known as Norfolk Spaniels, the name arising from the Duke of Norfolk's involvement with the breed. This name, however, was changed in the early part of this century to his current title. The word 'Springer' refers to the 'springing' of game from the undergrowth into the view of the huntsman.

In Britain and also in the U.S.A. he remains a highly regarded sporting dog, particularly for his prowess at bird work. He is a tireless and speedy worker, not at all inconvenienced by even the foulest weather. Training is no problem with such an intelligent dog and he thoroughly enjoys coping with whatever his master asks of him.

Nowadays there are two very distinct types of Springer, the worker and the show dog. The working dog tends to be more compact and rugged and the show specimen taller and moulded on more aesthetic lines, whilst still maintaining some of his natural fitness.

He is a dog of undoubted beauty and has an excellent disposition to match. A springer is the epitome of loyalty and fits very well into a family environment. Definitely a dog for the active, long periods of exercise on and off the lead are a must.

KEY TO CHARACTER	
INTELLIGENCE	****
TEMPERAMENT	*****
EASE OF COAT CARE	***
SUITABILITY FOR SMALL DWELLING	*
***** (5) = VERY GOOD	

BRITISH KENNEL CLUB STANDARD

SPANIEL (ENGLISH SPRINGER)

CHARACTERISTICS. — The English Springer is the oldest of our Sporting Gundogs and the taproot from which all of our sporting land spaniels (Clumbers excepted) have been evolved. It was originally used for the purpose of finding and springing game for the net, falcon, or greyhound, but at the present time it is used entirely to find, flush, and retrieve game for the gun. The breed is of ancient and pure origin, and should be kept as such.

GENERAL APPEARANCE. — The general appearance of the modern Springer is that of a symmetrical, compact, strong, upstanding, merry and active dog, built for endurance and activity. He is the highest on the leg and raciest in build of all British land Spaniels.

Head and Skull. — The skull should be of medium length and fairly broad and slightly rounded, rising from the foreface, making a brow or stop, divided by a fluting between the eyes gradually dying away along the forehead towards the occiput bone, which should not be peaked. The cheeks should be flat, that is not rounded or full. The foreface should be of proportionate length to the skull, fairly broad and deep without being coarse, well chiselled below the eyes, fairly deep and square in flew, but not exaggerated to such an extent as would interfere with comfort when retrieving. Nostrils well developed.

Eyes. — The eyes should be neither too full nor too small but of medium size, not prominent nor sunken but well set in (not showing haw) of an alert, kind expression. A mouse-like eye without expression is objectionable, as also is a light eye. The colour should be dark hazel.

Ears. — The ears should be lobular in shape, set close to the head, of good length and width, but not exaggerated. The correct set should be in line with the eye.

Mouth. — The jaws should be strong, with a perfect regular and complete scissor bite, i.e., the upper teeth closely overlapping the lower teeth and set square to the jaws.

Neck. — The neck should be strong and muscular, of nice length and free from throatiness, well set in the shoulders, nicely arched and tapering towards the head — thus giving great activity and speed. A ewe neck is objectionable.

Forequarters. — The forelegs should be straight and nicely feathered, elbows set well to body and with proportionate substance to carry the body, strong flexible pasterns.

Body. — The body should be strong and of proportionate length, neither too long nor too short, the chest deep and well developed with plenty of heart and lung room, well sprung ribs, loin muscular and strong with slight arch, and well coupled, thighs broad and msucular and well developed.

Hindquarters. — The hindlegs should be well let down from hip to hocks. Stifles and hocks moderately bent, inclining neither inwards nor outwards. Coarseness of hocks objectionable.

Feet. — Feet tight, compact, and well rounded with strong full pads.

Gait. — The Springer's gait is strictly his own. His forelegs should swing straight forward from the shoulder, throwing the feet well forward in an easy and free manner. His hocks should drive well under his body, following in a line with the forelegs. At slow movements many Springers have a pacing stride typical of the breed.

Tail. — The stern should be low and never carried above the level of the back, well feathered and with a lively action.

Coat. — The coat should be close, straight, and weather resisting without being coarse.

Colour. — Any recognised Land Spaniel colour is acceptable, but liver and white black and white,or either of these colours with tan markings preferred.

Weight and Size. — The approximate height should be 51cm (20″). The approximate weight should be 22.7Kg (50 lbs).

Note. — Male animals should have two apparently normal testicles fully descended into the scrotum.

MAIN AMERICAN KENNEL CLUB VARIATION TO STANDARD FOR THE ENGLISH SPRINGER SPANIEL —

Size and Proportion. — The ideal shoulder height for dogs is 20 inches; for bitches, 19 inches. Weight is dependent on the dog's other dimensions: a 20 inch dog, well proportioned, in good condition should weigh about 49 to 55 pounds.

ENGLISH SPRINGER SPANIEL REGISTRATIONS 1981 — 87 INCLUSIVE

1981 — 7055
1982 — 6984
1983 — 6825
1984 — 6235
1985 — 6666
1986 — 6474
1987 — 5999

YET TO WIN CRUFTS BEST-IN-SHOW.

FIELD SPANIEL

This is a rare Spaniel that, in the past, has suffered severely at the hands of thoughtless breeders. Having originally been developed from Cocker and Springer Spaniels around 1880, a craze set in for low-slung, thick-legged dogs which got so out of hand as to almost kill the breed off. After much dedicated work, conscientious breeders gradually bred out this almost Basset Hound-like appearance to give the pleasing form of today's Field Spaniels. Whilst still far from being long in the leg, this breed has become very agile and is a first class worker in the field.

His even temperament and responsiveness to training make him suitable both for sporting endeavours and as a fine dog for the home. Although he should be given a great deal of exercise, it would be difficult to point out a fault in this breed to a prospective owner. He would probably be happiest in a rural environment, but his easy going nature enables him to cope with most situations. Children are safe in his company and he thrives on all human affection.

We can only hope that such a beautiful dog does not disappear from the scene, as has been threatened in the past, for there is probably no better spaniel.

KEY TO CHARACTER	
INTELLIGENCE	****
TEMPERAMENT	*****
EASE OF COAT CARE	***
SUITABILITY FOR SMALL DWELLING	**
***** (5) = VERY GOOD	

BRITISH KENNEL CLUB STANDARD

SPANIEL (FIELD SPRINGER)

GENERAL APPEARANCE. — That of a well-balanced, noble, upstanding, sporting dog; built for activity and endurance; a combination of beauty and utility; of unusual docility.

Head and Skull. — The head should be characteristic as is that of the Bulldog or the Bloodhound; its very stamp and countenance should at once convey the impression of high breeding, character and nobility; skull well developed, with a distinct occipital protuberance, which gives the character alluded to; not too wide across the muzzle, long and lean, neither snipy nor squarely cut, and in profile curving gradually from nose to throat; lean beneath the eyes, a thickness here gives coarseness to the whole head. The great length of muzzle gives surface for the free development of the olfactory nerve, and thus secures the highest possible scenting powers. Nose, well developed, good with open nostrils.

Eyes. — Not too full, but not small, receding or overhung. The colour in all cases to match the coat and markings, except in livers which may be a light hazel. Grave in expression suggesting docility and intelligence and showing no haw.

Ears. — Moderately long and wide, sufficiently clad with nice Setter-like feather and set low. They should fall in graceful folds, the lower parts curling inwards and backwards.

Mouth. — The jaws should be strong, with a perfect regular and complete scissor bite, i.e., the upper teeth closely overlapping the lower teeth and set square to the jaws.

Neck. — Long, strong and muscular, so as to enable the dog to retrieve his game without undue fatigue.

Forequarters. — The shoulders should be long and sloping and well set back, thus giving great activity and speed. The foreleg should be of fairly good length, with straight, clean, flat bone and nicely feathered. Immense bone is not desirable.

Body. — Should be of moderate length, well ribbed up to a good strong loin, straight or slightly arched, never slack. The chest, deep and well developed, but not too round and wide. Back and loins very strong and muscular.

Hindquarters. — Strong and muscular. The stifles should be moderately bent and not twisted either in or out.

Feet. — Not too small, round with short, soft hair between the toes; good, strong pads.

Tail. — Well set on and carried low, if possible below the level of the back, in a straight line or with a slight downward inclination, never elevated above the back, and in action always kept low, nicely fringed with wavy feather of silky texture.

Coat. — Flat or slightly waved, and never curled, sufficiently dense to resist the weather and not too short. Silky in texture, glossy and refined without duffelness, curliness or wiriness. On the chest, under the belly and behind the legs, there should be abundant feather, but never too much, especially below the hocks, and that of the right sort — viz., Setter-like.

Colour. — The Field Spaniel should be a self-coloured dog, viz.: Black, Liver, Golden Liver, Mahogany Red, Roan; or any of these colours with Tan over the Eyes, on the Cheeks, Feet and Pasterns. Other colours, such as Black and White, Liver and White, Red or Orange and White, etc., while not debarring a dog, is a fault.

Weight and Size. — From about 16 to 23Kg (35 to 50½ lbs). Height: about 46cm (18″) at shoulder.

Faults. — Any departure from the foregoing points should be considered a fault and the seriousness with which the fault is regarded should be in exact proportion to its degree.

Note. — Male animals should have two aparently normal testicles fully descended into the scrotum.

FIELD SPANIEL REGISTRATIONS 1981 — 87 INCLUSIVE

1981 — 79
1982 — 86
1983 — 77
1984 — 83
1985 — 85
1986 — 127
1987 — 83

YET TO WIN CRUFTS BEST-IN-SHOW.

IRISH WATER SPANIEL

The Irish Water Spaniel owes the bulk of his development to an Irishman called Justin McCarthy, who established the breed in the mid nineteenth century. He probably used gundogs from Spain when working to perfect the breed, although exactly which ones is not certain. There had been other water spaniels in Ireland prior to this and McCarthy used selected specimens of these.

The coat of the Irish Water Spaniel is unique in the spaniel family. Some might say that the cascading curls on the head and ears give him a rather soft lap dog type of expression. But the truth is that he is probably the best wildfowling dog in existence, having all the necessary attributes of strength, stamina and intelligence. The dense coat is slightly oily, giving excellent waterproofing and insulation, so he will not waver if called to retrieve from the iciest water.

Training the Irish Water Spaniel in the home is not a great problem due to his great willingness to learn and responsiveness to human company. They are a breed of high spirits and might be a little overpowering for toddlers. Lots of free running exercise is essential so an owner should definitely be a lover of the outdoors.

KEY TO CHARACTER	
INTELLIGENCE	****
TEMPERAMENT	****
EASE OF COAT CARE	**
SUITABILITY FOR SMALL DWELLING	*
***** (5) = VERY GOOD	

BRITISH KENNEL CLUB STANDARD

SPANIEL (IRISH WATER)

CHARACTERISTICS. — The gait, peculiar to the breed, differs from that of any other variety of Spaniel.

GENERAL APPEARANCE. — The Irish Water Spaniel is a gundog bred for work in all types of shooting, and particularly suited for wild-fowling. His fitness for this purpose should be evident in his appearance; he is a strongly built, compact dog, intelligent, enduring and eager.

Head and Skull. — The head should be of good size. The skull high in dome, of good length and width sufficient to allow adequate brain capacity. The muzzle long, strong and somewhat square with a gradual stop. The face should be smooth and the skull covered with long curls in the form of a ponounced topknot growing in a well-defined peak to a point between the eyes. Nose large and well developed, dark liver colour. With all there should be an impression of fineness.

Eyes. — Comparatively small, medium to dark-brown colour, bright and alert.

Ears. — Very long and lobe-shaped in the leather, low set, hanging close to the cheeks and covered with long twisted curls of live hair.

Mouth. — The jaws should be strong, with a perfect regular and complete scissor bite, i.e., the upper teeth closely overlapping the lower teeth and set square to the jaws.

Neck. — strongly set into the shoulders, powerful, arching and long enough to carry the head well above the level of the back. The back and sides of the neck should be covered with curls similar to those on the body. The throat should be smooth, the smooth hair forming a V-shaped patch from the back of the lower jaw to the breast bone.

Forequarters. — The shoulders should be powerful and sloping. The chest deep and of large girth with ribs so well sprung behind the shoulders as to give a barrel-shaped appearance to the body but with normal width and curvature between the forelegs. The forelegs should be well boned and straight, with arms well let down and carrying the forearm at elbow and knee in a straight line with the point of the shoulder.

Body. — should be of good size. The back short, broad and level, strongly coupled to the hind quarters. The ribs carried well back. The loins deep and wide. The body as a whole being so proportioned as to give a barrel-shaped appearance accentuated by the springing of the ribs.

Hindquarters. — Powerful with long well-bent stifles and hocks set low.

Feet. — Should be large and somewhat round and spreading; well-covered with hair over and between the toes.

Tail. — Peculiar to the breed, should be short and straight, thick at the root and tapering to a fine point. It should be low set, carried straight and below the level of the back; and in length should not reach the hock joint. Three to four inches of the tail at the root should be covered by close curls which stop abruptly, the remainder should be bare or covered by straight fine hairs.

Coat. — Should be composed of dense, tight, crisp ringlets free from woolliness. The hair should have a natural oiliness. The forelegs covered with feather in curls or ringlets down to the feet. The feather should be abundant all round, though shorter in front so as only to give a rough appearance. Below the hocks the hindlegs should be smooth in front, but feathered behind down to the feet.

Colour. — A rich dark liver having the purplish tint or bloom peculiar to the breed and sometimes referred to as puce-liver.

Weight and Size. — Height to the shoulders: Dogs about 53 to 59cm (21″ to 23″). Bitches about 51 to 56cm (20″ to 22″).

Note. — Male animals should have two apparently normal testicles fully descended into the scrotum.

MAIN AMERICAN KENNEL CLUB VARIATION TO STANDARD FOR THE IRISH WATER SPANIEL —

Height and Weight. — dogs, 22 to 24 inches; bitches, 21 to 23 inches. Dogs, 55 to 65 pounds; bitches, 45 to 58 pounds.

IRISH WATER SPANIEL REGISTRATIONS 1981 — 87 INCLUSIVE

1981 — 98
1982 — 83
1983 — 117
1984 — 115
1985 — 122
1986 — 170
1987 — 144

YET TO WIN CRUFTS BEST-IN-SHOW.

SUSSEX SPANIEL

The Sussex Spaniel is one of the stockier of the Spaniel group and also one of the rarest. He goes back to the late eighteenth century and owes his early development to a breeder in Sussex called Fuller. Even then numbers were few and the Sussex Spaniel has often verged on extinction. Fortunately such features as his beautiful colour and handsomeness, coupled with renowned working ability in the field, have ensured that he has always kept a small yet devoted following.

Although not the speediest of the gun dogs, the Sussex has excellent stamina and stubbornly refuses to be thwarted by dense undergrowth in his search for prey. His luxurious coat is also an advantage when working amongst thorns and the like.

This is a breed of great beauty and the unique golden liver colour of the coat is a marvellous sight on a well groomed dog. He is as amiable as his kind facial expression would suggest and a commendable companion for someone who leads life at a leisurely pace. Exercise, however is important and walks of a fair length will be enjoyed by the Sussex. He is very even tempered and will prove easily house trained and loyal to his owner.

KEY TO CHARACTER	
INTELLIGENCE	****
TEMPERAMENT	*****
EASE OF COAT CARE	**
SUITABILITY FOR SMALL DWELLING	*
***** (5) = VERY GOOD	

BRITISH KENNEL CLUB STANDARD

SPANIEL (SUSSEX)

GENERAL APPEARANCE. — Massive and strongly built. An active, energetic, strong dog, whose characteristic movement is a decided roll, and unlike that of any other Spaniel.

Head and Skull. — The skull should be wide and show a moderate curve from ear to ear, neither flat nor apple headed, with a centre indentation and a pronounced stop. Brows frowning — occiput decided, but not pointed. Nostrils well developed and liver colour. A well balanced head.

Eyes. — Hazel colour, fairly large, not too full, but soft expression and not showing the haw over much.

Ears. — Thick, fairly large and lobe shape, set moderately low but above eye level. Should lie closely, hair soft and wavy, but not too profuse.

Mouth. — Strong and level, neither over nor undershot, with a scissor bite.

Neck. — Long, strong and slightly arched, not carrying the head much above the level of the back. Not much throatiness, but well marked frill.

Forequarters. — The shoulders should be sloping and free; arms well boned as well as muscular. Knees large and strong, pasterns short and well boned. Legs rather short and strong, moderately well feathered.

Body. — Chest deep and well developed; not too round and wide. Back and loin well developed and muscular both in width and depth. The back ribs must be deep. Whole body should be strong and level with no sign of waistiness from aitches to hips.

Hindquarters. — The thighs must be strongly boned as well as muscular; hocks large and strong, legs rather short and strong with good bone, moderately well feathered. The hind legs should not appear shorter than the fore legs, or be too much bent at the hocks so as to give a settery appearance, which is objectionable. The hind legs should be well feathered above the hocks, but not much hair below the hocks.

Feet. — Circular, well padded, well feathered between toes.

Tail. — Set low and not carried above level of the back. Free actioned, thickly clothed with hair, but no feather. Docked from 5 to 7 inches.

Coat. — Abundant and flat with no tendency to curl and ample undercoat for weather resistance.

Colour. — Rich golden liver and hair shading to gold at the tips: the gold predominating. Dark liver or puce is objectionable.

Weight and Size. — Ideal weight: Dogs 20.4Kg (45 lbs). Bitches 18.2Kg (40 lbs). Height 38 to 41cm (15″ to 16″).

Note. — Male animals should have two apparently normal testicles fully descended into the scrotum.

MAIN AMERICAN KENNEL CLUB VARIATION TO STANDARD FOR THE SUSSEX SPANIEL —

Weight — From 35 pounds to 45 pounds.

SUSSEX SPANIEL REGISTRATIONS 1981 — 87 INCLUSIVE

1981 — 55
1982 — 82
1983 — 62
1984 — 80
1985 — 93
1986 — 102
1987 — 75

YET TO WIN CRUFTS BEST-IN-SHOW.

WELSH SPRINGER SPANIEL

There is some debate as to which of the two Springer Spaniel breeds is the oldest. Some maintain that this honour goes to the Welsh variety, but most believe that the English Springer was crossed with other Spaniels to produce his smaller cousin. Nonetheless, this is a breed of many years standing, having been registered in 1902 and has a fine reputation amongst Welsh shooting enthusiasts. Although not quite as hardy as the English Springer, he thoroughly enjoys field work and his devotees will testify that he enjoys all aspects of it.

He can be a little scatter-brained at times and correct training, either for sport or general obedience is essential to allow his many good qualities to shine through.

If kept well groomed, which is not an enormous task, the rich red and white coat can be a superb sight. His head and muzzle are shaped slightly differently from the English Springer, but his facial expression is just as endearing.

Like all sporting dogs, maximum mental and physical condition can only be achieved through lengthy exercise each day. A prospective owner must prepare for this as the Welsh Springer Spaniel will be full of running long after his owner has tired.

This is a breed to be recommended to anyone who is seeking a loyal, affectionate, medium-sized dog for their home.

KEY TO CHARACTER	
INTELLIGENCE	****
TEMPERAMENT	****
EASE OF COAT CARE	***
SUITABILITY FOR SMALL DWELLING	**
***** (5) = VERY GOOD	

BRITISH KENNEL CLUB STANDARD

SPANIEL (WELSH SPRINGER)

CHARACTERISTICS. — The "Welsh Spaniel" or "Springer" is also known and referred to in Wales as a "Starter". He is of very ancient and pure origin, and is a distinct variety.

GENERAL APPEARANCE. — A symmetrical, compact, strong, merry, very active dog; not stilty; obviously built for endurance and hard work. A quick and active mover displaying plenty of push and drive.

Head and Skull. — Skull proportionate, of moderate length, slightly domed, with clearly defined stop and well chiselled below the eyes. Muzzle of medium length, straight, fairly square; the nostrils well developed and flesh-coloured or dark. A short chubby head is objectionable.

Eyes. — Hazel or dark, medium size, not prominent, nor sunken, nor showing haw.

Ears. — Set moderately low and hanging close to the cheeks, comparatively small and gradually narrowing towards the tip and shaped somewhat like a vine leaf, covered with setter-like feathering.

Mouth. — The jaws should be strong, with a perfect regular and complete scissor bite, i.e., the upper teeth closely overlapping the lower teeth and set square to the jaws.

Neck. — Long and muscular, clean in throat, neatly set into long, sloping shoulders.

Forequarters. — Forelegs of medium length, straight, well boned, moderately feathered.

Body. — Not long; strong and muscular with deep brisket, well-sprung ribs; length of body should be proportionate to length of leg, and very well balanced; muscular loins lightly arched and well coupled up.

Hindquarters. — Strong and muscular, wide and fully developed with deep second thighs. Hind legs well boned, hocks well let down; stifles moderately bent (neither turned in nor out), moderately feathered.

Feet. — Round, with thick pads. Firm and cat-like, not too large or spreading.

Tail. — Well set on and low, never carried above the level of the back; lightly feathered and lively in action.

Coat. — Straight or flat, of a nice silky texture, never wiry nor wavy. A curly coat is most objectionable.

Colour. — Rich red and white only.

Weight and Size. — A dog not to exceed 48cm (19″) in height at shoulder and a bitch 46cm (18″) approximately.

Faults. — Any departure form the foregoing points should be considered a fault and the seriousness of the fault should be in exact proportion to its degree.

Note. — Male animals should have two apparently normal testicles fully descended into the scrotum.

WELSH SPRINGER SPANIEL REGISTRATIONS 1981 — 87 INCLUSIVE

1981 — 596
1982 — 670
1983 — 710
1984 — 648
1985 — 702
1986 — 715
1987 — 528

YET TO WIN CRUFTS BEST-IN-SHOW.

WEIMARANER

The "grey ghost" as this breed is often nicknamed, has one of the strangest and some might say of of the most attractive colourations of all breeds. The slick, gleaming coat gives a steely appearance which is all the more striking on a muscualr dog such as the Weimaraner.

Officially recognised in his native Germany in the nineteenth century, the Weimaraner has been perfected over a period of many years. A type of German Bloodhound known as a Schweisshund was one of his main ancestors and as is plain to see by the Weimaraner's overall shape, Pointer blood was also introduced.

The Germans had been seeking to develop the ultimate gun dog and it was the court of Weimar which pursued this task with the greatest vigour. the early Weimaraners were referred to as Weimar hounds or Weimar Pointers and were used to hunt big game when it was abundant in Germany. Later, of course, the huntsmen had to be content with bird and small game and the Weimaraner excelled at this work.

German breeding was very secretive and disciplined and it was not until the late 1920's that specimens were allowed into the U.S.A., a nation which has taken a great liking to the Weimaraner. It was to be another thirty years before the breed reached Britain and numbers are now steadily on the increase.

The Weimaraner is a dog of good learning capacity with a lively and friendly disposition. They are one of the foremost sporting dogs in the world so exercise should be of paramount importance with lots of free running. Generally he lives very happily in the home environment but, his exuberant nature should be tempered by firm and careful training when young.

KEY TO CHARACTER	
INTELLIGENCE	****
TEMPERAMENT	****
EASE OF COAT CARE	*****
SUITABILITY FOR SMALL DWELLING	*
***** (5) = VERY GOOD	

BRITISH KENNEL CLUB STANDARD

WEIMARANER

CHARACTERISTICS. — In the case of the Weimaraner his hunting ability is the paramount concern and any fault of body or mind which detracts from this ability should be penalised. The dog should display a temperament that is fearless, friendly, protective and obedient.

GENERAL APPEARANCE. — A medium sized grey dog with light eyes, he should present a picture of great driving power, stamina, alertness and balance. Above all, the dog should indicate ability to work hard in the field. Movement should be effortless and ground-covering and should indicate smooth co-ordination. When seen from the rear, the hind feet should parallel the front feet. When seen from the side, the top line should remain strong and level.

Head and Skull. — Moderately long and aristocratic, with moderate stop and slight median line extending back over the forehead. Rather prominent occipital bone and ears set well back. Measurement from the top of the nose to stop to equal that from the stop to the occipital prominence. The flews should be moderately deep, enclosing a powerful jaw. Foreface perfectly straight, delicate at the nostrils. Skin tightly drawn. Neck clean cut and moderately long. Expression keen, kind and intelligent.

Eyes. — Medium-sized in shades of amber or blue-grey, not protruding or too deeply set, placed far enough apart to indicate good disposition and intelligence. When dilated under excitement the eyes may appear almost black.

Ears. — Long and lobular, slightly folded and set high. The ear when drawn alongside the jaw should end approximately one inch from the point of the nose.

Mouth. — Well-set, strong and even teeth, well developed and proportionate to jaw with correct scissor bite (the upper teeth protruding slightly over the lower teeth). Complete dentition is greatly desired. grey nose, lips and gums of pinkish flesh shade.

Forequarters. — Forelegs straight and strong, with measurement from elbow to the ground equalling the distance from the elbow to the top of the withers.

Body. — The length of the body from the highest point of the withers to the root of the tail should equal the measurement from the highest point of the withers to the ground. The top line should be level with a slightly sloping croup. The chest should be well developed and deep, shoulders well laid and snug. Ribs well sprung and long. Abdomen firmly held, moderately tucked up flank. The brisket should drop to the elbow.

Hindquarters. — Moderately angulated with well turned stifle. The hock joint well let down and tuned neither in nor out. Musculation well developed.

Feet. — Firm and compact. Toes well arched, pads closed and thick. Nails short and grey or amber in colour. Dew claws allowable only on imported dogs.

Tail. — Docked at a point such that the tail remaining shall just cover the scrotum in dogs and vulva in bitches. The thickness of the tail should be in proportion to the body and it should be carried in a manner expressing confidence and sound temperament. In the long-haired Weimaraner the tip of the tail should be removed.

Coat. — Short, smooth and sleek. In the long-haired Weimaraner the coat should be form 1-2 inches long on the body and somewhat longer on the neck, chest and belly. The tail and the backs of the limbs should be feathered.

Colour. — Preferably silver grey, shades of mouse or roe grey are admissible. The colour usually blends to a lighter shade on head and ears. A dark eel stripe frequently occurs along the back. The whole coat gives an appearance of metallic sheen. Small white mark allowable on chest but not on any other part of the body. White spots that have resulted from injuries should not be penalised. Colour of the long-haired Weimaraner as the short-haired.

Size. — Height at withers. Dogs 61 to 69cm (24″ to 27″), bitches 56 to 64cm (22″ to 25″).

Faults. — Shyness or viciousness. Any colour or marking other than specified in this Standard.

Note. — Male animals should have two apparently normal testicles fully descended into the scrotum.

MAIN AMERICAN KENNEL CLUB VARIATION TO STANDARD FOR THE WEIMARANER —

Height. — Height at the withers: Dogs, 25 to 27 inches; bitches, 23 to 25 inches.

WEIMARANER REGISTRATIONS 1981 — 87 INCLUSIVE

1981 — 671
1982 — 735
1983 — 845
1984 — 893
1985 — 1070
1986 — 1307
1987 — 1283

YET TO WIN CRUFTS BEST-IN-SHOW.

PEDIGREE DOGS IN COLOUR

BOOK THREE

TERRIERS

This is Book Three in a volume consisting of six books each dealing with a main group of dogs. The page numbering follows that used in the main volume.

Airedale Terrier

Bedlington Terrier

AIREDALE TERRIER

Easily the largest of the Terriers, the impressive Airedale possesses all the attributes of his smaller relatives in points of temperament, courage and hardiness.

He was bred around the mid 1800's and draws his name from the valley of Aire in Yorkshire where most of his development took place. Exactly which Terrier-types were involved in this breeding is not clear, but the Airedale's great size is thought to have come from the use of Otterhounds. In the formative years of the breed, it was known as the Waterside Terrier and an affinity with water is still to be seen in modern Airedales. Although these first specimens were far removed from the superbly proportioned dogs we see today, the foundations were laid for the breeders to build upon.

In Yorkshire the Airedale was widely used in vermin control and rats of any size were quickly exterminated with his powerful jaws. But since his official registration in 1886, the breed has been elevated above such unsavoury tasks and he is now a popular show dog. When trimmed and presented by an expert the Airedale will always create a lasting impression in a show-ring.

He makes a fine house dog, guarding his home with exteme forcefullness. With everyone in the family, though, the Airedale Terrier is friendly, co-operative and playful. He is not over-fond of his fellow dogs so on his exercise outings, which must be frequent, care should be taken to protect other people's pets.

KEY TO CHARACTER	
INTELLIGENCE	****
TEMPERAMENT	****
EASE OF COAT CARE	**
SUITABILITY FOR SMALL DWELLING	*
***** (5) = VERY GOOD	

BRITISH KENNEL CLUB STANDARD

AIREDALE TERRIER

CHARACTERISTICS. — Keen of expression, quick of movement, on the tip-toe of expectation at any movement. Character is denoted and shown by the expression of the eyes, and by the carriage of the ears and tail.

GENERAL APPEARANCE. — The various parts of the dog should be in proportion to each other giving a symmetrical appearance. In movement, the legs should be carried straight forward, the forelegs being perpendicular and parallel with the sides. The propulsive power is furnished by the hind legs, perfection of action being found in the Terrier possessing long thighs, and muscular second thighs well bent at the stifles, which admit of a strong forward thrust or snatch of the hocks. When approaching, the forelegs should form a continuatin of the straight line of the front, the feet being the same distance apart as the elbows; when stationary it is often difficult to determine whether a dog is slightly out at shoulder, but directly he moves, the defect if it exists, becomes most apparent, the forefeet having a tendency to cross. When, on the contrary, the dog is tied at the shoulder, the tendency of the feet is to move wider apart. When the hocks are turned in (cow-hocks) the stifles and feet are turned outward, resulting in a serious loss of propulsive power. When the hocks are turned outward, the tendency of the hind feet is to cross.

Head and Skull. — The skull should be long and flat, not too broad between the ears, and narrowing slightly to the eyes. It should be well balanced, with only little aparent difference in length between skull and foreface. The skull to be free from wrinkles, with stop hardly visible, and cheeks level and free from fullness. Foreface must be well filled up before the eyes, not dish-faced or falling away quickly below eyes, but on the other hand a little delicate chiselling should keep appearance from wedginess and plainness. Upper and lower jaws should be deep, powerful, strong and muscular, as strength of foreface is a great desideratum of the Airedale, but there must be no excess development of the jaws to give a rounded or bulging appearance to the cheeks, as "cheekiness" is not desired. Lips to be tight. The nose should be black.

Eyes. — Should be dark in colour, small, not prominent, full of terrier expression, keenness and intelligence.

Ears. — Should be "V" shaped with a side carriage, small, but not out of proportion to the size of the dog. The top line of the folded ear should be above the level of the skull. A pendulous ear, hanging dead by the side of the head like a hound's, is a fault.

Mouth. — Teeth strong and level being capable of closing together like a vice.

Neck. — Should be clean, muscular, of moderate length and thickness, gradually widening towards the shoulders, and free from throatiness.

Forequarters. — Shoulders should be long, well laid back, and sloping obliquely into the back, shoulder blades flat. Forelegs should be perfectly straight, with plenty of bone. Elbows should be perpendicular to the body, working free of the sides.

Body. — Back should be short, straight and level, with no appearance of slackness. Loins muscular. Ribs well sprung. In a well ribbed-up or short-coupled dog there is little space between ribs and hips. When the dog is long in couplings some slackness will be shown here. Chest to be deep but not broad.

Hindquarters. — Should be long and muscular with no droop. Thighs long and powerful with muscular second thigh, stifles well bent, not turned either in or out. Hocks well let down, parallel with each other when viewed form behind.

Feet. — Should be small, round and compact, with a good depth of pad, well cushioned, and the toes moderately arched, not turned either in or out.

Tail. — Should be set on high and carried gaily, but not curled over the back. It should be of good strength and substance, and of fair length.

Coat. — Should be hard, dense and wiry, and not too long as to appear ragged. It should also lie straight and close, covering the body and legs; the outer coat of hard, wiry, stiff hairs, the undercoat should be a shorter growth of softer hair. Some of the hardest coats are crinkling or just slightly waves; a curly coat is objectionable.

Colour. — The head and ears, with the exception of dark markings on each side of the skull, should be tan, the ears being of a darker shade than the rest. The legs up to the thighs and elbows also should be tan. The body to be black or dark grizzle.

Weight and Size. — Height about 23 inches to 24 inches for dogs, taken form top of shoulder, and bitches about 22 inches to 23 inches. Weight to be commensurate with height and type.

Note. — Male animals should have two apparently normal testicles fully descended into the scrotum.

MAIN AMERICAN KENNEL CLUB VARIATION TO STANDARD FOR THE AIREDALE TERRIER —

Size. — Dogs should measure approximately 23 inches in height at the shoulder; bitches slightly less.

AIREDALE TERRIER REGISTATIONS 1981 — 87 INCLUSIVE

1981 — 1383
1982 — 1327
1983 — 1356
1984 — 1401
1985 — 1369
1986 — 1454
1987 — 1238

CRUFTS BEST-IN-SHOW TWICE.

1961 CH. RIVERINA TWEEDSBAIRN — MISS P. McCAUGHEY AND MRS D. SCHUTH.
1986 CH. GINGER XMAS CAROL — MRS A. LIVRAGHI.

Border Terrier

BEDLINGTON TERRIER

Before 1825 this breed was referred to as the Rothbury Terrier after Rothbury Forest in Northumberland. It was there that gypsies kept dogs similar to todays Bedlington Terrier as pets and for small game hunting. In 1825 a dog enthusiast called Joseph Aynsley took a special interest in these dogs and intensive development was commenced. Aynsley re-named the breed after his home town of Bedlington.

The unique combination of this terrier's physical characteristics comes from Dandie Dinmont Terrier and Whippet blood. Two more different breeds you could not imagine, yet the Bedlington is a harmonious union of the Dandie Dinmont's toughness and attractive coat with the speed and agility of the Whippet. As a catcher of rats or rabbits there is none better than the fearless Bedlington Terrier and the working men of Northumberland used to exploit this talent to the full.

Around the home he conducts himself extremely well, being very easy to train and having a normally mild nature. When roused, however, the Bedlington shows great courage as a guard and will stand his ground against any man or animal who shows agression towards him.

A fair amount of varied exercise is needed to keep this athletic little dog well attuned both physically and mentally. To keep the thick coat clipped correctly does require a fair amount of work, although one advantage is that it does not shed.

KEY TO CHARACTER	
INTELLIGENCE	****
TEMPERAMENT	****
EASE OF COAT CARE	*
SUITABILITY FOR SMALL DWELLING	****
***** (5) = VERY GOOD	

BRITISH KENNEL CLUB STANDARD

BEDLINGTON TERRIER

GENERAL APPEARANCE. — A graceful, lithe, muscular dog, with no sign of either weakness or coarseness. The whole head should be pear or wedge-shaped, and expression in repose mild and gentle, though not shy or nervous. When roused, the eyes should sparkle and the dog look full of temper and courage. Bedlingtons are capable of galloping at great speed and should have the appearance of being able to do so. This action is very distinctive. Rather mincing, light and springy in the slower paces, could have slight roll when in full stride. When galloping must use the whole body.

Head and Skull. — Skull narrow, but deep and rounded; covered with profuse silky top-knot which should be nearly white. Jaw long and tapering. There must be no "stop," the line from occiput to nose end being straight and unbroken. Well filled up beneath the eye. Close fitting lips, without flew. The nostrils must be large and well-defined. Blues and blue-and-tans must have black noses; livers and sandies must have brown noses.

Eyes. — Small, bright and well sunk. The ideal eye has the appearance of being triangular. Blues should have a dark eye; blue-and-tans have lighter eyes with amber lights, and livers and sandies have a light hazel eye.

Ears. — Moderate sized, filbert shaped, set on low, and hanging flat to the cheek. They should be covered with short fine hair with a fringe of whiteish silky hair at the tip.

Mouth. — Teeth, level or pincer-jawed. The teeth should be large and strong.

Neck. — Long tapering neck, deep at the base; there should be no tendency to throatiness. The neck should spring well up from the shoulders, and the head should be carried rather high.

Forequarters. — The forelegs should be straight, but wider apart at the chest than at the feet. Pasterns long and slightly sloping without weakness. Shoulders flat and sloping.

Body. — Muscular, yet markedly flexible; flat-ribbed and deep through the brisket; well ribbed up. The chest should be deep and fairly broad. The back should be roached and the loin markedly arched. Muscular galloping quarters which are also fine and graceful.

Hindquarters. — Muscular and of moderate length. The hind legs, by reason of the roach back and arched loin, have the appearance of being longer than the forelegs. The hocks should be strong and well let down.

Feet. — Long hare feet with thick and well closed up pads.

Tail. — Of moderate length, thick at the root, tapering to a point and gracefully curved. Should be set on low, and must never be carried over the back.

Coat. — Very distinctive. Thick and linty, standing well out from the skin, but not wiry. There should be a distinct tendency to twist, particularly on the head and face.

Colour. — Blue, blue and tan, liver, or sandy. Darker pigment to be encouraged.

Weight and Size. — Height should be about sixteen inches at the shoulder. This allows of slight variation below in the case of a bitch and above in the case of a dog. Weight should be between eighteen and twenty-three pounds.

Note. — Male animals should have two apparently normal testicles fully descended into the scrotum.

MAIN AMERICAN KENNEL CLUB VARIATION TO STANDARD FOR THE BEDLINGTON TERRIER —

Height. — The preferred Bedlington Terrier dog measures 16½ inches at the withers, the bitch 15½ inches. Under 16 inches or over 17½ inches for dogs and under 15 inches or over 16½ inches for bitches are serious faults.

BEDLINGTON TERRIER REGISTRATONS 1981 — 87 INCLUSIVE

1981 — 200
1982 — 261
1983 — 157
1984 — 194
1985 — 198
1986 — 232
1987 — 217

YET TO WIN CRUFTS BEST-IN-SHOW.

BORDER TERRIER

Although diminutive in stature, the Border Terrier is far from being meek or fragile. He was bred from the hardy terriers that were native to the English/Scottish borderlands over a century ago. The goal of the men who began this breeding was to produce a compact yet speedy terrier who could keep pace with a fox hunt and who could stand his ground against a cornered badger. When used for fox hunting, the Border Terrier could make use of his size by burrowing through undergrowth to flush out the fox for his master's hounds. His very thick skin and hard, dense coat protected him well in this danger-frought activity. Modern breeders have endeavoured to maintain all his original characteristics and he is still kept by some of the hunting fraternity.

Since his registration over 60 years ago in Britain and subsequent recognition in the U.S.A., the Border Terrier has deservedly gathered a fair size following. He is a thoroughly genuine type with a first class dispositon and love of human company. He does not care for, or need, too much pampering but he will show great spirit and affection, especially if he is given plenty of outdoor exercise to work off his abundant energy. His size belies his guarding ability and he will defend his owner's home against all-comers.

KEY TO CHARACTER	
INTELLIGENCE	***
TEMPERAMENT	*****
EASE OF COAT CARE	*****
SUITABILITY FOR SMALL DWELLING	****
***** (5) = VERY GOOD	

BRITISH KENNEL CLUB STANDARD

BORDER TERRIER

CHARACTERISTICS. — The Border Terrier is essentially a working Terrier. It should be able to follow a horse and must combine activity with gameness.

Head and Skull. — Head like that of an otter, moderately broad in skull, with a short strong muzzle; a black nose is preferable but a liver or flesh-coloured one is not a serious fault.

Eyes. — Dark, with keen expression.

Ears. — Small, V-shaped, of moderate thickness and dropping forward close to the cheek.

Mouth. — Teeth should have a scissor-like grip, with the top teeth slightly in front of the lower, but level mouth is quite acceptable. An undershot or overshot mouth is a major fault and highly undesirable.

Neck. — Of moderate length.

Forequarters. — Forelegs straight and not too heavy in bone.

Body. — Deep and narrow and fairly long; ribs carried well back, but not over-sprung, as a terrier should be capable of being spanned by both hands behind the shoulder.

Hindquarters. — Racy. Loin strong.

Feet. — Small with thick pads.

Tail. — Moderately short and fairly thick at the base, then tapering, set high and carried gaily but not curled over the back.

Coat. — Harsh and dense with close undercoat. The skin must be thick.

Colour. — Red, wheaten, grizzle and tan or blue and tan.

Weight and Size. — Weight: Dogs, between 13 to 15½ lbs; Bitches, between 11½ to 14 lbs.

Note. — Male animals should have two apparently normal testicles fully descended into the scrotum.

BORDER TERRIER REGISTRATIONS 1981 — 87 INCLUSIVE

1981 — 1152
1982 — 1291
1983 — 1330
1984 — 1362
1985 — 1502
1986 — 1449
1987 — 1534

YET TO WIN CRUFTS BEST-IN-SHOW.

Bull Terrier

BULL TERRIER

The Bull Terrier first appeared in Britain in the mid-nineteenth century and owes his development to a breeder called James Hinks. Using the Old English White Terrier, The Bulldog and some believe the Dalmatian, he worked to perfect a dog that had the power of the Bulldog and the agility of the Terrier. As well as creating an attractive and popular breed, Hinks had produced the ultimate fighting dog, which in the nineteenth century was of great interest to the working classes. Organised dog fights were very popular and this new breed with a longer muzzle and greater speed than the other combatants, was invincible. When this dreadful pastime was abolished, the Bull Terrier's attractive appearance ensured that this was not the signal for his demise. He went on to become a hugely successful show-dog and although his heyday may have passed, he still takes many top honours all over the world.

Although the Bull Terrier can still be intolerant of other dogs, his behaviour with people is without fault. Even small children need have no fear of this gentle powerhouse. With firm training when young, he soon makes a clean, easily managed pet. It should be remembered, though, that a dog of such natural energy and stamina should be allowed plenty of free-running exercise and he will revel in long sessions of play.

As a guard of property he is awesome, any intruder being very foolish to dice with the great power of the Bull Terrier's jaws.

Although all early specimens where white, coloured Bull Terriers have existed for many years, brindle being the most popular. Deafness is a fairly common complaint in white puppies, so always check for this.

KEY TO CHARACTER	
INTELLIGENCE	***
TEMPERAMENT	****
EASE OF COAT CARE	*****
SUITABILITY FOR SMALL DWELLING	**
***** (5) = VERY GOOD	

BRITISH KENNEL CLUB STANDARD

BULL TERRIER

GENERAL APPEARANCE. — The Bull Terrier is the Gladiator of the canine race and must be strongly built, muscular, symmetrical and active, with a keen, determined and intelligent expression, full of fire and courageous but of even temperament and amenable to discipline. Irrespective of size, dogs should look masculine, and bitches feminine. Male animals should have two apparently normal testicles fully descended into the scrotum. The moving dog shall appear well-knit, smoothly covereing the ground with free easy strides and with a typical jaunty air. Fore and hind legs should move parallel each to each when viewed from in front or behind, the forelegs reaching out well and the hindlegs moving smoothly at the hip and flexing well at the stifle and hock with great thrust.

Head. — The head should be long, strong and deep, right to the end of the muzzle, but not coarse. Viewed from the front it should be egg-shaped and completely filled, its surface being free from hollows or indentations. The top of the skull should be almost flat from ear to ear. The profile should curve gently downwards from the top of the skull to the tip of the nose, which should be black and bent downwards at the tip. The nostrils should be well developed. The under-jaw should be strong.

Eyes. — The eyes should appear narrow, obliquely placed, and triangular, well sunken, black, or as dark brown as possible, so as to appear almost black, and with a piercing glint. The distance from the tip of the nose to the eyes should be perceptibly greater than that from the eyes to the top of the skull.

Ears. — The ears should be small, thin and placed close together. The dog should be able to hold them stiffly erect, when they should point straight upwards.

Mouth. — The teeth should be sound, clean, strong, of good size and perfectly regular. The upper front teeth should fit in front of and closely against the lower front teeth. The lips should be clean and tight.

Neck. — The neck should be very muscular, long, arched, tapering from the shoulders to the head, and free from loose skin.

Forequarters. — The shoulders should be strong and muscular but without loading. The shoulder blades should be wide, flat and attached closely to the chest wall, and should have a very pronounced backward slope of the front edge from bottom to top. The forelegs should have the strongest type of round quality bone and the dog should stand solidly upon them; they should be moderately long and perfectly parallel. The elbows should be held straight and the strong pasterns upright.

Body. — The body should be well rounded with marked spring of rib, and great depth from withers to brisket, so that the latter is nearer the ground than the belly. The back should be short and strong with the top line level behind the withers and arching or roaching slightly over the loin. The underline from brisket to belly should form a graceful upward curve. The chest should be broad viewed from the front.

Hindquarters. — The hindlegs should be in parallel viewed from behind. The thighs must be muscular and the second thigh well developed. The stifle joint should be well bent and the hock well angulated, with the bone to the foot short and strong.

Feet. — The feet should be round and compact with well arched toes.

Tail. — The tail should be short, set on low, it should be carried horizontally. Thick at the root it should taper to a fine point.

Coat. — The coat should be short, flat, even and harsh to the touch, with a fine gloss. The skin should fit the dog tightly.

Colour. — For white, pure white coat. Skin pigmentation and markings on the head should not be penalised. For coloured, the colour should predominate; all other things being equal, brindle to be preferred.

Weight and Size. — There are neither weight nor height limits but there should be the impression of the maximum of substance to the size of the dog.

Faults. — Any departure from the foregoing points should be considered a fault and the seriousness of the fault should be in exact proportion to its degree.
N.B. — Under Kennel Club Show Regulations, deafness is a disqualification.

BULL TERRIER REGISTRATIONS 1981 — 87 INCLUSIVE

1981 — 1426
1982 — 1626
1983 — 1676
1984 — 1965
1985 — 2178
1986 — 2263
1987 — 2532

CRUFTS BEST-IN-SHOW WINNER.

1972 CH. ABRAXAS AUDACITY — MISS V. DRUMMOND-DICK.

BULL TERRIER (MINIATURE)

The Miniature Bull Terrier is an exact scaled-down replica of the Bull Terrier. This type of Bull Terrier was developed simply by breeding from only the smallest specimens available. As the popularity of these dogs flourished in some quarters, so the breed was eventually established in it's own right.

All points relating to the Bull Terrier apply to the Miniature version and the standard differs only in the size and weight stipulatons.

Miniature Bull Terrier

KEY TO CHARACTER	
INTELLIGENCE	***
TEMPERAMENT	****
EASE OF COAT CARE	*****
SUITABILITY FOR SMALL DWELLING	*****
***** (5) = VERY GOOD	

BRITISH KENNEL CLUB STANDARD

BULL TERRIER (MINIATURE)

The standard of the Bull Terrier (Miniature) is the same as that of the Bull Terrier with the exception of the following:—

Weight and Size. — There should be an impression of the maximum of substance to the size of the dog. Height should not exceed 35cm (14″). The dog should at all times be balanced.

MINIATURE BULL TERRIER REGISTRATIONS 1981 — 87 INCLUSIVE

1981 — 65
1982 — 48
1983 — 49
1984 — 79
1985 — 65
1986 — 85
1987 — 124

YET TO WIN CRUFTS BEST-IN-SHOW.

Cairn Terrier

Dandie Dinmount Terrier

Smooth Fox Terrier

Wire Fox Terrier

CAIRN TERRIER

This is the breed from which all Scottish terriers are descended and he is one of the most ancient of all British terriers. It seems probable that the kennels which first developed the Cairn Terrier were on the Isle of Skye. The oldest of these kennels was a Captain MacLeod's who first bred these dogs approximately 150 years ago. These primitive Cairn Terriers were known as short-haired Skye Terriers until the official registration of the first Cairn in 1907. From then on he was developed steadily towards today's generally superior form.

His original use was as a hunter of small game and controller of vermin. Fox, badger, otter and rat being amongst his prey. He is ideally suited for this work due to his excellent burrowing ability. The Cairn's coat is well suited to the harsh conditions of his native environment, being hard, wiry and weather resistant.

He often lives to a good age and is basically hardy, confident, well balanced and fearless. The coat does not require too much attention, just an occassional brushing and he does not need lengthy periods of exercise to maintain his naturally fit and sturdy constitution. He has a lively and friendly nature, is never the neurotic type, and is loyal and amusing in the home. Both the elderly and young children alike will find the Cairn Terrier a commendable small dog.

KEY TO CHARACTER	
INTELLIGENCE	****
TEMPERAMENT	*****
EASE OF COAT CARE	****
SUITABILITY FOR SMALL DWELLING	*****
***** (5) = VERY GOOD	

BRITISH KENNEL CLUB STANDARD

CAIRN TERRIER

CHARACTERISTICS. — This terrier should impress with his fearless and gay disposition.

GENERAL APPEARANCE. — Active, game, hardy, and "shaggy" in appearance; strong, though compactly built. Should stand well forward on forepaws. Strong quarters, deep in ribs. Very free in movement. Coat hard enough to resist rain. Head small, but in proportion to body, a general foxy appearance is the chief characteristic of this working terrier.

Head and Skull. — Skull broad in proportion; strong, but not too long or heavy jaw. A decided indentation between eyes; hair should be full on forehead. Muzzle powerful but not heavy. Very strong jaw, which should be neither undershot nor overshot.

Eyes. — Set wide apart; medium in size; dark hazel, rather sunk, with shaggy eyebrows.

Ears. — Small, pointed, well carried and erect, but not too closely set.

Mouth. — Large teeth. Jaw strong and level.

Neck. — Well set on, but not short.

Forequarters. — Sloping shoulder and a medium length of leg; good, but not too large, bone. Forelegs should not be out at elbow. Legs must be covered with hard hair.

Body. — Compact, straight back; well sprung deep ribs; strong sinews. Back medium in length and well-coupled.

Hindquarters. — Very strong.

Irish Terrier

Kerry Blue Terrier

Lakeland Terrier

Manchester Terrier

Feet. — Forefeet, larger than hind, may be slightly turned out. Pads should be thick and strong. Thin and ferrety feet are objectionable.

Tail. — Short, well furnished with hair, but not feathery; carried gaily, but should not turn down towards back.

Coat. — Very important. Must be double-coated, with profuse, hard, but not coarse, outer coat, and undercoat which resembles fur, and is short, soft and close. Open coats are objectionable. Head should be well furnished.

Colour. — Red, sandy, grey, brindled, or nearly black. Dark points such as ears and muzzle, very typical.

Weight and Size. — Ideal weight, 14 lbs.

Faults. — Muzzle: undershot or overshot. Eyes: too prominent or too light. Ears: too large or round at points; they must not be heavily coated with hair. Coat: silkiness or curliness objectionable; a slight wave permissible. Nose: flesh or light coloured, most objectionable. In order to keep this breed to the best old working type, any resemblance to a Scottish Terrier will be considered objectionable.

Note. — Male animals should have two apparently normal testicles fully descended into the scrotum.

MAIN AMERICAN KENNEL CLUB VARIATION TO STANDARD FOR THE CAIRN TERRIER —

Ideal Size. — Weight for bitches, 13 pounds; for dogs, 14 pounds. Height at the withers — bitches, 9½ inches; dogs, 10 inches.

CAIRN TERRIER REGISTRATIONS 1981 — 87 INCLUSIVE

1981 — 2571
1982 — 2384
1983 — 2411
1984 — 2427
1985 — 2509
1986 — 2322
1987 — 2082

YET TO WIN CRUFTS BEST-IN-SHOW.

DANDIE DINMONT TERRIER

Not only is this breed unique in appearance, the origin of his name is also unusual. It is taken from a novel by Sir Walter Scott called "Guy Mannering", which features a character called Dandie Dinmont who keeps small terriers. Although the novel was published in 1814, it is thought that this breed goes back much further.

He first appeared in the early eighteenth century in the Scottish and English border counties. His ancestors were the various types of rough coated terriers of the region whose main function was the hunting of vermin. The early breeders wanted a low slung dog with sufficient burrowing ability to be able to easily root out badgers and foxes, amongst other prey. The long body could possibly come from the use of dogs similar to the Skye Terrier we know today and other suggestions of breeds used to formulate the modern Dandie Dinmont are the Dachsund and the Otterhound.

Although the Dandie Dinmont is not one of the most popular breeds with the general public, he has many good qualities. The relatively small number being bred has helped to keep a strong blood line and his courage and faithfullness have remained firmly implanted in his character. He is a very confident dog, a good guard whilst also being playful and patient. The attractive top-knot and the rest of the Dandie Dinmont's coat does require care to maintain the best appearance. Exercise should be brisk and very frequent.

Norfolk Terrier
Norwich Terrier

Scottish Terrier
Sealyham Terrier

KEY TO CHARACTER	
INTELLIGENCE	***
TEMPERAMENT	****
EASE OF COAT CARE	**
SUITABILITY FOR SMALL DWELLING	****
***** (5) = VERY GOOD	

BRITISH KENNEL CLUB STANDARD

DANDIE DINMONT TERRIER

Head and Skull. — Head strongly made and large, not out of proportion to the dog's size, the muscles showing extraordinary development, more especially the maxillary. Skull broad between the ears, getting gradually less towards the eye, and measuring about the same from the inner corner of the eye to back of skull as it does from ear to ear. The forehead well domed. The head is covered with very soft silky hair, which should not be confined to a mere top-knot, and the lighter in colour and silkier it is the better. The cheeks, starting from the ears proportionately with the skull, have a gradual taper towards the muzzle, which is deep and strongly made, and measures about three inches in length, or in proportion to skull as three is to five. The muzzle is covered with hair of a little darker shade than top-knot, and of the same texture as the feather of the forelegs. The top of the muzzle is generally bare for about an inch from the back part of the nose, the bareness coming to a point towards the eye, and being about one inch broad at the nose. The nose black.

Eyes. — Set wide apart, large, full, round but not protruding, bright, expressive of great determination, intelligence, and dignity, set low and prominent in front of the head, colour, a rich dark hazel.

Ears. — Pendulous, set well back wide apart and low on the skull, hanging close to the cheek, with a very slight projection at the base, broad at the junction of the head and tapering almost to a point, the for part of the ear coming almost straight down from its junction with the head to the tip. They shall harmonise in colour with the body colour. In the case of a pepper dog they are covered with a soft, straight, dark hair (in some cases almost black). In the case of a mustard dog, the hair should be mustard in colour, a shade darker than the body, but not black. All should have a thin feather of light hair starting about two inches from the tip, and of nearly the same colour and texture as the top-knot, which give the ear the appearance of a distinct point. The animal is often one or two years old before the feather is shown. The cartilage and skin of the ear should not be thick, but very thin. Lengh of ear, from three to four inches.

Mouth. — The inside of the mouth should be black or dark coloured. The teeth very strong, especially the canine, which are of extraordinary size for such a small dog. The canines fit well into each other, so as to give the greatest available holding and punishing power, and the teeth are level in front, the upper ones very slightly overlapping the under ones. Undershot or overshot mouths are equally objectionable.

Neck. — Very muscular, well developed, and strong, showing great power of resistance, being well set into the shoulders.

Forequarters. — The forelegs short, with immense muscular development and bone, set wide apart and chest coming well down between them. Bandy legs are objectionable. The hair on the forelegs of a pepper dog should be tan, varying according to the body colour from a rich tan to a pale fawn; of a mustard dog they are of a darker shade than its head, which is a creamy white. In both colours there is a nice feather about two inches long, rather lighter in colour than the hair on the fore part of the leg.

Body. — Long, strong, and flexible; ribs well sprung and round, chest well developed and let down between the forelegs; the back rather low at the shoulders having a slight downward curve and a corresponding arch over the loins, with a very slight gradual drop from top of loin to root of tail; both sides of backbone well supplied with muscle.

Hindquarters. — The hind legs are a little longer than the fore ones, and are set rather wide apart, but not spread out in an unnatural manner; the thighs are well developed, and the hair of the same colour and texture as the fore ones, but having no feather or dew claws.

Feet. — Flat feet are objectionable. The whole claws should be dark, but the claws of all vary in shade according to the colour of the dog's body. The feet of a pepper dog should be tan, varying according to the body colour from a rich tan to a pale fawn; of a mustard dog they are a darker shade than its head. Hind feet should be much smaller than the fore feet.

Tail. — Rather short, say from eight to ten inches, and covered on the upper side with wiry hair of a darker colour than that of the body, the hair on the under side being lighter in colour, and not so wiry, with a nice feather about two inches long, getting shorter as it nears the tip; rather thick at the root, getting thicker for about four inches, then tapering off to a point. It should not be twisted or curled in any way, but should come up with a curve like a scimitar, the tip, when excited, being in a perpendicular line with the root of the tail. It should neither be set too high nor too low. When not excited it is carried gaily, and a little above the level of the body.

Coat. — This is a very important point. The hair should be about two inches long; that from the skull to root of tail a mixture of hardish and soft hair, which gives a sort of crisp feel to the hand. The hard should not be wiry; the coat is what is termed pily or pencilled. The hair on the under part of the body is lighter in colour and softer than that on the top. The skin on the belly accords with the colour of the dog.

Colour. — The colour is pepper or mustard. The pepper ranges from a dark bluish black to a light silvery grey, the intermediate shades being preferred, the body colour coming well down the shoulder and hips, gradually merging into the leg colour. The mustards vary from a reddish brown to a pale fawn, the head being a creamy white, the legs and feet of a shade darker than the head. The claws are dark as in other colours. (Nearly all Dandie Dinmont Terriers have some white on the chest, and some have white claws.) White feet are objectionable.

Skye Terrier

Soft-Coated Wheaten Terrier

Staffordshire Bull Terrier
Welsh Terrier

Weight and Size. — The height should be from eight to eleven inches at the top of shoulder. Length from top of shoulder to root of tail should not be more than twice the dog's height, but, preferably, one or two inches less. The ideal weight as near eighteen pounds as possible. This weight is for dogs in good working order.

Note. — Male animals should have two apparently normal testicles fully descended into the scrotum.

MAIN AMERICAN KENNEL CLUB VARIATION TO STANDARD FOR THE DANDIE DINMONT TERRIER —

Weight. — The preferred weight from 18 to 24 pounds. These weights are for dogs in good working condition.

DANDIE DINMONT TERRIER REGISTRATIONS 1981 — 87 INCLUSIVE

1981 — 204
1982 — 154
1983 — 130
1984 — 184
1985 — 149
1986 — 204
1987 — 190

YET TO WIN CRUFTS BEST-IN-SHOW.

West Highland White Terrier

FOX TERRIER (SMOOTH AND WIRE)

The Fox Terrier as we know him today was developed purely for hunting purposes. Fox hunting enthusiasts of the early eighteenth century required a dog that was small and sturdy enough to burrow for foxes and was also long enough in the leg to keep up with a fast-paced hunt. The Beagle and Foxhound are likely to have been included in his production and the predominantly white coat was probably obtained from the introduction of Bull Terrier blood. This white colouration was an aid to the hunter as many darker terriers had been mistaken for the fox and attacked by the hounds.

The Smooth and Wire Fox Terriers are of identical origin with the coat being their only distinguishing feature. The Smooth Fox Terrier was undoubtedly the more popular of the two up until the start of this century. It was then that the Wire haired gradually became the more sought after, this being mainly due to development in coat care techniques which helped greatly with maintenance.

The Fox Terrier is a very manageable breed in the home, enjoying human companionship and standing no nonsense from potential intruders. They are very alert and sharp in reaction but never nervous or unpredictable. The more dense and hard the coat of the Wire Fox Terrier, the better and it should be given plenty of attention to avoid scruffiness. As he was bred for stamina when hunting, the Fox Terrier must have regular vigorous exercise.

KEY TO CHARACTER		
INTELLIGENCE		***
TEMPERAMENT		****
EASE OF COAT CARE	SMOOTH	*****
	WIRE	**
SUITABILITY FOR SMALL DWELLING		***
***** (5) = VERY GOOD		

BRITISH KENNEL CLUB STANDARD

FOX TERRIER (SMOOTH)

GENERAL APPEARANCE. — The dog must present a general gay, lively, and active appearance; bone and strength in a small compass are essentials, but this must not be taken to mean that a Fox Terrier should be cloggy, or in any way coarse, speed and endurance must be looked to as well as power, and the symmetry of the Foxhound taken as a model. The Terrier, like the Hound, must on no account be leggy, nor must he be too short in the leg. He should stand like a cleverly made Hunter, covering a lot of ground, yet with a short back. He will then attain the highest degree of propelling power, together with the greatest length of stride that is compatible with the length of his body.

Head and Skull. — The skull should be flat and moderately narrow, and gradually decreasing in width to the eyes. Not much "stop" should be apparent, but there should be more dip in the profile between the forehead and the top jaw than is seen in the case of the Greyhound. The cheeks must not be full. The jaw, upper and under, should be strong and muscular, should be of fair punishing strength, but not so in any way to resemble the Greyhound. There should not be much falling away below the eyes. This part of the head should, however, be moderately chiselled out, so as not to go down in a straight line like a wedge. The nose, towards which the muzzle must gradually taper, should be black.

Eyes. — Should be dark in colour, small and rather deep set, full of fire, life, and intelligence; as nearly as possible circular in shape.

Ears. — Should be V-shaped and small, of moderate thickness, and dropping forward close to the cheek, not hanging by the side of the head like a Foxhound's.

Mouth. — The teeth should be nearly as possible level, i.e., the upper teeth on the outside of the lower teeth.

Neck. — Should be clean and muscular, without throatiness, of fair length, and gradually widening to the shoulders.

Forequarters. — The shoulders should be long and sloping, well laid back, fine at the points, and clearly cut at the withers.

Body. — Chest deep and not too broad. Back should be short, straight and strong, with no appearance of slackness. Loin should be powerful and very slightly arched. The fore ribs should be moderately arched, the back ribs deep; and the dog should be well ribbed up.

Hindquarters. — Should be strong and muscular, quite free from droop or crouch; the thighs long and powerful; hocks near the ground, the dog standing well up on them like a Foxhound, and not straight in stifle.

Feet. — Should be round, compact and not large. The soles hard and tough. The toes moderately arched, and turned neither in nor out.

Tail. — Should be set on rather high, and carried gaily, but not over the back nor curled. It should be of good strength.

Coat. — White should predominate; brindle, red or liver markings are objectionable. Otherwise this point is of litle or no importance.

Weight and Size. — Weight is not a certain criterion of a Terrier's fitness for his work — general shape, size and contour are the main points — and if a dog can gallop and stay, and follow his fox up a drain, it matters little what his weight is to a pound or so, though, roughly speaking, 15 to 17 lbs. for a bitch and 16 to 18 lbs. for a dog in Show condition are appropriate weights.

Faults. — Nose, white, cherry, or spotted to a considerable extent with either of these colours. Ears, prick, tulip or rose. Mouth, much undershot or much overshot.

Note. — Male animals should have two apparently normal testicles fully descended into the scrotum.

MAIN AMERICAN KENNEL CLUB VARIATION TO STANDARD FOR THE SMOOTH FOX TERRIER —

Size. — According to present-day requirements, a full-sized well-balanced dog should not exceed 15½ inches at the withers.

SMOOTH FOX TERRIER REGISTRATIONS 1981 — 87 INCLUSIVE

1981 — 316
1982 — 308
1983 — 318
1984 — 305
1985 — 319
1986 — 251
1987 — 344

YET TO WIN CRUFTS BEST-IN-SHOW.

FOX TERRIER (WIRE)

CHARACTERISTICS. — The Terrier should be alert, quick of movement keen of expression, on the tip-toe of expectation at the slightest provocation. Character is imparted by the expression of the eyes and by the carriage of ears and tail.

GENERAL APPEARANCE. — The dog should be balanced and this may be defined as the correct proportions of a certain point or points, when considered in relation to a certain other point or points. It is the keystone of the Terrier's anatomy. The chief points for consideration are the relative proportions of skull and foreface; head and back; height at withers; and length of body from shoulder-point to buttock — the ideal of proportion being reached when the last two measurements are the same. It should be added that, although the head measurements can be taken with absolute accuracy, the height at withers and length of back are approximate, and are inserted for the information of breeders and exhibitors rather than as a hard-and-fast rule. The movement or action is the crucial test of conformation. The Terrier's legs should be carried straight forward while travelling, the forelegs hanging perpendicular and swinging parallel to the sides, like the pendulum of a clock. The principal propulsive power is furnished by the hind legs, perfection of action being found in the Terrier possessing long thighs and muscular second-thighs well bent at the stifles, which admit of a strong forward thrust or "snatch" of the hocks. When approaching the forelegs should form a continuation of the straight of the front, the feet being the same distance apart as the elbows. When stationary it is often difficult to determine whether a dog is slightly out at shoulder but directly he moves the defect — if it exists — becomes more apparent, the fore-feet having a tendency to cross, "weave" or "dish". When on the contrary, the dog is tied at the shoulder, the tendency of the feet is to move wider apart, with a sort of padding action. When the hocks are turned in — cow hocks — the stifles and feet are turned outwards, resulting in a serious loss of propulsive power. When the hocks are turned outwards the tendency of the hind feet is to cross, resulting in an ungainly waddle.

Head and Skull. — The top line of the skull should be almost flat, sloping slightly and gradually decreasing in width towards the eyes. In a well-balanced head there should be little apparent difference in length between skull and foreface. If, however, the foreface is noticeably shorter, it amounts to a fault, the head looking weak and "unfinished". On the other hand, when the eyes are set too high up in the skull, and too near the ears, it also amounts to a fault, the head being said to have a "foreign appearance". Although the foreface should gradually taper from eye to muzzle and should dip slightly at its juncture with the forehead, it should not "dish" or fall away quickly below the eyes, where it should be full and well made up, but relieved from "wedginess" by a little delicate chiselling. While well-developed jaw bones, armed with a set of strong white teeth, impart that appearance of strength to the foreface which is desirable. An excessive bony or muscular development of the jaws is both unnecessary and unsightly, as it is partly responsible for the full and rounded contour of the cheeks to which the term "cheeky" is applied. Nose should be black.

Eyes. — Should be dark in colour, moderately small and not prominent, full of fire, life, and intelligence; as nearly as possible, circular in shape and not too far apart. Anything approaching a yellow eye is most objectionable.

Ears. — Should be small and V-shaped and of moderate thickness, the flaps neatly folded over and drooping forward close to the cheeks. The top line of the folded ear should be well above the level of the skull. A pendulous ear, hanging dead by the side of the head like a hound's is uncharacteristic of the Terrier, while an ear which is semi-erect is still more undesirable.

Mouth. — Both upper and lower jaws should be strong and muscular, the teeth as nearly as possible level and capable of closing together like a vice — the lower canines locking in front of the upper and the points of the upper incisors slightly overlapping the lower.

Neck. — Should be clean, muscular, of fair length, free from throatiness and presenting a graceful curve when viewed from the side.

Forequarters. — Shoulders when viewed from the front, should slope steeply downwards from their juncture, with the neck towards the points, which should be fine. When viewed from the side they should be long, well laid back, and should slope obliquely backwards from points to withers, which should always be clean cut. A shoulder well laid back gives the long fore-hand, which, in combination with a short back, is so desirable in Terrier or Hunter. Chest deep and not broad, a too narrow chest being almost as undesirable as a very broad one. Excessive depth of chest and brisket is an impediment to a Terrier when going to ground. Viewed from any direction the legs should be straight, the bone of the forelegs strong right down to the feet. The elbows should hang perpendicular to the body, working free of the sides, carried straight through in travelling.

Body. — The back should be short and level, with no appearance of slackness — the loins muscular and very slightly arched. The brisket should be deep, the front ribs moderately arched, and the back ribs deep, and well sprung. The term "slackness" is applied both to the portion of the back immediately behind the withers when it shows any tendency to dip, and also the flanks when there is too much space between the back-ribs and hip-bone. When there is little space between the ribs and hips, the dog is said to be "short in couplings", "short-coupled", or "well-ribbed up". A Terrier can scarcely be too short in back, provided he has sufficient length of neck and liberty of movement. The bitch may be slightly longer in couplings than the dog.

Hindquarters. — Should be strong and muscular, quite free from droop or crouch; the thighs long and powerful; the stifles well curved and turned neither in nor out; the hock-joints well bent and near the ground; the hocks perfectly upright and parallel with each other when viewed from behind. The worst possible form of hindquarters consists of a short second-thigh and a straight stifle, a combination which causes the hind-legs to act as props rather than instruments of propulsion. The hind-legs should be carried straight through in travelling.

Feet. — Should be round, compact, and not large — the pads tough and well cushioned, and the toes moderately arched and turned neither in nor out. A Terrier with good-shaped fore-legs and feet will wear his nails down short by contact with the road surface, the weight of the body being evenly distributed between the toe-pad and the heels.

Tail. — Should be set on rather high and carried gaily but not curled. It should be of good strength and substance and of fair length — a three-quarter dock is about right — since it affords the only safe grip when handling working Terriers. A very short tail is suitable neither for work nor show.

Coat. — The principal difference between that of the Smooth and Wire variety is that, whereas the former is straight and flat, that of the latter appears to be broken — the hairs having a tendency to twist. The best coats are of a dense, wiry texture — like cocoa-nut matting — the hairs growing so closely and strongly together that when parted with the fingers the skin cannot be seen. At the base of these stiff hairs is a shorter growth of finer and softer hair — termed the under coat. The coat on the sides is never quite so hard as that on the back and quarters. Some of the hardest coats are "crinkly" or slightly waved, but a curly coat is very objectionable. The hair on the upper and lower jaws should be crisp and only sufficiently long to impart an appearance of strength to the fore-face, thus effectually differentiating them from the Smooth variety. The hair on the fore-legs should also be dense and crisp. The coat should average in length from ¾ to 1 inch on shoulders and neck, lengthening to 1½ inches on withers, backs, ribs and quarters. These measurements are given rather as a guide to exhibitors than as an infallible rule, since the length of coat varies in different specimens and seasons. The judge must form his own opinion as to what constitutes a "sufficient" coat.

Colour. — White should predominate: brindle, red, liver, or slaty blue are objectionable. Otherwise, colour is of little or no importance.

Weight and Size. — Bone and strength in a small compass are essential, but this must not be taken to mean that a Terrier should be "cloddy", or in any way coarse — speed and endurance being requisite as well as power. The Terrier must on no acount be leggy, nor must he be too short on the leg. He should stand like a cleverly-made, short-backed Hunter, covering a lot of ground. According to present-day requirements, a full-sized, well-balanced dog should not exceed 15½ inches at the withers — the bitch being proportionately lower — nor should the length of back from withers to root of tail exceed 12 inches, while to maintain the relative proportions, the head — as before mentioned — should not exceed 7¼ inches or be less than 7 inches. A dog with these measurements should scale 18 lbs. in show condition — a bitch weighing some 2 lbs. less — with a margin of 1 lb. either way.

Faults. — Nose: white, cherry, or spotted to a considerable extent with either of these colours. Ears: prick, tulip, or rose. Mouth: much undershot or much overshot.

N.B. — Old scars or injuries, the result of work or accident, should not be allowed to prejudice a Terrier's chance in the show-ring, unless they interfere with its movement or with its utility for work or stud.

Note. — Male animals should have two apparently normal testicles fully descended into the scrotum.

WIRE FOX TERRIER REGISTRATIONS 1981 — 87 INCLUSIVE

1981 — 738
1982 — 677
1983 — 681
1984 — 681
1985 — 747
1986 — 661
1987 — 656

CRUFTS BEST-IN-SHOW WINNER 3 TIMES.

1962 CH. CRACKWYN COCKSPUR — H.L. GILL
1975 CH. BROOKEWIRE BRANDY OF LAYVEN — MESSRS. BENELLI AND DONDINA
1978 CH. HARROWHILL HUNTSMAN — MISS E. HOWLES.

IRISH TERRIER

At first glance this ancient breed from the Emerald Isle looks like a scaled-down Airedale or an over-blown Lakeland Terrier. But apart from the colour difference the Irish Terrier has a unique head and a conformation all of his own.

Much legend and uncertainty surrounds the breed's beginnings, some Irishmen even maintaining that he is a close relation of the Irish Wolfhound. But in all corners of the Britissh Isles small wire-haired hunting terriers have existed for centuries and Ireland is no exception. So it would seem very probable that the Irish Terrier is from stock of this sort, and his efficiency as a ratter and catcher of small game adds weight to that idea.

Until the late 1870's when the breed became more standardised, the colouring had varied quite widely. Now the colours of bright red, red wheaten or yellow red are insisted upon by the breed standard.

As might be expected of a true Terrier, expecially an Irish one, he is full of spirit, mischief and courage. He has gained, rather unfairly, a reputation as a vicious fighter, but whilst he will take no nonsense from any dog, he will normally mind his own business.

He is easily trained for the home and is naturally adaptable to any environment that his owner lives in. Children will enjoy his company and if exercised regularly he makes a high-spirited, good-natured companion.

KEY TO CHARACTER	
INTELLIGENCE	****
TEMPERAMENT	****
EASE OF COAT CARE	***
SUITABILITY FOR SMALL DWELLING	***
***** (5) = VERY GOOD	

BRITISH KENNEL CLUB STANDARD

IRISH TERRIER

CHARACTERISTICS. — Dogs that are very game are usually surly or snappish. The Irish Terrier as a breed is an exception, being remarkably good tempered, notably so with humans, it being admitted, however, that he is perhaps a little too ready to resent interference on the part of other dogs. There is a heedless, reckless pluck about the Irish Terrier which is characteristic, and coupled with the head-long dash, blind to all consequence, with which he rushes at his adversary, has earned for the breed the proud epithet of "The Dare Devils". When "off duty" they are characterised by a quiet caress-inviting appearance, and when one sees them endearingly, timidly pushing their heads into their master's hands, it is difficult to realise that on occasions, at the "set on", they can prove that they have the courage of a lion, and will fight unto the last breath in their bodies. They develop an extraordinary devotion for, and have been known to track their masters almost incredible distances.

GENERAL APPEARANCE. — The dog must present an active, lively, lithe and wiry appearance; with lots of substance, at the same time free of clumsiness, as speed and endurance, as well as power, are very essential. They must be neither "cloddy" nor "cobby", but should be framed on the "lines of speeds", showing a graceful "racing outline".

Head and Skull. — Head long; skull flat, and rather narrow between ears, getting slightly narrower trowards the eye; free from wrinkles; stop hardly visible except in profile. The jaw must be strong and muscular, but not too full in the cheek, and of a good punishing length. The foreface should not "dish" or fall away quickly between or below the eyes, where it should be well made up, being relieved of "wedginess" by delicate chiselling. The hiar should be crisp and only sufficiently long to impart an appearance of additional strength to the foreface. Lips should be well fitting and externally almost black in colour. The nose must be black.

Eyes. — A dark colour, small not prominent, and full of life, fire and intelligence. A light or yellow eye is a fault.

Ears. — Small and V-shpaed, of moderate thickness, set well on the head, and dropping forward closely to the cheek. The top of the folded ear should be well above the level of the skull. The ear must be free of fringe, and the hair thereon shorter and darker in colour than the body.

Mouth. — The teeth should be even, strong and free from discoloration, the top teeth slightly overlapping the lower.

Neck. — Should be of a fair length and gradually widening towards the shoulders, well carried, and free of throatiness. There is generally a slight frill at each side of the neck, running nearly to the corner of the ear.

Forequarters. — The shoulders must be fine, long, and sloping well into the back. The legs moderately long, well set from the shoulders, perfectly straight, with plenty of bone and muscle; the elbows working freely clear of the sides; pasterns short and straight, hardly noticeable. The forelegs should be moved straight forward when travelling. The hair on the legs should be dense and crisp.

Body. — Chest deep and muscular, but neither full nor wide. Body moderately long; back should be strong and straight, with no appearance of slackness behind the shoulders; the loin muscular and slightly arched; ribs fairly sprung, rather deep than round, and well-ribbed back.

Hindquarters. — Should be strong and muscular, the thighs powerful, hocks near the ground, stifles moderately bent. The hind legs should be moved straight forward when travelling, the stifles not turned outwards. The hair on the legs should be dense and crisp.

Feet. — Should be strong tolerably round, and moderately small, toes arched, and neither turned out not in; black toe nails most desirable. Pads must be sound and free from cracks or horny excrescences.

Tail. — Generally docked to about three quarters; should be free of fringe or feather, but well covered with rough hair, set on pretty high, carried gaily, but not over the back or curled.

Coat. — Hard and wiry, having a broken appearance, free of softness or silkiness, not so long as to hide the outline of the body, particularly in the hindquarters, straight and flat, no shagginess and free of lock or curl. At the base of these stiff hairs is a growth of finer and softer hair, usually termed the undercoat.

Colour. — Should be "whole-coloured", the most preferable colours being a bright red, red wheaten, or yellow red. White sometimes appears on chest and feet and is more objectionable on the latter than on the former, as a speck of white on chest is frequently to be seen in all self-coloured breeds.

Weight and Size. — The most desirable weight in Show condition is, for a dog, 27 lbs., and for a bitch, 25 lbs. Height at shoulders, approximately 18 inches.

Note. — Male animals should have two apparently normal testicles fully descended into the scrotum.

IRISH TERRIER REGISTRATIONS 1981 — 87 INCLUSIVE

1981 — 139
1982 — 130
1983 — 146
1984 — 165
1985 — 184
1986 — 137
1987 — 135

YET TO WIN CRUFTS BEST-IN-SHOW.

KERRY BLUE TERRIER

The Kerry Blue Terrier is a tough, no nonsense dog in the finest terrier tradition.

Hailing from County Kerry in Eire, he has been used for a variety of useful jobs for many years. Among these tasks have geen guarding, small hunting and even herding sheep and cattle.

It was not until the early 1920's that England began to show interest in this fine breed and although he could not be called a common breed, he has made a good impact on the English show world and given great pleasure to many as a house pet.

Although he is the soul of good manners when in human company, the Kerry Blue is noted as a ferocious fighter with his own kind. This behaviour should naturally be discouraged from puppyhood, but total success in that endeavour would be difficult.

The Kerry Blue is an excellent guard dog and is of sufficiently solid proportions to discourage any unwanted visitor. He is easily house trained and does not shed any hairs although the dense coat does requre very frequent clipping.

Plenty of boisterous play and rigoroous exercise is enjoyed by this breed, so an elderly or infirm owner would not be advised.

KEY TO CHARACTER	
INTELLIGENCE	****
TEMPERAMENT	****
EASE OF COAT CARE	**
SUITABILITY FOR SMALL DWELLING	**
***** (5) = VERY GOOD	

BRITISH KENNEL CLUB STANDARD

KERRY BLUE TERRIER

CHARACTERISTICS. — Disciplined gameness. The Kerry Blue Terrier is a compact, powerful Terrier, showing gracefulness and an attitude of alert determination, with definite Terrier style and character throughout.

GENERAL APPEARANCE. — The typical Kerry Blue Terrier should be upstanding, well knit and well proportioned, showing a well-developed and muscular body.

Head and Skull. — Well balanced, long, proportionately lean, with slight stop and flat over the skull. Foreface and jaw very strong, deep and punishing; nose black; nostrils of due proportion.

Eyes. — Dark as possible. Small to medium with keen Terrier expression.

Ears. — Small to medium and V-shaped, carried forward but not as high as in some Terrier breeds.

Mouth. — Teeth level with upper teeth just closing over the lower; dark gums and roof.

Neck. — Strong and reachy, running into sloping sholders.

Forequarters. — Shoulders flat as possible with elbows carried close to the body while the dog is standing or in action. Legs straight, bone powerful. Front straight, neither too wide nor too narrow.

Body. — Short coupled with good depth of brisket and well sprung ribs. Chest to be deep. Topline level.

Hindquarters. — Large and well developed, stifle bent and hocks close to the ground giving perfect freedom of hind action.

Feet. — Round and small. Toe nails black.

Tail. — Set on high to complete a perfectly staight back and carried erect.

Coat. — Soft and silky, plentiful and wavy.

Colour. — Any shade of blue, with or without black points. A shade of tan is permissible in puppies, as is also a dark colour up to the age of 18 months. A small white patch on chest should not be penalised.

Weight and Size. — The most desirable weight for a fully-developed dog is from 33 to 37 lbs., and bitches should weigh proportionately less, but 35 lbs., is the most desirable weight to aim for. Ideal height: dogs 18 to 19 inches at shoulder; bitches slightly less.

Faults. — Hard or woolly coat. Solid black after 18 months. In excess of 19 inches in height. Bumpy cheek bones, teeth undershot or very overshot. Rose ears. Snipy foreface. Light-coloured or full eyes. Roach or hollowback. Close, stilted or cow-hocked hind action.

Note. — Male animals should have two apparently normal testicles fully descended into the scrotum.

MAIN AMERICAN KENNEL CLUB VARIATION TO STANDARD FOR THE KETTY BLUE TERRIER —

Height. — The ideal Kerry should be 18½ inches at the withers for a dog, slightly less for a bitch.

Weight. — The most desirable weight for a fully developed dog is from 33 to 40 pounds, bitches weighing proportionately less.

KERRY BLUE TERRIER REGISTRATIONS 1981 — 87 INCLUSIVE

1981 — 260
1982 — 299
1983 — 305
1984 — 302
1985 — 316
1986 — 315
1987 — 256

CRUFTS BEST-IN-SHOW WINNER.

1979 ENG. AM. CH. CALLAGHAN OF LEANDER — MRS W. STREATFIELD.

LAKELAND TERRIER

This tough, energetic terrier originated in the Lake District and was officially registered in 1921. Before then there had been several varieties of Terrier in the area, each named after it's particular region. All these dogs, though, were of similar type and all were used for fox hunting as they were very adept at burrowing in the difficult Lakeland terrain. Various owners of these Terrier packs eventually formed a Lakeland Terrier club and from then onwards there has been but one distinct variety.

Although only a moderately popular Terrier, the Lakeland has won his fair share of top show honours. When trimmed by an expert and presented in prime condition, he can be the epitome of smartness. The coat can come in any of several colour schemes and this adds to the interest created by the breed amongst Terrier enthusiasts.

The Lakeland Terrier has all the classic Terrier features of gameness, high spirits and love of human company. He is a manageable size for almost any home and his sharp bark is sufficient to discourage any would-be intruder.

This breed possesses great stamina and loves vigorous exercise, this provision being made, the Lakeland makes a fine companion.

KEY TO CHARACTER	
INTELLIGENCE	***
TEMPERAMENT	****
EASE OF COAT CARE	***
SUITABILITY FOR SMALL DWELLING	****
***** (5) = VERY GOOD	

BRITISH KENNEL CLUB STANDARD

LAKELAND TERRIER

GENERAL APPEARANCE. — Smart and workman-like, with gay fearless demeanour.

Head and Skull. — Well balanced. Skull flat and refined. The jaws powerful and the muzzle should be broad but not too long. The length of the head from the stop to the tip of the nose should not exceed that from the occiput to the stop. Nose black.

Eyes. — Should be dark or hazel.

Ears. — Moderately small, V-shaped and carried alertly. They should not be placed too high or too low on the head.

Mouth. — Teeth even, closing scissor fashion, i.e., top teeth fitting closely over lower.

Neck. — Reachy.

Forequarters. — Shoulders well laid back. Forelegs straight, well boned.

Body. — Chest reasonably narrow. Back strong, moderately short, well coupled.

Hindquarters. — Strong and muscular, thighs long and powerful, well turned stifles, hocks low to ground and straight.

Feet. — Small, compact, round and well padded.

Tail. — Well set on, carried gaily but not to curl over the back.

Coat. — Dense and weather resisting, harsh with good undercoat.

Colour. — Black and tan, blue and tan, red, wheaten, red grizzle, liver, blue or black. Small tips of white on feet and chest not to debar. Mahogany or deep tan is not typical.

Weight and Size. — The average weight of dogs is 17 lbs., bitches 15 lbs. The height should not exceed 14½ inches at the shoulder.

Faults. — A true Lakeland Terrier expression is determined by head, ears and eyes. Too long a head, ears set on the top of the head, and slanting eyes are faults.

Note. — Male animals should have two apparently normal testicles fully descended into the scrotum.

MAIN AMERICAN KENNEL CLUB VARIATION TO STANDARD FOR THE LAKELAND TERRIER —

Size. — The ideal height of the mature dog is 14½ inches from the withers to the ground, with up to a ½ inch deviation either way permissible. Bitches may measure as much as one inch less than dogs. The weight of the well-balanced, mature specimen in hard, show condition, averages approximately 17 pounds, those of other heights proportionately more or less.

LAKELAND TERRIER REGISTRATIONS 1981 — 87 INCLUSIVE

1981 — 273
1982 — 268
1983 — 270
1984 — 303
1985 — 292
1986 — 236
1987 — 257

CRUFTS BEST-IN-SHOW WINNER TWICE.

1963 ROGERHOLM RECRUIT — W. ROGERS
1967 CH. STINGRAY OF DERRYABAH — MR & MRS W. POSTLEWAITE.

MANCHESTER TERRIER

The spirited Manchester Terrier descends directly from the old Black and Tan Terriers that were once common in nothern England. These hardy little dogs were principally used for ratting and their skill at this work was reputed to be unsurpassed. In fact their prowess was such that a grisly form of entertainment known as the 'rat pit' flourished among working men. At these events dozens of rats would be released in a pit and a Black and Tan Terrier would be thrown amongst them. Bets were taken on how quickly the dog would kill a given number of rats.

A crossing of one of these rather coarse dogs with a Whippet is thought to have laid the foundations of today's Manchester Terrier. The ealry dogs would often vary greatly in size and when they were first exhibited at dog shows there were two distinct weight categories. Both these types were bracketed as Black and Tan Terriers but over a century ago the two were given the distinct titles of English Toy Terrier for the smaller and Manchester Terrier for the larger.

Although not a widespread breed by any means, the Manchester Terrier has many fine attributes. In the home he is extremely clean, has no odour and is of an uncomplaining and unfussy disposition. He enjoys human company and makes a tireless and friendly playmate for children. The sleek coat and appealing markings make this an attractive small dog and he will maintain his well-being on only a moderate amount of exercise.

KEY TO CHARACTER	
INTELLIGENCE	***
TEMPERAMENT	****
EASE OF COAT CARE	*****
SUITABILITY FOR SMALL DWELLING	*****
***** (5) = VERY GOOD	

BRITISH KENNEL CLUB STANDARD

MANCHESTER TERRIER

GENERAL APPEARANCE. — The dog shall be compact in appearance with good bone and free from any resemblance to the Whippet.

Head and Skull. — Long, flat in skull and narrow, level and wedge-shaped, without showing cheek muscles; well-filled up under the eyes, with tapering, tight lipped jaws.

Eyes. — Small, dark and sparkling, oblong in shape, set close in head, not prominent.

Ears. — Small and V-shaped, carried well above the top line of the head and hanging to the head above the eyes.

Mouth. — Should be level.

Neck. — The neck should be fairly long and tapering from the shoulder to the head and slightly arched at the crest, free from throatiness.

Forequarters. — The shoulders should be clean and well sloped. The chest narrow and deep. The forelegs must be quite straight, set on well under the dog; and of proportionate length to the body.

Body. — Short with well-sprung ribs, slightly roached and well cut up behind the ribs.

Hindquarters. — The hind legs should be neigher cow-hocked nor with the feet turned in and well bent at the stifle.

Feet. — Small, semi-harefooted, and strong with well-arched toes.

Tail. — Short and set on where the arch of the back ends, thick where it joins the body and tapering to a point, carried not higher than the level of the back.

Coat. — Close, smooth, short and glossy, of a firm texture.

Colour. — Jet black and rich mahogany tan distributed as follows: on the head, the muzzle to be tanned to the nose, the nose and nasal bone to be jet black. There shall be a small tan spot on each cheek and above each eye, the under-jaw and throat to be tanned with a distinct tan V. The legs from the knee downward to be tanned with the exception of the toes which shall be pencilled with black, and a distinct black mark (thumb mark) immediately above the feet. Inside the hind legs tanned but divided with black at the stifle joint. Under the tail tanned, the vent tanned but as narrow as possible so that it is covered by the tail. A slight tan mark on each side of the chest. Tan outside the hind legs, commonly called breeching, a defect. In all cases the black should not run into the tan or vice versa, but the division between the colours shall be clearly defined.

Weight and Size. — Desired height at shoulders 16 inches dogs, 15 inches bitches.

Note. — Male animals should have two apparently normal testicles fully descended into the scrotum.

MAIN AMERICAN KENNEL CLUB VARIATION TO STANDARD FOR THE MANCHESTER TERRIER —

Weith. — Over 12 pounds and not exceeding 22 pounds.

Ears. — Erect, or button, small and thin; smaller at the root and set as close together as possible at the top of the head. If cropped, to a point, long and carried erect.

MANCHESTER TERRIER REGISTRATIONS 1981 — 87 INCLUSIVE

1981 — 91
1982 — 102
1983 — 160
1984 — 135
1985 — 186
1986 — 160
1987 — 103

YET TO WIN CRUFTS BEST-IN-SHOW.

NORFOLK TERRIER

The Norfolk Terrier existed in similar form for many years under te same title as today's Norwich Terrier. It was only in 1964 that he became a fully-fledged breed in his own right. The only marked difference between the two is still the ears, the Norwich having erect, pointed ears.

He has always been used for hunting and has the sturdiness and strong character that such work often requires. His short but powerful legs are ideal for digging after badgers and foxes and the hard coat serves as good protection from the weather and from the hazards of thorns and the like.

Being almost identical to his fellow East Anglian, he too shares the friendly nature of the Norwich. He enjoys being with children and makes a fine playmate for them. Given plenty of attention and regular exercise he makes a rewarding addition to any family who want a small but unfussy dog.

KEY TO CHARACTER	
INTELLIGENCE	***
TEMPERAMENT	****
EASE OF COAT CARE	****
SUITABILITY FOR SMALL DWELLING	*****
***** (5) = VERY GOOD	

BRITISH KENNEL CLUB STANDARD

NORFOLK TERRIER

CHARACTERISTICS. — The Norfolk Terrier is one of the smallest of the Terriers, but a "demon" for its size. Of a lovable disposition, not quarrelsome, with a hardy constitution. Temperament: Alert and fearless.

GENERAL APPEARANCE. — A small low keen dog, compact and strong with short back, good substance and bone. Honourable scars from fair wear and tear should not be penalised unduly.

Head and Skull. — Skull wide and slightly rounded with good width between the ears. Muzzle wedge-shaped and strong; length of muzzle slightly less than half the length of skull. Stop should be well defined.

Eyes. — Oval shaped and deep set, in colour dark brown or black. Expression alert, keen and intelligent.

Ears. — Size medium "V"-shaped but slightly rounded at tip, dropping forward close to the cheek.

Mouth. — Tight lipped, jaw strong; teeth strong and rather large; scissor bite.

Neck. — Medium length and strong.

Forequarters. — Clean and powerful shoulders with short powerful and straight legs.

Body. — Compact with short back, level topline, well sprung ribs.

Hindquarters. — Well muscled, good turn of stifle, hocks well let down and straight when viewed from rear; with great powers of propulsion.

Feet. — Round with thick pads.

Tail. — Medium docked, not excessively gay.

Coat. — Hard, wiry and straight, lying close to the body. It is longer and rougher on the neck and shoulders. Hair on head and ears short and smooth, except for slight whiskers and eyebrows.

Colour. — All shades of red, red wheaten, black and tan or grizzle. White marks or patches are undesirable but shall not disqualify.

Size. — Ideal height 10 in. at withers.

Faults. — Any departure from the foregoing points should be considered a fault and the seriousness of the fault should be in exact proportion to its degree.

Note. — Male animals should have two apparently normal testicles fully descended into the scrotum.

MAIN AMERICAN KENNEL CLUB VARIATION TO STANDARD FOR THE NORFOLK TERRIER —

Size. — Height at the withers 9 to 10 inches at maturity. Bitches tend to be smaller than dogs. Weight 11 to 12 pounds or that which is suitable for each individual dog's structure and balance.

NORFOLK TERRIER REGISTRATIONS 1981 — 87 INCLUSIVE

1981 — 272
1982 — 302
1983 — 295
1984 — 316
1985 — 360
1986 — 349
1987 — 398

YET TO WIN CRUFTS BEST-IN-SHOW.

NORWICH TERRIER

The beginnings of this fine Terrier go back to the mid-nineteenth century. Small short-legged Terriers were used for hunting fox and badger at that time in East Anglia and the courage and hardness of these dogs was renowned. They also gained favour amongst Cambridge students who used to hunt vermin and small game with them as a means of recreation. The small size of these Terriers enabling the undergraduates to keep them in their rooms.

Most credit for the development of the Norwich Terrier we see today goes to a breeder called Jones. He crossed local dogs with Glen of Imaal and Irish Terriers, the resulting breed taking it's name from the breeder. These 'Jones' Terriers were possibly the first modern Norwich-types.

Until 1964 Norwich Terriers had existed in two forms, the prick-eared and the drop-eared. But demand grew from followers of each variety for a separating of the two. the new standard for the Norwich was then drawn up and the two breeds have been kept pure ever since, the Norfolk, therefore being a relatively new distinct breed.

He is a very manageable and good-tempered little dog to have around the home and he revels in human attention from all age groups. He is full of spirit and due to his hunting past will love to chase anything that moves. Exercise should consist of regular walks at least and he will enjoy running free in the countryside whenever possible.

KEY TO CHARACTER	
INTELLIGENCE	***
TEMPERAMENT	****
EASE OF COAT CARE	****
SUITABILITY FOR SMALL DWELLING	*****
***** (5) = VERY GOOD	

BRITISH KENNEL CLUB STANDARD

NORWICH TERRIER

CHARACTERISTICS. — The Norwich Terrier is one of the smallest of the terriers. Of a lovable disposition, not quarrelsome, tremendously active and with a hardy constitution. Temperament gay and fearless.

GENERAL APPEARANCE. — A small, low, keen dog, compact and strong with good substance and bone. Honourable scars from fair wear and tear should not be penalised unduly.

Head and Skull. — Muzzle wedge-shaped and strong; length about one third less than a measurement form the occiput to the bottom of the stop, which should be well defined. Skull wide, good width between the ears, and slightly rounded.

Eyes. — Small and oval shaped, dark, full of expression, bright and keen.

Ears. — Erect, set well apart on top of skull. Of medium size with pointed tips. Held perfectly erect when aroused. Can be laid back when not at attention.

Mouth. — Tight lipped, jaws clean and strong. Teeth strong, rather large. Scissor bite.

Neck. — Neck strong of good length, commensurate with correct overall balance, flowing into well laid back shoulders.

Forequarters. — Legs short, powerful and straight; elbows close to body. Pasterns firm and upright. Legs should be moving straight forward when travelling.

Body. — Short back, compact body with good depth. Rib cage should be long and well sprung with short loin. Level topline.

Hindquarters. — Broad, strong and muscular, with well turned stifle. Low set hock with great powers of propulsion. Hind legs should follow in the track of the forelegs when moving, showing the pads and with hocks parallel.

Feet. — Round, well padded and catlike. To point straight forward standing and moving.

Tail. — Medium docked. Set on high to complete a perfectly level topline. Carried erect.

Coat. — Hard, wiry and straight, lying close to the body with a thick undercoat. Longer and rougher on the neck forming a ruff to frame the face. Hair on head and ears short and smooth, except for slight whiskers and eyebrows.

Colour. — All shades of red, wheaten, black and tan, or grizzle. White marks or patches are undesirable.

Size. — Ideal height 10 inches (25.4cm) at withers. This ideal height should not be attained by excessive length of leg.

Faults. — Any departure form the foregoing points should be considered a fault and the seriousness of the fault should be in exact proportion to its degree.

Note. — Male animals should have two apparently normal testicles fully descended into the scrotum.

NORWICH TERRIER REGISTRATIONS 1981 — 87 INCLUSIVE

1981 — 117
1982 — 135
1983 — 114
1984 — 131
1985 — 121
1986 — 165
1987 — 142

YET TO WIN CRUFTS BEST-IN-SHOW.

SCOTTISH TERRIER

There have been various strains of Terrier in Scotland for many centuries and accurate records of them are scarce. It seems though, that the Scottish Terrier descends from dogs that were used to hunt vermin and small game in the Perthshire region. Although the breed was not officially registered until 1879, he existed in a smilar form for many years before then.

Many of the early Terriers from Scotland became known simply as Scottish Terriers but since many of them resembled Cairn Terriers, Sky Terriers and others, this led to extreme confusion among the dog fanciers of the 19th century. But after much uncertainty and argument, a standardised version was agreed upon and the Scottish Terrier has gone on to become a very successful show dog and highly esteemed pet.

Sometimes called the Aberdeen Terrier, due to the famous efforts of early breeders in that city, this breed is one of the gamest terriers. His totally fearless approach to hunting has remained in his make-up to this day. He is generally very good natured and loves plenty of spirited play, but he will take no nonsense if teased or mistreated. Although black is by far the most common colour, wheaten and brindle specimens also occur. All of these colours can look very attactive if care is taken with grooming.

KEY TO CHARACTER	
INTELLIGENCE	***
TEMPERAMENT	***
EASE OF COAT CARE	**
SUITABILITY FOR SMALL DWELLING	*****
***** (5) = VERY GOOD	

BRITISH KENNEL CLUB STANDARD

SCOTTISH TERRIER

GENERAL APPEARANCE. — A Scottish Terier is a sturdy thick-set dog of a suitable size to go to ground, placed on short legs, alert in carriage, and suggestive of great power and activity in small compass. The head gives the impression of being long for a dog of its size. The body is covered with a close-lying, broken, rough-textured coat; with its keen intelligent eyes and sharp prick ears, the dog looks willing to go anywhere and do anything. In spite of its short legs, the construction is such that it is a very agile and active dog. The movement of the dog is smooth, easy, and straight forward, with free action at shoulder, stifle and hock.

Head and Skull. — Without being out of proportion to the size of the dog, it should be long, the length of skull enabling it to be fairly wide and yet retain a narrow appearance. The skull is nearly flat and the cheek-bones do not protrude. There is a slight, but distinct stop between skull and foreface just in front of the eye. The nose is large, and in profile the line from the nose towards the chin appears to slope backwards.

Eyes. — Should be almond-shaped, dark brown, fairly wide apart and set deeply under the eyebrows.

Ears. — Neat, of fine texture, pointed and erect.

Mouth. — The teeth large, the upper incisors closely overlapping the lower.

Neck. — Muscular, of moderate length.

Forequarters. — The head is carried on a muscular neck of moderate length, showing quality, set into a long sloping shoulder; the brisket well in front of the forelegs, which are straight and well-boned to straight pasterns. The chest fairly broad and hung between the forelegs, which must not be out at elbows nor placed under the body.

Body. — The body has well-rounded ribs, which flatten to a deep chest and are carried well back. The back is proportionately short and very muscular. In general the top line of the body should be straight and level; the loin muscular and deep, thus powerfully coupling the ribs to the hindquarters.

Hindquarters. — Remarkably powerful for the size of the dog. Big and wide buttocks. Thighs deep and muscular, well bent at stifle. Hocks strong and well bent and turned neither inwards nor outwards.

Feet. — Of good size and well padded, toes well arched and close-knit.

Tail. — Of moderate length to give a general balance to the dog, thick at the root and tapering towards the tip, set on with an upright carriage or with a slight bend.

Coat. — The dog has two coats, the undercoat short, dense, and soft; the outer coat harsh, dense, and wiry; the two making a weather-resisting covering to the dog.

Colour. — Black, wheaten or brindle of any colour.

Weight and Size. — The ideally-made dog in hard show condition should weigh from 19 lbs. to 23 lbs. Height, 10 to 11 inches.

Note. — Male animals should have two apparently normal testicles fully descended into the scrotum.

MAIN AMERICAN KENNEL CLUB VARIATION TO STANDARD FOR THE SCOTTISH TERRIER —

Size and Weight. — Height at the shoulder for either sex should be about 10 inches. Generally, a well-balanced Scottish Terrier dog of correct size should weigh from 19 to 22 pounds and a bitch, from 18 to 21 pounds.

SCOTTISH TERRIER REGISTRATIONS 1981 — 87 INCLUSIVE

1981 — 904
1982 — 849
1983 — 882
1984 — 961
1985 — 853
1986 — 902
1987 — 1009

CRUFTS BEST-IN-SHOW WINNER.

1929 HEATHER NECESSITY — E. CHAPMAN.

SEALYHAM TERRIER

The Sealyham Terrier was developed in Pembrokeshire during the latter part of the nineteenth century.

The town of Sealyham just outside Haverfordwest gave the breed it's name. Around this region the hunting men of the time worked to obtain the ideal terrier for hunting small game, particularly the badger. The dogs used in this quest were an interesting cocktail of personalities. The Welsh Corgi, Cheshire Terrier which was a small Bull Terrier type, Fox Terrier and Dandie Dinmont Terrier were all introduced in varying degrees. Early results were not always consistent, some dogs being barely similar to todays Sealyham, but the general pattern was set, sturdy, short-legged physique, strong jaws, mainly white coat and boundless courage and tenacity.

The breed was eventually registered in 1910 and became fairly popular between the two world wars, but numbers have slowly declined ever since. This, however, ensures a purer breed and todays Sealyham is surely one of the most striking terriers.

Firm, careful handling is essential with the Sealyham puppy as there can be a streak of bad temper in his character, which should not be allowed to flourish. Most, however, are playful and manageable with a good guarding instinct.

The coat can look very unsightly if not constantly cared for, so a prospective owner should be prepared for a daily grooming. Exercise must be frequent and fairly energetic.

KEY TO CHARACTER	
INTELLIGENCE	***
TEMPERAMENT	***
EASE OF COAT CARE	**
SUITABILITY FOR SMALL DWELLING	*****
***** (5) = VERY GOOD	

BRITISH KENNEL CLUB STANDARD

SEALYHAM TERRIER

CHARACTERISTICS. — Alert and fearless but of friendly dispositon.

GENERAL APPEARANCE. — Should be that of a freely moving and active dog, presenting a balanced picture of great substance in a small compass. General outline oblong, not square.

Head and Skull. — The skull slightly domed and wide between the ears. Cheek bones should not be prominent. Punishing square jaw, powerful and long. Nose black.

Eyes. — Dark, deep set, oval but not small. Unpigmented eye rims permissible.

Ears. — Size medium, slightly rounded at tip, and carried at side of cheek.

Mouth. — Teeth level and strong, with canine teeth fitting well into each other, and long for the size of the dog. A scissor bite is preferred viz the jaws should be strong, with a perfect, regular and complete scissor bite i.e., the upper teeth closely overlapping the lower teeth and set square to the jaws. A level bite is permissible.

Neck. — Fairly long, thick and muscular, on well-laid shoulders.

Forequarters. — Forelegs should be short, strong and as straight as possible consistent with the chest being well let down. Point of shoulder should be in line with point of elbow which should be close to side of chest.

Body. — Medium length, level and flexible with ribs well sprung. Chest broad and deep, well let down between forelegs.

Hindquarters. — Notably powerful for size of dog. Thighs deep and muscular with well bent stifle. Hocks strong, well bent and parallel to each other.

Feet. — Round and cat-like with thick pads. Feet pointing directly forward.

Gait. — Brisk and vigorous with plenty of drive.

Tail. — Set in line with back and carried erect. Quarters should protrude beyond set of tail.

Coat. — Long, hard and wiry topcoat with weather resistant under-coat.

Colour. — All white, or white with lemon, brown or badger pied markings on head and ears. Much black and heavy ticking undesirable.

Weight and Size. — Ideal weight: Dogs about 9Kg (20 lbs); Bitches about 8.2Kg (18 lbs). Height should not exceed 31cm (12") at the shoulder. General conformation, overall balance, type and substance are the main criteria.

Faults. — Any departure from the foregoing points should be considered a fault and the seriousness with which the fault should be regarded should be in exact proportion to its degree.

Note. — Male animals should have two apparently normal testicles fully descended into the scrotum.

MAIN AMERICAN KENNEL CLUB VARIATION TO STANDARD FOR THE SEALYHAM TERRIER —

Height. — At withers about 10½ inches.

Weight. — 23 to 24 pounds for dogs; bitches slightly less. It should be borne in mind that size is more important than weight.

SEALYHAM TERRIER REGISTRATIONS 1981 — 87 INCLUSIVE

1981 — 140
1982 — 123
1983 — 107
1984 — 114
1985 — 63
1986 — 116
1987 — 86

YET TO WIN CRUFTS BEST-IN-SHOW.

SKYE TERRIER

Many Terriers of varying shape, size and character have been known throughout Scotland for centuries. The same can be said for the islands off the Scottish coast, Skye being one of these. There is no hard evidence as to how the Skye Terrier first appeared, most suggestions being based on folklore rather than fact. It is known that he was always a valued hunter being used mainly for badger, otter and fox and it seems from ancient writings that in essence he has changed very little over the years. He still has the short muscular legs, weatherproof coat and strong jaws that stood his ancestors in good stead in the harsh environment of their homeland.

Although far from the most popular of the Terriers, the Skye makes a fine show dog and devoted companion. He is quite a substantial dog and if the coat is well prepared and he is handled skilfully then he makes an impressive sight in the show-ring. He is to be seen in a variety of interesting colours which also adds appeal. In the U.S.A. he was once an extremely popular breed for showing and he is still very much in evidence there.

The Skye Terrier is very loyal to his master at all times and he can be very cool with strangers. Generally, though, he is good-natured and blends in well with a family. Plenty of outdoor activity is needed as the Sky still has a lot of the hunter's energy and stamina.

KEY TO CHARACTER	
INTELLIGENCE	***
TEMPERAMENT	****
EASE OF COAT CARE	*
SUITABILITY FOR SMALL DWELLING	***
***** (5) = VERY GOOD	

BRITISH KENNEL CLUB STANDARD

SKYE TERRIER

CHARACTERISTICS. — A one-man dog, distrustful of strangers but not vicious.

Head and Skull. — Head long with powerful jaws. Nose black.

Eyes. — Hazel, preferably dark brown, medium size, close set and full of expression.

Ears. — Prick or drop. When prick, gracefully feathered, not large, erect at outer edges and slanting towards each other at inner edge, from peak to skull. When drop, larger hanging straight, lying flat and close at front.

Mouth. — Teeth closing level.

Neck. — Long and slightly crested.

Forequarters. — Shoulders broad and close to body, chest deep. Legs short and muscular.

Body. — Long and low. Back level. Ribs well sprung, giving flattish appearance to sides. sides.

Hindquarters. — The hindquarters and flanks full and well developed. Legs short and muscular, no dew claws.

Feet. — Large and pointing forward.

Tail. — When hanging, upper part pendulous and lower half thrown back in a curve. When raised, a prolongation of the incline of the back, not raising higher nor curling up.

Coat. — Double. Under-coat short, close, soft and woolly. Overcoat long, hard, straight, flat and free from crisp and curl. Hair on head shorter, softer, veiling forehead and eyes. On ears overhanging inside, falling down and mingling with side locks, surrounding the ears like a fringe and allowing their shape to appear. Tail gracefully feathered.

Colour. — Dark or light grey, fawn, cream, black, with black points. In fact, any self colour allowing shading of the same colour and lighter undercoat, so long as the nose and ears are black. A small white spot on the chest is permissible.

Weight and Size. — Height 10 inches, total length 41½ inches, weight 25 lbs. Bitch, slightly smaller in same proportions.

Faults. — Yellow eyes, tail curled over back or any deformity.

Note. — Male animals should have two apparently normal testicles fully descended into the scrotum.

MAIN AMERICAN KENNEL CLUB VARIATION TO STANDARD FOR THE SKYE TERRIER —

Size. — Dogs: Shoulder height, 10 inches. Length, chest bone over tail at rump, 20 inches. Head, 8½ inches. Tail, 9 inches. Bitches: Shoulder height, 9½ inches. Length, chest bone over tail at rump, 19 inches. Head, 8 inches. Tail 8½ inches.

SKYE TERRIER REGISTRATIONS 1981 — 87 INCLUSIVE

1981 — 163
1982 — 100
1983 — 148
1984 — 103
1985 — 114
1986 — 110
1987 — 136

YET TO WIN CRUFTS BEST-IN-SHOW.

SOFT-COATED WHEATEN TERRIER

The Soft-Coated Wheaten Terrier is a truly Irish breed, not often seen outside his homeland. He is almost certainly the oldest of the breeds native to Ireland and under the abundant coat he bears a marked resemblance to another fine Irish terrier, the Kerry Blue. It is believed that these dogs share the same ancestry.

For centuries the Soft-Coated Wheaten has been used as an all purpose dog on the many small farms throughout Ireland. Breeding has been hap-hazard until this century and it was not until 1937 that the Irish Kennel Club officially recognised the breed.

Many Irish farmers would testify that the Soft-Coated Wheaten is a versatile and indispensable member of their family. He is a good ratter, can be used for herding and will fearlessly guard anything in his charge. They have slightly less natural aggression than many other terriers and are as fond of people as any breed.

In England and the U.S.A. the breed has made some headway but has not had the success that perhaps he deserves.

He is a dog of high spirits who needs a good deal of vigorous exercise. An owner who prefers a natural, totally unspoilt breed will suit the Soft-Coated Wheaten. He can be easily house-trained and will show great devotion if treated well. An added attraction is that the coat does not shed.

KEY TO CHARACTER	
INTELLIGENCE	****
TEMPERAMENT	****
EASE OF COAT CARE	***
SUITABILITY FOR SMALL DWELLING	**
***** (5) = VERY GOOD	

BRITISH KENNEL CLUB STANDARD

SOFT-COATED WHEATEN TERRIER

CHARACTERISTICS. — The Soft-Coated Wheaten Terrier should be good tempered, spirited and game. Full of confidence and humour; a delightful, affectionate, intelligent companion. A natural terrier with strong sporting instincts, hardy and of strong constitution.

GENERAL APPEARANCE. — A medium-sized, compact, upstanding terrier well covered with a soft, wheaten coloured, natural coat that falls in loose curls or waves. An active, short-coupled dog, strong and well built; well balanced in structure and movement, not exaggerated in any way. Standing four square with head and tail up, giving the appearance of a happy dog, full of character.

Head and Skull. — Head moderately long and profusely covered with coat which should fall forward over the eyes. The skull, while not being coarse, should not be narrow. Skull flat and not too wide between the ears. The stop should be well defined and the cheek bones not prominent. The distance from the eyes to nose not longer, and preferably shorter, than the distance from the eye to the occiput. Jaws strong and punishing, muzzle square with no suggestion of snipiness. The top-line of the muzzle absolutely straight and parallel with skull. The nose should be black and large for the size of dog. Head in general, powerful without being coarse.

Eyes. — A clear bright dark hazel. Squarely set under a strong brow and of medium size, Eye rims black.

Ears. — V-shaped and folded at level of skull. The forward edge should drop down and slightly forward to lie closely along the cheek, the back edge standing slightly away from the side of the head. Thin, small to medium in size, covered with coat and with a fringe.

Mouth. — Teeth large. Bite scissors (the tips of the upper incisors should lie tightly in front of the lower incisors.) Overshot and undershot are equally objectionable. Lips tight and black.

Neck. — Moderately long, strong, muscular and slightly arched. Without throatiness. Gradually widening toward, and running cleanly into, the shoulders.

Forequarters. — Shoulders long, well laid back, and slope inwards from points to withers. Well knit in, fine, but muscular. Viewed from any angle, the forelegs perfectly straight. Good bone and muscle. Pasterns strong and springy. Chest moderately wide. Dew claws on the front legs may be removed.

Body. — Compact, with powerful short loins. Back strong and level. Ribs well sprung, without roundness, providing a deep chest with relatively short coupling. Length of back from point of withers to base of tail should measure about the same as, or slightly less than, from point of withers to ground. Male animals should have two apparently normal testicles fully descended into the scrotum.

Hindquarters. — Thighs strong and muscular. Hindlegs well developed with powerful muscle and well bent stifles. Hocks well let down and turning neither in nor out. Dew claws on the hind legs should be removed.

Feet. — Strong and compact, turned neither in nor out. Good depth of pad. Toenails black.

Gait. — Movement free, graceful and lively. Well co-ordinated with long, low strides. Having reach in front and good drive behind; straight action fore and aft. The head and tail should be carried high, the backline remaining level.

Tail. — Docked. The tail of the fully grown dog should be about 4 to 5 inches long. Set on high, carried gaily, but never over the back. Not curled and not too thick.

Coat. — Soft and silky. Neither woolly nor wiry. Loosely waved or curly, but if curly, the curls should be large, light and loose. The coat should not stand off but should flow and fall naturally. The coat should be abundant all over the body and escpecially profuse on the head and legs. The length of the leg coat should be sufficient to give good balance to the length of coat on the head and body. There is no seasonal change in the length or texture of the mature coat. The Soft-Coated Wheaten Terrier is a natural dog and should so appear. Dogs that appear to be over trimmed or stylized should be penalised. For show purposes the coat may be tidied up to present a neat outline. Coat colour and texture do not stabilize until about 18 months and should be given some latitude in young dogs.

Colour. — A good clear wheaten. A shade of ripening wheat. A white coat and a red coat are equally objectionable. Dark shading on the ears is not untypical. There is often a slight fluctuation in the intensity of colour in the mature coat, but the overall effect should be light wheaten. Dark overall colour and the even darker markings often present in the immature coat clear by about 18 months, if not before.

Weight and Size. — Height: Dogs approximately 18 to 19½ inches measured at the withers. Bitches slightly less. Weight: Dogs approximately 35 to 45 pounds. Bitches somewhat less.

Faults. — Any departure from the foregoing points should be considered a fault and the seriousness of the fault should be in exact proportion to its degree.

MAIN AMERICAN KENNEL CLUB VARIATION TO STANDARD FOR THE SOFT-COATED WHEATEN TERRIER —

Size. — A dog shall be 18 to 19 inches at the withers, the ideal being 18½. A bitch shall be 17 to 18 inches at the withers, the ideal being 17½. dogs should weigh 35 to 40 pounds; bitches 30 to 35 pounds.

SOFT-COATED WHEATEN TERRIER REGISTRATIONS 1981 — 87 INCLUSIVE

1981 — 104
1982 — 89
1983 — 132
1984 — 141
1985 — 119
1986 — 148
1987 — 99

YET TO WIN CRUFTS BEST-IN-SHOW.

STAFFORDSHIRE BULL TERRIER

This powerful little dog came into being over 150 years ago. He was the result of crossing the Old English Bulldog with a Terrier of the period, the idea being to combine the brute strength of the Bulldog with the athleticism of the Terrier.

As well as being employed as a successful ratter, the Staffordshire Bull Terrier was the favourite breed amongst followers of the odious practice of organised dog fighting. Many dogs would be terribly injured or killed in these matches and a great deal of money was often wagered on the result. This appalling pastime has long since been banned, although it is sad to say that some illegal fights still take place.

The enormous agression of this breed is evident only when in combat with another dog and in the company of people there is no gentler breed. There is still an aura attached to the Saffordshire Bull Terrier and his bloody past and unfortunately some people seem to think it good for the ego to own a "ferocious" dog. This must surely be a poor reason for deciding upon a dog and an unworthy insult to such a fine breed.

He is well behaved in the home, but will be more manageable if given firm training as a puppy. He is extremely sociable and affectionate, especially with children. His boundless energy is best used up on frequent periods of exercise and this will keep his stocky physique in top condition.

KEY TO CHARACTER	
INTELLIGENCE	***
TEMPERAMENT	****
EASE OF COAT CARE	*****
SUITABILITY FOR SMALL DWELLING	***
***** (5) = VERY GOOD	

BRITISH KENNEL CLUB STANDARD

STAFFORDSHIRE BULL TERRIER

CHARACTERISTICS. — From the past history of the Staffordshire Bull Terrier, the modern dog draws his character of indomitable courage, high intelligence and tenacity. This coupled with his affection for his friends, and children in particular; his off-duty quietness and trustworthy stability, makes him the foremost all-purpose dog.

GENERAL APPEARANCE. — The Staffordshire Bull Terrier is a smooth coated dog. He should be of great strength for his size and although muscular, should be active and agile.

Head and Skull. — Short, deep through, broad skull, very pronounced cheek muscles, distinct stop, short foreface, black nose.

Eyes. — Dark preferable but may bear some relation to coat colour. Round, of medium size, and set to look straight ahead.

Ears. — Rose or half-pricked and not large. Full drop or prick to be penalised.

Mouth. — The mouth should be level, i.e., the incisors of the bottom jaw should fit closely inside the incisors of the top jaw, and the lips should be tight and clean. The badly undershot or overshot mouth to be heavily penalised.

Neck. — Muscular, rather short, clean in outline and gradually widening towards the shoulders.

Forequarters. — Legs straight and well-boned, set rather wide apart, without looseness at the shoulders, and showing no weakness at the pasterns, from which point the feet turn out a little.

Body. — The body should be close-coupled, with a level topline, wide front, deep brisket, well-sprung ribs and rather light in the loins.

Hindquarters. — The hindquarters should be well muscled, hocks let down with stifles well bent. Legs should be parallel when viewed from behind.

Feet. — The feet should be well padded, strong and of medium size.

Tail. — The tail should be of medium length, low set, tapering to a point and carried rather low. It should not curl much and may be likened to an old-fashioned pump handle.

Coat. — Smooth, short and close to the skin.

Colour. — Red, fawn, white, black or blue, or any of these colours with white. Any shade of brindle or any shade of brindle with white. Black-and-tan or liver-colour not to be encouraged.

Weight and Size. — Weight: Dogs, 28 lbs. to 38 lbs. Bitches, 24 lbs. to 34 lbs. Height (at shoulder), 14 to 16 inches, these heights being related to the weights.

Faults. — To be penalised in accordance with the severity of the fault:— Light eyes or pink eye-rims. Tail too long or badly curled. Non-conformation to the limits of weight or height. Full drop and prick ears. Undershot or overshot mouths. The following faults should debar a dog from winning any prize:— Pink (Dudley) nose. Badly undershot or overshot mouth. Badly undershot — where the lower jaw protrudes to such an extent that the incisors of the lower jaw do not touch those of the upper jaw. Badly overshot — where the upper jaw protrudes to such an extent that the incisors of the upper jaw do not touch those of the lower jaw.

Note. — Male animals should have two apparently normal testicles fully descended into the scrotum.

STAFFORDSHIRE BULL TERRIER REGISTRATIONS 1981 — 87 INCLUSIVE

1981 — 3374
1982 — 3968
1983 — 4709
1984 — 4809
1985 — 6419
1986 — 6473
1987 — 6233

YET TO WIN CRUFTS BEST-IN-SHOW.

WELSH TERRIER

Although only registered by the Kennel Club in 1886, dogs similar to today's Welsh Terrier had been known before then for more than a century. His most likely forebear was the old Black and Tan Terrier, a dog that was once widespread throughout Britain. The Welsh developed their own particular strain of this tough working breed and resisted any attempts to make him more like English Terriers.

The Welsh Terrier has always been used for hunting and he has the classic Terrier trademarks of stamina, great courage, strong jaw and sturdy legs for digging. He is know to be an adaptable hunter and will pursue all manner of small game in any weather.

The ease of handling, characteristic of this breed, is a great asset in the show-ring and he has a very keen if not enormous following in this field. He stands very well which the handler appreciates both in preparing his dog and when in actual competition.

The Welsh Terrier is an unfussy dog who combines even temperament with a love of play and mischief. He is of a nice, compact size, large enough to be quite an effective guard and small enough to be managed by an elderly owner. House-training should not be a great problem with this breed and generally he will be found to be a faithful and obedient companion. He will enjoy regular exercise, a good daily walk being the minimum requirement.

KEY TO CHARACTER	
INTELLIGENCE	***
TEMPERAMENT	****
EASE OF COAT CARE	***
SUITABILITY FOR SMALL DWELLING	****
***** (5) = VERY GOOD	

BRITISH KENNEL CLUB STANDARD

WELSH TERRIER

CHARACTERISTICS. — The Welsh Terrier is of a gay, volatile disposition and is rarely of a shy nature. He is affectionate, obedient and easily controlled, thus making him an eminently suitable dog for town life. His size and colour render him ideal as a house dog, as the former point is in his favour where accommodation is limited, whilst the latter feature precludes the necessity for frequent washing as in the case of a white terrier. He is game and fearless, but definitely not of a pugnacious disposition, although at all times able to hold his own when necessary. He is ideally constituted to be a perfect town or country companion. Welsh Terriers are normally hardy and of robust constitution, and need no pampering, whilst as working terriers they are second to none, being easily trained to all sorts of game and vermin to work with gun or ferrets, and are generally found to be capital water dogs.

Head and Skull. — The skull should be flat and rather wider between the ears than the Wire-Haired Fox Terrier. The jaw should be powerful, clean cut, rather deeper, and more punishing — giving the head a more masculine appearance than that usually seen on a Fox Terrier. Stop not too defined, fair length from stop to end of nose, the latter being of a black colour.

Eyes. — Should be small, well set in, of a dark colour, expressive and indicating abundant keenness. A round full eye is undesirable.

Ears. — Should be V-shaped, small, not too thin, set on fairly high, carried forward and close to the cheek.

Mouth. — Should be level with strong teeth.

Neck. — The neck should be of moderate length and thickness, slightly arched and sloping gracefully into the shoulders.

Forequarters. — The shoulders should be long, sloping and well set back. The legs should be straight and muscular, possessing ample bone, with upright and powerful pasterns.

Body. — The back should be short, and well ribbed up, the loin strong, good depth, and moderate width of chest.

Hindquarters. — Should be strong, thighs muscular, and of good length, with the hocks well bent, well let down and with ample bone.

Feet. — The feet should be small, round and catlike.

Tail. — The tail should be well set on, but not too gaily carried.

Coat. — Should be wiry, hard, very close and abundant. A single coat is undesirable.

Colour. — The colour should be black and tan for preference, or black grizzle and tan, free from black pencilling on toes. Black below the hocks is a fault.

Weight and Size. — The height at shoulder should not exceed 15½ inches. 20 to 21 lbs. shall be considered a fair average weight in working condition.

Faults. — A white, cheery or spotted nose. Prick, tulip or rose ears. An appreciable amount of black below the hocks.

Note. — Male animals should have two apparently normal testicles fully descended into the scrotum.

MAIN AMERICAN KENNEL CLUB VARIATION TO STANDARD FOR THE WELSH TERRIER —

Size. — Males are about 15 inches at withers, with an acceptable range between 15 and 15½ inches. Bitches may be proportionately smaller. Twenty pounds is considered an average weight, varying a few pounds depending on the height of the dog, and the density of bone.

WELSH TERRIER REGISTRATIONS 1981 — 87 INCLUSIVE

1981 — 272
1982 — 214
1983 — 251
1984 — 258
1985 — 259
1986 — 217
1987 — 201

CRUFTS BEST-IN-SHOW WINNER TWICE.

1951 TWYNSTAR DYMA-FI — CAPT. AND MRS I.M. THOMAS
1959 CH. SANDSTORM SARACEN — MESDAMES LEACH & THOMAS.

WEST HIGHLAND WHITE TERRIER

The West Highland White is deservedly one of the most popular terriers in Britain and has been in that position for a great many years.

It is probable that he is of the same descent as the Cairn Terrier and it is easy to see the similarities between the two. Like the Cairn, he is an ancient breed, similar dogs being known in Scotland some 400 years ago. There were various types of white terriers in the Highland regions and these were used as efficient working dogs on the bleak terrain thereabouts. They were unrivalled in their burrowing ability and their stubborness in the pursuit of rats, badgers and others and their white colouring made them easily visible on a murky winter's day.

In the 19th century there were two main strains of white Scottish terrier. These were the Poltalloch Terrier and the White Roseneath Terrier and they were the forerunners of todays West Highland White. Having been in evidence in one form or another for hundreds of years he finally was given official recognition by the Kennel Club in 1907.

Much of the Cairn Terrier's qualities are also to be found in the West Highland White, his closest relative. He requires only moderate grooming, is hardy and fearless, yet friendly and lively. Exercise is not as vital as with some breeds, but a daily walk and some energetic play will do much to maintain his good natured disposition.

KEY TO CHARACTER	
INTELLIGENCE	***
TEMPERAMENT	****
EASE OF COAT CARE	***
SUITABILITY FOR SMALL DWELLING	*****
***** (5) = VERY GOOD	

BRITISH KENNEL CLUB STANDARD

WEST HIGHLAND WHITE TERRIER

GENERAL APPEARANCE. — The general appearance of the West Hightland White Terrier is that of a small, game, hardy-looking Terrier, possessed of no small amount of self-esteem; with a varminty appearance; strongly built, deep in chest and back ribs; level back and powerful quarters on muscular legs, and exhibiting in a marked degree a great combination of strength and activity. Movement should be free, straight and easy all round. In the front the legs should be freely extended forward by the shoulder. The hind movement should be free, strong and close. The hocks should be freely flexed and drawn close in under the body, so that when moving off the foot, the body is pushed forward with some force. Stiff, stilted movement behind is very objectionable.

Head and Skull. — The skull should be slightly domed and when gripped across the forehead, should present a smooth contour. There should only be a very slight tapering from the skull at the level of the ears to the eyes. The distance from the occiput to the eyes should be slightly greater than the length of the foreface. The head should be thickly coated with hair, and carried at a right-angle or less, to the axis of the neck. On no account should the head be carried in the extended position. The foreface should gradually taper from the eye to the muzzle. There should be a distinct stop formed by heavy, bony ridges, immediately above and slightly overhanging the eye, and a slight indentation between the eyes. The foreface should not dish or fall away quickly below the eyes where it should be well made up. The jaws should be strong and level. The nose must be black. Should be fairly large, and forming a smooth contour with the rest of the muzzle. The nose must not project forward giving rise to a snipy appearance.

Eyes. — Should be widely set apart, medium in size, as dark as possible in colour, slightly sunk in head, sharp and intelligent, which, looking from under the heavy eyebrows, imparts a piercing look. Full or light-coloured eyes are objectionable.

Ears. — Small, erect and carried firmly, terminating in a sharp point. The hair on them should be short, smooth (velvety) and should not be cut. The ears should be free from any fringe at the top. Round pointed, broad, large or thick ears are very objectionable, also ears too heavily coated with hair.

Mouth. — Should be as broad between the canine teeth as is consistent with the sharp varminty expression required. The teeth should be large for the size of the dog, and should articulate in the following manner:— the lower canines should lock in front of the upper canines. There should be six teeth between the canines of the upper and lower incisors. The upper incisors should slightly overlap the lower incisors, the inner side of the upper incisors being in contact with the outer side of the lower incisors. There should be no appreciable space between the incisors when the mouth is closed ensuring a keen bite; a dead level mouth is not a fault.

Neck. — Should be sufficiently long to allow the proper set on of head required, muscular and gradually thickening towards the base allowing the neck to merge into nicely sloping shoulders, thus giving freedom of movement.

Forequarters. — The shoulders should be sloped backwards. The sholder blades should be broad and lie close to the chest wall. The joint formed by the shoulder blade and the upper arm should be placed forward, on account of the obliquity of the shoulder blades, bringing the elbows well in, and allowing the foreleg to move freely, parallel to the axis of the body, like the pendulum of a clock. Forelegs should be short and muscular, straight and thickly covered with short hard hair.

Body. — Compact. Back level, loins broad and strong. The chest should be deep and the ribs well arched in the upper half presenting a flattish side appearance. The back ribs should be of a considerable depth and the distance from the last rib of the quarters as short as is compatible with free movement of the body.

Hindquarters. — Strong, muscular and wide across the top. Legs should be short muscular and sinewy. The thighs very muscular and not too wide apart. The hocks bent and well set in under the body so as to be fairly close to each other when standing, walking or trotting. Cow-hocks detract from the general appearance. Straight or weak hocks are undesirable and are a fault.

Feet. — The forefeet are larger than the hind ones, are round, proportionate in size, strong, thickly padded and covered with short hard hair. The hind feet are smaller and thickly padded. The under-surface of the pads of feet and all nails should be preferably black.

Tail. — 5 to 6 inches long, covered with hard hair, no feather, as straight as possible, carried jauntily, not gay nor carried over the back. A long tail is objectionable and on no account should tails be docked.

Coat. —Colour pure white, must be doublecoated. The outer coat consists of hard hair, about 2 inches long, free from any curl. The under coat, which resembles fur, is short, soft and close. Open coats are objectionable.

Colour. — Pure white.

Weight and Size. — Size about 11 inches at the withers.

Note. — Male animals should have two apparently normal testicles fully descended into the scrotum.

WEST HIGHLAND WHITE TERRIER REGISTRATIONS 1981 — 87 INCLUSIVE

1981 — 3525
1982 — 3485
1983 —3950
1984 — 4153
1985 — 4864
1986 — 5155
1987 — 5339

CRUFTS BEST-IN-SHOW WINNER.

1976 CH. DIANTHUS BUTTONS — MRS K. NEWSTEAD.

PEDIGREE DOGS IN COLOUR

BOOK FOUR

UTILITY GROUP

This is Book Four in a volume consisting of six books each dealing with a main group of dogs. The page numbering follows that used in the main volume.

Boston Terrier

BOSTON TERRIER

This good-natured, attractive little dog was developed in the U.S.A. from English breeds. As the face would suggest, one of these breeds was the Bulldog and the athletic lines of the torso and legs are derived from terrier stock. This early breeding work took place in Boston, Massachusetts in the mid-nineteenth century, hence the naming of the breed. He became a popular dog almost immediately and show appearances inevitably followed. When enthusiasts formed a breed club, they had wanted to call their dogs American Bull Terriers but this was opposed by Bull Terrier breeders and the present name was eventually settled upon.

At one time the Boston Terrier was the most popular dog in the U.S.A., and whilst not enjoying quite such success now, he is still very much an American favourite. He is also far from rare in Britain, although devotees of the breed are surprised that his following is not even larger here. He is certainly an appealing breed, combining all the manageability and charm of a small dog with the toughness and courage of a much larger breed. He guards his master's property very keenly and is loyal and affectionate with the whole family.

If feeding is kept at a sensible level, the Boston Terrier's exercise needs are not too great, but he will enjoy regular walks and occasional runs in the open.

KEY TO CHARACTER	
INTELLIGENCE	****
TEMPERAMENT	*****
EASE OF COAT CARE	*****
SUITABILITY FOR SMALL DWELLING	*****
***** (5) = VERY GOOD	

BRITISH KENNEL CLUB STANDARD

BOSTON TERRIER

CHARACTERISTICS. — A proportionate combination of "Colour" and "Ideal Markings" is a particularly distinctive feature of a representative specimen. A dog with a preponderance of white on body or without the proper proportion of brindle and white on head is at a disadvantage. The ideal "Boston Terrier Expression" as indicating "a high degree of intelligence" is also an important characteristic of the breed. "Colour and Markings" and "Expression" should be given particular consideration in determining the relative value of "General Appearance" to other points.

GENERAL APPEARANCE. — The general appearance of the Boston Terrier should be that of a lively, highly intelligent, smooth-coated, short-headed, compactly built, short-tailed, well balanced dog of medium size, of brindle colour and evenly marked with white. The head should indicate a high degree of intelligence and should be in proportion to the size of the dog; the body rather short and well knit; the limbs strong and neatly turned; tail short and no feature to be so prominent that the dog appears badly proportioned. The dog should convey an impression of determination, strength and activity, with style of a high order; carriage easy and graceful. The gait of the Boston Terrier is that of a sure-footed straight-gaited dog, forelegs and hindlegs moving straight ahead in time with perfect rhythm, each step indicating grace and power.

Head and Skull. — Skull square, flat on top, free from wrinkles; cheeks flat; brow abrupt, stop well defined. Muzzle short, square, wide and deep, and in proportion to the skull; free form wrinkles; shorter in length than in width and depth, not exceeding in length approximately one-third of length of skull; width and depth carried out well to end; the muzzle from stop to end of nose on a line parallel to the top of the skull; nose black and wide with well-defined line between nostrils. The jaws broad and square. The chops of good depth but not pendulous, completely covering the teeth when mouth is closed.

Eyes. — Wide apart, large and round, dark in colour, expression alert but kind and intelligent. The eyes should set square in the skull, and the outside corners should be on a line with the cheeks as viewed from the front.

Ears. — Carried ererct; small and thin; situated as near corner of skull as possible.

Mouth. — Teeth short and regular, bite even, or sufficiently undershot to square muzzle.

Neck. — Of fair length, slightly arched and carrying the head gracefully; neatly set into the shoulders.

Forequarters. — Legs set moderately wide apart and on a line with the point of the shoulders; straight in bone and well muscled; pasterns short and strong. Elbows standing neither in nor out.

Body. — Deep with good width of chest; shoulders sloping, back short; ribs deep and well sprung, carried well back to loins; loins short and muscular; rump curving slightly to set-on of tail; flank very slightly cut up. The body should appear short but not chunky.

Hindquarters. — Legs set true, bent at stifles, short from hocks to feet; hocks turning neither in nor out; thighs strong and well muscled.

Feet. — Round, small and compact, and turned neither in nor out; toes well arched.

Tail. — Set-on low; short, fine and tapering; straight or screw; devoid of fringes or coarse hair, and not carried above horizontal.

Coat. — Short, smooth, bright and fine in texture.

Colour. — Brindle with white markings; brindle must show throughout the body distinctly; black and white markings are permissible, but brindles with white markings are preferred. (Ideal colour shall be one in which the brindle colouring is evenly distributed throughout the body). Ideal markings: white muzzle, even white blaze over head, collar, breast, part or whole of forelegs, and hind legs below hocks.

Weight and Size. — Weight should not exceed 11.4 kg (25 lbs) divided by classes as follows: Lightweight, under 6.8 kg (15 lbs); Middleweight, 6.8 kg (15 lbs) and under 9.1 kg (20 lbs); Heavyweight, 9.1 kg (20 lbs) and under 11.4 kg (25 lbs).

Faults. — Solid black, black and tan; liver or mouse colour; Dudley nose; docked tail. Skull "domed" or inclined; furrowed by a medial line; skull too long for breadth, or vice versa; stop too shallow; brow and skull too slanting. Eyes small or sunken; too prominent; light colour or wall eye; showing too much white or haw. Muzzle wedge-shaped or lacking depth; down faced; too much cut out below the eyes; pinched or wide nostrils; butterfly nose; protruding teeth; weak lower jaw; showing "turn-up". Ears poorly carried or in size out of proportion to the head. Neck: ewe-necked; throaty, short or thick. Body: flat sides; narrow chest; long or slack loins; roach back; sway back; too much cut-up in flank. Loose shoulders or elbows; hind legs too straight at stifles; hocks too prominent; long or weak pasterns; splay feet. A long or gaily carried tail; extremely gnarled or curled against body. (Note — The preferred tail should not exceed in length approximately half the distance from the set-on to hock). Colour and markings: all white; absence of white markings; preponderance of white on body; without the proper proportion of brindle and white on head; or any variations detracting from the general appearance. Coat: long or coarse; lacking lustre.

Note. — Male animals should have two apparently normal testicles fully descended into the scrotum.

MAIN AMERICAN KENNEL CLUB VARIATION TO STANDARD FOR THE BOSTON TERRIER —

Ears. — Carried erect, either cropped to conform to the shape of the head, or natural bat, situated as near the corners of skull as possible.

BOSTON TERRIER REGISTRATIONS 1981 — 87 INCLUSIVE

1981 — 93
1982 — 93
1983 — 94
1984 — 75
1985 — 101
1986 — 102
1987 — 112

YET TO WIN CRUFTS BEST-IN-SHOW.

BULLDOG

The Bulldog is a direct descendant of the Molossian Dog of ancient Greece, a type of dog used for ceremonial fighting against men and various kinds of beast. It is most probable that these huge vicious dogs were the common ancestors for all short faced heavily built dogs, the Mastiff and Bullmastiff being others which fall into this category.

The Bulldog had developed into something like his present form by the thirteenth century. He was then widely used for the grisly pastime of bull baiting. This would involve a bull being tethered to a stake in the centre of a ring where it was goaded into a fury by onlookers. A Bulldog, similar in appearance to today's only larger, would then be set to it. The idea was for the dog to clamp it's jaws on the bull's nose or mouth and for the bull to exhaust itself in it's efforts to shake it off. The Bulldog had been specially bred to have jaws that locked when they were engaged and, so, once the dog had taken firm hold he would be flung into the air but his grip could rarely be broken.

This appalling sport was banned in the early nineteenth century but this did result in a decline in the Bulldog's numbers. However, it was soon realised that this breed had more to offer than it's prowess in the bull ring and conscientious breeding began.

The Bulldog of today harbours no trace of his gruesome beginnings and is perfectly trustworthy with all age groups. Exercise should be very regular but not too frantic as heart attacks can sometimes result. He is a dog of great character and prescence who enjoys human company and he makes an easy going, faithful companion.

KEY TO CHARACTER	
INTELLIGENCE	****
TEMPERAMENT	*****
EASE OF COAT CARE	*****
SUITABILITY FOR SMALL DWELLING	****
***** (5) = VERY GOOD	

BRITISH KENNEL CLUB STANDARD

BULLDOG

GENERAL APPEARANCE. — In forming a judgment on any specimen of the breed, the general appearance, which is the first impression the dog makes as a whole on the eye of the judge, should be first considered. Secondly should be noticed its size, shape and make, or rather its proportions in the relation they bear to each other. No point should be so much in excess of the others as to destroy the general symmetry, or make the dog appear deformed, or interfere with its powers of motion, etc. Thirdly its style, carriage, gait, temper and its several points should be considered separately in detail, due allowance being made for the bitch, which is not so grand or as well developed as the dog.

Thegeneral appearance of the Bulldog is that of a smooth-coated, thick-set dog, rather low in stature, but broad, powerful, and compact. The head strikingly massive and large in proportion to the dog's size.. The face extremelv short. The muzzle very broad, blunt, and inclined upwards. The body short and well knit; the limbs stout and muscular. The hindquarters high and strong but rather lightly made in comparison with its heavily made foreparts. The dog should convey an impression of determination, strength, and activity, similar to that suggested by the appearance of a thick-set Ayreshire Bull.

From its formation the dog has a peculiar heavy and constrained gait, appearing to walk with short, quick steps on the tips of its toes, its hind-feet not being lifted high, but appearing to skim the ground, and running with the right shoulder rather advanced, similar to the manner of a horse in cantering.

Head and Skull. — The skull should be very large — the larger the better — and in circumference should measure (round in front of the ears) at least the height of the dog at the shoulders. Viewed from the front it should appear very high from the corner of the lower jaw to the apex of the skull, and also very broad and square. The cheeks should be well rounded and extended sideways beyond the eyes. Viewed at the side, the head should appear very high, and very short from its back to the point of the nose. The forehead should be flat, neither prominent nor overhanging the face; the skin upon it and about the head very loose and well wrinkled. The projections of the frontal bones should be very prominent, broad, square, and high, causing a deep and wide indentation between the eyes termed the "stop". From the "stop" a furrow both broad and deep should extend up to the middle of the skull, being traceable to the apex. The face, measured from the front of the cheek-bone to the nose, should be as short as possible, and its skin should be deeply and closely wrinkled. The muzzle should be short, broad, turned upwards and very deep from the corner of the eye to the corner of the mouth. The nose should be large, broad and black, and under no circumstances should it be liver coloured or brown; its top should be deeply set back almost between the eyes. The distance from the inner corner of the eye (or from the centre of the stop between the eyes) to the extreme tip of the nose should not exceed the length from the tip of the nose to the edge of the under lip. The nostrils should be large, wide, and black, with a well-defined vertical straight line between them. The flews, called the "chop" should be thick, broad, pendant, and very deep, hanging completely over the lower jaw at the sides (not in front). They should join the under lip in front and quite cover the teeth. The jaws should be broad, massive and square, the lower jaw should project considerably in front of the upper and turn up. Viewed from the front, the various properties of the face must be equally balanced on either side of an imaginary line down the centre of the face.

Eyes. — The eyes seen from the front, should be situated low down in the skull, as far from the ears as possible. The eyes and "stop" should be in the same straight line, which should be at right angles to the furrow. They should be as wide apart as possible, provided their outer corners are within the ouline of the cheeks. They should be quite round in shape, of moderate size, neither sunken nor prominent, and in colour should be very dark — almost, if not quite, black, showing no white when looking directly forward.

Ears. — The ears should be set high on the head — i.e., the front inner edge of each ear should (as viewed from the front) join the outline of the skull at the top corner of such outline, so as to place them as wide apart, and as high and as far from the eyes as possible. In size they should be small and thin. The shape termed "rose ear" is correct, and folds inwards at its back, the upper or front edge curving over outwards and backwards, showing part of the inside of the burr.

Mouth. — The jaw should be broad and square and have the six small front teeth between the canines in an even row. The canine teeth or tusks wide apart. The teeth should not be seen when the mouth is closed. The teeth should be large and strong. When viewed from the front, the underjaw should be centrally under the upper jaw to which it should also be parallel.

Neck. — Should be moderate in length (rather short than long) very thick, deep and strong. It should be well arched at the back, with much loose, thick and wrinkled skin about the throat, forming a dewlap on each side, from the lower jaw to the chest.

Forequarters. — The shoulders should be broad, sloping and deep, very powerful and muscular, and giving the appearance of having been "tacked on" to the body. The brisket should be capacious, round and very deep from the top of the shoulders to the lowest part where it joins the chest, and be well let down between forelegs. It should be large in diameter and round behind the forelegs (not flat-sided, the ribs being well rounded). The forelegs should be very stout and strong, set wide apart, thick, muscular, and straight, with well-developed forearms, presenting a rather bowed outline, but the bones of the legs should be large and straight, not bandy or curved. They should b rather short in proportion to the hind-legs, but not so short as to make the back appear long, or detract from the dog's activity, and so cripple him. The elbows should be low, and stand well away from the ribs. The pasterns should be short, straight and strong.

Body. — The chest should be very wide, laterally round, prominent, and deep, making the dog appear very broad and short-legged in front. The body should be well ribbed up behind, with the belly tucked up and not pendulous. The back should be short and strong, very broad at the shoulders, and comparatively narrow at the loins. There should be a slight fall to the back close behind the shoulders (its lowest part), whence the spine should rise to the loins (the top of which should be higher than the top of the shoulders), thence curving again more suddenly to the tail, forming an arch — a distinctive characteristic of the breed — termed "roach back".

Hindquarters. — the legs should be large and muscular, and longer in proportion than the forelegs, so as to elevate the loins. The hocks should be slightly bent and well let down, so as to be long and muscular from the loins to the point of the hock. The lower part of the leg should be short, straight and strong. The stifles should be round and turned slightly outwards away from the body. The hocks are thereby made to approach each other, and the hind feet to turn outwards.

Feet. — The hind feet, like the fore feet, should be round and compact, with the toes well split up and the knuckles prominent. The fore feet should be straight and turn very slightly outward, of medium size and moderately round. The toes compact and thick, being well split up, making the knuckles prominent and high.

Tail. — The tail, termed the "stern", should be set on low, jut out rather straight, then turn downwards. It should be round, smooth and devoid of fringe or coarse hair. It should be moderate in length — rather short than long — thick at the root, and tapering quickly to a fine point. It should have a downward carriage (not having a decided upward curve at the end), and the dog should not be able to raise it over its back.

Coat. — Should be fine in texture, short, close and smooth (hard only from the shortness and closeness, not wiry).

Colour. — The colour should be whole or smut (that is, a whole colour with a black mask or muzzle). The only colours (which should be brilliant and pure of their sort) are whole colours — viz., brindles, reds, with their varieties, fawns, fallows, etc., white and also pied (i.e., a combination of white with any other of the foregoing colours). Dudley, black and black with tan are extremely undesirable colours.

Weight and Size. — The most desirable weight for the Bulldog is 25 kg (55 lbs) for a dog and 22.7 kg (50 lbs) for a bitch.

Note. — Male animals should have two apparently normal testicles fully descended into the scrotum.

MAIN AMERICAN KENNEL CLUB VARIATION TO STANDARD FOR THE BULLDOG —

Size. — The size for mature dogs is about 50 pounds for mature bitches about 40 pounds.

BULLDOG REGISTRATIONS 1981 — 87 INCLUSIVE

1981 — 805
1982 — 832
1983 — 792
1984 — 888
1985 — 1003
1986 — 1003
1987 — 1040

CRUFTS BEST-IN-SHOW WINNER

1952 CH. NOWAYS CHUCKLES — J.T. BARNARD

CHOW CHOW

It is very possible that this breed goes back to the eleventh century B.C. that being when the first mention of Chow Chow type dogs was made. Due to the area of origin being in the remote areas of northern China, hard facts on his history are hard come by. But he was used probably in hunting and as a guard dog with an almost certain link with the dogs of the Arctic, his coat and great physical strength giving weight to this theory. There are some rare blue Chow Chows in China, but these are not to be seen in Britain. He was first recognised in this country in 1894 and from then until the second World War he was extremely popular. He is still very much in evidence but not quite to the same extent.

The straight hind leg formation of the Chow Chow gives him a distinctive rather wooden gait, but this somehow adds to his imposing physique and earnest expression. The indigo blue tongue of this breed is unique to him.

The Chow Chow is a breed of rugged beauty and will respond to strong-minded thoughtful training. However, he is not to be recommended to families with small children as he can be a little impatient with them and a Chow Chow's bite is not be be flirted with.

Abhorrent as it is to contemplate, this excellent breed has been used as a food source in it's native China.

KEY TO CHARACTER	
INTELLIGENCE	***
TEMPERAMENT	***
EASE OF COAT CARE	*
SUITABILITY FOR SMALL DWELLING	**
***** (5) = VERY GOOD	

BRITISH KENNEL CLUB STANDARD

CHOW CHOW

CHARACTERISTICS. — A well-balanced dog, leonine in appearance, with proud dignified bearing; loyal yet aloof; unique in its stilted gait and bluish-black tongue.

GENERAL APPEARANCE. — An active, compact, short-coupled and well-balanced dog, well knit in frame, with tail carried well over the back.

Head and Skull. — Skull flat and broad, with little stop, well filled out under the eyes. Muzzle moderate in length, broad from the eyes to the point (not pointed at the end like a fox). Nose black, large and wide in all cases (with the exception of cream and white in which case a light-coloured nose is permissible and in blues and fawns a self-coloured nose); but in all colours a black nose is preferable.

Eyes. — Dark and small, preferably almond-shaped (in blue or fawn dog a light colour is permissible).

Ears. — Small, thick, slightly rounded at the tip, carried stiffly erect but placed well forward over the eyes and wide apart, which gives the dog the peculiar characteristic expression of the breed, viz., a scowl.

Mouth. — Teeth strong and level, giving scissor bite. Tongue bluish black. Flews and roof of mouth black. Gums preferably black.

Neck. — Strong, full, set well on the shoulders and slightly arched.

Forequarters. — Shoulders muscular and sloping. Forlegs perfectly straight of moderate length and with good bone.

Body. — Chest broad and deep. Back short, straight and strong. Loins powerful.

Bulldog

Chow Chow

Dalmatian

French Bulldog

Hindquarters. — Hindlegs muscular and hocks well let down and perfectly straight which are essential in order to produce the Chow's characteristic stilted gait.

Feet. — Small, round and catlike, standing well on the toes.

Tail. — Set high and carried well over the back.

Coat. — Abundant, dense, straight and stand-off. Outer coat rather coarse in texture and with a soft woolly undercoat. The Chow Chow is a profusely coated dog and balance should therefore be assessed when the coat is at its natural length.

Colour. — Whole coloured black, red, blue, fawn, cream or white, frequently shaded but not in patches or parti-coloured (the underpart of tail and back of thighs frequently of a light colour).

Weight and Size. — Minimum height for Chows to be 45.7 cm (18″) but in every case balance should be the outstanding feature and height left to the discretion of the judges.

Faults. — Drop ears, tongue splashed or patchy, tail not carried over the back, parti-coloured, off black noses except in the colours specified, viz., creams, whites, blues or fawns. Any artificial shortening of the coat which alters the natural outline or expression of the dog should be penalised. (The standard of the smooth variety is identical with the above except that the coat is smooth).

Note. — Male animals should have two apparently normal testicles fully descended into the scrotum.

CHOW CHOW REGISTRATIONS 1981 — 87 INCLUSIVE

1981 — 1155
1982 — 1096
1983 — 1096
1984 — 929
1985 — 977
1986 — 942
1987 — 773

CRUFTS BEST-IN-SHOW

1936 CH. CHOONAM HUNG KWONG — MRS. V.A.M. MANOOCH

DALMATIAN

The Dalmatian is an energetic, loyal and affectionate breed, with a genuine liking for people of all ages.

His history is uncertain, with serveral differing views being voiced. Despite his name, it is now thought unlikely that he comes from the Yugoslavian province of Dalmatia, the British having probably introduced him there. Some contend that he has Danish origins, others favour the eastern Mediterranean regions. It is possible that the Dalmatian has existed in a fairly unaltered form for many hundreds of years. A spotted dog can be seen in many paintings dating from the 17th century and before and some of these were quite similar to today's specimens.

In the 19th century the Dalmatian was widely known as the "carriage dog". This nickname stems from his apparent affinity for horses, and a liking for running alongside them as they pulled the coaches of the gentry. It became extremely fashionable, in fact, to be seen with Dalmatians accompanying you in this way.

All Dalmatian owners will testify to the breed's affable, playful disposition and equally to it's surprisingly forceful guarding qualities. They are lively, highly strung dogs with endless stamina, so exercise is of a paramount importance. With application they can be trained into excellent house dogs, especially enjoying the company of children, who cope well with their endless appetite for play.

KEY TO CHARACTER	
INTELLIGENCE	***
TEMPERAMENT	***
EASE OF COAT CARE	*****
SUITABILITY FOR SMALL DWELLING	**
***** (5) = VERY GOOD	

BRITISH KENNEL CLUB STANDARD

DALMATIAN

GENERAL APPEARANCE. — The Dalmatian should be a balanced, strong, muscular, active dog of good demeanour. Symmetrical in outline, free from coarseness and lumber, capable of great endurance with a fair amount of speed.

Head and Skull. — The head should be of fair length, the skull flat, reasonably broad between the ears but refined, moderately well defined at the temples, i.e. exhibiting a moderate amount of Stop; not in one straight line from nose to occiput bone. Entirely free from wrinkle. The muzzle should be long and powerful, never snipy, the lips clean, fitting the jaw moderately close. The nose in the black-spotted variety should always be black, in the liver spotted variety always brown.

Eyes. — The eyes, set moderately well apart should be of medium size, round, bright and sparkling, with an intelligent expression, their colour, depending on the marking of the dog; dark in the black spotted, amber in the liver spotted. The rim round the eyes should be complete; black in the black spotted and liver brown in the liver spotted.

Ears. — The ears should be set on rather high, of moderate size, rather wide at the base, gradually tapering to a rounded point. Fine in texture, carried close to the head. The marking should be well broken up, preferably spotted.

Mouth. — The teeth should meet. The upper slightly overlapping the lower (Scissor bite).

Neck. — The neck should be fairly long, nicely arched, light and tapering. Entirely free from throatiness.

Forequarters. — The shoulders should be moderately oblique, clean and muscular. Elbows close to the body. The forelegs perfectly straight with strong round bone down to the feet, with a slight spring at the pastern joint.

Body. — The chest should not be too wide but deep and capacious with plenty of lung and heart room. The ribs well sprung, well defined wither, powerful level back, loins strong, clean and muscular, and slightly arched.

Hindquarters. — Rounded, muscles clean with well developed second thigh, good turn of stifle and hocks well defined.

Tail. — In length reaching approximately to the hocks. Stong at the insertion gradually tapering towards the end, it should not be inserted too low or too high, be free from coarseness and carried with a slight upward curve, never curled. Preferably spotted.

Feet. — Round, compact, with well arched toes (cat feet) and round tough elastic pads. Nails black or white in the black spotted variety, in the liver spotted variety — brown or white.

Gait. — The Dalmatian should have great freedom of movement. A smooth, powerful rhythmic action with a long stride. Viewed from behind, the legs should move in parallel the hindlegs tracking the fore. A short stride and paddling action is incorrect.

Coat. — The coat should be short, hard and dense, sleek and glossy in appearance. The ground colour should be pure white. Black spotted dogs should have dense black spots and liver spotted dogs liver-brown spots. They should not run together but be round and well defined the size of sixpence to a half crown, as well distributed as possible. Spots on the extremities should be smaller than those on the body.

Size. — Overall balance of prime importance, but the ideal height to be aimed at is: Dog 58.4 cm to 61 cm (23″ to 24″). Bitch 55.9 cm to 58.4 cm (22″ to 23″).

Faults. — Patches, black and liver spots on the same dog (tri colours). Lemon spots; Blue eyes; Bronzing and other faults of pigmentation.

Note. — Male animals should have two apparently normal testicles fully descended into the scrotum.

SCALE OF POINTS

Build and symmetry	20
Colour	20
Head and expression	9
Spotted ears	4
Neck and breast	10
Legs and feet	15
Forequarters	8
Hindquarters	8
Spotted tail	6
Total	100

MAIN AMERICAN KENNEL CLUB VARIATION TO STANDARD FOR THE DALMATIAN —

Size. — The desirable height of dogs and bitches is between 19 and 23 inches at the withers.

DALMATIAN REGISTRATIONS 1981 — 87 INCLUSIVE

1981 — 745
1982 — 699
1983 — 756
1984 — 681
1985 — 911
1986 — 752
1987 — 773

CRUFTS BEST IN SHOW WINNER

1968 CH. FANHILL FAUNE — MRS. E.J. WOODYATT

FRENCH BULLDOG

Although he carries the name of French Bulldog, this breed is a direct descendant of the early British Bulldog. It is believed that over three hundred years ago small Bulldog specimens were imported by the French and crossed with dogs native to France. Exactly which crossings took place is unclear although the accent was always on keeping the size down. As was the unhappy fate of many bull breeds, the French Bulldog was often used for pit fighting. This was not surprising as he possesses all the courage and pound-for-pound strength of his larger cousins.

It was not until the early 1900's that the breed was registered with the Kennel Club in Britain and it was only a short time before then that the first French Bulldogs appeared in the U.S.A. The breed has built up a solid following in both countries.

Apart from the very conspicuous and appealing bat-ears, the French Bulldog is almost a Bulldog in miniature both in his physical proportions and in his friendly, outgoing nature. He makes a lively companion who loves rough and tumble games and the company of children. He is a good choice of pet for someone who wants a small dog that has no trace of frailty or timidity. If his owner's family indulge in his play sessions, then the French Bulldog will derive a good deal of exercise from this, but he will still enjoy plenty of outdoor excursions.

KEY TO CHARACTER	
INTELLIGENCE	****
TEMPERAMENT	*****
EASE OF COAT CARE	*****
SUITABILITY FOR SMALL DWELLING	*****
***** (5) = VERY GOOD	

BRITISH KENNEL CLUB STANDARD

FRENCH BULLDOG

GENERAL APPEARANCE. — A French Bulldog should be sound, active and intelligent, of compact build, medium or small sized, with good bone, a short smooth coat, and the various points so evenly balanced that the dog does not look iil-proportioned.

Head and Skull. — Head massive, square and broad. Skull nearly flat between the ears, with a domed forehead, the loose skin forming symmetrical wrinkles. Muzzle broad, deep and laid back with the muscles of the cheek well developed; nose and lips black. Stop well defined. Lower jaw should be deep square, broad, slightly undershot and well turned up. Nose extremely short, black and wide, with open nostrils and the line between well defined. Lips thick, the lower meeting the upper in the middle, completely hiding the teeth. The upper lip should cover the lower on each side with plenty of cushion, but not so exaggerated as to hang too much below the level of the lower jaw.

Eyes. — Should be dark, of moderate size, round, neither sunken nor prominent showing no white when looking straight, set wide apart and low down in the skull.

Ears. — "Bat ears" of medium size, wide at the base, rounded at the top, set high, carried upright and parallel, a sufficient width of skull preventing them being too close together; the skin soft and fine and the orifice, as seen from the front, showing entirely.

Mouth. — Teeth sound and regular, but not visible when the mouth is closed. Tongue must not protrude.

Neck. — Should be powerful, with loose skin at the throat, but not exaggerated. Well arched and thick, but not too short.

Forequarters. — Legs set wide apart, straight boned, strong, muscular and short.

Body. — Should be short, cobby, muscular and well rounded, with deep wide brisket, roach back, strong, wide at the shoulders and narrowing at the loins, good "cut up" and well sprung.

Hindquarters. — Legs strong, muscular and longer than the forelegs so as to raise the loins above th shoulders. Hocks well let down and with very fine movement.

Feet. — Should be small, compact and placed in continuation of the line of the leg, with absolutely sound pasterns. The hind rather longer than the fore-feet. Toes compact, knuckle high, nails short, thick and preferably black.

Tail. — Very short, set low, thick at the root, and tapering quickly towards the tip, either straight or kinked, but never curling over the back. A good tail is placed so that it cannot be carried gaily.

Coat. — Texture fine, smooth, lustrous, short and close.

Colour. — The colours allowed are brindle, pied and fawn.

(1) The brindle is a mixture of black and coloured hairs. This variety may contain white on condition that brindle predominates.

(2) The pied is a dog in which the white predominates over the brindle. White dogs are classified with the pieds, but their eyelashes and eyerims should be black. In pieds the white should be clear with definite brindle patches and no ticking or black spots.

(3) The fawn dog may contain brindle hairs but must have black eyerims and eyelashes.

Weight and Size. — The ideal weight is 12.7 kg (28 lbs) for dogs and 10.9 kg (24 lbs) for bitches but soundness must not be sacrificed to smallness.

Faults. — Nose other than black. Eyes of different colours. Ears not erect. Hare lip. Tail docked. Colour-Tan, Mouse Grey (blue).

Note. — Male animals should have two apparently normal testicles fully descended into the scrotum.

MAIN AMERICAN KENNEL CLUB VARIATION TO STANDARD FOR THE FRENCH BULLDOG —

Weight. — A lightweight class under 22 pounds; heavyweight class, 22 pounds, and not over 28 pounds.

FRENCH BULLDOG REGISTRATIONS — 1981 — 87 INCLUSIVE

1981 — 141
1982 — 128
1983 — 103
1984 — 146
1985 — 123
1986 — 163
1987 — 176

YET TO WIN CRUFTS BEST-IN-SHOW.

JAPANESE SPITZ

At first glance, the Japanese Spitz looks very much like a Samoyed in miniature. This is not surprising since both dogs belong to the Spitz group and therefore share the same ancestry. This ancestry lies in the dogs of the Arctic regions and it seems probable that dogs reached Japan centuries ago from northern Europe to be later developed into something close to today's Japanese Spitz.

Outside Japan, this breed is very uncommon, although in Britain he is beginning to make headway in the show world. He is very suited to the show-ring with his luxurious white coat and his air of alertness and intelligence.

As with all the Spitz breeds, he is not short on courage and energy and in the home he makes an engaging pet. He does not tolerate strangers easily and becomes very strongly attached to his owner. He enjoys the outdoor life but can live in the town if allowed plenty of outings.

Despite the length of the coat, grooming is not too much of a headache but a frequent brushing is necessary to keep the Japanese Spitz at his impressive best.

KEY TO CHARACTER	
INTELLIGENCE	****
TEMPERAMENT	****
EASE OF COAT CARE	***
SUITABILITY FOR SMALL DWELLING	***
***** (5) = VERY GOOD	

BRITISH KENNEL CLUB STANDARD

JAPANESE SPITZ

CHARACTERISTICS. — Intelligent, bold, and lively.

GENERAL APPEARANCE. — Profuse, pure white offstanding coat. The dog should have a sharply pointed muzzle and triangular shaped ears standing erect. Bushy tail carried over the back. The overall quality of the body should be firm and strong, full of flexibility. Fore and hind quarters should be well proportioned and balanced.

Head and Skull. — Head of medium size without coarseness; moderately broad and slightly rounded. Skull broadest at occiput; well defined stop; cheeks rounded; forehead not protruding. Muzzle sharply pointed neither too thick nor too long. Lips firm and tightly closed, with black colour desirable. The nose round and small and black in pigmentation.

Eyes. — Of moderate size, almond shape, set rather obliquely and not too wide apart; dark in colour with black eye rims.

Ears. — Small, triangular and standing erect. Set high, forward facing and not too wide apart.

Mouth. — The jaws should be strong, with a perfect regular and complete scissor bite, i.e. the upper teeth closely overlapping the lower teeth and set square to the jaw.

Neck. — Strong and of moderate length.

Forequarters. — Shoulders well laid. Forelegs straight with elbows firm and tight and pasterns slightly sloping.

Body. — Chest broad and deep. Ribs powerfully sprung; belly moderately firm with good tuck-up. Withers should be highly developed and back should be straight and short. Loins should be broad and firm. Croup should be comparatively long and slightly arched.

Hindquarters. — Muscular and moderately angulated. Hind legs paralled to each other viewed from the rear.

Feet. — Toes should be small, round and cat-like. Well padded with good pigment. Nails should be hard and black or dark.

Gait. — Light and nimble, active, energetic and very smooth.

Tail. — Moderate in length with root set high and curled over the back.

Coat. — The outer coat should be straight and stand-off. Profuse undercoat, short, dense and soft in texture. Shorter on the face, ears, front parts of fore and hind legs and below hocks. All the other parts of the body covered with long coat. Mane on the neck and shoulder, reaching down to the brisket. Tail profusely covered with long hair.

Colour. — Pure white.

Size. — Height at shoulder: 30 to 40 cm (12″ to 16″) for males, 25 to 35 cm (10″ to 14″) for females.

Faults. — Any departure from the foregoing points should be considered a fault and the seriousness with which the fault is regarded should be in exact proportion to its degree.

Note. — Male animals should have two apparently normal testicles fully descended into the scrotum.

JAPANESE SPITZ REGISTRATIONS 1981 — 87 INCLUSIVE

1981 — 41
1982 — 77
1983 — 106
1984 — 109
1985 — 219
1986 — 143
1987 — 180

YET TO WIN CRUFTS BEST-IN-SHOW.

KEESHOND

This member of the Spitz family of breeds hails from Holland. During his early history the Keeshond was used extensively as a guard dog on the barges of Holland's many canals. His alertness and loud bark were well suited to this post and his medium size was sufficient to back up his agression.

The breed's name is taken from a famous dog lover called Kees de Gyselaer who was a leading dutch patriot in the 18th century when Holland was on the verge of upheaval.

The wild arctic ancestry of the Keeshond has long since vanished from his character and centuries of working for man and living with his families have produced a first class house dog. His temperament is usually very sound and house training and indeed training for the show bench, is no problem. He becomes very attached to his owner, often being a little wary of strangers but he will live harmoniously with all the owner's family.

The glorious, dense double coat is obviously an asset in the winter and when given fairly regular attention is the Keeshond's most striking feature.

Feeding and exercise requirements are not excessive and he could be said to be generally an easily managed breed.

KEY TO CHARACTER	
INTELLIGENCE	***
TEMPERAMENT	*****
EASE OF COAT CARE	**
SUITABILITY FOR SMALL DWELLING	***
***** (5) = VERY GOOD	

BRITISH KENNEL CLUB STANDARD

KEESHOND

GENERAL APPEARANCE. — A short, compact body; alert carriage, foxlike head; small pointed ears; a well-feathered, curling tail, carried over the back; hair very thick on the neck, forming a large ruff; head, ears and lets covered with short thick hair. Dogs should move cleanly and briskly (not lope like an Alsatian) but movement should be straight and sharp. Dogs should show boldly.

Head and Skull. — Head well proportioned to the body, wedge-shaped when seen from above; from the side showing definite stop. Muzzle should be of medium length, neither coarse nor snipy.

Eyes. — Dark with well-defined spectacles.

Ears. — Small and well set on head, not wide and yet not meeting.

Mouth. — Should be neither over nor undershot, upper teeth should just overlap under teeth and should be white, sound and strong (but discoloration from distemper not to penalize severely).

Forequarters. — Forelegs feathered, straight, with good bone and cream in colour.

Hindquarters. — Hind legs should be straight, showing very little hock and not feathered below the hock. Cream in colour.

Feet. — Round and cat-like with black nails.

Tail. — Tightly curled, a double curl at the end is desirable. Plume to be white on the top where curled, with black tip.

Coat. — Dense, and harsh (off-standing), dense ruff and well feathered, profuse trousers; a soft, thick, light-coloured undercoat. Coat should not be silky, wavy or woolly, nor should it form a parting on the back.

Colour. — Should be wolf, ash-grey; not all black or all white, and markings should be definite.

Weight and Size. — The ideal height is 45.7 cm (18″) for dogs and 43.2 cm (17″) for bitches, but type is of more importance.

Faults. — Light eyes, prominent eyes. Curly or wavy tendency in coat. Silky coat. Absence of spectacles. Nervous demeanour. Drop ears. Whole white foot or feet. Black marks below the knee, pencilling excepted. White chest. Apple head or absence of stop.

Note. — Male animals should have two apparently normal testicles fully descended into the scrotum.

KEESHOND REGISTRATIONS 1981 — 87 INCLUSIVE

1981 — 198
1982 — 142
1983 — 216
1984 — 253
1985 — 177
1986 — 242
1987 — 221

CRUFTS BEST-IN-SHOW WINNER

1957 CH. VOLKRIJK OF VORDEN — MRS. I.M. TUCKER.

LHASA APSO

This is another of the attractive small dogs that has his roots in Tibet. The Lhasa Apso was the favourite breed of the Dalai Lama, the supreme religious leader of Tibet. There are many stories of some of the finest Lhasa Apso specimens being presented as gifts to visiting Europeans and this is most probably how this breed reached the west. After the Chinese takeover of Tibet and the exile of the Dalai Lama, it has not been clear how these dogs are faring, but certainly before the invasion they were held in the highest regard by the monks who kept them in their monastries.

Nowadays in Britain, the Lhasa Apso has become quite well established and has been a great success in the show world. The solid little frame is covered with an abundant coat which is hard in texture yet flows beautifully smooth and straight when correctly groomed. It is mainly this feature which has always guaranteed these dogs a second look by all who attend breed shows.

The Lhasa Apso is a dog with a self confidence which belies his stature and he is often aloof with strangers. His loyalty to his owner is very pronounced and he will adopt a guarding role whenever necessary. Within the family he mixes well with all age groups and he will enjoy lengthy sessions of play in the home. This play should be supplemented with frequent walks. To do the Lhasa Apso full justice, the coat must be given a great deal of attention.

KEY TO CHARACTER	
INTELLIGENCE	***
TEMPERAMENT	****
EASE OF COAT CARE	*
SUITABILITY FOR SMALL DWELLING	*****
***** (5) = VERY GOOD	

BRITISH KENNEL CLUB STANDARD
LHASA APSO

CHARACTERISTICS. — The Apso should give the appearance of a well-balanced, solid dog. Gay and assertive, but chary of strangers. Free and jaunty in movement.

Head and Skull. — Heavy head furnishings with good fall over the eyes, good whiskers and beard.

Skull moderately narrow, falling away behind the eyes in a marked degree; not quite flat, but not domed or apple shaped.

Straight foreface, with medium stop. Nose black. Muzzle about 1½ inches long, but not square; the length from tip of nose to be roughly one-third the total length from nose to back of skull.

Eyes. — Dark. Medium sized eyes to be frontally placed, not large or full, or small and sunk. No white showing at base or top of eye.

Ears. — Pendant, heavily feathered. Dark tips an asset.

Mouth. — Upper incisors should close just inside the lower, i.e., a reverse scissor bite. Incisors should be nearly in a staight line. Full dentition is desirable.

Neck. — Strong, well covered with a dense mane which is more pronounced in dogs than in bitches.

Forequarters. — Shoulders should be well laid back. Forelegs straight, heavily furnished with hair.

Body. — The length from point of shoulders to point of buttocks greater than height at withers. Well ribbed up. Level top-line. Strong loin. Well balanced and compact.

Hindquarters. — Well developed with good muscle. Good angulation. Heavily furnished. The hocks when viewed from behind should be parallel and not too close together.

Feet. — Round and cat-like, with good pads. Well-feathered.

Tail. — High set, carried well over back and not like a pot-hook. There is often a kink at the end. Well feathered.

Coat. — Top coat heavy, straight and hard, not wooly or silky, of good length. Dense under-coat.

Colours. — Golden, sandy, honey, dark grizzle, slate, smoke, parti-colour, black, white or brown.

Size. — Ideal height: 25.4 cm (10″) at shoulder for dogs; bitches slightly smaller.

Note. — Male animals should have two apparently normal testicles fully descended into the scrotum.

MAIN AMERICAN KENNEL CLUB VARIATION TO STANDARD FOR THE LHASA APSO —

Size. — Variable, but about 10 inches or 11 inches at shoulder for dogs, bitches slightly smaller.

LHASA APSO REGISTRATIONS 1981 — 87 INCLUSIVE

1981 — 965
1982 — 952
1983 — 1303
1984 — 1304
1985 — 1404
1986 — 1485
1987 — 1447

CRUFTS BEST-IN-SHOW WINNER

1984 CH. SAXONSPRINGS HACKENSACK — MRS. J. BLYTH

MINIATURE SCHNAUZER

This attractive small breed is a scaled-down carbon copy of his larger relative the Schnauzer, sometimes called the Standard Schnauzer. It seems that to produce the Miniature Schnauzer, small Schnauzer specimens were crossed by German breeders with other small breeds. Some maintain that one of the breeds involved in this miniaturisation process was the Affenpinscher, although the Miniature Schnauzer's physical appearance might belie this.

He has the strength of character and cool temperament of a larger dog and this has ensured a very strong following for him, particularly in the U.S.A. where he is classed as a Terrier, an idea strongly resisted by European fanciers. But he does share one of the talents of the Terrier family, that of being an excellent ratter.

As a show competitor he has made a great impact. If expertly prepared the Miniature Schnauzer is a picture of smartness and he is renowned for his ability to stand statue-like for long periods. He has also shown his worth in the obedience ring.

It would be difficult to find a better small dog for a family. Apart from his grooming needs, he is easily maintained, robust and healthy. He loves playful exercise but is quite happy to have short regular walks if, for instance, his owner is elderly.

Japanese Spitz
Keeshond

Lhasa Apso

Miniature Schnauzer

KEY TO CHARACTER	
INTELLIGENCE	****
TEMPERAMENT	*****
EASE OF COAT CARE	**
SUITABILITY FOR SMALL DWELLING	*****
***** (5) = VERY GOOD	

BRITISH KENNEL CLUB STANDARD

MINIATURE SCHNAUZER

GENERAL APPEARANCE. — The Miniature Schnauzer is a powerfully built, robust, sinewy, nearly square, dog (length of body equal to height at shoulders). His temperament combines high spirits, reliability, strength, endurance and vigour. Expression keen and attitude alert. Correct conformation is of more importance than colour or other purely "beauty" points.

Head and Skull. — Head strong and elongated, gradually narrowing from the ears to the eyes and thence forward toward the tip of the nose. Upper part of the head (occiput to the base of the forehead) moderately broad between the ears — with flat, creaseless, forehead and well muscled, but not too strongly developed cheeks. Medium stop to accentuate prominent eyebrows. The powerful muzzle formed by the upper and lower jaws (base of forehead to the tip of the nose) should end in a moderately blunt line, with bristly, stubby moustache and chin whiskers. Ridge of the nose straight and running almost parallel to the extension of the forehead. The nose is black and full. Lips tight and not overlapping.

Eyes. — Medium sized, dark, oval, set forward, with arched bushy eyebrows.

Ears. — Neat and V shaped, set high and dropping forward to temple.

Mouth. — Scissor teeth, slightly overlapping from the top; with strongly developed fangs; healthy and pure white.

Neck. — Moderately long, nape strong and slightly arched, skin close to throat, neck set cleanly on shoulders.

Forequarters. — Shoulders flat and sloping. Forelegs straight viewed from any position. Muscles smooth and lithe rather than prominent; bone strong, straight and carried well down to the feet; elbows set close to the body and pointing directly backward.

Body. — Chest moderately broad, deep, with visible strong breast bone reaching down to at least the height of elbow and slightly rising backward to loins. Back strong and straight, slightly higher at the shoulder than at the hindquarters, with short, well developed loins. Ribs well sprung. Length of body equal to height from top of withers to ground.

Hindquarters. — Thighs slanting and flat, but strongly muscled. Hindlegs (upper and lower thighs) at first vertical to the stifle, from stifle to hock, in line with the extension of the upper neck line, from hock, vertical to ground.

Feet. — Short, round, extremely compact with close-arched toes, (cat's paws), dark nails and hard soles. The feet also deep or thickly padded, pointing forward.

Tail. — Set on and carried high, cut down to three joints.

Coat. — Hard and wiry and just short enough for smartness, clean on neck, shoulder, ears and skull, plenty of good hard hair on front legs. Good undercoat is essential.

Colour. — All pepper and salt colours in even proportions, or pure black.

Height. — The ideal height for bitches shall be 33 cm (13″) and for dogs 35.6 cm (14″). Too small, toyish-appearing dogs are not typical and should be penalised.

Faults. — Too heavy or too light; too low or high on the leg. Head too heavy or round, creased forehead, sticking-out, or badly carried, ears; light eye, with yellow or light grey rings; strongly protruding cheek-bones; flabby throat skin; undershot or overshot jaw. Muzzle too pointed or too small. Back too long, sunken or roached; barrel-shaped ribs; slanting crupper; elbows turned out); heels turned in, hindpart overbuilt (too steep). Toes spread open; paws long and flat (hare). Coat too short and sleek, or too long, soft or curled. All white, spotty, tigered or red colours. Small white breast spot or marking is not a fault. Among other serious faults are cow-hocks, sunken pasterns, or any weakness of joint, bones or muscular development.

Note. — Male animals should have two apparently normal testicles fully descended into the scrotum.

MAIN AMERICAN KENNEL CLUB VARIATION TO STANDARD FOR THE MINIATURE SCHNAUZER —

Ears. — When cropped the ears are identical in shape and length, with pointed tips.

Size. — From 12 to 14 inches. Ideal size 13½ inches.

MINIATURE SCHNAUZER REGISTRATIONS 1981 — 87 INCLUSIVE

1981 — 751
1982 — 813
1983 — 907
1984 — 943
1985 — 1192
1986 — 1214
1987 — 1192

YET TO WIN CRUFTS BEST-IN-SHOW.

Poodle

Schipperke

POODLE

The official standard for all three types of Poodle is exactly the same save for the obvious height differences. The first Standard Poodle was registered in 1874, the first Miniature in 1911 and the first Toy in 1957.

A similar breed seems to have reared it's head in the 16th century. This cannot be substantiated, however, as many early poodle-like dogs depicted in paintings and engravings might well have been more closely related to the Portugese water dog which is often clipped similarly to a poodle.

Both the French and the Germans stake a claim to being the Poodle's originator, and until recently it was common to hear the breed referred to as the French Poodle. But Germany has a strong case for there is record of an ancient German breed known as the Pudel, the name changing to Poedel when the breed sprang up in Belgium and Holland.

Surprising as it may seem, the Poodle has been successfully employed as a hunting dog, having excellent retrieving qualities. His intelligence is beyond question as is clearly illustrated by the amazingly complex tricks performed by circus poodles. His athleticism, too, is displayed at these shows.

If shown plenty of affection and attention, the Poodle makes a truly interesting companion, but they can become touchy if left too long to their own devices.

The coat can be clipped in a variety of different styles with perhaps the most popular being the "Lion Clip", so called as it features a heavy mane around the neck and shoulders.

The three Poodle varieties offer a good choice for many prospective owners, with the Toy being currently the most popular, due to his manageable size and undemanding exercise needs.

KEY TO CHARACTER		
INTELLIGENCE		*****
TEMPERAMENT		***
EASE OF COAT CARE		*
SUITABILITY FOR SMALL DWELLING	STANDARD	*
	MINIATURE	****
	TOY	*****
***** (5) = VERY GOOD		

BRITISH KENNEL CLUB STANDARD

POODLE (STANDARD)

CHARACTERISTICS & GENERAL APPEARANCE. — That of a very active, intelligent, well balanced and elegant looking dog with good temperament, carrying himself very proudly.

Gait. — Sound, free movement and light gait are essential.

Head and Skull. — Long and fine with slight peak at the back. The skull not broad and with a moderate stop. Foreface strong and well chiselled, not falling away under the eyes; bones and muscle flat. Lips tight fitting. Chin well defined, but not protruding. The whole head must be in proportion to the size of the dog.

Eyes. — Almond shaped, dark, not set too close together, full of fire and intelligence.

Ears. — The leather long and wide, low set on, hanging close to the face.

Mouth. — Teeth — white, strong, even, with scissor bite. A full set of 42 teeth is desirable.

Neck. — Well proportioned, of good length and strong to admit of the head being carried high and with dignity. Skin fitting tightly at the throat.

Forequarters. — Shoulders — strong and muscular, sloping well to the back, legs set straight from the shoulders, well muscled.

Body. — Chest — deep and moderately wide. Ribs — well sprung and rounded. Back — short, strong, slightly hollowed, loins broad and muscular.

Hindquarters. — Thighs well developed and muscular, well bent stifles, well let down hocks, hind legs turning neither in nor out.

Schnauzer

Shih Tzu

Feet. — Pasterns strong, tight feet proportionately small, oval in shape, turning neither in nor out, toes arched, pads thick and hard, well cushioned.

Tail. — Set on rather high, well carried at a slight angle away from the body, never curled or carried over the back, thick at the root.

Coat. — Very profuse and dense of good harsh texture without knots or tangles. All short hair close, thick and curly. It is strongly recommended that the traditional lion clip be adhered to.

Colour. — All solid colours. White and cream poodles to have black nose, lips and eyerims, black toenails desirable, brown poodles to have dark amber eyes, dark liver nose, lips, eyerims and toenails. Apricot poodles to have dark eyes with black points or deep amber eyes with liver points. Black, silver and blue poodles to have black nose, lips, eyerims and toenails. Cream, apricot, born, silver and blue poodles may show varying shades of the same colour up to 18 months. Clear colours preferred.

Size. — 38 cm (15″) and over.

Faults. — Heavy build, clumsiness, long back, snipy in foreface, light or round or prominent eyes, lippiness, bad carriage, heavy gait, coarse head, over or undershot or pincer mouth, flesh coloured nose, coarse legs and feet, long flat toes, open soft coats with no curl, particolours — white markings on black or coloured poodles, lemon or other markings on white poodles, vicious temperament.

Note. — Male animals should have two apparently normal testicles fully descended into the scrotum.

POODLE (MINIATURE)

The Poodle (Miniature) should be in every respect a replica, in miniature, of the Poodle (Standard). Height at shoulder should be under 38 cm (15″) but not under 28 cm (11″).

POODLE (TOY)

The standard of the Poodle (Toy) is the same as that of the Poodle (Standard) and Poodle (Miniature) except that the height at shoulder should be under 28 cm (11″).

MAIN AMERICAN KENNEL CLUB VARIATION TO STANDARD FOR THE POODLE —

Size. — The Miniature Poodle is 15 inches or under at the highest point of the shoulders, with a minimum height in excess of 10 inches. The Toy Poodle is 10 inches or under at the highest point of the shoulders.

STANDARD POODLE REGISTRATIONS 1981 — 87 INCLUSIVE

1981 — 794
1982 — 745
1983 — 923
1984 — 885
1985 — 1103
1986 — 1103
1987 — 1113

CRUFTS BEST-IN-SHOW WINNER TWICE

1955 CH. TZIGANE AGGRI OF NASHEND — MRS. A. PROCTOR
1985 CH. MONTRAVIA TOMMY-GUN — MISS M. GIBBS.

MINIATURE POODLE REGISTRATIONS 1981 — 87 INCLUSIVE

1981 — 1781
1982 — 1538
1983 — 1627
1984 — 1542
1985 — 1475
1986 — 1233
1987 — 1190

YET TO WIN CRUFTS BEST-IN-SHOW.

TOY POODLE REGISTRATIONS 1981 — 87 INCLUSIVE

1981 — 3567
1982 — 3100
1983 — 3037
1984 — 2799
1985 — 2740
1986 — 2166
1987 — 2162

CRUFTS BEST-IN-SHOW WINNER TWICE

1966 OAKINGTON PUCKSHILL AMBER SUNBLUSH — MRS. C.E. PERRY
1982 CH. GRAYCO HAZLENUT — MRS. L.A. HOWARD.

Tibetan Spaniel

Tibetan Terrier

SCHIPPERKE

The early history of this breed's development is open to argument but the Belgain's can rightly claim to have originated the modern Schipperke. He was used in Belgium as a watchdog and vermin controller on the canals. Their nimbleness and size enabled them to scurry around the barges with great ease and his very strong guarding instinct was put to good use. The name Schipperke is Flemish for "little skipper", a title well suited to this breed's jaunty demeanour.

He first appeared in Britain some 100 years ago and has a comparatively small, but devoted band of followers. It is perhaps surprising that registrations for the Schipperke are not higher as he has an endearing and interesting personality. He loves to play and children are perfectly safe in his company. He is far more robust than his diminutive size would indicate and longevity is well known as a Schipperke trait.

Feeding requirements and grooming needs are minimal and he will be happy with long or short periods of daily exercise, whichever the owner prefers. The tail is usually docked when very young although some dogs are born tail-less.

KEY TO CHARACTER	
INTELLIGENCE	***
TEMPERAMENT	****
EASE OF COAT CARE	*****
SUITABILITY FOR SMALL DWELLING	*****
***** (5) = VERY GOOD	

BRITISH KENNEL CLUB STANDARD

SCHIPPERKE

GENERAL APPEARANCE. — A small cobby animal, with sharp expression, intensely lively, presenting the appearance of being always on the alert.

CHARACTERISTICS. — Intelligent, lively and alert.

Head and Skull. — Head foxy in type, skull not round, but fairly broad, flat and with little stop. The muzzle should be moderate in length, fine but not weak, should be well filled out under the eyes. Nose black and small.

Eyes. — Dark brown, small, more oval than round and not full; bright and full of expression.

Ears. — Sharp, of moderate length, not too broad at the base, tapering to a point. Carried stiffly erect and strong enough not be be bent other than lengthways.

Mouth. — Teeth strong and level.

Neck. — Strong and full, rather short set, broad on the shoulders, and slightly arched.

Forequarters. — Shoulders muscular and sloping. Legs perfectly straight, well under the body, with bone in proportion to the body.

Body. — Chest broad and deep in brisket. Back short, straight and strong. Loins powerful, well drawn up from brisket.

Hindquarters. — Fine compared to the foreparts, muscular and well-developed thighs; tailless rump well rounded. Legs strong, muscular, hocks well let down.

Feet. — Should be small, cat-like, and standing well on the toes.

Coat. — Abundant, dense and harsh, smooth on the head, ears and legs, lying close on the back and sides, but erect and thick round the neck, forming a mane and frill and with a good culotte on the back of the thighs.

Colour. — Should be black but other whole colours are permissible.

Weight and Size. — Weight about 5.4 to 7.3 kg (12 to 16 lbs).

Faults. — Drop or semi-erect ears, Dudley noses in the coloured variety. A light-coloured eye. Head narrow and elongated, or too short. Coat sparse, wavy or silky. Absence of the mane and "culotte". Coat too long, and white spots. Undershot or overshot mouth.

Note. — Male animals should have two apparently normal testicles fully descended into the scrotum.

MAIN AMERICAN KENNEL CLUB VARIATION TO STANDARD FOR THE SCHIPPERKE —

Weight. — Up to 18 pounds.

SCHIPPERKE REGISTRATIONS 1981 — 87 INCLUSIVE

1981 — 76
1982 — 95
1983 — 107
1984 — 82
1985 — 109
1986 — 84
1987 — 129

YET TO WIN CRUFTS BEST-IN-SHOW.

SCHNAUZER

The Schnauzer, sometimes known as the Standard Schnauzer, is a fine combination of good looks and toughness, the latter characteristic having been developed through a hard working past. Originating in the Wurttemberg and Bavaria regions of Germany in the early seventeenth century, he was used as a cattle drover, ratter and small game huner. Among his main ancestors is the Wire-haired German Pinscher which would account for the Schnauzer's Terrier-like qualities, 'Pinscher' translating roughly to 'Terrier'.

As Germany became more industrialised, so the need for the Schnauzer's working expertise dwindled. Instead he was put to good use as a guard dog in the towns and latterly he became a successful show breed. Shortly after his first show bench appearance in 1879 a standard was arrived at and his future was secured.

It was over twenty years later that the Schnauzer reached the U.S.A. and a further twenty until the British saw their first specimens. There is a liking for cropping the ears in the U.S.A., a practice banned in Britain.

Although not as popular as the smallest of the three types of Schnauzer, the Miniature, this breed is of a commendable disposition and is reliable in the home. The guarding of property, children or anything in his charge is second nature and he also has a great facility for play. Plenty of vigorous exercise is recommended and he will enjoy the challenge of being trained for specific tasks.

KEY TO CHARACTER	
INTELLIGENCE	****
TEMPERAMENT	****
EASE OF COAT CARE	**
SUITABILITY FOR SMALL DWELLING	***
***** (5) = VERY GOOD	

BRITISH KENNEL CLUB STANDARD

SCHNAUZER

GENERAL APPEARANCE. — The Schnauzer is a powerfully built, robust, sinewy, nearly square dog (length of body equal to height at shoulders). His temperament combines high spirits, reliability, strength, endurance and vigour. Expression keen and attitude alert. Correct conformation is of more importance than colour or other purely "beauty" points.

Head and Skull. — Head strong and elongated, gradually narrowing from the ears to the eyes and thence forward toward the tip of the nose. Upper part of the head (occiput to the base of the forehead) moderately broad between the ears — with flat, creaseless, forehead and well muscled, but not too strongly developed cheeks. Medium stop to accentuate prominent eyebrows. The powerful muzzle formed by the upper and lower jaws (base of forehead to the tip of the nose) should end in a moderately blunt line, with bristly, stubby moustache and chin whiskers. Ridge of the nose straight and running almost parallel to the extension of the forehead. The nose is black and full. Lips tight and not overlapping.

Eyes. — Medium sized, dark, oval, set forward, with arched bushy eyebrows.

Ears. — Neat and V shaped, set high and dropping forward to temple.

Mouth. — Scissor teeth, slightly overlapping from the top; with strongly developed fangs; healthy and pure white.

Neck. — Moderately long, nape strong and slightly arched, skin close to throat, neck set cleanly on shoulders.

Forequarters. — Shoulders flat and sloping. Forelegs straight veiwed from any position. Muscles smooth and lithe rather than prominent; bone strong, straight and carried well down to the feet; elbows set close to the body and pointing directly backward.

Body. — Chest moderately broad, deep, with visible strong breast bone reaching down to at least the height of elbow and slightly rising backward to loins. Back strong and straight, slightly higher at the shoulder than at the hindquarters, with short, well developed loins. Ribs well sprung. Length of body equal to height from top of withers to ground.

Hindquarters. — Thighs slanting and flat, but strongly muscled. Hindlegs (upper and lower thighs) at first vertical to the stifle, from stifle to hock, in line with the extension of the upper neck line, from hock, vertical to ground.

Feet. — Short, round, extremely compact with close-arched toes, (cat's paws) dark nails and hard soles. The feet also deep or thickly padded, pointing forward.

Tail. — Set on and carried high, cut down to three joints.

Coat. — Hard and wiry and just short enough for smartness, clean on neck, shoulder, ears and skull, plenty of good hard hair on front legs. Good undercoat is essential.

Colour. — All pepper and salt colours in even proportions, or pure black.

Height. — The ideal height for bitches shall be 45.7 cm (18″) and for dogs 48.3 cm (19″). Any variation of more than 2.5 cm (1″) in these heights should be penalised.

Faults. — Too heavy or too light; too low or high on the leg. Head too heavy or round, creased forehead, sticking-out, or badly carried, ears; light eye, with yellow or light grey rings; strongly protruding cheek-bones; flabby throat skin; undershot or overshot jaw. Muzzle too pointed or too small. Back too long, sunken or roached; barrel-shaped ribs; slanting crupper; elbows turned out; heels turned in, hindpart overbuilt (too steep). Toes spread open; paws long and flat (hare). Coat too short and sleek, or too long, soft or curled. All white, spotty, tigered or red colours. Small white breast spot or markings is not a fault. Among other serious faults are cow-hocks, sunken pasterns, or any weakness of joint, bones or muscular development.

Note. — Male animals should have two apparently normal testicles fully descended into the scrotum.

MAIN AMERICAN KENNEL CLUB VARIATION TO STANDARD FOR THE SCHNAUZER —

Known as the Standard Schnauzer in the U.S.A.

Ears. — Evenly shaped, set high and carried erect when cropped.

Height. — Ideal height at the highest point of the shoulder blades, 18½ to 19½ inches for males and 17½ inches to 18½ inches for females.

MAIN AMERICAN KENNEL CLUB VARIATION TO STANDARD FOR THE GIANT SCHNAUZER —

Ears. — When cropped, identical in shape and length with pointed tips. They are in balance with the head and are not exaggerated in length. They are set high on the skull and carried perpendicularly at the inner edges with as little bell as possible along the other edges.

SCHNAUZER REGISTRATIONS 1981 — 87 INCLUSIVE

1981 — 98
1982 — 122
1983 — 153
1984 — 125
1985 — 167
1986 — 144
1987 — 195

YET TO WIN CRUFTS BEST-IN-SHOW.

SHIH TZU

The energetic little Shih Tzu is one of the several small flat-faced breeds that herald from the Far East. All of these breeds obviously have a common ancestry stretching back thousands of years, but details are very sketchy. It seems very possible, though that the Shih Tzu was produced by crossing the Pekingese with Tibetan dogs of the type kept by the Dalai Lama, the all-powerful religious leader of Tibet. Much mystique surrounded dogs of the East in those far ancient times, and Pekingese/Shih Tzu — type dogs were known as 'Lion Dogs' after a half dog and half lion creature in Chinese mythology.

So prized were these dogs that the Chinese and Tibetans refused to allow them out of the East and the first Shih Tzu specimens to reach Europe in the early part of this century, were probably taken illegally. Since the breed's official recognition in Britain in 1934, there has been a steadily growing interest here. All major dog shows feature a large Shih Tzu entry and he is a dog suited admirably to the show environment. He always looks keen to impress, has a cheeky extrovert nature and an exotic attractiveness.

The Shih Tzu is a sociable dog and an ideal family pet provided enough time is spent on daily maintenance of the luxurious coat. He likes the company of children and never misses an opportunity to play, this being undertaken with great gusto. He is quite a hardy little dog with a sturdy frame and he will enjoy moderate amounts of daily exercise.

KEY TO CHARACTER	
INTELLIGENCE	***
TEMPERAMENT	****
EASE OF COAT CARE	*
SUITABILITY FOR SMALL DWELLING	*****
******* (5) = VERY GOOD**	

BRITISH KENNEL CLUB STANDARD

SHIH TZU

GENERAL APPEARANCE. — Very active, lively and alert, with a distinctly arrogant carriage. The Shih Tzu is neither a terrier nor a toy dog.

Head and Skull. — Head broad and round; wide between the eyes. Shock-headed with hair falling well over the eyes. Good beard and whiskers; the hair growing upwards on the nose gives a distinctly chrysanthemum-like effect. Muzzle square and short, but not wrinkled like a Pekingese; flat and hairy. Nose black for preference and about one inch from tip to stop.

Eyes. — Large, dark and round but not prominent.

Ears. — Large, with long leathers, and carried drooping. Set slightly below the crown of the skull; so heavily coated that they appear to blend with the hair of the neck.

Mouth. — Level or slightly underhung.

Forequarters. — Legs short and muscular with ample bone. The legs should look massive on account of the wealth of hair.

Body. — Body between withers and root of tail should be longer than height at withers; well-coupled and sturdy; chest broad and deep, shoulders firm, back level.

Hindquarters. — Legs short and muscular with ample bone. They should look straight when viewed from the rear. Thighs well-round and muscular. Legs should look massive on account of the wealth of hair.

Feet. — Firm and well-padded. They should look big on account of the wealth of hair.

Tail. — Heavily plumed and curled well over back; carried gaily, set on high.

Coat. — Long and dense, but not curly, with good undercoat.

Colour. — All colours permissible, but a white blaze on the forehead and a white tip to the tail are highly prized. Dogs with liver markings may have dark liver noses and slightly lighter eyes. Pigmentation on muzzle as unbroken as possible.

Weight and Size. — 4.5 to 8.2 kg (10 to 18 lbs). Ideal weight 4.5 to 7.3 kg (10 to 16 lbs). Height at withers not more than 26.7 cm (10½"); type and breed characteristics of the utmost importance and on no account to be sacrificed to size alone.

Faults. — Narrow heads, pig-jaws, snipyness, pale pink noses and eye-rims, small or light eyes, legginess, sparse coats.

Note. — Male animals should have two apparently normal testicles fully descended into the scrotum.

MAIN AMERICAN KENNEL CLUB VARIATION TO STANDARD FOR THE SHIH TZU —

Size. — Height at withers 9 to 19½ inches, should be no more than 11 inches nor less than 8 inches. Weight of mature dogs 12 to 15 pounds, should be no more than 18 pounds nor less than 9 pounds.

SHIH TZU REGISTRATIONS 1981 — 87 INCLUSIVE

1981 — 1528
1982 — 1397
1983 — 1425
1984 — 1531
1985 — 1576
1986 — 1532
1987 — 1743

YET TO WIN CRUFTS BEST-IN-SHOW.

TIBETAN SPANIEL

Often mistaken for the shorter-faced Pekingese by the layman, the Tibetan Spaniel has unclear beginnings like most of the breeds from the east.

There is record of similar dogs being kept by the Tibetan monks for hundreds of years. Apparently the dogs would perform the quaint practice of turning their master's prayer wheels for them and this was probably still a common sight up until Tibet was invaded by the Chinese.

Although the Tibetan Spaniel, Pekingese, Tibetan Terrier and Lhasa Apso are all almost certainly related, it is not certain which of these breeds is the oldest. Any statements concerning the Tibetan Spaniel's early ancestry would be pure conjecture.

In 1958 the Tibetan Spaniel Association was formed in Britain and this perky, intelligent breed has experienced a steady if not meteoric rise in popularity. He is renowned as a first class show dog, being of convenient size, outgoing yet inoffensive nature and striking appearance when well groomed.

In the home he is safe in the company of small children and he will enjoy plenty of playful romps and regular walks, although his exercise needs are not excessive. Although slow to accept strangers, the Tibetan Spaniel is basically a sociable and commendable small dog.

KEY TO CHARACTER	
INTELLIGENCE	****
TEMPERAMENT	****
EASE OF COAT CARE	**
SUITABILITY FOR SMALL DWELLING	*****
***** (5) = VERY GOOD	

BRITISH KENNEL CLUB STANDARD

TIBETAN SPANIEL

CHARACTERISTICS. — Gay and assertive, highly intelligent, aloof with strangers.

GENERAL APPEARANCE. — Should be small, active and alert. The outline should give a well balanced appearance, slightly longer in body than height at withers.

Head and Skull. — Small in proportion to body and proudly carried giving an impression of quality. Masculine in dogs but free from coarseness. Skull slightly domed, moderate width and length. Stop slight, but defined. Medium length of muzzle, blunt with cushioning, free from wrinkle. The chin should show some depth and width. Nose black preferred.

Eyes. — Dark brown in colour, oval in shape, bright and expressive, of medium size set fairly well apart but forward looking giving an ape-like expression. Eye rims black.

Ears. — Medium size, pendant, well feathered in the adult and set fairly high. They may have a slight lift from the skull, but should not fly. Large heavy low set ears are not typical.

Mouth. — Ideally slightly undershot, the upper incisors fitting neatly inside and touching the lower incisors. Teeth should be evenly placed and the lower jaw wide between the canine tusks. Full dentition desired. A level mouth is permissible providing there is sufficient width and depth of chin to preserve the blunt appearance of muzzle. Teeth must not show when mouth is closed.

Neck. — Moderately short, strong and well set on. Covered with a mane or "shawl" of longer hair which is more pronounced in dogs than bitches.

Forequarters. — The bones of the forelegs slightly bowed but firm at shoulder. Moderate bone. Shoulder well placed.

Body. — Slightly longer from point of shoulder to root of tail than the height at withers, well ribbed with good depth, level back.

Hindquarters. — Well made and strong, hocks well let down and straight when viewed from behind. Stifle well developed, showing moderate angulation.

Feet. — Harefooted, small and neat with feathering between toes often extending beyond the feet. White markings allowed.

Gait. — Quick moving, straight, free, positive.

Tail. — Set high, richly plumed and carried in a gay curl over the back when moving. Should not be penalised for dropping tail when standing.

Coat. — Double coat, silky in texture, smooth on face and front of legs, of moderate length on body, but lying rather flat. Ears and back of forelegs nicely feathered, tail and buttocks well furnished with longer hair. Should not be over-coated and bitches tend to carry less coat and mane than dogs.

Colour. — All colours and mixture of colours allowed.

Weight and Size. — 4.1 to 6.8 kg (9 to 15 lbs) being ideal. Height about 25.4 cm (10″).

Faults. — Large full eyes, broad flat muzzle, very domed or flat wide skull, accentuated stop, pointed weak or wrinkled muzzle, overshot mouth, long plain down face without stop, very bowed or loose front, straight stifle, cow hocks, nervousness, cat feet, coarseness of type, mean expression, liver or putty coloured pigmentation, light eyes, protruding tongue.

Note. — Male animals should have two apparently normal testicles fully descended into the scrotum.

TIBETAN SPANIEL REGISTRATIONS 1981 — 87 INCLUSIVE

1981 — 430
1982 — 445
1983 — 493
1984 — 517
1985 — 462
1986 — 444
1987 — 400

YET TO WIN CRUFTS BEST-IN-SHOW.

TIBETAN TERRIER

The Tibetan Terrier is in fact not a true Terrier at all, such a name being given to dogs that burrow underground to locate game or vermin. Although this activity does not feature in the history of the Tibetan Terrier, his is still a working past.

In his homeland of Tibet he was known for thousands of years as the 'holy dog' and like most Tibetan breeds his early development was probably in the monastries. But he led a more rugged life than the other more pampered breeds and was used widely as a sheepdog and even in a guarding role. Although he was a more practically employed dog than, for instance the Tibetan Spaniel, he was still a breed that the Tibetans guarded jelously.

But eventually specimens did reach Europe. In Britain, it was very unclear at first as to what exactly constituted a Tibetan Terrier. Early dogs were known as Lhasa Terriers and some bore resemblance to the Shih Tzu or the Lhasa Apso and some were more like the modern Tibetan Terrier. It was not until the 1930's that the Tibetan Breeds Association was formed in a concerted effort to sort things out.

Since his proper classification, he has won a fair size following here and features quite strongly in the show world. Looking a little like a scaled-down Old English Sheepdog, he has a marvellous outgoing nature and strong prescence. His greatest physical asset is his coat which is stunning if properly prepared.

His guarding instinct is used to full effect in the home but that is normally the only aggression the Tibetan Terrier will show. He is full of fun and will enjoy plenty of exercise and play sessions.

KEY TO CHARACTER	
INTELLIGENCE	***
TEMPERAMENT	****
EASE OF COAT CARE	**
SUITABILITY FOR SMALL DWELLING	***
***** (5) = VERY GOOD	

BRITISH KENNEL CLUB STANDARD

TIBETAN TERRIER

CHARACTERISTICS. — Alert, intelligent and game, not fierce nor pugnacious. Chary of strangers.

GENERAL APPEARANCE. — A well muscled medium sized dog, in general appearance not unlike an Old English Sheepdog in miniature.

Head and Skull. — Skull of medium length, not broad or coarse, narrowing slightly from ear to eye, not domed but not absolutely flat between the ears. The malar bones are curved, but should not be over developed so as to bulge. There should be a marked stop in front of the eyes, but this must not be exaggerated. The head should be well furnished with long hair, falling forward over the eyes. The lower jaw should carry a small, but not exaggerated amount of beard. The length from eye to tip of nose equal to length from eye to base of skull; not broad nor massive. Nose black.

Eyes. — Large, dark, neither prominent nor sunken: should be set fairly wide apart. Eyelids dark.

Ears. — Pendent, not too close to head, V shaped, not too large, heavily feathered.

Mouth. — Level by preference but if slightly undershot not to be penalised.

Forequaters. — Legs parallel and heavily furnished. Pasterns slightly sloping.

Body. — Compact and powerful. Length from point of shoulder to root of tail equal to height at withers. Well ribbed up. Loin slightly arched.

Hindquarters. — Heavily furnished, should be slightly longer than forelegs with well bent stifles and low set hocks giving a level back.

Feet. — The feet should be large, round, heavily furnished with hair between the toes and pads. The dog should stand well down on its pads. There should be no arch in the feet.

Gait. — When walking or trotting the hind legs should neither go inside nor outside the front ones but run on the same track.

Tail. — Medium length, set on fairly high and carried in a gay curl over the back. Very well feathered. There is often a kink near the tip.

Coat. — Double coated. The undercoat fine wool, the top coat profuse, fine but not silky or woolly; long; either straight or waved.

Colour. — White, golden, cream, grey or smoke, black, particolour, and tri-colours; in fact any colour except chocolate or liver colour.

Size. — Height at shoulders, dogs should be from 35.6 to 40.6 cm (14 to 16″), bitches slightly smaller.

Faults. — A weak snipy foreface should be penalised. Lack of double coat, Cat feet.

Note. — Male animals should have two apparently normal testicles fully descended into the scrotum.

MAIN AMERICAN KENNEL CLUB VARIATION TO STANDARD FOR THE TIBETAN TERRIER —

Weight and Size. — Average weight 22 to 23 pounds, but may be 18 to 30 pounds.

TIBETAN TERRIER REGISTRATIONS 1981 — 87 INCLUSIVE

1981 — 404
1982 — 411
1983 — 571
1984 — 522
1985 — 601
1986 — 662
1987 — 625

YET TO WIN CRUFTS BEST-IN-SHOW.

PEDIGREE DOGS IN COLOUR

BOOK FIVE

WORKING GROUP

This is Book Five in a volume consisting of six books each dealing with a main group of dogs. The page numbering follows that used in the main volume.

BEARDED COLLIE

The Bearded Collie or "Beardie" as he is nicknamed, has the alert, eager expression that is found in all the more intelligent breeds. This intelligence is matched by a perfect temperament and he makes a pet and companion of great interest and loyalty.

The far north of England and in particular Scotland, saw the birth of the breed, but the exact crosses made for his production are unclear. It is generally thought, though, that the Collie and Scottish Deerhound were involved with perhaps a European breed. The idea behind the Bearded Collie's conception was to develop a breed that would suit all the needs of the Scottish and North England farmers who worked bleak, rugged farms. As is plain to see the coat is an ideal weather combatant and of course a quick thinking, natural herding dog was the primary aim. So the dog arrived at was an outstanding worker in all weathers, with a sociable disposition in the home. In his early days the Beardie was called the Highland Collie or Scottish Highland Collie, the name not being altered until much later.

It takes some eighteen months for the magnificent coat to fully develop and the colour tends to lighten with age. This coat and of course "beard" are often the first attraction to this breed, but it should be remembered that it will become terribly matted and unsightly without regular care. An active, outdoor-type owner would be ideal for a Beardie.

KEY TO CHARACTER	
INTELLIGENCE	*****
TEMPERAMENT	*****
EASE OF COAT CARE	**
SUITABILITY FOR SMALL DWELLING	*
***** (5) = VERY GOOD	

BRITISH KENNEL CLUB STANDARD

BEARDED COLLIE

CHARACTERISTICS. — The Bearded Collie should be alert, lively, self confident and active. The temperament should be that of a steady intelligent working dog, with no signs of nervousness or aggression.

GENERAL APPEARANCE. — A lean active dog, longer than it is high in an approximate proportion of 5-4, measured from point of chest to point of buttock. Bitches may be slightly longer. The breed, though strongly made, should show plenty of daylight under the body and should not look too heavy. A bright, enquiring expression is a distinctive feature of the breed.

Head and Skull. — The head should be in proportion to the size of the dog. The skull broad and flat and square, the distance between stop and occiput being equal to the width between the orifices of the ears. The muzzle strong and equal in length to the distance from the stop to the occiput, the whole effect being that of a dog with strength of muzzle and plenty of brain room. The stop should be moderate. The nose large and square, generally black but normally following the coat colour in blues and browns. The nose and lips should be of solid colour without spots or patches. Pigmentation of lips and eye rims should follow nose colour.

Eyes. — The eyes should tone with coat in colour, be set widely apart and be large, soft and affectionate, but not protruding. The eyebrows arched up and forward but not so long as to obscure the eyes.

Ears. — The ears of medium size and drooping. When the dog is alert, the ears should lift at the base level with, but not above, the top of the skull, increasing the apparent breadth of the skull.

Mouth. — The teeth large and white, the incisors of the lower jaw fitting tightly behind those of the upper jaw. However, a pincer bite is acceptable.

Neck. — Moderate length, muscular and slightly arched.

Forequarters. — The shoulders should slope well back: a line drawn through the centre of the shoulder blade should form a right angle (90°) with the humerus. The shoulder blades at the withers should be separated only by the vertebrae but should slope outwards from there sufficiently to accommodate the desired spring of rib. Legs straight and vertical, with good bone, and covered with shaggy hair all round. Pasterns flexible without weakness.

Body. — The length of the back should come from the length of the ribcage and not that of the loin. The back level and ribs well sprung but not barrelled. The loins should be strong and the chest deep, giving plenty of heart and lung room.

Hindquarters. — Well muscled with good second thighs, well bent stifles and low hocks. The lower leg should fall at the right angle to the ground and, in normal stance, should be just behind a line vertically below the point of the buttock.

Feet. — Oval in shape with the soles well padded. The toes arched and close together, well covered with hair including between the pads.

Gait. — Movement should be supple, smooth and long reaching, covering the ground with the minimum of effort.

Tail. — Set low, without kink or twist, and long enough for the end of the bone to reach at least the point of the hock. Carried low with an upward swirl at the tip whilst standing or walking, but may be extended at speed. Never carried over the back. Covered with abundant hair.

Coat. — Double with the undercoat soft, furry and close. Outercoat flat, harsh, strong and shaggy, free from woolliness and curl, though a slight wave is permissible. Length and density of the hair should be sufficient to provide a protective coat and to enhance the shape of the dog, but not enough to obscure the natural lines of the body. The coat must not be trimmed in any way. On the head, the bridge of the nose should be sparsely covered with hair which is slightly longer on the side just to cover the lips. From the cheeks, the lower lips and under the chin, the coat should increase in length towards the chest, forming the typical beard.

Colour. — Slate grey, reddish fawn, black, blue, all shades of grey, brown and sandy, with or without white markings. Where white occurs it should appear on the foreface, as a blaze on the skull, on the tip of the tail, on the chest, legs and feet and, if round the collar, the roots of the white hair should not extend behind the shoulder. White should not appear above the hocks on the outside of the hind legs. Slight tan markings are acceptable on the eyebrows, inside the ears, on the cheeks, under the root of the tail, and on the legs where white joins the main colour.

Size. — Ideal height at the shoulder: Dogs 53 to 56cm (21 to 22 in) Bitchess 51 to 53cm (20 to 21 in). Overall quality and proportions should be considered before size but excessive variation from the ideal height should be discouraged.

Faults. — Any departure from the foregoing points should be considered a fault and the seriousness with which the fault is regarded should be in exact proportion to its degree.

Note. — Male animals should have two apparently normal testicles fully descended into the scrotum.

BEARDED COLLIE REGISTRATIONS 1981 — 87 INCLUSIVE

1981 — 1179
1982 — 1179
1983 — 1371
1984 — 1487
1985 — 1443
1986 — 1487
1987 — 1496

YET TO WIN CRUFTS BEST-IN-SHOW.

BELGIAN SHEPHERD DOG (GROENENDAEL)

The Groenendael is the most well known of the four Belgain Sheepdogs registered with the Kennel Club. Although similar in conformation to the others, he possesses a rich black coat, not present in any of his relatives.

Named after the Belgian town of Groenendael which was responsible for his early development, this breed was first registered in 1891.

The Belgians have always rated the Groenendael's working abilities extremely highly and have also extolled the virtues of his excellent behaviour in the family environment. These features coupled with his attractive appearance have also led to the Groenendael's growing popularity in the U.S.A., the first specimens having been imported there in the early part of this century. He is known simply as the Belgian Sheepdog in the U.S.A., the Malinois and Tervueren varieties being given their normal titles (the Laekenois is not officially recognised in the U.S.A.).

Although still something of a minority breed in Britain, the Groenendael is slowly becoming more popular with many appearing at the larger dog shows. This is not surprising as a well groomed specimen can look stunning.

The Groenendael makes a first class pet for any active owner. His intelligence, good nature even with small children and strong guarding instinct make him a faultless house dog. Brushing must be fairly frequent and exercise should be as lengthy and interesting as possible.

KEY TO CHARACTER	
INTELLIGENCE	*****
TEMPERAMENT	*****
EASE OF COAT CARE	***
SUITABILITY FOR SMALL DWELLING	*
***** (5) = VERY GOOD	

BRITISH KENNEL CLUB STANDARD
BELGIAN SHEPHERD DOG (GROENENDAEL)

GENERAL APPEARANCE. — A medium-sized dog, well proportioned, intelligent, hardy, and bred to withstand adverse weather. It should be alert and attentive with a lively and enquiring mien.

CHARACTERISTICS. — With its fine proportions and proud carriage of the head, the Belgian Shepherd Dog should convey an impression of that graceful strength which has become the mark of selected representatives of a working breed. In addition to its inborn skill as a sheep-dog, it has a great potential as a guard dog. Should be wary, but not timid, nervous or overly aggressive.

Head and Skull. — The head should be finely chiselled, long, but not excessively so, and gaunt. The skull and muzzle should be roughly equal in length, with at most a slight bias in favour of the muzzle, giving the impression of a balanced whole. The skull should be of medium width in proportion to the length of the head, flattened rather than rounded forehead and centre line not very pronounced; seen in profile it should be parallel to an imaginary line extending the muzzle line. The muzzle should be of medium length tapering gradually towards the nose. The nose should be black with well-flared nostrils. Moderate stop.

Eyes. — Of medium size, neither protruding nor sunken, slightly almond-shaped, brownish coloured and preferably dark; black ringed eyelids. Direct, lively and inquiring look. Arches above the eyes not prominent the muzzle finely chiselled under the eyes.

Ears. — Distinctly triangular appearance, stiff and erect, set high, of proportionate length, with the external ear well rounded at the base.

Mouth. — Wide, Lips thin-textured, very firm, strongly pigmented, not showing the red of the mucous membranes. Cheeks spare, quite flat but well-muscled. Strong, white, regular teeth firmly set in well-developed jaws. Scissor bite, i.e., the incisors of the upper jaw fitting closely over those of the lower jaw, extending slightly beyond them without losing contact with them. Edge to edge bite tolerated.

Neck. — Very supple. The neck should be slightly elongated, well-muscled and without dewlap, broadening slightly towards the shoulders. The nape should be very slightly arched.

Forequarters. — Strongly boned throughout with wiry and powerful muscle structure. The shoulder blades should be long and oblique, firmly attached, flat, forming an angle with the humerus, so as to enable the elbows to work easily. The forelegs should be long and well-muscled, and should move parallel. The bones joining the feet and pastern joint should be strong and short. Pastern joint clearly defined. Feet round, toes arched and very close together; soles thick and springy with large dark claws. Dew claws are permitted.

Body. — The body should be powerful without being bulky. The length from the point of the shoulder to the point of the buttocks should be approximately equal to the height at the withers in the case of the male; in the female it may be slightly greater. The chest should not be very broad but deep and low. Ribs should be well sprung. The upper line of the body (back and lumbar region) should be straight, broad and powerfully muscled. The belly should be moderately developed neither drooping nor unduly cut-up, continuing the lower line of the chest in a graceful curve. The rump should be very slightly sloping, broad but not excessively so. Male animals should have two apparently normal testicles fully descended into the scrotum.

Hindquarters. — The hindquarters should be well muscled and powerful but not bulky. Good, but not excessive, angulation, with hocks close to the ground. Viewed from behind the legs should be parallel. Dew claws are not permitted. Feet slightly oval, toes arched and very close together; soles thick and springy with large dark claws.

Tail. — The tail should be firmly set, strong at the base and of medium length. At rest it should hang down, with the tip slightly bent backwards at the level of the hock; on the move it should lift, accentuating the curve towards the tip; however it should under no circumstances curl up or bend to one side and at no time should any part of the tail be lifted above the line of the back.

Gait. — Movement should be brisk and even, covering the maximum amount of ground.

Coat. — The outer coat should be long, straight and abundant. It should not be silky or wiry, the texture should be of medium harshness. The undercoat should be extremely dense. The hair should be shorter on the head, outside of the ears and lower part of the legs. The opening of the ear should be protected by hair. The hair should be especially long and abundant, like a ruff around the neck, particularly in the male. There should be a fringe of long hair down the back of the forearm, long and abundant hair evident on the hindquarters and the tail. The male should be longer coated than the female.

Colour. — Black. May be completely black or black with limited white as follows:— Small to moderate patch or stip on chest, between pads of the feet and on the tips of the hind toes. Frosting (white or grey) on the muzzle.

Skin. — Springy but quite taut over the whole body. All external mucous membranes highly pigmented.

Size. — The desired height for the male is 61 to 66cm (24 to 26 in) and for the female: 56 to 61cm (22 to 24 in).

Faults. — Any departure form the foregoing points should be considered a fault and the seriousness with which the fault is regarded should be in exact proportion to its degree.

Note. — Male animals should have two apparently normal testicles fully descended into the scrotum.

MAIN AMERICAN KENNEL CLUB VARIATION TO STANDARD FOR THE BELGIAN SHEPHERD DOG (GROENENDAEL) —

Known as the Belgian Sheepdog in the U.S.A.

GROENENDAEL REGISTRATIONS 1981 — 87 INCLUSIVE

1981 — 149
1982 — 145
1983 — 148
1984 — 109
1985 — 170
1986 — 168
1987 — 244

YET TO WIN CRUFTS BEST-IN-SHOW.

BELGIAN SHEPHERD DOG (TERVUEREN)

The attractive Tervueren is very similar to his close relative the Groenendael. In all aspects except coat colour they are practically identical. The Tervueren has a glorious red coat with the hairs tipped black to give a striking overlay effect.

His development ran parallel with the other Belgian Shepherd Dogs and he was recognised in his home country in 1891. The colour seems to have been developed purely as a result of the personal preference of some early Belgian Shepherd Dog enthusiasts.

He has been and still is used as a herding dog, a job which makes use of his high level of intelligence and physical toughness. Tervuerens have also distinguished themselves in wartime when acting as messenger dogs in the very heart of battle. He combines this fine working ability with striking good looks and he has slowly made his presence felt in the show worlds of the U.S.A. and Britain as well as Europe.

At first glance the Tervueren could conceivably be mistaken for a German Shepherd Dog and the similarity goes beyond the physical appearance.

This is a very active, demanding breed who will enjoy a good deal of mental stimulation and off-the-lead exercise. With perserverance he can reach a high standard of obedience and can make an excellent house-dog. He will guard his master's home very effectively and will show great devotion to all members of the family.

KEY TO CHARACTER	
INTELLIGENCE	*****
TEMPERAMENT	****
EASE OF COAT CARE	***
SUITABILITY FOR SMALL DWELLING	*
***** (5) = VERY GOOD	

BRITISH KENNEL CLUB STANDARD

ITERIM STANDARD OF THE BELGIAN SHEPHERD DOG (TERVUEREN)

GENERAL APPEARANCE. — A medium-sized dog, well proportioned, intelligent, hardy, and bred to withstand adverse weather. It should be alert and attentive with a lively and enquiring mien.

CHARACTERISTICS. — With its fine proportions and proud carriage of the head, the Belgian Shepherd Dog should convey an impression of that graceful strength which has become the mark of selected representatives of a working breed. In addition to its inborn skill as a sheep-dog, it has a great potential as a guard dog. Should be wary, but not timid, nervous or overly aggressive.

Head and Skull. — The head should be finely chiselled, long, but not excessively so, and gaunt. The skull and muzzle should be roughly equal in length, with at most a slight bias in favour of the muzzle, giving the impression of a balanced whole. The skull should be of medium width in proportion to the length of the head, flattened rather than rounded forehead and centre line not very pronounced; seen in profile it should be parallel to an imaginary line extending the muzzle line. The muzzle should be of medium length tapering gradually towards the nose. The nose should be black with well-flared nostrils. Moderate stop.

Eyes. — Of medium size, neither protruding nor sunken, slightly almond-shaped, brownish coloured and preferably dark; black ringed eyelids. Direct, lively and inquiring look. Arches above the eyes not prominent the muzzle finely chiselled under the eyes.

Ears. — Distincly triangular appearance, stiff and erect, set high, of proportionate length, with the external ear well rounded at the base.

Mouth. — Wide. Lips thin-textured, very firm, strongly pigmented, not showing the red of the mucous membranes. Cheeks spare, quite flat but well-muscled. Strong, white, regular teeth firmly set in well-developed jaws. Scissor bite, i.e., the incisors of the upper jaw fitting closely over those of the lower jaw, extending slightly beyond them without losing contact with them. Edge to edge bite tolerated.

Neck. — Very supple. The neck should be slightly elongated, well-muscled and without dewlap, broadening slightly towards the shoulders. The nape should be very slightly arched.

Forequarters. — Strongly boned throughout with wiry and powerful muscle structure. The shoulder blades should be long and oblique, firmly attached, flat, forming an angle with the humerus, so as to enable the elbows to work easily. The forelegs should b long and well-muscled, and should move parallel. The bones joining the feet and pastern joint should be strong and short. Pastern joint clearly defined. Feet round, toes arched and very close together; soles thick and springy with large dark claws. Dew claws are permitted.

Body. — The body should be powerful without being bulky. The length from the point of the shoulder to the point of the buttocks should be approximately equal to the height at the withers in the case of the male; in the female it may be slightly greater. The chest should not be very broad but deep and low. Ribs should be well sprung. The upper line of the body (black and lumbar region) should be straight, broad and powerfully muscled. The belly should be moderately developed neither drooping nor unduly cut-up, continuing the lower line of the chest in a graceful curve. The rump should be very slightly sloping, broad but not excessively so.

Hindquarters. — The hindquarters should be well muscled and powerful but not bulky. Good, but not excessive, angulation, with hocks close to the ground. Viewed from behind the legs should be parallel. Dew claws are not permitted. Feet slightly oval, toes arched and very close together; soles thick and springy with large dark claws.

Tail. — The tail should be firmly set, strong at the base and of medium length. At rest it should hang down, with the tip slightly bent backwards at the level of the hock; on the move it should lift, accentuating the curve towards the tip; however it should under no circumstances curl up or bend to one side and at no time should any part of the tail be lifted above the line of the back.

Gait. — Movement should be brisk and even, covering the maximum amount of ground.

Coat. — The outer coat should be long, straight and abundant. It should not be silky or wiry, the texture should be of medium harshness. The undercoat should be extremely dense. The hair should be shorter on the head, outside of the ears and lower part of the legs. The opening of the ear should be protected by hair. The hair should be especially long and abundant, like a ruff around the neck, particularly in the male. There should be a fringe of long hair down the back of the forearm, long and abundant hair evident on the hindquarters and the tail. The male should be longer coated than the female.

Colour. — Colour may include all shades of red, fawn, also grey with black overlay. The coat should be characteristically double pigmented, wherein the tip of each light coloured hair is blackened. On mature males this blackening should be especially pronouned on the shoulders, back and rib section. The face should have a black mask, not to extend above the line of the eyes, and the ears should be mostly black. The tail should typically have a darker or black tip. Small to moderate white patch or strip permitted on chest, between pads of feet and on the tips of the hind toes. Frosting (white or grey) on the muzzle. Beyond the age of 18 months a washed out colour or colour too black resembling a Groenendael should be considered a fault.

Skin. — Springy but quite taut over the whole body. All external mucous membranes highly pigmented.

Size. — The desired height for the male is 61 to 66cm (24 to 26 in) and for the female: 56 to 61cm (22 to 24 in).

Faults. — Any departure from the foregoing points should be considered a fault and the seriousness with which the fault is regarded should be in exact proportion to its degree.

Note. — Male animals should have two apparently normal testicles fully descended into the scrotum.

MAIN AMERICAN KENNEL CLUB VARIATION TO STANDARD FOR THE BELGAIN SHEPHERD DOG (TERVUEREN) —

Known as the Belgian Tervueren in the U.S.A.

TERVUEREN REGISTRATIONS 1981 — 87 INCLUSIVE

1981 — 109
1982 — 137
1983 — 241
1984 — 255
1985 — 299
1986 — 321
1987 — 286

YET TO WIN CRUFTS BEST-IN-SHOW.

BERNESE MOUNTAIN DOG

The Bernese Mountain Dog must surely be one of the most striking of all the larger breeds, combining good looks with a friendly, yet positive personality.

He is one of the four Sennenhunde of Switzerland, the others being the Great Swiss, the Appenzell and the Entlebuch. All three of these breeds are short coated and are virtually unknown outside Switzerland.

Like all of the heavy mountain dogs of the world, the Bernese can trace his ancestry to the first Mastiff-types of thousands of years ago. His more recent history though, has been centred around the town from which he takes his name, Berne. For centuries the people of Berne have used this breed to haul small carts and as a herder, both tasks suiting his nartural attributes of strength and adaptability.

The breed fell into decline upon the demise of carts as a popular form of goods delivery and a certain Professor Heim was responsible for the resurrection of the Bernese into a common breed once more. He carefully began a breeding programme which incorportated only the finest remaining specimens. His work was a great success and by the 1930's, Britain and the U.S.A., has acquired specimens. The popularity of the Bernese has, not surprisingly, increased in both these countries since the second World War.

Space must be a major consideration for anybody contemplating owning a Bernese Mountain Dog, ideally he would live in rural surroundings but, if considerable time and effort can be given to exercise and training, then this is a breed to grace any home. He is quick to learn, has a superb disposition and is a forthright and confident guard.

KEY TO CHARACTER	
INTELLIGENCE	****
TEMPERAMENT	*****
EASE OF COAT CARE	***
SUITABILITY FOR SMALL DWELLING	*
***** (5) = VERY GOOD	

BRITISH KENNEL CLUB STANDARD

ITERIM STANDARD OF THE BERNESE MOUNTAIN DOG

CHARACTERISTICS. — Self confident, good natured. Agressiveness must not be tolerated. Slow to mature.

GENERAL APPEARANCE. — Above medium sized, strong, sturdy working dog, active, alert, well boned, of striking colour.

Head and Skull. — Strong with flat skull and slightly developed furrow, well defined stop, strong straight muzzle. Lips slightly developed.

Eyes. — Dark brown and almond-shaped, eyelids tight.

Ears. — Medium sized ears, set high, triangular shaped, lying flat in repose, when alert brought slightly forward, and raised at the base.

Mouth. — Scissor bite.

Neck. — Strong, muscular and of medium length.

Forequarters. — Shoulders long, strong and sloping, with upper arm forming a distinct angle, flat lying and well muscled. Appears straight from all sides. Pastern flexing slightly.

Body. — Compact rather than long. Ratio height to length 9:10. Broad chest with, good depth of brisket reaching at least to the elbow. Well ribbed; strong loins. Back firm and straight. rump smoothly rounded.

Hindquarters. — Quarters broad, strong and well muscled. Stifes well bent. Hock strong, well let down and turning neither in nor out. Dewclaws should be removed.

Feet. — Short, round and compact.

Gait. — Stride reaching out well in front, following well through behind, balanced stride in all gaits.

Tail. — Bushy, reaching just below hock; may be raised when dog alert or moving but never curled or carried above level of back.

Coat. — Soft and silky with bright natural sheen, long and slightly wavy, but should not curl when mature.

Colour. — Jet black, with rich reddish brown on the cheeks, over the eyes, on all four legs and on chest. Slight to medium sized symmetrical white head marking (blaze) and white chest marking (cross), are essential. Preferred but not essential, white paws, white not reaching higher than the pastern, white tip to tail. A few white hairs at nape of neck, and white anal patch undesirable but tolerated.

Weight and Size. — Dogs: 64 to 70cm. (25 to 27½ in) at the withers, preferred size 66 to 68cm. (26 to 26¾ in). Bitches: 58 to 66cm. (23 to 26 in) at the withers, preferred size 60 to 63cm. (23½ to 25 in).

Temperament. — Self-confident, good natured, friendly and fearless.

Faults. — Any departure from the foregoing points should be considered a fault and the seriousness of the fault should be in exact proportion to its degree.

Note. — Male animals should have two apparently normal testicles fully descended into the scrotum.

MAIN AMERICAN KENNEL CLUB VARIATION TO STANDARD FOR THE BERNESE MOUNTAIN DOG —

Height. — Dogs: 24½ inches to 27½ inches at the withers. Bitches: 22½ inches to 25½ inches at the withers.

BERNESE MOUNTAIN DOG REGISTRATIONS 1981 — 87 INCLUSIVE

1981 — 199
1982 — 246
1983 — 301
1984 — 301
1985 — 557
1986 — 485
1987 — 565

YET TO WIN CRUFTS BEST-IN-SHOW.

BORDER COLLIE

The Border Collie is to be found all over the world working as a skilful herder of sheep and cattle. This talent was nurtured in his place of origin, the country of the English-Scottish border. Many Collie-type dogs have always existed in this area and their appearance was of little importance. But eventually a single supreme strain of sheepdog began to appear and, with some variation, this dog resembled today's Border Collie.

For many years he was used virtually exclusively as a working dog, but he also has fine qualities as a companion for man and demand grew for a standardised breed. This was arrived at as recently as 1976 and now as well as continuing as the most successful of all sheepdogs, he has gained a following in the show world. Although he does have an attractive appearance, it is in obedience competitions and sheepdog trials where he really excels. He combines uncanny trainability and intelligence with great speed and agility.

One of the kindest natured dogs, the Border Collie is well suited to a home with children and his love of games will constantly amuse them. Town living is possible but the ideal situation for this breed would be a rural existence with many long walks and runs. He will thrive on being constantly active, both physically and mentally.

KEY TO CHARACTER	
INTELLIGENCE	*****
TEMPERAMENT	*****
EASE OF COAT CARE	***
SUITABILITY FOR SMALL DWELLING	**
***** (5) = VERY GOOD	

BRITISH KENNEL CLUB STANDARD

INTERIM STANDARD OF THE BORDER COLLIE

CHARACTERISTICS. — Should be neither nervous nor agressive, but keen, alert, responsive and intelligent.

GENERAL APPEARANCE. — The general appearance should be that of a well proportioned dog, the smooth outline showing quality, gracefulness and perfect balance, combined with sufficient substance to convey the impression that it is capable of endurance. Any tendency to coarseness or weediness is undesirable.

Head and Skull. — Skull fairly broad, occiput not pronounced. Cheeks should not be full or rounded. The muzzle, tapering to the nose, should be moderately short and strong, and the skull and foreface should be approximately the same length. Nose black, nostrils well developed. Stop very distinct.

Eyes. — The eyes should be set wide apart, oval shaped of moderate size and dark brown in colour, except in the case of merles where one or both, or part of one or both, may be blue. The expression should be mild yet keen.

Ears. — The ears should be of medium size and texture, set well apart, carried semi-erect and sensitive in their use. Inside the ear should be well furnished with hair.

Mouth. — The teeth should be strong, with perfect regular and complete scissor bite, i.e. the upper teeth closely overlapping the lower teeth and set square to the jaws.

Neck. — The neck should be of good length, strong and muscular, slightly arched and broadening to the shoulders.

Forequarters. — Front legs parallel when viewed from front, pasterns sloping slightly when viewed from side. Bone should be round and strong but not heavy. Shoulders well laid back, elbows close to the body.

Body. — Ribs well sprung, chest deep and rather broad. The back should be broad and strong, and loins deep, muscular and slightly arched. The body should be slightly longer than it is high at the shoulder.

Hindquarters. — The hindquarters should be broad and muscular, in profile sloping gracefully to the set on of the tail. The thighs should be long, broad, deep, muscular with well turned stifles and strong hocks, well let down. From hock to ground the hind legs should be well boned and parallel when viewed from the rear.

Feet. — Oval in shape, pads deep, strong and sound, toes arched and close together. Nails short and strong.

Gait. — The movement should be free, smooth and tireless, with a minimum lift to feet, conveying the impression of the ability to move with great stealth and speed.

Tail. — The tail should be moderately long, the bone reaching at lest to the hock joint, set on low, well furnished and with an upward swirl towards the end, completing the graceful contour and balance of the dog. The tail may be raised in excitement but never carried over the back.

Coat. — There are two varieties of coat, one moderately long, the other smooth. In both, the topcoat should be dense and medium textured, the undercoat short, soft and dense to give good weather resistance. In the moderately long coated variety, there should be abundant coat to form a mane, breeching and brush. On face, ears, forelegs (except for feather) hindlegs from hock to ground, the hair should be short and smooth.

Colour. — A variety of colours is permissible, but white should never predominate.

Size. — Ideal height: Dogs about 53cm (21 in). Bitches slightly less.

Faults. — Any departure from the foregoing points should be considered a fault and the seriousness of the fault should be in exact proportion to its degree.

Note. — Male animals should have two apparently normal testicles fully descended into the scrotum.

BORDER COLLIE REGISTRATIONS 1981 — 87 INCLUSIVE

1981 — 718
1982 — 756
1983 — 768
1984 — 968
1985 — 1052
1986 — 1131
1987 — 1158

YET TO WIN CRUFTS BEST-IN-SHOW.

BOUVIER DES FLANDRES

This powerful working dog takes his name from Flanders in Belgium where he has been established for almost a century. He was developed from many varieties of Belgian herding dogs, at first in a rather slap-dash manner. But by 1912 some sort of rational attempt was made at standardising the Bouvier des Flandres. There was great debate amongst Belgian dog fanciers and a single undisputed standard was not formulated until 1961. Part of the reason for this enormous delay was that the Bouvier was a breed that suffered badly during World War 1 and was in fact nearly decimated.

This breed is one of the worlds finest cattle droving dogs and it is small wonder when you consider his prodigious strength and industrious nature. His willingness and ability to learn any task is well known to Belgian farmers and cart pulling and tracking have featured in his working repertoire. As a house guard there is none better and his ferocious appearance is enhanced by the cropped ears seen on all Bouviers in Belgium.

Anyone considering owning this breed must have plenty of room and a willingness to give his dog lengthy and frequent outdoor exercise. He makes a good housedog but he should be treated with respect that a dog of such power deserves and sensible training should begin very early in the Bouvier's life. Given these provisions his intelligence and good nature will flourish and make him a valued, loyal companion.

KEY TO CHARACTER	
INTELLIGENCE	****
TEMPERAMENT	****
EASE OF COAT CARE	***
SUITABILITY FOR SMALL DWELLING	*
***** (5) = VERY GOOD	

BRITISH KENNEL CLUB STANDARD

ITERIM STANDARD OF THE BOUVIER DES FLANDRES

CHARACTERISTICS. — By his lively appearance he should reveal his intelligence, energy and audacity. His temperament should be calm and sensible.

GENERAL APPEARANCE. — Rather short legged and cobby, the body set on well muscled, strong legs, giving the impression of great strength without clumsiness.

Head and Skull. — The head should appear big, the moustache and beard making it appear even more so, in proportion to the body and height. When handled it should be found to be well chiselled. Well developed and flat, the skull should be slightly broader than it is long. The lines of the under side of the skull and the top should be parallel. The proportion of the length of the skull in relation to the muzzle should be as 3 is to 2. A very slight furrow in the forehead. The stop not very deep, but appearing so, due to the heavy eyebrows. The muzzle broad, strong and bony, rectangular when seen from the front, gradually narrowing towards the nose, but never becoming pointed. The circumference, measured just in front of eyes, should be approximately equal to the length of the head. Extending the foreface in a slightly convex line towards its tip, the nose should be very well developed, rounded at its edges and always black. Nostrils wide. Cheeks flat and clean.

Eyes. — Honest, alert in expression. Neither protruding nor set too deeply. Slightly oval in shape and horizontally placed. As dark as possible in colour in relation to the coat. Light or wild looking eyes to be strongly penalised. Eyelids black, with no sign of loss of pigment. Conjunctiva should never be visible.

Ears. — Set on high, very flexible; in proportion to the head.

Mouth. — Jaws strong and of equal length. Teeth strong and white with a perfect regular and complete scissor bite i.e. the upper teeth closely overlapping the lower teeth and set square to the jaws.

Neck. — Strong, well muscled and thickening slightly towards the shoulders. A little longer than the length of the head, nape strong and arched. No sign of dewlap.

Forequarters. — Forelegs very strong and absolutely straight. Shoulders relatively long, muscular without heaviness and placed obliquely. Shoulder blade and upper arm of equal length. Elbows set well into body and parallel, never turning in or out. Forearms, seen either from the front or the side, absolutely straight, parallel to each other and perpendiculr to the ground. Well muscled and heavy boned. Pasterns strong, fairly short, sloping very slightly.

Body. — Strong, deep, broad and compact with very little tuck-up. Length from point of shoulder to point of buttock about equal to height at withers. Chest should descend to level of elbows and should not be cylindrical, although the ribs should be well sprung. Croup should continue, as far as possible, the horizontal line of the back and blend imperceptibly with the curve of the rump. Broad but not excessively so in the dog, broader in the bitch. A rising croup, or one which falls away, is a very serious fault.

Hindquarters. — Hindlegs very strong with pronounced muscle. They should move in the same plane as the forelegs. Thighs broad and well muscled. Hocks well let down. Dew claws should be removed.

Feet. — Short, round and compact. Toes tight and well arched. Nails black and strong. Pads thick and hard.

Gait. — Proud, upright bearing. Ambling is permitted.

Tail. — Docked to 2 to 3 vertebrae. It should continue the normal line of the vertebral column and be carried gaily when moving. Dogs born tailless should not be faulted for this.

Coat. — Hair coarse to touch, dry and matt. Neither too long nor too short (about 6cms (2½ in)) unkept looking but never woolly nor curly. On the head it should be shorter and the outside of the ears almost bare, with the inside of the ear protected by fairly long hair. The coat should be particularly thick and "crackly" on the top of the back, gradually becoming shorter as it comes down the legs. It should be always harsh. A flat coat is to be avoided since it denotes lack of undercoat, which should be normally fine and close grained. The upper lip well moutached, the lower carrying a full harsh beard, which gives the forbidding expression so characteristic of the breed. Eyebrows formed of backward sweeping hairs which accentuate the shape of the eyebrows but which never hide the eyes.

Colour. — Usually fawn or grey, often brindled or shaded. Black is also permissible and no colour shall have preference. Light, washed out shades are undesirable.

Weight and Size. — Ideal Weight: Dogs 35 to 40 kgs (77 to 88 lbs). Bitches 27 to 35 kgs (59½ to 77 lbs). Ideal Height: Dogs 62 to 68 cms (24½ to 27 in); Bitches 59 to 65 cms (23 to 25½ in). In either sex the ideal is midway between the measurements.

Faults. — Any departure from the foregoing points should be considered a fault and the seriousness with which the fault is regarded should be in exact proportion to its degree.

Note. — Male animals should have two apparently normal testicles fully descended into the scrotum.

MAIN AMERICAN KENNEL CLUB VARIATION TO STANDARD FOR THE BOUVIER DES FLANDRES —

Height. — The height as measured at the withers from 24½ to 27½ inches. Bitches, from 23½ to 26½ inches. In each sex, the ideal height is the median of the two limits, i.e. 26 inches for a dog and 25 inches for a bitch.

BOUVIER DES FLANDRES REGISTRATIONS 1981 — 87 INCLUSIVE

1981 — 56
1982 — 68
1983 — 151
1984 — 125
1985 — 134
1986 — 136
1987 — 228

YET TO WIN CRUFTS BEST-IN-SHOW.

BOXER

As his heavily muscled physique would suggest, the Boxer is descended from powerful fighting dogs. He has ancestors going as far back as the days of the Roman Empire when huge, ferocious Mastiff type dogs were common. These were used mainly for purposes of gory entertainment in the fighting arena. This type of dog gave rise to all the thicker set Mastiff types we know now and one such breed, now extinct was the Bullenbeiser. This was a breed much in evidence in Germany prior to 1800 and was a fearless hunting dog of solid proportions. Used for the pursuit of wild ox ("Bullenbeiser" translating to "Bull biter"), these dogs were a larger, more athletic type of Bulldog and it was the crossing of the Bullenbeiser with the English Bulldog which produced the early Boxers.

Breeding of the Boxer began in earnest at the end of the 19th Century. The meticulous German breeders went through much painstaking selective breeding and dispute among themselves before finally drawing up the perfected Boxer standard in 1910. It was about ten years later that the first dogs reached Britain and from then on the breed has become hugely successful here.

Despite the grisly past of his forefathers, the Boxer is an excellent family dog. He loves human company and is kind and affectionate with even the most boisterous of children. He needs firm training but has the necessary intelligence to grasp many tasks and has shown his worth in police and military service. The Boxer is an excellent guard and is clean and manageable. Plenty of vigorous exercise is essential to maintain his naturally superb muscle tone.

KEY TO CHARACTER	
INTELLIGENCE	****
TEMPERAMENT	****
EASE OF COAT CARE	*****
SUITABILITY FOR SMALL DWELLING	*
***** (5) = **VERY GOOD**	

BRITISH KENNEL CLUB STANDARD

BOXER

CHARACTERISTICS. — The character of the Boxer is of the greatest importance and demands the most careful attention. He is renowned from olden times for his great love and faithfulness to his master and household, his alertness and fearless courage as a defender and protector. The Boxer is docile but distrustful of strangers. He is bright and friendly in play but brave and determined when roused. His intelligence and willing tractability, his modesty, and cleanliness make him a highly desirable family dog and cheerful companion. He is the soul of honesty and loyalty. He is never false or treacherous even in his old age.

GENERAL APPEARANCE. — The Boxer is a medium sized, sturdy, smooth haired dog of short square figure and strong limb. The musculation is clean and powerfully developed, and should stand out plastically from under the skin. Movement of the Boxer should be alive with energy. His gait, although firm, is elastic. The stride free and roomy; carriage proud and noble. As a service and guard dog he must combine a considerable degree of elegance with the substance and power essential to his duties; those of an enduring escort dog whether with horse, bicycle or carriage and as a splendid jumper. Only a body whose individual limbs are built to withstasnd the most strenuous "mechanical" effort and assembled as a complete and harmonious whole, can respond to such demands. Therefore to be at its highest efficiency, the Boxer must never be plump or heavy. Whilst equipped for great speed, it must not be racy. When judging the Boxer the first thing to be considered is general appearance, the relation of substance to elegance and the desired relationship of the individual parts of the body to each other. Consideration, too, must be given to colour. After these, the individual parts should be examined for their correct construction and their functions. Special attention to be devoted to the head.

Head and Skull. — The head imparts to the Boxer a unique individual stamp peculiar to the breed. It must be in perfect proportion to his body; above all it must never be too light. The muzzle is the most distinctive feature. The greatest value is to be placed on its being of correct form and in absolute proportion to the skull. The beauty of the head depends upon the harmonious proportion between the muzzle and the skull. From whatever direction the head is viewed, whether from the front, from the top or from the side, the muzzle should always appear in correct relationship to the skull. That means that the head should never appear too small or too large. The length of the muzzle to the whole of the head should be as 1 is to 3. The head should not show deep wrinkles. Normally wrinkles will spring up on the top of the skull when the dog is alert. Folds are always indicated from the root of the nose running downwards on both sides of the muzzle. The dark mask is confined to the muzzle. It must be in distinct relief to the colour of the head so that the face will not have a "sombre" expression. The muzzle must be powerfully developed in length, in breadth and in height. It must not be pointed or narrow; short or shallow. Its shape is influenced through the formation of both jaw-bones, the placement of teeth in the jaw-bones, and through the quality of the lips. The top of the skull should be slightly arched. It should not be so short that it is rotund, too flat, or too broad. The occiput should not be too pronounced. The forehead should form a distinct stop with the top line of the muzzle, which should not be forced back into the forehead like that of a Bulldog. Neither should it slope away (downfaced). The tip of the nose should lie somewhat higher than the root of the muzzle. The forehead should show a suggestion of furrow which, however, should never be too deep, especially between the eyes. Corresponding with the powerful set of teeth, the cheeks accordingly should be well developed without protruding from the head with "too bulgy" an appearance. For preference they should taper into the muzzle in a slight, graceful curve. The nose should be broad and black, very slightly turned up. The nostrils should be broad with a naso-labial line between them. The two jaw-bones should not terminate in a normal perpendicular level in the front but the lower jaw should protrude beyond the upper jaw and bend slightly upwards. The Boxer is normally undershot. The upper jaw should be broad where attached to the skull, and maintain this breadth except for a very slight tapering to the front.

Eyes. — The eyes should be dark brown; not too small or protruding; not deep set. They should disclose an expression of energy and intelligence, but should never appear gloomy, threatening or piercing. The eyes must have a dark rim.

Ears. — Some American and Continental Boxers are cropped and are ineligible for competition under Kennel Club Regulations. The boxer's natural ears are defined as: moderate in size (small rather than large), thin to the touch, set on wide apart at the highest points of the sides of the skull and lying flat and close to the cheek when in repose. When the dog is alert the ears should fall forward with a definite crease.

Mouth. — The canine teeth should be as widely separated as possible. The incisors (6) should all be in one row, with no projection of the middle teeth. In the upper jaw they should be slightly concave. In the lower they should be in a straight line. Both jaws should be very wide in front; bite powerful and sound, the teeth set in the most normal possible arrangement. The lips complete the formation of the muzzle. The upper lip should be thick and padded and fill out the hollow space in front formed by the projection of the lower jaw and be supported by the fangs of the jaw. These fangs must stand as far apart as possible and be of good length so that the front surface of the muzzle becomes broad and almost square; to form on obtuse (rounded) angle with the top line of the muzzle. The lower edge of the upper lip should rest on the edge of the lower lip. The repandous (bent upward) part of the under-jaw with the lower lip (sometimes called the chin) must not rise above the front of the upper lip. On the other hand it should not disappear under it. It must, however, be plainly perceptible when viewed from the front as well as the side, without protruding and bending upward as in the English Bulldog. The teeth of the under-jaw should not be seen when the mouth is closed, neither should the tongue show when the mouth is closed.

Neck. — The neck should be not too thick and short but of ample length, yet strong, round, muscular and clean-cut throughout. There should be a distinctly marked nape and an elegant arch down to the back.

Forequarters. — The chest should be deep and reach down to the elbows. The depth of the chest should be half the height of the dog at the withers. The ribs should be well arched but not barrel-shaped. They should extend far to the rear. The loins should be short, close and taut and slightly tucked up. The lower stomach line should blend into an elegant curve to the rear. The shoulders should be long and sloping, close lying but not excessively covered with muscle. The upper arm should be long and form a right-angle to the shoulder-blade. The forelegs when seen from the front should be straight, parallel to each other and have strong, firmly articulated (joined) bones. The elbows should not press too closely to the chest-wall or stand off too far from it. The underarm should be perpendicular, long and firmly muscled. The pastern joint of the foreleg should be clearly defined, but not distended. The pastern should be short, slightly slanting and almost perpendicular to the ground.

Body. — The body viewed in profile should be of square appearance. The length of the body from the front of the chest to the rear of the body should equal the height from the ground to the top of the shoulder, giving the Boxer a short-coupled, square profile. The torso rests on trunk-like straight legs with strong bones. The withers should be clearly defined. The whole back should be short, straight, broad, and very muscular.

Hindquarters. — The hindquarters should be strongly muscled. The musculation should be hard and stand out plastically through the skin. The thighs should not be narrow and flat but broad and curved. The breech musculation should also be strongly developed. The croup should be slightly sloped, flat arched and broad. The pelvis should be long and, in females especially, broad. The upper and lower things should be long. The hip and knee joints should have as much angle as possible. In a standing position the knee should reach so far forward that it would meet a vertical line drawn from the hip protuberance to the floor. The hock angle should be about 140 degrees; the lower part of the foot at a slight slope of about 95 to 100 degrees from the hock joint to the floor; that is, not completely vertical. Seen from behind, the hind legs should be straight. The hocks should be clean and not distended, supported by powerful rear pads.

Feet. — The feet should be small with tightly-arched toes (cat feet) and hard soles. The rear toes should be just a little longer than the front toes, but similar in all other respects.

Tail. — The tail attachment should be high. The tail should be docked and carried upwards and should not be more than 2 inches long.

Coat. — The coat should be short and shiny, lying smooth and tight to the body.

Colour. — The permissible colours are fawn, brindle and fawn in various shades from light yellow to dark deer red. The brindle variety should have black stripes on a golden-yellow or red-brown background. The stripes should be clearly defined and above all should not be grey or dirty. Stripes that do not cover the whole of the top are not desirable. White markings are not undesirable, in fact, they are often very attractive in appearance. The black mask is essential but when white stretches over the muzzle, naturally that portion of the black mask disappears. It is not possible to get black toe-nails with white feet. It is desirable, however, to have an even distribution of head markings.

Weight and Size. — Dogs: 22 to 24 inches at the withers. Bitches: 21 to 23 inches at the withers. Heights above or below these figures not to be encouraged. Dogs around 23 inches should weigh about 66 lbs. and Bitches of about 11 inches should weigh about 62 lbs.

Faults. — Viciousness; treachery; unreliability; lack of temperament; cowardice. Head: a head that is not typical. A plump, bulldoggy appearance. Light bone. Lack of proportion. Bad physical conditions. Lack of nobility and expression. "Sombre" face. Unserviceable bite whether due to disease or to faulty tooth placement. Pinscher or Bulldog head. Showing the teeth or the tongue. A sloping top line of the muzzle. Too pointed or too light a bite (snipy). Eyes: visible conjunctiva (Haw). Light eyes. Ears: flying ears; rose ears; semi-erect or erect ears. Neck: dewlap. Front: too broad and low in front; loose shoulders; chest hanging between the shoulders; hare feet; turned legs and toes. Body: carp (roach) back; sway back; thin, lean back; long narrow, sharp-sunken in loins. Weak union with the croup, hollow flanks; hanging stomach. Hindquarters: a falling off or too arched or narrow croup. A low-set tail; higher in back than in front; steep, stiff or too little angulation of the hindquarters; light thighs; cow-hocks; bow-legs; hind dewclaws; soft hocks, narrow heel, tottering, waddling gait; hare's feet; hinquarters too far under or too far behind. Colour: Boxers with white or black ground colour, or entirely white or black or any other colour than fawn or brindle. (White markings are allowed but must not exceed one-third (⅓) of the ground colour).

Note. — Male animals should have two apparently normal testicles fully descended into the scrotum.

MAIN AMERICAN KENNEL CLUB VARIATION TO STANDARD FOR THE BOXER —

Head. — The ears are set at the highest points of the sides of the skull, cut rather long without too broad a shell, and are carried erect.

Height. — Adult males: 22½ to 25 inches; Females: 21 to 23½ inches at the withers.

BOXER REGISTRATIONS 1981 — 87 INCLUSIVE

1981 — 3947
1982 — 4077
1983 — 4693
1984 — 4759
1985 — 5321
1986 — 5185
1987 — 4911

YET TO WIN CRUFTS BEST-IN-SHOW.

BRIARD

This strong herding dog hails from Brie in France. There have been similar working dogs in France for many centuries but the Brie area can claim credit for the Briard's modern development. His full title is Chien Berger de Brie, Briard bing a convenient abbreviation.

He is still a very popular breed in his home country and since 1900 there has been a club in France that is regarded as the breed's ruling body, this club being known as Les Amis du Briard.

These dogs have a first class record as skilled herders with sheep and cattle and the breed has also been used for police and military work. His responsiveness to training, even temper and hardy constitution are all attributes which well qualify the Briard for these tasks. The heavy, wavy coat is also useful as it resists all types of weather.

Although the Briard's is very much a disciplined, working past, he will happily settle into a domesticated existence. If reared correctly and allowed a fair amount of space he will make a faultless companion. Children and the elderly alike will find the Briard most agreeable and there is no trace of viciousness in his make-up.

A dog of such natural vigour deserves plenty of off the lead exercise and to keep him at his best, the coat must recieve frequent attention.

KEY TO CHARACTER	
INTELLIGENCE	****
TEMPERAMENT	*****
EASE OF COAT CARE	**
SUITABILITY FOR SMALL DWELLING	*
***** (5) = VERY GOOD	

BRITISH KENNEL CLUB STANDARD

BRIARD

CHARACTERISTICS. — Very intelligent, gay and lively, fearless with no trace of timidity.

GENERAL APPEARANCE. — A dog of rugged appearance; supple, muscular and well proportined.

Head and Skull. — The skull slightly rounded and a little longer from occiput to stop than it is wide when measured through the points of the cheekbones. Emphasis should be placed on the fact that the head is composed of two equal rectangles, occiput to stop and stop to end of nose, when viewed in profile and from above. The muzzle square and very strong, any tendency to snipiness being severely penalised. The nose large and square and always black no matter what colour the dog. The head should carry hair forming a moustache, beard and eyebrows lightly veiling the eyes.

Mouth. — The teeth very strong, white and with a perfect regular and complete scissor bite, i.e. the upper teeth closely overlapping the lower teeth and set square to the jaws. Lips black, no matter what colour the dog.

Eyes. — Horizontally placed, well open and rather large, not oblique. Intelligent and gentle in expression. Dark brown, eye-rims always black, no matter what colour the dog.

Ears. — Set on high. The ears, covered with long hair, should not lie too flat against the side of the head. They should be fairly short, the length of the ear being equal to or slightly less than half the length of the head. When the dog is alerted, the ears should be lifted slightly and swing very slightly forward.

Neck. — Of good length, strong and muscular, arched to give proud carriage of the head and flowing smoothly into well placed shoulders.

Forequarters. — Shoulders well angulated and well laid back; forelegs well muscled and with strong bone.

Body. — The back firm and level, chest broad and well let down, there should be a very slight slope at the croup, which determines the set of the tail. The Briard should be very slightly longer in body than he is high at the shoulder.

Hindquarters. — Well angulated with hocks set not too low and turning neither in nor out, but the leg below the hock not quite vertical. Hindlegs, particularly the thighs, well muscled. Double dewclaws set low on the hind legs of the utmost importance.

Feet. — Strong, turning neither in nor out, slightly rounded, about mid-way between a cat foot and a hare-foot. Nails always black. Pads firm and hard and toes close together.

Gait. — Effortless and, when the dog extends himself, covers a great deal of ground. Extremely supple enabling the dog to turn quickly. The gait strong, firm vey smooth and with plenty of drive.

Coat. — Long (not less than 7cm (3 in)) on the body. Slightly wavy and very dry. A fine dense undercoat is required all over the body.

Tail. — Long, well covered with hair and with an upward hook at the tip. Carried low but held neither to none side nor the other. The bone of the tail should reach at least to the point of the hock.

Colour. — All black, or with white hairs scattered through the black coat. Fawn in all its shades, but the darker shades preferred. Fawns may have dark shadings on the ears, muzzle, back and tail, but these shadings must blend gradually into the rest of the coat, since any demarcation line denotes a bi-colour which is unacceptable. Briards may also be slate grey.

Size. — Dogs 61 to 69cm at withers (24 to 27 in). Bitches 58 to 64cm at withers (23 to 25½ in). Slight undersize is not to be considered a fault in an animal under eighteen months of age. A well balanced animal should never be penalised for being slightly over the maximum size.

Faults. — Any departure from the foregoing points should be considered a fault and the seriousness with which the fault is regarded should be in exact proportion to its degree.

Note. — Male animals should have two apparently normal testicles fully descended into the scrotum.

MAIN AMERICAN KENNEL CLUB VARIATION TO STANDARD FOR THE BRIARD —

Size. — Males 23 to 27 inches at the withers; bitches 22 to 25½ inches at the withers.

BRIARD REGISTRATIONS 1981 — 87 INCLUSIVE

1981 — 176
1982 — 170
1983 — 288
1984 — 224
1985 — 254
1986 — 274
1987 — 281

YET TO WIN CRUFTS BEST-IN-SHOW.

Bearded Collie
Belgian Shepherd Dog (Groenendael)

Belgian Shepherd Dog (Tervueren)

Bernese Mountain Dog

BULLMASTIFF

This imposing breed was officially registered in 1924, although similar dogs had existed long before then. Various crosses had been tried, usually with some sort of Mastiff or Wolfhound and the Bulldog. The most successful combination proved to be the English Mastiff with the Bulldog and these two breeds formed the basis for all today's Bullmastiffs. The Bulldog of the time was not as squat as today's and the Bullmastiff probably bears more overall resemblance to that breed than to the giant Mastiff.

He was particularly prized as a gamekeeper's dog and was the scourge of poachers for many decades. Despite his great bulk, he can move well and his technique was to lunge on the trespasser and pin him to the spot without actually causing serious injury. He has always been widely used as a guard of country estates and the like, often his sheer size being sufficient to discourage anyone with ideas of illegal entry.

To control this size of dog, early training must be methodical and disciplined or the owner, especially a woman, would find it impossible to restrain him.

Not, perhaps, a dog to take on lightly, but if handled correctly he makes an immensely rewarding companion. He revels in the attentions of all the family and children are quite safe with him. Exercise must be regular, the more the better.

KEY TO CHARACTER	
INTELLIGENCE	***
TEMPERAMENT	****
EASE OF COAT CARE	*****
SUITABILITY FOR SMALL DWELLING	*
***** (5) = VERY GOOD	

BRITISH KENNEL CLUB STANDARD

BULLMASTIFF

CHARACTERISTICS. — The temperament of the Bullmastiff combines high spirits, reliability, activity, endurance and alertness.

GENERAL APPEARANCE. — The Bullmastiff is a powerfully built, symmetrical dog, showing great strength, but not cumbersome.

Head and Skull. — The skull should be large and square, viewed from every angle, with fair wrinkle when interested, but not when in repose. The circumference of the skull may equal the height of the dog measured at the top of the shoulder; it should be broad and deep with good cheeks. The muzzle short, the distance from the tip of the nose to the stop should be approximately one-third of the length from the tip of the nose to the centre of the occiput, broad under the eyes and nearly parallel in width to the end of the nose; blunt and cut off square, forming a right-angle with the upper line of the face, and at the same time proportionate with the skull. Underjaw broad to the end. Nose broad with widely spreading nostrils when viewed from the front; flat, not pointed or turned up in profile. Flews not pendulous, and not hanging below the level of the bottom of the lower jaw. Stop definite.

Eyes. — Dark or hazel, and of medium size, set apart with width of the muzzle with furrow between. Light or yellow eyes a fault.

Ears. — Dark or hazel, and of medium size, set apart the width of the muzzle with furrow between. Light or yellow eyes a fault.

Ears. — V-shaped, or folded back, set on wide and high, level with occiput, giving a square appearance to the skull, which is most important. They should be small and deeper in colour than the body, and the point of the ear should be level with the eye when alert. Rose ears to be penalised.

Border Collie

Bouvier des Flandres

Boxer

Newfoundland

Mouth. — Mouth to be level, slight undershot allowed, but not preferred. Canine teeth large and set wide apart, other teeth strong, even and well-placed. Irregularity of teeth a fault.

Neck. — Well-arched, moderate length, very muscular and almost equal to the skull in circumference.

Forequarters. — Chest, wide and deep, well set down between forelegs, with deep brisket. Shoulders muscular sloping and powerful, not overloaded. Forelegs powerful and straight, well boned and set wide apart, presenting a straight front. Pasterns straight and strong.

Body. — Back short and straight, giving a compact carriage, but not so short as to interfere with activity. Roach and sway backs a fault.

Hindquarters. — Loins wide and muscular with fair depth of flank. Hindlegs strong and muscular, with well developed second thighs, denoting power and activity, but not cumbersome. Hocks moderately bent. Cow-hocks a fault.

Feet. — Not large, with rounded toes, well-arched (cat feet), pads hard. Splay feet a fault.

Tail. — Set high, strong at root and tapering, reaching to the hocks, carried straight or curved, but not hound fashion. Crank tails a fault.

Coat. — Short and hard, giving weather protection, lying flat to the body. A tendency to long silky or woolly coats to be penalised.

Colour. — Any shade of brindle, fawn or red, but the colour to be pure and clear. A slight white marking on chest permissible but not desirable. Other white markings a fault. A dark muzzle is esential, toning off towards the eyes, with dark markings around the eyes, giving expression. Dark toenails desirable.

Weight and Size. — Dogs should be 25 to 27 inches at shoulder, and 110 lbs. to 130 lbs., in weight. Bitches should be 24 to 26 inches at the shoulder and 90 lbs. to 110 lbs., in weight. It must be borne in mind that size must be proportionate with weight, and soundness and activity is most essential.

Note. — Male animals should have two apparently normal testicles fully descended into the scrotum.

MAIN AMERICAN KENNEL CLUB VARIATION TO STANDARD FOR THE BULLMASTIFF —

Size. — Bitches, 24 to 26 inches at the shoulder, and 100 to 120 pounds weight.

BULLMASTIFF REGISTRATIONS 1981 — 87 INCLUSIVE

1981 — 422
1982 — 394
1983 — 464
1984 — 530
1985 — 752
1986 — 817
1987 — 801

YET TO WIN CRUFTS BEST-IN-SHOW.

Bullmastiff

Rough Collie

ROUGH COLLIE

For many centuries there has existed in Scotland a long-coated working Collie, the name having been taken from a strain of Scottish sheep called Colleys. This dog has a high level of intelligence and excellent herding ability but tends to vary in physical appearance from one dog to another. In the mid-nineteenth century enthusiastic dog fanciers made efforts to standardise this breed. After much experimentation and selective breeding, the details of which are sketchy, the beautiful Rough Collie of today was arrived at. By 1860 he had made his first appearance in the show ring. This remodelled Scottish Collie stood taller and was longer in the head than his predecessors. The semi-erect ears are another in-bred characteristic, not to be seen on all of the working dogs.

It is true to say that the show-type Rough Collie has lost a great deal of his strong working instinct, this having been sacrificed in the search for a more aesthetic form and quality of coat. All the same he is still a dog of good intelligence and one to be recommended to anyone who can manage him correctly. He responds well to training and when fully involved in the family life, will show great loyalty and affection to all age groups.

The superb coat, which makes him impervious to cold, is not too much of a headache to maintain and when presented properly, there is no more attactive a coat in the dog world.

Exercise is of paramount importance and short walks on the lead will not suffice.

KEY TO CHARACTER	
INTELLIGENCE	****
TEMPERAMENT	****
EASE OF COAT CARE	***
SUITABILITY FOR SMALL DWELLING	*
***** (5) = VERY GOOD	

BRITISH KENNEL CLUB STANDARD

COLLIE (ROUGH)

CHARACTERISTICS. — To enable the Collie to fulfil a natural bent for sheepdog work, its physical structure should be on the lines of strength and activity, free from cloddiness and without any trace of coarseness. Expression, one of the most important points in considering relative values, is obtained by the perfect balance and combination of skull and foreface; size, shape, colour and placement of eye, correct position and carriage of ears.

GENERAL APPEARANCE. — The Collie should instantly appeal as a dog of great beauty, standing with impassive dignity, with no part out of proportion to the whole.

Head and Skull. — The head properties are of great importance and must be considered in proportion to the size of the dog. When viewed from the front or the side the head bears a general resemblance to a well-blunted, clean wedge, being smooth in outline. The skull should be flat. The sides should taper gradually and smoothly from the ears to the end of the black nose, without prominent cheek bones or pinched muzzle. Viewed in profile the top of the skull and the top of the muzzle lie in two parallel, straight lines of equal length, divided by a slight, but perceptible "stop" or break. A mid-point between the inside corner of the eyes (which is the centre of a correctly placed "stop") is the centre of balance in length of head. The end of the smooth, well-rounded muzzle is blunt, but not square. The underjaw is strong, clean cut and the depth of the skull from the brow to the underpart of the jaw, must never be excessive (deep though). Whatever the colour of the dog, the nose must be black.

Eyes. — These are a very important feature and give a sweet expression to the dog. They should be of medium size, set somewhat obliquely, of almond shape and of dark brown colour, except in the case of blue merles when the eyes are frequently (one or both, or part of one of both), blue or blue flecked. Expression full of intelligence, with a quick, alert look when listening.

Smooth Collie

Dobermann

Ears. — These should be small and not too close together on top of the skull, not too much to the side of the head. When in repose they should be carried thrown back, but when on the alert brought forward and caried semi-erect, that is, with approximately two-thirds of the ear standing erect, the top third tipping forward naturally, below the horizontal.

Mouth. — The teeth should be of good size, with the lower incisors fitting closely behind the upper incisors; a very slight space not to be regarded as a serious fault.

Neck. — The neck should be muscular, powerful, of fair length and well arched.

Forequarters. — The shoulders should be sloped and well-angulated. The forelegs should be straight and muscular, neither in nor out at elbows, with a moderate amount of bone.

Body. — The body should be a trifle long compared to the height, back firm with a slight rise over the loins; ribs well-sprung, chest deep and fairly broad behind the shoulders.

Hindquarters. — The hind legs should be muscular at the thighs, clean and sinewy below, with well bent stifles. Hocks well let-down and powerful.

Feet. — These should be oval in shape with soles well padded, toes arched and close together. The hind feet slightly less arched.

Gait. — Movement is a distinct characteristic of this breed. A sound dog is never out at elbow, yet it moves with its front feet comparatively close together. Plaiting, crossing or rolling are highly undesirable. The hind legs, from the hock joint to the ground, when viewed from the rear, should be parallel. The hind legs should be powerful and full of drive. Viewed from the side the action is smooth. A reasonably long stride is desirable and this should be light and appear quite effortless.

Tail. — The tail should be long with the bone reaching at least to the hock joint. To be carried low when the dog is quiet, but with a slight upward swirl at the tip. It may be carried gaily when the dog is excited, but not over the back.

Coat. — The coat should fit the outline of the dog and be very dense. The outer coat straight and harsh to the touch, The undercoat soft, furry and very close, so close as to almost hide the skin. The mane and frill should be very abundant; the mask or face, smooth, also the ears at the tips, but they should carry more hair towards the base; the fore-legs well feathered, the hind legs above the hocks profusely so, but smooth below. Hair on the tail very profuse.

Colour. — The three recognised colours are sable and white, tricolour and blue merle.

Sable. — Any shade from light gold to rich mahogany or shaded sable. Light straw or cream colour is highly undesirable.

Tricolour. — Predominantly black with rich tan markings about the legs and head. A rusty tinge in the top coat is highly undesirable.

Blue Merle. — Predominantly clear, silvery blue, splashed and marbled with black. Rich tan markings to be preferred, but their absence should not be counted as a fault. Large black markings, slate colour, or a rusty tinge either of the top or undercoat are highly undesirable.

White Markings. — All the above may carry the typical white Collie markings to a greater or lesser degree. The following markings are favourable — White collar, full or part; white shirt, legs and feet; white tail tip. A blaze may be carried on muzzle or skull or both.

Weight and Size. —Dogs 22 to 24 inches at shoulder, bitches 20 to 22 inches. Dogs 45 to 65 lbs., bitches 40 to 55 lbs.

Faults. — Length of head apparently out of proportion to body; receding skull or unbalanced head to be strongly condemned. Weak, snipy muzzle; domed skull; high peaked occiput, prominent cheek bones; dish-faced or Roman-nosed; under-shot or over-shot mouth; missing teeth; round or light coloured and glassy or staring eyes are highly objectionable. Body flat sided, short or cobby; straight shoulder or stifle; out at elbow; crooked fore-arms; cow-hocks or straight hocks, large, open or hare feet; feet turned in or out; long weak pasterns; tail short, kinked or twisted to one side or carried over the back; a soft, silky or wavy coat or insufficient undercoat; prick ears, low-set ears; nervousness.

Note. — Male animals should have two apparently normal testicles fully descended into the scrotum.

MAIN AMERICAN KENNEL CLUB VARIATION TO STANDARD FOR THE ROUGH COLLIE —

Size. — Dogs are from 24 to 26 inches at the shoulder and weigh from 60 to 75 pounds. Bitches are from 22 to 24 inches at the shoulder weighing from 50 to 65 pounds.

ROUGH COLLIE REGISTRATIONS 1981 — 87 INCLUSIVE

1981 — 6059
1092 — 5663
1983 — 5572
1984 — 5226
1985 — 4998
1986 — 4479
1987 — 4259

YET TO WIN CRUFTS BEST-IN-SHOW.

SMOOTH COLLIE

Until 1974 the breed standards for the Rough Collie and the smooth Collie differed only in the obvious area of coat. Even then the wording was only changed slightly for the new standard. Every detail of each breed is identical, bar the coat of course. Some have put forward the theory that the Rough Collie was crossed with the Greyhound to produce the smooth coat, but this is now thought unlikely as no trace of the Greyhound is to be seen in the Smooth Collie. It is more probable that the coat appeared through natural genetic variation.

As would be expected of a Collie he is a fine worker and excellent pet. Rough and Smooth Collies have worked on Scottish farms together for many years although the Rough has always been the more popular, purely for appearance, it seems. Nowadays the Smooth Collie is far from common but his future seems safe in the hands of a hard core of loyal followers.

He is easy to house-train, very friendly with all age groups in the family and displays intelligence and loyalty. Plenty of exercise is required and he will thrive on regular off-the-lead runs.

KEY TO CHARACTER	
INTELLIGENCE	****
TEMPERAMENT	****
EASE OF COAT CARE	*****
SUITABILITY FOR SMALL DWELLING	*
***** (5) = VERY GOOD	

BRITISH KENNEL CLUB STANDARD

COLLIE (SMOOTH)

CHARACTERISTICS. — To enable the Collie to fulfil a natural bent for sheepdog work, its physical structure should be on the lines of strength and activity, free from cloddiness and without any trace of coarseness. Expression, one of the most important points in considering relative values, is obtained by the perfect balance and combination of skull and foreface, size, shape, colour and placement of eye, correct position and carriage of ears. Temperament should be gay and friendly, never nervous nor aggressive.

GENERAL APPEARANCE. — The Collie should instantly appear as gifted with intelligence, alertness and activity. He should stand with dignity, and his movements, governed by perfect anatomical formation, with no part out of proportion, should be smooth and graceful. He should give the appearance of a dog capable of working.

Head and Skull. — The head properties are of great importance and must be considered in proportion to the size of the dog. When viewed from both front and profile the head should bear a general resemblance to a well-blunted, clean wedge, being smooth in outline. The skull should be flat. The sides should taper gradually and smoothly from the ears to the end of the black nose, without prominent cheek bones or pinched muzzle. Viewed in profile the top of the skull and the top of the muzzle should lie in two parallel, straight planes of equal length, divided by a slight but perceptible "stop" or break. A mid-point between the insdie corners of the eyes (which is the centre of a correctly placed "stop") should be the centre of balance in length of head. The end of the smooth, well-rounded muzzle should be blunt, but not square. The underjaw should be strong, clean cut, and the depth of the skull from the brow to the underpart of the jaw should never be excessive (deep through). Whatever the colour of the dog, the nose must be black.

Eyes. — Are a very important feature and should give a sweet expression to the dog. They should be of medium size, set somewhat obliquely, of almond shape and of dark brown colour, except in the case of blue merles when one or both eyes may be wall or jewelled. Expression full of intelligence with a quick, alert look when listening.

Ears. — Should be moderately large, wider at the base, and placed not too close together nor too much on the side of the head. When in repose they should be carried thrown back, but when on the alert brought forward and carried semi-erect, that is, with approximately two-thirds of the ear standing erect, the top third tipping forward naturally, below the horizontal.

Mouth. — The teeth should be of good size, with the lower incisors fitting closely behind the upper incisors; a very slight space not to be regarded as a serious fault.

Neck. — Should be muscular, powerful, of fair length and well arched.

Forequarters. — The shoulders should be sloped and well angulated. The forelegs should be straight and muscular, neither in nor out at the elbows, with a moderate amount of bone. The forearm somewhat fleshy with pasterns showing flexibility without weakness.

Body. — Should be a trifle long compared with the height, back level and firm with a slight rise over the loins; ribs well-sprung; chest deep and fairly broad behind the shoulders.

Hindquarters. — The hind legs should be muscular at the thighs, clean and sinewy below, with well bent stifles. Hocks well let-down and powerful. Male animals should have two apparently normal testicles fully descended into the scrotum.

Feet. — Should be oval with soles well padded. Toes arched and close together. Hind feet slightly less arched.

Gait. — Movement is a distinct characteristic of the breed. A sound dog is never out at elbow, yet it moves with its front feet comparatively close together. Plaiting, crossing or rolling are highly undesirable. The hind legs, from the hock joint to the ground, when viewed from the rear, should be parallel, powerful and full of drive. Viewed from the side the action should be smooth. A reasonably long stride is desirable and this should be light and appear quite effortless.

Tail. — Should be long with the bone reaching at least to the hock joint. To be carried low when the dog is quiet but with a slight upward swirl at the tip. It may be carried gaily when the dog is excited, but never over the back.

Coat. — A very important feature of the Smooth Collie is his short, flat top coat of harsh texture, with a very dense undercoat.

Colour. — The three recognised colours are: Sable and White, Tricolour and Blue Merle.

Sable. — Any shade from light gold to rich mahogany or shaded sable. Light straw or cream colour is highly undesirable.

Tricolour. — Predominantly black with rich tan markings about the legs and head. A rusty tinge in the top coat is highly undesirable.

Blue Merle. — Predominantly clear, silvery blue, splashed and marbled with black. Rich ran markings to be preferred but their absence should not be counted as a fault. Large black markings, slate colour or a rusty tinge on the top or undercoat are highly undesirable.

White Markings. — All the above may carry the typical white Collie markings to a greater or lesser degree. The following markings are favourable: white collar, full or part; white front, legs and feet; white tail tip. A blaze may be carried on muzzle or skull or both. All white or predominantly white is most undesirable.

Weight and Size. — Dogs 22 to 24 inches at shoulder; Bitches 20 to 22 inches at shoulder. Dogs 45 to 65 pounds; Bitches 40 to 55 pounds.

Faults. — Any departure from the foregoing points should be considered a fault and the seriousness of the fault should be in exact proportion to its degree.

SMOOTH COLLIE REGISTRATIONS 1981 — 87 INCLUSIVE

1981 — 49
1982 — 48
1983 — 53
1984 — 105
1985 — 126

YET TO WIN CRUFTS BEST-IN-SHOW.

DOBERMANN

Towards the end of the nineteenth century a certain Louis Dobermann was the warden of the local dog pound in Apolda, Germany. He had an obsession with guard dogs and set out to develop a dog of unequalled ferocity, bravery and learning capacity. From his large collection in the pound, it is thought he interbred the German Pinscher with the Rottweiler and the German Shepherd and Manchester Terrier were possibly used. Herr Dobermann's efforts undoubtedly laid the foundations for the dogs of today although selective breeding since then has honed the breed down to the ultra efficient form we now see.

Although not a massive dog, pound for pound the Dobermann is one of the most fearsome guard dogs known. This intensely strong instinct has caused problems in managing the breed, but the temperament of modern Dobermanns is far more predictable than was always the case. The police and military have illustrated that with very firm training, this is a dog of great potential able to fulfil many tasks with courage and skill.

The Dobermann is always a huge success in the show ring with his gleaming, slick coat perfectly complementing his taut musculature.

This is not a breed to be feared as many unfortunately do, but intelligent training is advised and an owner would do well to join an obedience class with his puppy. He is a supremely loyal dog who will get on well with all the family if reared correctly. Teasing from children though, is to be strongly discouraged.

The Dobermann requires a great deal of daily exercise to maintain peak condition of body and mind.

KEY TO CHARACTER	
INTELLIGENCE	****
TEMPERAMENT	***
EASE OF COAT CARE	*****
SUITABILITY FOR SMALL DWELLING	*
***** (5) = VERY GOOD	

BRITISH KENNEL CLUB STANDARD

DOBERMANN

CHARACTERISTICS. — The Dobermann is a dog of good medium size with well-set body, muscular and elegant. He has a proud carriage and a bold, alert temperament. His form is compact and tough and owing to his build capable of great speed. His gait is light and elastic. His eyes show intelligence and firmness of character, and he is loyal and obedient. Shyness or viciousness must be heavily penalised.

Head and Skull. — Has to be proportionate to the body. It must be long, well filled under the eyes and clean cut. Its form seen from above and from the side must resemble a blunt wedge. The upper part of the head should be as flat as possible and free from wrinkle. The top of the skull should be flat with a slight stop, and the muzzle line extend parallel to the top line of the skull. The cheeks must be flat and the lips tight. The nose should be solid black in black dogs, solid dark brown in brown dogs, and solid dark grey in blue dogs. Head out of balance in proportion to body, dish-faced, snipy or cheeky should be penalised.

Eyes. — Should be almond-shaped, not round, moderately deep set, not prominent, with vigorous, energetic expression. Iris of uniform colour, ranging from medium to darkest brown in black dogs, the darker shade being the more desirable. In browns or blues the colour of the iris should blend with that of the markings, but not be of lighter hue than that of the markings. Light eyes in black dogs to be discouraged.

Ears. — Should be small, neat and set high on the head. Erect or dropped, but erect preferred.

Mouth. — Should be very well developed, solid and strong, with a scissor bite. The incisors of the lower jaw must touch the inner face of the incisors of the upper jaw. Overshot or undershot mouths, badly arranged or decayed teeth to be penalised.

Neck. — Should be fairly long and lean carried erect and with considerable nobility, slightly convex and proportionate to the whole shape of the dog. The region of the nape has to be muscular. Dewlap and loose skin are undesirable.

Forequarters. — The shoulder blade and upper arm should meet at an angle of 90 degrees. Relative length of shoulder and upper arm should be as one, excess length of upper arm being much less undesirable than excess length of shoulder blade. The legs, seen from the front and side, are perfectly straight and parallel to each other from elbow to pastern, muscled and sinewy, with round bone proportionate to body structure. In a normal position and when gaiting, the elbow should lie close to the brisket.

Body. — Should be square, height measured vertically from the ground to the highest point of the withers, equalling the length measured horizontally, from the forechest to rear projection of the upper thigh. The back should be short and firm with the topline sloping slightly from the withers to the croup, the female needing room to carry litters may be slightly longer to loin. The belly should be fairly well tucked up. ribs should be deep and well-sprung, reaching to elbow. Long, weak or roach backs to be discouraged.

Hindquarters. — Should be parallel to each other and wide enough apart to fit in with a properly built body. The hip bone should fall away from the spinal column at an angle of about 30 degrees. Croup well filled out. The hindquarters should be well developed and muscular, with long bent stifle and their hocks turning neither in nor out. While the dog is at rest, hock to heel should be perpendicular to the ground.

Feet. — Fore-feet should be well arched, compact and cat-like, turning neither in nor out. All dew claws to be removed. Long, flat deviating paws and weak pasterns should be penalised. Hind-feet should be well arched, compact and cat-like, turning neither in nor out.

Gait. — Should be free, balanced and vigorous with good reach in the forequarters, and a driving power in the hindquarters. When trotting, there should be a strong rear action drive with rotary motion of hindquarters. Rear and front legs should be thrown neither in nor out. Back should remain strong and firm.

Tail. — The tail should be docked at the first or second joint and should appear to be a continuation of the spine, without material drop.

Coat. — Should be smooth-haired, short, hard, thick and close lying. Invisible grey undercoat on neck permissible.

Colour. — Colours allowed are definite black, brown, blue or fawn with rust red markings. Markings must be sharply defined and appearing above each eye and on the muzzle, throat and fore-chest, and on all legs and feet, and below tail. White markings of any kind are highly undesirable.

Weight and Size. — Ideal height at withers: Males 27 inches; Females 25½ inches. Considerable deviation from this ideal to be discouraged.

Faults. — Shyness or viciousness must be heavily penalised. Head out of balance in proportion to body, dish-faced, snipy or cheeky should be penalised. Light eyes in black dogs to be discouraged. Overshot or undershot mouths, badly arranged or decayed teeth to be penalised. Dewlap and loose skin are undesirable. Long, weak or roach back to be discouraged. White markings of any kind are highly undesirable. Hair forming a ridge on the back of the neck and/or along the spine should be classed as a serious fault.

Note. — Male animals should have two apparently normal testicles fully descended into the scrotum.

MAIN AMERICAN KENNEL CLUB VARIATION TO STANDARD FOR THE DOBERMANN —

Known as the Dobermann Pinscher in the U.S.A.

Ears. — Normally cropped and carried erect. The upper attachment of the ear, when held erect, is on a level with the top of the skull.

Height. — At the withers: Dogs 26 to 28 inches; ideal about 27½ inches; Bitches 24 to 26 inches, ideal about 25½ inches.

DOBERMANN REGISTRATIONS 1981 — 87 INCLUSIVE

1981 — 4824
1982 — 6244
1983 — 8499
1984 — 8905
1985 — 9953
1986 — 8564
1987 — 6413

YET TO WIN CRUFTS BEST-IN-SHOW.

THE GERMAN SHEPHERD DOG

For a considerable period the German Shepherd Dog was known as the Alsatian and even today the latter is still used and recognized.

Records indicate that the breed has existed since the seventh century, but nothing appears to have been recorded. In fact, the first written of the breed came in 1606 when P.C. Gessner described the 'Schaffhunde' (sheepdogs) stating they must be "large, strong, courageous and enterprising and must possess a very strong voice".

The modern type dog dates from around 1880 when the Alsatian appeared in Germany. This was followed by the formation of the German Sheepdog Club. Clubs for the breed are now established world wide; indeed, the dog has become one of the most popular.

Like all large dogs the German Shepherd Dog has its staunch followers and, conversely, those who make statements on its unreliability, occasionally turning on its owners. There, are also references to the 'Wolf Dog' indicating that the German Shepherd Dog came from a line of wolves. Modern thinking has now concluded that the breed is *not* closely related to the wolf. Moreover, the temperament of the modern dog is far removed from being aggressive to its owners. It is a loyal companion which mixes well with all the family. At the same time it is an excellent guard dog.

There has to be recognition though that German Shepherd Dogs will not suit all potential owners. They are strong and large and require a firmness and understanding to cope with them. Moreover, they have large appetites which make them expensive dogs to keep.

Besides requiring physical exercise the German Shepherd Dog requires plenty to keep him occupied. He is a very intelligent dog and being part of a family and its activities will be natural for him.

In conclusion it can be said that the German Shepherd Dog is one of the most popular breeds in the world. In the past it has been maligned, but nowadays is accepted as an intelligent dog, loyal to its owners, but feared by those who tresspass or are up to no good on other people's property. In a suitable environment, with adequate space, the German Shepherd Dog is an excellent companion.

KEY TO CHARACTER	
INTELLIGENCE	*****
TEMPERAMENT	****
EASE OF COAT CARE	***
SUITABILITY FOR SMALL DWELLING	*
***** (5) = VERY GOOD	

BRITISH KENNEL CLUB STANDARD

GERMAN SHEPHERD DOG (Alsatian)

CHARACTERISTICS. — The characteristic expression of the German Shepherd Dog gives the impression of perpetual vigilance, fidelity, liveliness and watchfulness, alert to every sight and sound, with nothing escaping atention; fearless, but with decided suspiciousness of strangers — as opposed to the immediate friendliness of some breeds. The German Shepherd Dog possesses highly developed senses, mentally and temperamentally. He should be strongly individualistic and possess a high standard of intelligence. Three of the most outstanding traits are incorruptibility, discernment and ability to reason.

GENERAL APPEARANCE. — The general appearance of the German Shepherd Dog is a well-proportioned dog showing great suppleness of limb, neither massive nor heavy, but at the same time free from any suggestion of weediness. It must not approach the greyhound type. The body is rather long, strongly boned, with plenty of muscle, obviously capable of endurance of speed and of quick and sudden movement. The gait should be supple, smooth and long-reaching, carrying the body along with the minimum of up-and-down movement, entirely free from stiltiness.

Head and Skull. — The head is proportionate to the size of the body, long, lean and clean cut, broad at the back of the skull, but without coarseness, tapering to the nose with only a slight stop between the eyes. The skull is slightly domed and the top of the nose should be parallel to the forehead. The cheeks must not be full or in any way prominent and the whole head, when viewed from the top, should be much in the form of a V, well filled in under the eyes. There should be plenty of substance in foreface, with a good depth from top to bottom. The muzzle is strong and long and, while tapering to the nose, it must not be carried to such an extreme as to give the appearance of being overshot. It must not show any weakness, or be snipy or lippy. The lips must be tight fitting and clean. The nose must be black.

Eyes. — The eyes are almond-shaped as nearly as possible matching the surrounding coat but darker rather than lighter in shade and placed to look straight forward. They must not be in any way bulging or prominent, and must show a lively, alert and highly intelligent expression.

Ears. — The ears should be of moderate size, but rather large than small, broad at the base and pointed at the tips, placed rather high on the skull and carried erect — in adding to the alert expression of the dog as a whole. (It should be noted, in case novice breeders may be misled, that in German Shepherd Dog puppies the ears often hang until the age of six months and sometimes longer, becoming erect with the replacment of the milk teeth.)

Mouth. — The teeth should be sound and strong, gripping with a scissor-like action, the lower incisors just behind, but touching the upper.

Neck. — The neck should be strong, fairly long with plenty of muscle, fitting gracefully into the body, joining the head without sharp angles and free from throatiness.

Forequarters. — The shoulders should slope well back, the ideal being that a line drawn through the centre of the shoulder blade should form a right-angle with the humerus when the leg is perpendicular to the ground in stance. Upright shoulders are a major fault. They should show plenty of muscle, which is distinct from, and must not be confused with, coarse or loaded bone, which is a fault. The shoulder-bone should be clean. The forelegs should be perfectly straight viewed from the front, but the pasterns should show a slight angle with the forearm when regarded from the side, too great an angle denotes weakness, and while carrying plenty of bone, it should be of good quality. Anything approaching the massive bone of the Newfoundland, for example, being a decided fault.

Body. — The body is muscular, the back is broadish and straight, strongly boned and well developed. The belly shows a waist without being tucked up. There should be a good depth of brisket or chest, the latter should not be too broad. The sides are flat compared to some breeds, and while the dog must not be barrel ribbed, it must not be so flat as to be actually slabsided. The German Shepherd Dog should be quick in movement and speedy but not like a greyhound in body.

Hindquarters. — The hindquarters should show breadth and strength, the loins being broad and strong, the rump rather long and sloping and the legs, when viewed from behind, must be quite straight, without any tendency to cow-hocks, or bow-hocks, which are both extremely serious faults. The stifles are well turned and the hocks strong and well let down. The ability to turn quickly is a necessary asset to the German Shepherd Dog, and this can only be if there is good length of thigh-bone and leg, and by the bending of the hock.

Feet. — The feet should be round, the toes strong, slightly arched and held close together. The pads should be firm, the nails short and strong. Dewclaws are neither a fault nor a virtue, but should be removed from the hind legs at 4 to 5 days old, as they are liable to spoil the gait.

Tail. — When at rest the tail should hang in a slight curve, and reach at least as far back as the hock. During movement and excitement it will be raised, but in no circumstances should the tail be carried past a vertical line drawn through the root.

Coat. — The coat is smooth, but it is at the same time a double coat. The under-coat is woolly in texture, thick and close and to it the animal owes its characteristic resistance to cold. The outer-coat is also close, each hair straight, hard, and lying flat, so that it is rain-resisting. Under the body, to being the legs, the coat is longer and forms near the thigh a mild form of breeching. On the head (including the inside of the ears). to the front of the legs and feet, the hair is short. Along the neck it is longer and thicker, and in Winter approaches a form of ruff. A coat either too long or too short is a fault. As an average, the hairs in the back should be from 1 to 2 inches in length.

Colour. — The colour of the German Shepherd Dog is in itself not important and has no effect on the character of the dog or in its fitness for work and should be a secondary consideration for that reason. All white or near white unless possessing black points are not desirable. The final colour of a young dog can only be ascertained when the outer coat has developed.

Weight and Size. — The ideal height (measured to the highest point of the shoulder) is 22 — 26 inches for dogs. The proportion, of length to height, may vary between 10:9 and 10:8·5.

Faults. — A long, narrow, Collie or Borzoi head. A pink or liver-coloured nose. Undershot or overshot mouth. Tail with curl or pronounced hook. The lack of heavy undercoat.

Note. — Male animals should have two apparently normal testicles fully descended into the scrotum.

MAIN AMERICAN KENNEL CLUB VARIATION TO STANDARD FOR THE GERMAN SHEPHERD DOG —

Proportion. — The German Shepherd Dog is longer than tall, with the most desirable proportion as 10 to 8½.

GERMAN SHEPHERD DOG REGISTRATIONS 1981 — 87 INCLUSIVE

1981 — 16068
1982 — 18124
1983 — 20593
1984 — 21009
1985 — 21649
1986 — 19309
1987 — 16976

CRUFTS BEST IN SHOW WINNER 3 TIMES.

1965 CH. FENTON OF KENTWOOD — MISS S.H. GODDEN.
1969 CH. HENDRAWEN'S NIBELUNG OF CHARAVIGNE —
MR. & MRS. E.J. WHITE.
1971 CH. RAMACON SWASHBUCKLER — PRINCE AHMED HUSAIN.

GIANT SCHNAUZER

The Miniature and Standard Schnauzers both feature attractive beards and moustaches on the muzzle and the Giant variety is no exception. The name for these breeds is derived from the German word "schnauze" which translates to "snout".

Outside Germany, the Giant Schnauzer is the least common of the three. But in his native land, a similar breed has existed for centuries and has been widely used as a working dog. It is difficult to assess the exact ancestry of the modern Giant Schnauzer, but it seems probable thast a wire-coated terrier has been used with possibly the Bouvier des Flandres contributing to the great size.

As well as working in rural Germany as a guard and cattle droving dog, he has been used by the police and military. This reflects a good level of intelligence and his strength and endurance are an obvious asset in the testing situations that this work entails.

In the U.S.A. and Britain this is still a minority breed, although this is due simply to public taste and not attributable to any major faults in his make-up.

As a house-guard, the Giant Schnauzer is highly effective and all of the owner's family can feel very safe in his presence. House-training should prove no problem and when reared correctly he shows a playful and affectionate nature that belies his fierce appearance.

His exercise needs are great, so this is definitely not a dog for the inactive or elderly.

KEY TO CHARACTER	
INTELLIGENCE	****
TEMPERAMENT	****
EASE OF COAT CARE	**
SUITABILITY FOR SMALL DWELLING	*
***** (5) = VERY GOOD	

BRITISH KENNEL CLUB STANDARD

INTERIM STANDARD OF THE GIANT SCHNAUZER

GENERAL APPEARANCE. — The Schnauzer should be a powerfully built, robust, sinewy, nearly square dog (length of body equal to height at shoulders). His temperament should combine high spirits, reliability, strengthh, endurance and vigour. Expression keen and attitude alert. Correct conformation is of more importance than colour or other purely "beauty" points.

Head and Skull. — Head strong and elongated, gradually narrowing from the ears to the eyes and thence forward toward the tip of the nose. Upper part of the head (occiput to the base of the forehead) moderately broad between the ears — with flat, creaseless forehead and well muscled, but not too strongly developed cheeks. The powerful muzzle formed by the upper and lower jaws (base of forehead to the tip of nose) should end in a moderately blunt line, with bristly, stubby moustache and chin whiskers. Ridge of the nose straight and running almost parallel to the extension of the forehead. The nose should be black and full. Lips tight and not overlapping. Medium stop to accentuate eyebrows.

Eyes. — Medium sized, dark, oval, set forward, with arched bushy eyebrows.

Ears. — Neat and V shaped, set high and dropping forward to temple.

Mouth. — Scissor teeth, slightly overlapping from the top; with strongly developed fangs; healthy and pure white.

Neck. — Moderately long, nape strong and slightly arched, skin close to throat, neck set cleanly on shoulders.

Forequarters. — Shoulders flat and sloping. Forelegs straight viewed from any position. Muscles smooth and lithe rather than prominent; bones strong, straight and carried well down to the feet, elbows set close to the body and pointing directly backward.

Body. — Chest moderately broad, deep, with visible strong breast bone reaching down to at least the height of elbow and slightly rising backward to loins. Back strong and straight, slightly higher at the shoulder than at the hindquarters, with short well developed loins. Ribs well sprung. Length of body equal to height from top of withers to ground.

Hindquarters. — Thighs slanting and flat, but strongly muscled. Hindlegs (upper and lower thighs) at first vertical to the stifle, from stifle to hock in line with the extension of the upper neck line, from hock vertical to ground.

Feet. — Short, round, extremely compact with close-arched toes (cat's paws) dark nails and hard soles. The feet also deep or thickly padded, pointing forward.

Tail. — Set on and carried high, cut down to three joints.

Coat. — Hard and wiry and just short enough for smartness, clean on neck, shoulder, ears and skull, plenty of good hard hair on front legs. Good undercoat is essential.

Colour. — All pepper and salt colours in even proportions, or pure black.

Height. — The ideal height for bitches shall be between 60 cms. and 65 cms. (23½ inches and 25½ inches) and for dogs between 65 cms. and 70 cms. (25½ inches and 27½ inches). Any variation of more than 3 cms (1 inch) in these heights should be penalised.

Faults. — Too heavy or too light; too low or high on the leg. Head too heavy or round; creased forehead; sticking out or badly carried ears; light eye, with yellow or light grey rings; strongly protruding cheek-bones; flabby throatskin; undershot or overshot jaw. Muzzle too pointed or too small. Back too long, sunken or roached; barrel-shaped ribs; slanting crupper; elbows turned out; heels turned in, hindpart overbuilt (too steep). Toes spread open; paws long and flat (hare). Coat too short and sleek, or too long, soft or curled. All white, spotty, tigered or red colours. Small white breast spot or marking is not a fault. Among other serious faults are cow-hocks, sunken pasterns, or any weakness of joint, bone or muscular development.

Note. — Male animals should have two apparently normal testicles fully descended into the scrotum.

GIANT SCHNAUZER REGISTRATIONS 1981 — 87 INCLUSIVE

1981 — 89
1982 — 128
1983 — 162
1984 — 214
1985 — 218
1986 — 218
1987 — 184

YET TO WIN CRUFTS BEST-IN-SHOW.

GREAT DANE

Despite his name, this colossal breed does not definitely have his origins in Denmark, his exact place of origin being unascertainable. There is record of Great Dane-like dogs being present throughout Europe as far back as the Middle Ages. They were probably related to the Mastiffs although they developed along more graceful, athletic lines. These early specimens were employed in the hunting of boar, where their great power and agility were put to great effect. However, the struggling boar would often rip the dog's large ears and this eventually led to them being cropped, a practice still seen in the U.S.A. and Germany.

A British breed known as the Lyme Mastiff existed some 400 years ago and it can be seen from paintings of the period that it bore a strong resemblance to today's Great Dane and was probably used in his development.

But the people who have put the most work into perfecting this breed are the Germans. Through tireless selective breeding in the 19th Century they established all the major characteristics of the present day Danes. The breed is often referred to as the German Mastiff, especially in Europe and he is, as ever, a prized breed in Germany itself.

The most obvious consideration for anyone contemplating keeping a Great Dane is his immense size. Anyone who has anything less than a very large house, large garden and plenty of time and energy for consistent exercise should steer away from the breed. Although a truly terrifying guard dog, he has a gentle and friendly side to him and the right owner will derive great satisfaction from his company.

KEY TO CHARACTER	
INTELLIGENCE	***
TEMPERAMENT	****
EASE OF COAT CARE	*****
SUITABILITY FOR SMALL DWELLING	*
***** (5) = VERY GOOD	

BRITISH KENNEL CLUB STANDARD

GREAT DANE

GENERAL APPEARANCE. — The Great Dane should be remarkable in size and very muscular, strongly though elegantly built; the head and neck should be carried high, and the tail in line with the back, or slightly upwards but not curled over the hindquarters. Elegance of outline and grace of form are most essential to a Dane; size is absolutely necessary, but there must be that alertness of expression and briskness of movement without which the Dane character is lost. He should have a look of dash and daring, of being ready to go anywhere and do anything. The action should be lithe, springy and free, the hocks move freely and the head be carried high except when galloping.

Head and Skull. — The head, taken altogether, should give the idea of great length and strength of jaw. The muzzle or foreface is broad, and the skull proportionately narrow, so that the whole head, when viewed from above and in front, has the appearance of equal breadth throughout. The entire length of head varies with the height of the dog; 13 inches from the top of the nose to the back of the occiput is a good measurement for a dog of 32 inches at the shoulder. The length from the end of the nose to the point between the eyes should be about equal, or preferably of greater length than from this point to the back of the occiput. The skull should be flat and have a slight indentation running up the centre, the occipital peak not prominent. There should be a decided rise or brow over the eyes but no abrupt stop between them; the face should be well chiselled, well filled in below the eyes with no appearance of being pinched; the foreface long, of equal depth throughout. The cheeks should show as little lumpiness as possible, compatible with strength. The underline of the head, viewed in profile, should run almost in a straight line from the corner of the lip to the corner of the jawbone, allowing for the fold of the lip, but with no loose skin to hang down. The bridge of the nose should be very wide, with a slight ridge where the cartilage joins the bone. (This is a characteristic of the breed). The nostrils should be large, wide and open, giving a blunt look to the nose. A butterfly or flesh-coloured nose is not objected to in Harlequins. The lips should hang squarely in front, forming a right-angle with the upper line of foreface.

Eyes. — Fairly deep set, of medium size and preferably dark. Wall or odd eyes permissible in Harlequins.

Ears. — Should be small, set high on the skull and carried slightly erect with the tips falling forward.

Mouth. — The teeth should be level and not project one way or the other.

Neck. — The neck should be long, well arched, and quite clean and free from loose skin, held well up, well set in the shoulders, and the junction of the head and neck well defined.

Forequarters. — The shoulders should be muscular but not loaded, and well sloped back, with the elbows well under the body. The forelegs should be perfectly straight with big bone, which must be flat.

Body. — The body should be very deep, with ribs well sprung and belly well drawn up. The back and loins should be strong, the latter slightly arched.

Hindquarters. — The hindquarters and thighs should be extremely muscular giving the idea of great strength and galloping power. The second thigh is long and well developed, the stifle and hock well bent, the hocks set low, turning neither in nor out.

Feet. — The feet should be catlike and should not turn in or out. The toes well arched and close, the nails strong and curved. Nails should be black but light nails are permissible in Harlequins.

Tail. — The tail should be thick at the root, and taper towards the end, reaching to or just below the hocks. It should be carried in a straight line level with the back, when the dog is in action, slightly curved towards the end, but in no case should it curl or be carried over the back.

Coat. — The hair is short and dense and sleek-looking, and in no case should it incline to roughness.

Colour. — (a) Brindles must be striped, ground colour from the lightest yellow to the deepest orange, and the stripes must always be black. Eyes and nails preferably dark. (b) Fawns, the colour varies from lightest buff to deepest orange, darker shadings on the muzzle and the ears and around the eyes are by no means objectionable. Eyes and nails preferably dark. (c) Blues, the colour varies from light grey to deepest slate. (d) Blacks, black is black. (In all the above colours white is only admissible on the chest and feet, but it is not desirable even there. The nose is always black (except in blues). Eyes and nails preferably dark). (e) Harlequins, pure white underground with preferably black patches (blue patches permitted), having the appearance of being torn. In Harlequins, wall eyes, pink noses or butterfly noses are permissible but are not desirable.

Weight and Size. — The minimum height of an adult dog over eighteen months must be 30 inches, that of a bitch, 28 inches. Weight, the minimum weight of an adult dog over eighteen months should be 120 lbs., that of a bitch, 100 lbs.

Faults. — Cow-hocks. Out at elbows. Straight stifles. Undershot or overshot mouth. Round bone. Snipy muzzle. Straight shoulders. Shelly body. Ring tail.

Note. — Male animals should have two apparently normal testicles fully descended into the scrotum.

MAIN AMERICAN KENNEL CLUB VARIATION TO STANDARD FOR THE GREAT DANE —

Ears. — Cropped ears: high set, not set too far apart, well pointed but always in proportion to the shape of the head and carried uniformally erect.

Size. — The male should not be less than 30 inches at the shoulders, but it is preferable that he be 32 inches or more providing he is well proportioned to his height. The female should not be less than 28 inches at the shoulders, but it is preferable that she be 30 inches or more, providing she is well proportioned to her height.

GREAT DANE REGISTRATIONS 1981 — 87 INCLUSIVE

1981 — 2381
1982 — 2255
1983 — 2555
1984 — 2548
1985 — 2432
1986 — 2068
1987 — 2242

CRUFTS BEST-IN-SHOW WINNER

1953 CH. ELCH ELDER OF OUBOROUGH — W. G. SIGGERS.

KOMONDOR

A Komondor always creates a stir amongst people who are viewing one for the first time. His size and incredible coat formation give him an almost unreal air. The thick cords form naturally and on a mature dog barely resemble hair at all.

The breed most likely originated in Asia, although exactly where is unknown. Several centuries ago Hungary found the Komondor to be ideal for the needs of their shepherds and breeding was begun there in great quantity. He was particularly suitable for the herding of a large species of sheep known as Racka. These sheep were large and aggressive and the imposing figure of the Komondor proved very successful at keeping them in order. His coat, too, ensured that he was impervious to the bitter cold of the Hungarian plains.

The Komondor is still very popular in Hungary where he is still in use as a herding dog and as a forceful and intelligent guard.

He has reached a fair degree of popularity in the U.S.A. where he was introduced in 1935 but, Britain has imported only a small number of specimens.

This is not a breed to be taken on lightly due to his size and coat care needs. Although the coat is not brushed, the cords have to be meticulously tended to keep them clean and unmatted, especially in the young dog.

His conduct in the home is excellent as he is easily trained and friendly to all these he trusts. Space is an obvious consideration and exercise must be regular.

KEY TO CHARACTER	
INTELLIGENCE	****
TEMPERAMENT	****
EASE OF COAT CARE	*
SUITABILITY FOR SMALL DWELLING	*
***** (5) = VERY GOOD	

BRITISH KENNEL CLUB STANDARD

INTERIM STANDARD OF THE KOMONDOR

CHARACTERISTICS. — The Komondor is a shepherd's dog of Asiatic origin, an excellent guard, wary of strangers, courageous, faithful and devoted to its master, whom he will defend against any attack. Because of this trait, it was not used for driving the herds, but only for guarding. The Komondor's special task was to protect the herds against wolves, bears, and strange dogs, etc. The Komondor is noted for his imposing strength and courageous manner.

GENERAL APPEARANCE. — A large muscular dog, with plenty of bone and substance. Powerful in conformation.

Head and Skull. — The head should look somewhat short in comparison to the wide forehead. The skull should be slightly arched when viewed from the side. Stop moderate, muzzle slightly shorter than the length of skull. Broad rather coarse muzzle, not pointed. Nostrils wide. Nose black, though a dark grey or dark brown nose is acceptable but not desirable.

Eyes. — Medium sized, not too deeply set, the darker the eye the better; eye rims dark grey or black and close fitting.

Ears. — Medium sized and hanging U-shaped. Erect or partially erect ears are incorrect.

Mouth. — Powerful jaws, strong teeth. Scissor bite ideal (pincer bite acceptable but not desirable). Lips tight fitting and black. Ideally gums and roof of mouth should be black or dark grey.

Neck. — Strong, medium length, moderately arched, no dewlap.

Forequarters. — Straight, well boned and muscular, viewed from any side the forelegs should be like vertical columns; well laid tight shoulders.

Body. — Broad, deep, muscular chest, back level. Rump broad, slightly sloping towards root of tail. The body should be slightly longer than height at withers. Belly tucked up.

Hindquarters. — Strong in bone structure and very muscular. Viewed from rear, legs fairly wide apart, parallel, well angulated. Dewclaws should be removed.

Feet. — Strong, large and compact, well arched toes. Claws strong, grey or black, toes slightly longer on hindfeet. Pads hard, elastic and dark.

Gait. — Light and easy, should move with very long strides.

Tail. — Continuation of rump line, should reach down to hocks, slightly curved at tip; when excited, raised in line with body.

Coat. — The coat texture should consist of a longer coarse outer coat, which may be wavy or curly, and a softer undercoat. The hair should tend to cling together like tassels, giving a corded appearance, even when combed. When corded, the cords of an adult coat should be stong and heavy and felty to the touch, if neglected will form into large matted "plates". Coat should be longest on rump, loins and tail, of medium length on back, shoulders and chest, and shorter on cheeks around eyes, mouth and lower parts of legs. Coat is fairly slow in cording and may not be fully formed before two years of age. Puppy coat should be soft and fluffy, adult coat usually appearing 6-9 months of age. Should be presented corded.

Colour. — Always white. Ideally the skin should be grey; pink skin is acceptable and is no evidence of albinism.

Weight and Size. — Weight for dogs, about 110 lbs to 135 lbs. Weight for bitches, about 80 to 110 lbs.

Size. — Dogs, average 80 cms. (31 ins.). Minimum 65 cms. (26 ins.). Bitches, average 70 cms. (27½ ins.). Minimum 55 cms. (23½ ins.). Whilst the average height is given, of the Komondor it can be said that there is no maximum height, but height should always be taken into consideration with the overall picture of the dog, which should be strong, well balanced and give the impression of vast strength.

Faults. — Any departure from the foregoing points should be considered a fault and the seriousness of the fault should be in exact proportion to its degree.

Note. — Male animals should have two apparently normal testicles fully descended into the scrotum.

MAIN AMERICAN KENNEL CLUB VARIATION TO STANDARD FOR THE KOMONDOR —

Size. — Dogs, 25½ inches and upwards at withers; bitches, 23½ inches and upward at withers.

KOMONDOR REGISTRATIONS 1981 — 87 INCLUSIVE

1981 — 9
1982 — 1
1983 — 5
1984 — 0
1985 — 5
1986 — 12
1987 — 0

YET TO WIN CRUFTS BEST-IN-SHOW.

MAREMMA SHEEPDOG

The Maremma region of Italy contains vast areas of open plain and it is there that this breed has been used for centuries as a guard of sheep. His ancestry probably dates back 2000 years to when the Magyars brought a dog similar to the Kuvasz into Central Europe. The Maremma Sheepdog's kinship with the Kuvasz is very evident so these ancient dogs were almost certainly the originators of both breeds.

He has all the attributes essential for an effective guard, namely strength, stamina and unfaltering courage. The Maremma Sheepdog is highly prized in Italy and farmers there have kept the breed extremely pure, so much so that it is doubtful if today's dogs differ at all from the earliest specimens. This pure blood has meant that the Maremma is still very much a dog with a working mentality, still possessing the great independence that is such an asset when guarding large flocks in the open countryside. Having this innate self-confidence can often mean that the Maremma finds training pointless. This being said, a healthy, mutual respect should develop between dog and owner although this is not a breed that enjoys being totally dominated.

Needless to say he makes an excellent house guard and whilst he can be 'stand-offish' he will attach himself to the family in his own undemonstrative way. He will enjoy plenty of exercise and a rural environment would be ideal.

KEY TO CHARACTER	
INTELLIGENCE	****
TEMPERAMENT	****
EASE OF COAT CARE	***
SUITABILITY FOR SMALL DWELLING	*
***** (5) = VERY GOOD	

BRITISH KENNEL CLUB STANDARD
MAREMMA SHEEPDOG

CHARACTERISTICS. — Majestic, lively, sturdy, distinguished and intelligent. Courageous without being aggressive.

GENERAL APPEARANCE. — Lithe and strongly built. The expression should be one of aloof awareness. This reserve should not be mistaken for nervousness, any tendency to which should be penalised.

Head and Skull. — When viewed from the front the head is of triangular shape and in proportion to the size of the body. The skull wider between the ears, narrowing towards the facial area. The head somewhat rounded, with the occipital ridge slightly emphasized. The area under the eyes gently chiselled. Medium stop. The length of the muzzle fractionally less than that of the cranium and the muzzle slightly tapering without showing snipiness. The lips close fitting and not pendulous. Pigmentation of the lips and nose black.

Eyes. — The eyes bold, neither large nor small; neither sunk nor protruding. The aperture almond-shaped. A dark eye preferred. Eyerims black.

Ears. — Small in relation to the size of the head, V-shaped, set high and covered with short hair. Hanging flat to the side of the head in repose; mobile when alert. The extremities of the ear forming a narrow point, never a rounded end.

Mouth. — The teeth should be white, strong, regularly spaced and set in a level jaw. The inner faces of the upper incisors should close on the outer faces of the lower incisors.

Neck. — The neck should be strong, of medium length. Devoid of dewlap.

Forequarters. — The shoulders should be long, sloping, well muscled and free moving; the forelegs well boned and muscled without heaviness, straight when viewed from the front, the elbows held close to the ribcage, neither in nor out. The pasterns should show a very slight angle in profile.

Body. — The body strong, the muscles well developed, the shoulders slightly above the level of the back, which should be broad and straight, rising to a slight arch on the loins and falling to a broad, strong rump. The length of the body, measured from the point of the shoulder to the point of the buttocks, slightly longer than the height at the shoulder. The ribcage full, descending to the level of the elbows, with well sprung ribs; not barrel-chested. The sternum long, gradually curving up to the abdomen which shows a waist without excessive tuck up.

Hindquarters. — The hindquarters broad and powerful, with strongly muscled thighs, legs straight when viewed from behind; hocks well let down and strong with a moderate bend of stifle.

Feet. — Large and almost round. Hind feet slightly more oval. Toes close together and well arched. Pads black.

Gait. — Movement should be free and active, giving the impression of a nimble dog, able to turn quickly.

Tail. — Set on low, reaching below the joint of the hock; hangs down when the dog is quiet but carried level with the back when the dog is alerted; with the tip gently curved. Well covered with thick hair, but without forming fringes.

Coat. — The coat should fit the outline of the dog and be long, plentiful and rather harsh. A slight waviness, but not curliness, is permissible. It should form a thick collar on the neck. The hair should be short on the muzzle, cranium, ears, feet and front of limbs but should form a slight feathering on the rear edges of the limbs. There should be a thick, close undercoat especially in winter.

Colour. — White. A little shading of ivory, pale orange or lemon is permissible.

Weight and Size. — Ideal Height: Dogs 65 to 73 cm. (25½ in. to 28½ in.). Bitches 60 to 68 cm. (23½ in. to 26¾ in.). Ideal weight: Dogs 35 to 45 Kgs. (77 to 99 lbs.). Bitches 30 to 40 Kgs. (66 to 88 lbs.).

Faults. — Any departure from the foregoing points should be considered a fault and the seriousness with which the fault should be regarded should be in exact proportion to its degree.

Note. — Male animals should have two apparently normal testicles fully descended into the scrotum.

MAREMMA SHEEPDOG REGISTRATIONS 1981 — 87 INCLUSIVE

1981 — 77
1982 — 19
1983 — 91
1984 — 49
1985 — 49
1986 — 29
1987 — 55

YET TO WIN CRUFTS BEST-IN-SHOW.

MASTIFF

The giant Mastiff, or Old English Mastiff as he has been known, is the closest living relative of the Molossian Dog of Ancient Greece. This dog was the main ancestor of all the large, heavy-set breeds of Europe. One such breed in its early form was kept by the Romans for use as a fighting dog. These fights were grand affairs staged in amphitheatres with the dog's pitted against various wild animals. It was the Romans, in fact who probably introduced the first Mastiff-type dogs to Britain where they flourished as guards and hunters. In the Middle Ages in particular, when hunting was so widespread, dogs not far removed from the Mastiffs of today were used effectively for the bringing down of large game.

Despite his distant European origins, the Mastiff is now regarded as a British breed. He makes the classic guard for an English Country gentleman's estate and radiates a nobility and authority that well befits his immense size.

Although unfortunately not as numerous as he once was, this being largely due to the ravages of the Second World War, the Mastiff still has a devoted band of enthusiasts who have kept him true to type.

As would be expected he makes an intimidating guard, so his owner need have no fear of intruders. He is the epitome of gentleness and tolerance when in the company of children and he warms to all human attention. If a prospective owner has a sufficiently large house and will provide his dog with regular exercise, a Mastiff makes a truly magnificent companion.

KEY TO CHARACTER	
INTELLIGENCE	****
TEMPERAMENT	*****
EASE OF COAT CARE	*****
SUITABILITY FOR SMALL DWELLING	*
***** (5) = VERY GOOD	

BRITISH KENNEL CLUB STANDARD

MASTIFF

GENERAL APPEARANCE. — Large, massive, powerful, symmetrical and well-knit frame. A combination of grandeur and good nature, courage and docility. The head, in general outline giving a square appearance when viewed from any point. Breadth greatly to be desired, and should be in ratio to length of the whole head and face as 2 to 3. Body, massive, broad, deep, long, powerfully built, on legs wide apart and squarely set. Muscles sharply defined. Size a great desideratum, if combined with quality. Height and substance important if both points are proportionately combined.

Head and Skull. — Skull broad between the ears, forehead flat, but wrinkles when attention is excited. Brows (superciliary ridges) slightly raised. Muscles of the temples and cheeks (temporal and masseter) well developed. Arch across the skull of a rounded, flattened curve, with a depression up the centre of the forehead from the median line between the eyes, to half-way up the sagittal suture. Face or muzzle, short, broad under the eyes, and keeping nearly parallel in width to the end of the nose; truncated, i.e., blunt and cut off squarely, thus forming a right-angle with the upper line of the face, of great depth from the point of the nose to under jaw. Under jaw broad to the end. Nose broad, with widely spreading nostrils when viewed from the front, flat (not pointed or turned up) in profile. Lips diverging at obtuse angles with the septum, and slightly pendulous so as to show a square profile. Length of muzzle to whole head and face as 1 to 3. Circumference of muzzle (measured mid-way between the eyes and nose) to that of the head (measured before the ears) as 3 to 5.

Eyes. — Small, wide apart, divided by at least the space of two eyes. The stop between the eyes well marked but not too abrupt. Colour hazel brown, the darker the better, showing no haw.

Ears. — Small, thin to the touch, wide apart, set on at the highest points of the sides of the skull, so as to continue the outline across the summit, and lying flat and close to the cheeks when in repose.

Mouth. — Canine teeth healthy; powerful and wide apart; incisors level, or the lower projecting beyond the upper but never so much as to become visible when the mouth is closed.

Neck. — Slightly arched, moderately long, very muscular, and measuring in circumference about one or two inches less than the skull before the ears.

Forequarters. — Shoulder and arm slightly sloping, heavy and muscular. Legs straight, strong, and set wide apart; bones being large. Elbows suare. Pasterns upright.

Body. — Chest wide, deep and well let down between the forelegs. Ribs arched and well rounded. false ribs deep and well set back to the hips. Girth should be one-third more than the height at the shoulder. Back and loins wide and muscular; flat and very wide in a bitch, slightly arched in a dog. Great depth of flanks.

Hindquarters. — Broad, wide and muscular, with well-developed second thighs, hocks bent, wide apart, and quite squarely set when standing or walking.

Feet. — Large and round. Toes well arched up. Nails black.

Tail. — Put on high up, and reaching to the hocks, or a little below them, wide at its root and tapering to the end, hanging straight in repose, but forming a curve with the end pointing upwards, but not over the back, when the dog is excited.

Coat. — Short and close-lying, but not too fine over the shoulders, neck and back.

Colour. — Apricot or silver, fawn, or dark fawn-brindle. In any case, muzzle, ears and nose should be black with black round orbits, and extending upwards between them.

Note. — Male animals should have two apparently normal testicles fully descended into the scrotum.

MAIN AMERICAN KENNEL CLUB VARIATION TO STANDARD FOR THE MASTIFF —

Size. — Dogs, minimum 30 inches at the shoulder, bitches, minimum 27½ inches at the shoulder.

MASTIFF REGISTRATIONS 1981 — 87 INCLUSIVE

1981 — 241
1982 — 239
1983 — 215
1984 — 238
1985 — 295
1986 — 247
1987 — 291

YET TO WIN CRUFTS BEST-IN-SHOW.

NEWFOUNDLAND

This massive breed hails from the land he is named after, although exactly how he developed there is a matter for speculation. It seems probable that dogs native to Newfoundland were crossed with dogs brought from europe by settlers or traders. His very heavy build would suggest that somewhere along the line Mastiff-type blood was introduced, the predominant black of the coat coming from local dogs.

He has won great fame for his affinity with water and has assisted the fishermen of Newfoundland for centuries. He is the most powerful swimmer in the canine world and he has been used extensively as a rescue dog, being able to reach a man in distress in the coldest and most dangerous of seas. This rescuing instinct undoubtedly stems from his skill at carrying fish to shore.

Eventually the Newfoundland reached Britain and by the mid-nineteenth century was quite popular here. When a black and white variety of the breed was developed, it was called the Landseer after the famous Victorian artist Sir Edward Landseer who produced some celebrated studies of the dog.

If a prospective owner has a sufficiently large home and garden, the Newfoundland is a magnificent breed to own. He has a kind, even disposition and loves children. As a guard he is truly formidable and no intruder would be a match for him. He will like as much outdoor life as possible and to keep him in muscular condition, a large amount of exercise is required.

KEY TO CHARACTER	
INTELLIGENCE	****
TEMPERAMENT	*****
EASE OF COAT CARE	***
SUITABILITY FOR SMALL DWELLING	*
***** (5) = VERY GOOD	

BRITISH KENNEL CLUB STANDARD

NEWFOUNDLAND

CHARACTERISTICS. — A water dog, used for life-saving; he should have an exceptionally gentle and docile nature.

GENERAL APPEARANCE. — The dog should impress the eye with strength and great activity. He should move freely on his legs with the body swung loosely between them, so that a slight roll in gait should not be objectionable. Bone massive throughout, but not to give a heavy, inactive appearance.

Head and Skull. — Head should be broad and massive, the occipital bone well developed; there should be no decided stop; the muzzle should be short, clean cut and rather square in shape and covered with short, fine hair.

Eyes. — Should be small, of a dark brown colour; rather deeply set, but not showing any haw; should be set rather wide apart.

Ears. — Should be small, set well back, square with the skull, lie close to the head, and covered with short hair without a fringe.

Mouth. — Should be soft and well covered by the lips, should be neither undershot nor overshot but teeth should be level or scissor bite.

Neck. — Should be strong, well set on to shoulders and back.

Forequarters. — Legs should be perfectly straight, well covered with muscle elbows in but well let down; feathered all down.

Body. — Should be well ribbed up with broad back and strong muscular loins. Chest should be deep and fairly broad; well covered with hair, but not to such an extent as to form a frill.

Hindquarters. — Should be very strong. The legs should have great freedom of action; slightly feathered. Slackness of loins and cow-hocks are a defect. Dew-claws are objectionable and should be removed.

Feet. — Should be large and well shaped. Splayed or turned out feet are objectionable.

Tail. — Should be of moderate length, reaching down a little below the hocks. It should be of fair thickness and well covered with hair, but not to form a flag. When the dog is standing still and not excited it should hang downwards with a slight curve at the end; but when the dog is in motion it should be carried up, and when he is excited straight out with only a slight curve at the end. Tails with a kink or curled over the back are very objectionabe.

Coat. — Should be flat and dense, of a coarsish texture and oily nature, and capable of resisting water. If brushed the wrong way it should fall back into its place naturally.

Colour. — The colours allowed are black, brown, white with black markings (Landseer).

Dull jet black. A slight tinge of bronze or splash of white on chest and toes is acceptable. Black dogs having only white toes and white chest and white tip of tail should be exhibited in classes provided for black.

Brown — can be chocolate or bronze. Should in all other aspects follow the black except in colour. Splash of white on chest and toes is acceptable. brown dogs to be exhibited in classes provided for blacks.

White with black markings only — Landseers. For preference black head with narrow blaize, even marked saddle and black rump extending on the tail. Beauty in markings to be taken greatly into consideration. Ticking is not desirable.

Weight and Size. — Size and weight are very desirable so long as symmetry is maintained. A fair average height at the shoulders is 28 inches for a dog and 26 inches for a bitch, and a fair average weight is, respectively: Dogs, 140 to 150 lbs. Bitches, 110 to 120 lbs.

Faults. — Weak or hollow back, slackness of the loins or cow-hocks. Dewclaws. Splayed or turned-out feet. Tails with a kink in them or curled over the back.

Note. — Male animals shuld have two apparently normal testicles fully descended into the scrotum.

MAIN AMERICAN KENNEL CLUB VARIATION TO STANDARD FOR THE NEWFOUNDLAND —

Size. — The approximate weight of adult dogs is 130 to 150 pounds, of adult bitches 100 to 120 lbs.

German Shepherd Dog

Giant Schnauzer

NEWFOUNDLAND REGISTRATIONS 1981 — 87 INCLUSIVE

1981 — 349
1982 — 346
1983 — 517
1984 — 511
1985 — 655
1986 — 715
1987 — 726

YET TO WIN CRUFTS BEST-IN-SHOW.

NORWEGIAN BUHUND

The Norwegian Buhund is instantly recognisable as one of the Spitz group of breeds. This is the group that includes all the dogs of the very far north, the Siberian Husky, the Keeshond and the Ellkhound being good examples. All these breeds have common ancestry but it is unclear as to exactly when some of the Spitz-types emerged. Such is the case with the Buhund, although it is well known that he has been widespread in Norway for centuries. He has always been held in very high esteem by Norwegian farmers who have used him as a herder of all manner of livestock. In the home, too, they will testify to his loyal, affectionate nature.

The Buhund has slowly but surely begun to make an impact in Britain and show appearances are now commonplace. There seems little doubt that his popularity will increase as he is one of the more intelligent and interesting of the smaller breeds.

A family with children would do well to acquire a Buhund as they love boisterous play and have a character of the most reliable type. He will also guard his owner's family with force and courage. Stamina and speed are natural to this breed so he must be allowed a great deal of exercise, several outings a day being ideal.

Great Dane

Komondor

KEY TO CHARACTER	
INTELLIGENCE	****
TEMPERAMENT	*****
EASE OF COAT CARE	****
SUITABILITY FOR SMALL DWELLING	***
***** (5) = VERY GOOD	

BRITISH KENNEL CLUB STANDARD

NORWEGIAN BUHUND

CHARACTERISTICS. — The Norwegian Buhund should be fearless and brave.

GENERAL APPEARANCE. — The Norwegian Buhund is a typical Spitz dog of under middle size, lightly built, with a short compact body, fairly smooth-lying coat, erect pointed ears, tail carried over the back, and with an energetic character.

It is of prime importance that the Buhund should be a well-balanced dog, free from all exaggeration and should be capable of the arduous work for which it is bred.

Head and Skull. — Head — lean, light, rather broad between the ears, wedge shaped, narrowing towards the point of the nose. Skull and back of head almost flat; marked but not sharp stop; muzzle of medium length, tapering evenly from above and side, with straight bridge; lips tightly closed.

Eyes. — Not protruding, colour dark brown, lively with a fearless expression.

Ears. — Placed high, erect, the height greater than the base; sharply pointed and very mobile.

Neck. — Medium length, lean without loose skin, good carriage.

Forequarters. — Legs lean, straight and strong, elbows tightly placed.

Body. — Strong and short, but light; chest deep with good ribs; straight line of back, good loins, strong couplings, slightly drawn up.

Hindquarters. — Only a little angulated, straight when seen from behind.

Feet. — Rather small, oval in shape, with tightly closed toes.

Tail. — Placed high on, short, thick and hairy, but without long hair, tightly curled.

Coat. — Close and harsh, but smooth; on head and front legs — short close and smooth; longer on chest, neck and shoulders and back of legs and inside of tail curl. The coat is made up of a harsh top hair, with soft wool undercoat.

Colour. — Wheaten (biscuit), black, red (if the red is not too dark), wolf-sable. Preferably self-coloured but small symmetric markings such as white on chest and legs, blaize on head and narrow ring on neck, black masks and ears and black tips to the tail are permissible.

Size. — Dogs not more than 45 cms. (17¾ inches); bitches somewhat less.

Faults. — White dogs. Light eyes. Light nose. Undershot or overshot mouth. Drop ear.

Note. — Male animals should have two apparently normal testicles fully descended into the scrotum.

NORWEGIAN BUHUND REGISTRATIONS 1981 — 87 INCLUSIVE

1981 — 81
1982 — 106
1983 — 114
1984 — 123
1985 — 102
1986 — 99
1987 — 60

YET TO WIN CRUFTS BEST-IN-SHOW.

OLD ENGLISH SHEEPDOG

The Old English Sheepdog or "Bobtail" as he is widely known, has very unclear origins. It seems that the breed has developed slowly over hundreds of years rather than suddenly appeared from cross-breeding. Some authorities believe he is from the same stock as a Russian breed called the Owtchah which was common at the turn of the century. This seems quite possible as these dogs were of similar conformation and coat type, but they were heavier and more aggressive than the Bobtail. There is also a view that the Briard is a close relative, the similarities there being very obvious. The Komondor, too has been mentioned as possibly sharing the same blood line.

There has been reference to large, dock-tailed shaggy coated sheepdogs in England for centuries, many ancient accounts extolling the virtues of these dog's faithfullness and intelligence. As well as showing his worth as an excellent herding dog, the Bobtail has occasionally been used as a gun dog and with great success.

It was towards the end of the 19th Century that the breed became recognised and was first exhibited. After a slightly uncertain start he became well established soon after.

With the help of some memorable advertising appearances, the Bobtail has now reached a peak of great esteem in British hearts and he does indeed make an excellent companion. He is every bit as gentle as he appears, mixing well with all age groups. His coat needs plenty of care and attention but the effort is well worthwhile when you see the end product. The Bobtail is lively and intelligent and will appreciate energetic play and lengthy exercise to ensure he does not become bored.

KEY TO CHARACTER	
INTELLIGENCE	****
TEMPERAMENT	****
EASE OF COAT CARE	*
SUITABILITY FOR SMALL DWELLING	*
***** (5) = VERY GOOD	

BRITISH KENNEL CLUB STANDARD
OLD ENGLISH SHEEPDOG

GENERAL APPEARANCE. — A strong, compact-looking dog of great symmetry; absolutely free of legginess; profusely coated all over; very elastic in a gallop but in walking or trotting has a characteristic ambling or pacing movement; and his bark should be loud, with a peculiar "pot casse" ring in it. All round he is a thick-set, muscular, able-bodied dog, with a most intelligent expression, free of all Poodle or Deerhound character.

Head and Skull. — Skull capacious and rather squarely formed, giving plenty of room for brain power. The parts over the eyes should be well arched and the whole well-covered with hair. Jaw fairly long, strong, square, and truncated; the stop should be defined to avoid a Deerhound face. Nose always black, large, and capacious.

Eyes. — Dark or wall eyes are to be preferred.

Ears. — Small and carried flat to side of head, coated moderately.

Mouth. — Teeth strong and large, evenly placed and level.

Neck. — The neck should be fairly long, arched gracefully, and well coated with hair.

Forequarters. — The forelegs should be dead straight, with plenty of bone, holding the body well from the ground, without approaching legginess; well coated all round. The shoulders sloping and narrow at the points, the dog standing lower at the shoulders than at the loin.

Body. — Rather short and very compact, ribs well sprung, and brisket deep and capacious. The loin should be very stout and gently arched.

Hindquarters. — The hindquarters should be round and muscular, hocks well let down and the hams densely coated with a thick, long jacket in excess of that of any part of the body.

Feet. — Small, round; toes well arched, and pads thick and round.

Tail. — Puppies requiring docking should have the operation performed within a week from birth, preferably within four days.

Coat. — Profuse, and of good hard texture; not straight, but shaggy and free from curl. The undercoat should be a waterproof pile when not removed by grooming.

Colour. — Any shade of grey, grizzle, blue or blue merle, with or without white markings; any shade of brown or sable to be considered distinctly objectionable and not to be encouraged.

Weight and Size. — Twenty-two inches and upwards for dogs, slightly less for bitches. Type, symmetry and character of the greatest importance, and on no account to be sacrificed to size alone.

Faults. — A long, narrow head.

Note. — Male animals should have two apparently normal testicles fully descended into the scrotum.

OLD ENGLISH SHEEPDOG REGISTRATIONS 1981 — 87 INCLUSIVE

1981 — 3940
1982 — 2807
1983 — 2364
1984 — 2050
1985 — 1958
1986 — 1725
1987 — 1598

YET TO WIN CRUFTS BEST-IN-SHOW.

PYRENEAN MOUNTAIN DOG

Several of Europe's giant mountain dogs are direct descendants of the Tibetan Mastiff and the Pyrenean variety is one such breed. He began as a predominantly brown coloured dog but has evolved in accordance with his native surroundings to become almost totally white.

The farmers of the Pyrenees have used this formidably powerful breed to guard their sheep. Such was the ferocity of some of the early dogs that it was said that even wolves would not approach them.

The vigilance of the Pyrenean Mountain Dog at work is legendary. If necessary he would guard his flock throughout the night using his acute sense of smell to detect any marauders. The shepherds would often don their dogs with large spiked collars to assist them in combat but, even without such aids no opponent would ever overcome them.

Great efforts have been made in the breeding of the modern day Pyrenean to eliminate any excess aggression, which would, of course, be a legacy from his early days. Although much success has been achieved in this area, the Pyrenean can still be a little touchy with strangers and small children might be at risk if they were to continually tease him. This being said, he can make an outstanding companion and if firmly and thoughtfully trained will become an important part of a household. To maintain his stunning appearance, his coat must be kept spotless and exercise should be regular. Definitely not for a small house.

KEY TO CHARACTER	
INTELLIGENCE	****
TEMPERAMENT	***
EASE OF COAT CARE	**
SUITABILITY FOR SMALL DWELLING	*
***** (5) = VERY GOOD	

BRITISH KENNEL CLUB STANDARD

PYRENEAN MOUNTAIN DOG

CHARACTERISTICS. — The Pyrenean is a natural guard dog and was originally employed as a protector of the shepherd and of his flocks.

GENERAL APPEARANCE. — The Pyrenean should possess great size, substance and power, giving an impression of an immesely strong yet well-balanced dog. These qualities should be accompanied by a certain elegance resulting from a combination of the attractive coat, the correct head and a general air of quiet confidence. It is of the utmost importance that nervousness or unprovoked aggression should be heavily penalised.

Head and Skull. — It is very important that the head should give an impression of strength with no sign of coarseness; it should not be too heavy in proportion to the size of the dog. The top of the skull, as viewed from front and side, should show a definite curve so as to give a somewhat domed effect and the breadth of the skull at its widest point should be about equal to the length from occiput to stop. The sides of the head should be nearly flat and of a good depth. There should be no obvious stop and only a slight furrow so that the skull and muzzle are joined by a gentle slope. The muzzle should be strong, of medium length and with a slight taper near its tip. The nose should be absolutely black. When viewed from above the head should have the general form of a blunt "V" well filled in below the eyes.

Eyes. — The eyes should be almond-shaped and of a dark amber-brown colour. The close-fitting eyelids should be set somewhat obliquely and should be bordered with black. Drooping lower eyelids should be penalised. The expression should be intelligent and contemplative.

Ears. — The ears should be fairly small and triangular with rounded tips, the root of the ear being on a level with the eyes. Normally the ears lie flat against the head, but may be slightly raised when the dog is alert.

Mouth. — There should be a complete set of healthy strong even teeth, the incisors meeting in either a scissor or a pincer bite. The two central lower incisors may be set a little deeper than the others but this should not be regarded as a serious fault.
The lips should be close fitting, the upper ones extending downwards just sufficiently to cover the lower. They should be black or heavily marked with black in common with the roof of the mouth.

Neck. — The neck should be fairly short, thick and muscular. Some dewlap is permitted.

Forequarters. — The shoulders should be powerful and lie close to the body. There should be medium angulation between the shoulder-blade and the upper arm. The forelegs should be straight, heavily boned and well muscled. The elbows should not be too close to the chest nor should they stand off too far from it, so that a good width of stance and a free striding movement are obtained. Pasterns should show flexibility, but no weakness.

Body. — The chest should be broad and of sufficient depth to reach just below the elbows. The sides should be slightly rounded and the rib cage should extend well to the rear.
The back should be of a good length, broad, muscular, straight and level. Dogs usually have a more pronounced waist than bitches, giving a greater curve to the lower body line.

Hindquarters. — The loins should be broad and muscular with fairly prominent haunches, the rump should be slightly sloping and the tail should be set on so that the topline curves smoothly into it. Male animals should have two apparently normal testicles fully descended into the scrotum.
The thighs should have great strength and be heavily muscled, tapering gradually down to strong hocks. The stifle and hock joints should both have medium angulation as seen from the side.
The hindlegs should each carry strongly-made double dewclaws and lack of this identifying characteristic is a very serious fault.
The hind feet may turn out slightly, but the legs themselves when viewed from behind should be straight. Pronounced cow hocks should be heavily penalised.

Feet. — The feet should be short and compact, the toes being slightly arched and equipped with strong nails.

Gait. — It is very important that the gait should be unhurried, and one should gain the impression of a large dog propelled by powerful hindquarters moving steadily and smoothly well within its capacity, yet able to produce bursts of speed. At slow speeds the Pyrenean tends to pace.

Tail. — The tail should be thick at the root and should taper gradually towards the tip, for preference, should have a slight curl. It should be of sufficient length to reach below the hocks and the thick coating of fairly long hair should form an attractive plume. In repose, the tail should be carried low with the tip turned slightly to one side, but as the dog becomes interested the tail rises and when he is fully alert it should be curled high above the back in a circle.

Coat. — The undercoat should be profuse and composed of very fine hairs whilst the longer outercoat should be of coarser texture, thick and straight or slightly wavy but never curly or fuzzy. The coat should be longer around the neck and shoulders, where it forms a mane, and towards the tail. The forelegs should be fringed. The hair on the rear of the thighs should be long, very dense and more woolly in texture, giving a "pantaloon" effect. Bitches tend to be smoother-coated than dogs and usually have a less developed mane.

Colour. — (a) Mainly white with patches of badger, wolf-grey or pale yellow; and (b) White.

(a) and (b) are of equal merit and judges should show no preference for either. Areas of black hair, where the black goes right down to the roots, are a serious fault.

The coloured markings can be on the head, the ears and at the base of the tail, but a few patches on the body are permitted.

The nose and eye rims should be black. The presence of liver pigmentation or pink is a serious fault.

Weight and Size. — The shoulder height of a bitch should be at least 26 inches (66 cm) and of a dog 28 inches (71 cm). Most specimens will exceed these heights by several inches and great size should be regarded as absolutely essential, provided that correct type and character are retained. The weight of a bitch should be at least 90 lbs (40 kg) and of a dog 110 lbs (50 kg). (These weights apply only to speicmens of minimum height and taller ones should weigh considerably more.) Weight should always be in proportion to height, giving a powerful dog of great strength. Excess weight due to fat should be penalised.

Note. — Male animals should have two apparently normal testicles fully descended into the scrotum.

MAIN AMERICAN KENNEL CLUB VARIATION TO STANDARD FOR THE PYRENEAN MOUNTAIN DOG —

Known as the Great Pyrenees in the U.S.A.

Size. — The average height at the shoulder is 27 inches to 32 inches for dogs and 25 inches to 29 inches for bitches. The weight for dogs runs 100 to 125 pounds and 90 to 115 pounds for bitches.

PYRENEAN MOUNTAIN DOG REGISTRATIONS 1981 — 87 INCLUSIVE

1981 — 430
1982 — 339
1983 — 347
1984 — 279
1985 — 372
1986 — 302
1987 — 346

CRUFTS BEST-IN-SHOW WINNER.

1970 BERGERIE KNUR — MR. & MRS. F.S. PRINCE.

ROTTWEILER

The Rottweiler takes his name from his town of origin, Rottweil in West Germany. He is thought to have been developed there probably from Mastiff-types and ancient hunting dogs. Known in his homeland as the Rottweiler Metzgerhund, he has been used as a working dog for a great many years.

Originally he was most widely used as a cattle droving dog, driving large herds to market with great efficiency. Also the pulling of heavy carts and the guarding of the farmer and his family figured in his working repertoire.

Despite a period when the Rottweiler was threatened with extinction, he has since gone on to be a valued working dog and pet in many parts of the world. The police and military, particularly in his home country, were quick to see the dogs great potential and they have utilised his strength and intelligence with great effort.

Today's Rottweiler is generally even-tempered and affectionate, due to careful work by breeders, but he is a dog of enormous power and not one to be treated without respect. Not surprisingly he makes a formidable guard and anyone or anything in his charge need never fear attack. He is also an extremely handsome breed which has no doubt been reflected in his increased popularity in recent years.

An active owner would suit his large exercise needs.

Maremma Sheepdog

Mastiff

KEY TO CHARACTER	
INTELLIGENCE	****
TEMPERAMENT	****
EASE OF COAT CARE	*****
SUITABILITY FOR SMALL DWELLING	*
***** (5) = VERY GOOD	

BRITISH KENNEL CLUB STANDARD

ROTTWEILER

GENERAL APPEARANCE. — The Rottweiler is an above average sized stalwart dog. His correctly proportioned, compact and powerful form permits of great stength, manoeuvrability and endurance. His bearing displays boldness and courage; his tranquil gaze manifests good nature and devotion.

Head and Skull. — The head is of medium length, the skull between the ears is broad. The forehead line is moderately arched as seen from the side. Occipital bone well developed but not conspicuous. Cheeks well muscled but not prominent, with the zygomatic arch well formed. The skin on the head should not be loose although it is allowed to form moderate wrinkle when the dog is attentive. Muzzle fairly deep with topline level and length not longer than the length from stop to occiput.

Nose. — The nose is well developed with proportionately large nostrils and is always black.

Eyes. — The eyes should be of medium size, almond shaped and dark brown in colour; eyelids close lying.

Ears. — The ears are pendant, small in proportion rather than large, set high and wide apart on the head, lying flat and close to the cheek.

Mouth. — The teeth are strong and the incisors of the lower jaw must touch the inner surface of the upper incisors. The flews are black and firm; they fall gradually away towards the corners of the mouth, which do not protrude excessively.

Neck. — The neck should be of fair length, strong, round and very muscular. It should be slightly arched and free from throatiness.

Forequarters. — The shoulders should be well placed on the body, long and sloping with the elbows well let down, but not loose. The legs should be muscular with plenty of bone and substance. The pasterns should be bent slightly forward and not be completely vertical. The front legs seen from all sides must be straight and not placed too closely to one another.

Body. — The chest should be roomy, broad and deep with the ribs well sprung. The depth of brisket will not be more, and not much less than 50% of the shoulder height. The back should be straight, strong and not too long; ratio of shoulder height to length of body should be a 9 is to 10; the loins short strong and deep, the flanks should not be tucked up. The croup should be broad, of proportionate length, and very slightly sloping.

Hindquarters. — The upper thigh not too short, broad and strongly muscled. The lower thigh well muscled at the top and strong and sinewy lower down. Stifles fairly well bent. Hocks well angulated without exaggeration and not completely vertical.

Feet. — The feet should be strong, round and compact with the toes well arched. The hind feet are somewhat longer than the front. The pads should be very hard and the toenails short, dark and strong. Rear dewclaws removed.

Gait. — In movement the Rottweiler should convey an impression of supple strength, endurance and purpose. While the back remains firm and stable there is a powerful hind thrust and good stride. First and foremost, movement should be harmonious, positive and unrestricted.

Tail. — Carried horizontally. It is short, strong and not set too low. It should be docked at the first joint.

Coat. — The coat, which consists of top coat and undercoat, should be of medium length, coarse and flat. The undercoat, which is essential on the neck and thighs, should not show through the outer coat. The hair may also be a little longer on the back of the forelegs and breachings.

Colour. — The colour is black with clearly defined markings on the cheeks, muzzle, chest and legs, as well as over both eyes and the area beneath the tail. Colour of markings ranges from rich tan to mahogany brown.

Size. — For males the height at the shoulder should be between 25 and 27 inches and for females between 23 and 25 inches. However, height should always be considered in relation to the general appearance of the dog.

Faults. — The following faults are noted for the clarification of the Standard.
1. Too lightly or too heavily built.
2. Sway backed or roach backed.
3. Cow hocked, bow hocked, or weak hocked.
4. Long or excessively wavy coat.
5. Any white markings.
6. Nervousness and viciousness are highly undesirable.

Note. — Male animals should have two apparently normal testicles fully descended into the scrotum.

MAIN AMERICAN KENNEL CLUB VARIATION TO STANDARD FOR THE ROTTWEILER —

Briard

Norwegian Buhund
Old English Sheepdog

Size. — Males: 24 inches to 27 inchs, Females: 22 inches to 25 inches.

ROTTWEILER REGISTRATIONS 1981 — 87 INCLUSIVE

1981 — 1641
1982 — 2466
1983 — 3526
1984 — 4690
1985 — 6836
1986 — 8374
1987 — 9088

YET TO WIN CRUFTS BEST-IN-SHOW.

SAINT BERNARD

The first image conjured up by the mention of the St. Bernard is of the benevolent rescue dog trudging through the snow with a brandy barrel swinging from his neck. This is not a wholly untrue picture but this magnificent breed has generally been employed in more up to date methods of mountain rescue.

He was developed by the monks of the Hospice of St. Bernard in Switzerland. Still in existence, the Hospice is set high in the mountains and in the often appalling weather conditions, a powerful dog can often seek out stranded or buried climbers far quicker than any man.

The first specimens were produced around the early part of the eighteenth century. The St. Bernard's main forerunner was the Apline Mastiff, a massive breed that was most likely crossed with the Pyrenean Mountain Dog and other Mastiffs.

The breeding work of the monks produced a rough coated dog and a smooth coated. The smooth coated were generally held higher in their esteem, so the rough coated were more often exported. This explains the greater ocurrence of the latter type in Britain.

As it is the heaviest breed in the canine world, a prospective owner should examine his finances before committing himself to the St. Bernard's awesome food bill. Around the home, he is the proverbial gentle giant, affectionate and lovable but, to maintain his even temperament, plenty of space and regular exercise is vital. Firm, careful training is advocated with the St. Bernard puppy as a fully grown dog of some 170 lbs plus, can be a nightmare if allowed to run riot.

Pyrenean Mountain Dog

Rottweiler

Saint Bernard

Samoyed

KEY TO CHARACTER	
INTELLIGENCE	****
TEMPERAMENT	*****
EASE OF COAT CARE	****
SUITABILITY FOR SMALL DWELLING	*
***** (5) = VERY GOOD	

BRITISH KENNEL CLUB STANDARD

ST. BERNARD

GENERAL APPEARANCE. — Expression should be token benevolence, dignity, and intelligence. Movement is most important, and St. Bernards have often failed in this direction, the hind legs being especially faulty.

Head and Skull. — Large and massive, circumference of skull being rather more than double the head from nose to occiput. Muzzle short, full in front of the eye, and square at nose end. Cheeks flat; great depth from eye to lower jaw. Lips deep, but not too pendulous. From nose to stop perfectly straight and broad. Stop somewhat abrupt and well defined. Skull broad, slightly rounded at the top, with somewhat prominent brow. Nose large and black, with well developed nostrils.

Eyes. — Rather small and deep set, dark in colour, not too close together, the lower eyelid drooping so as to show a fair amount of haw at the inner corner, the upper eyelid falling well over the eye.

Ears. — Of medium size lying close to the cheeks, and not heavily feathered.

Mouth. — Level.

Neck. — Lengthy, thick, muscular, and slightly arched, with dewlap well developed.

Forequarters. — Shoulders broad and sloping, well up at the withers. Legs perfectly straight, strong in bone and of good length.

Body. — Back broad and straight, ribs well rounded. Loin wide and very muscular. Chest wide and deep. The lower part should not project below the elbows.

Hindquarters. — Legs heavy in bone, hocks well bent and thighs very muscular.

Feet. — Large and compact with well-arched toes. Dewclaws should be removed.

Tail. — Set on rather high, long, and in long-coated variety well feathered. Carried low when in repose, and when excited or in motion should not be curled over the back.

Coat. — In Rough specimens, should be dense and flat, rather fuller round the neck; thighs well feathered. In Smooth specimens it should be close and hound-like, slightly feathered on thighs and tail.

Colour. — Orange, mahogany-brindle, red-brindle; white with patches on body of any of the above-named colours. The markings should be as follows:— White muzzle, white blaze up face, white collar round neck, white chest, white forelegs, feet and end of tail; black shadings on face and ears.

Weight and Size. — The taller the better, provided that symmetry is maintained; thoroughly well proportioned, and of great substance. The general outline should suggest great power and capability of endurance.

Faults. — Dudley, liver, flesh-coloured or split nose; over or under-shot mouth; snipy muzzle; light or staring eyes; cheek bumps; wedge head; flat skull; badly set or carried, or heavily feathered ears; too much peak; short neck; curly coat; flat sides; hollow back; roach back; flat thighs; ring tail; open or hare feet; cow-hocks; fawn or self-coloured, straight hocks.

Note. — Male animals should have two apparently normal testicles fully descended into the scrotum.

MAIN AMERICAN KENNEL CLUB VARIATION TO STANDARD FOR THE ST. BERNARD —

Size. — Height at shoulder: Dog should be 27½ inches minimum, of the bitch 25½ inches.

ST. BERNARD REGISTRATIONS 1981 — 87 INCLUSIVE

1981 — 559
1982 — 626
1983 — 515
1984 — 513
1985 — 516
1986 — 486
1987 — 521

CRUFTS BEST-IN-SHOW WINNER

1974 CH. BURTONSWOOD BOSSY BOOTS — MISS M. HINDES.

Cardigan Welsh Corgi

Pembroke Welsh Corgi

Shetland Sheepdog
Siberian Husky

SAMOYED

One of the most striking of the Spitz breeds, the Samoyed hails from the northern wastes of Siberia. Nomadic tribes were once common there and one such people were the Samoyeds. They used their dogs to pull sleds and herd livestock, tasks at which they excelled. European explorers came across the Samoyed people towards the end of the last century and were immediately impressed with the pulling power of these dogs so they purchased dogs from them to incorporate in their own teams. Some of these early specimens were not pure white, patches of black or brown often occurring.

Although working qualities have taken a back seat in the modern Samoyed's make-up, he still revels in physical exertion and the fulfilling of a task.

Despite the great strength and self confidence of this breed, he is very affectionate and easily trained. He is renowned for his liking of children and will play endlessly with anyone who has the stamina. The beautiful coat is not as big a headache to maintain as might be imagined but, regular brushing and cleaning are a must. The Samoyed's extensive extensive exercise needs make him an unwise choice of pet for anyone who is inactive.

KEY TO CHARACTER	
INTELLIGENCE	****
TEMPERAMENT	****
EASE OF COAT CARE	***
SUITABILITY FOR SMALL DWELLING	**
***** (5) = VERY GOOD	

BRITISH KENNEL CLUB STANDARD

SAMOYED

CHARACTERISTICS. — The Samoyed is intelligent, alert, full of action but above all displaying affection towards all mankind.

GENERAL APPEARANCE. — The Samoyed being essentially a working dog should be strong and active and graceful, and as his work lies in cold climates his coat should be heavy and weather-resisting. He should not be too long in back, as a weak back would make him practically useless for his legitimate work; but at the same time a cobby body, such as a Chow's, would also place him at a great disadvantage as a draught dog. Breeders should aim for the happy medium, viz, a body not long, but muscular, allowing liberty, with a deep chest and well sprung ribs, strong neck proudly arched, straight front and exceptionally strong loins. Both dogs and bitches should give the appearance of being capable of great endurance but should be free from coarseness. A full grown dog should stand about 21 inches at the shoulder. On account of the depth of chest required the legs should be moderately long, a very short-legged dog is to be deprecated. Hindquarters should be particularly well developed, stifles well angulated, and any suggestion of unsound stifles or cow hocks severely penalised.

Head and Skull. — Head powerful and wedge-shaped with a broad, flat skull, muzzle of medium length, a tapering foreface not too sharply defined. Lips black. Hair short and smooth before the ears. Nose black for preference, but maybe brown or flesh-coloured. Strong jaws.

Eyes. — Almond shaped, medium to dark brown in colour, set well apart with alert and intelligent expression. Eyerims should be black and unbroken.

Ears. — Thick, not too long and slightly rounded at the tips, set well apart and well covered inside with hair. The ears should be fully erect in the grown dog.

Mouth. — Upper teeth should just overlap the underteeth in a scissor bite.

Neck. — Proudly arched.

Forequarters. — Legs straight and muscular with good bone.

Body. — Back medium in length, broad and very muscular. Chest broad and deep ribs well sprung, giving plenty of heart and lung room.

Hindquarters. — Very muscular, stifles well angulated; cow hocks or straight stifles very objectionable.

Feet. — Long, flattish and slightly spread out. Soles well cushioned with hair.

Gait. — should move freely with a strong agile drive showing power and elegance.

Tail. — Long and profuse, carried over the back when alert; sometimes dropped when at rest.

Coat. — The body should be well covered with a thick, close, soft and short undercoat, with harsh hair growing through it, forming the outer coat, which should stand straight away from the body and be free from curl.

Colour. — Pure white; white and biscuit; cream.

Weight and Size. — Dogs 20 to 22 inches at the shoulder. Bitches 18 to 20 inches at the shoulder. Weight in proportion to size.

Faults. — Big ears with little feathering. Drop ears. Narrow width between ears. Long foreface. Blue or very light eyes. A bull neck. A long body. A soft coat; a wavy coat; absence of undercoat. Slack tail carriage; should be carried well over th back, though it may drop when the dog is at rest. Absence of feathering. Round, cat-like feet. Black or black spots. Severe unprovoked aggressiveness. Any sign of unsound movement.

Note. — Male animals should have two apparently normal testicles fully descended into the scrotum.

MAIN AMERICAN KENNEL CLUB VARIATION TO STANDARD FOR THE SAMOYED —

Height. — Males: 21 to 23½ inchs; Females: 19 to 21 inches at the withers.

SAMOYED REGISTRATIONS 1981 — 87 INCLUSIVE

1981 — 749
1982 — 719
1983 — 750
1984 — 708
1985 — 827
1986 — 732
1987 — 851

YET TO WIN CRUFTS BEST-IN-SHOW.

SHETLAND SHEEPDOG

Not surprisingly this breed hails from the most northerly reaches of Britain, the Shetland Islands. Although he appears to be an exact replica in miniature of a Rough Collie there are some small differences. Although the Rough and Border Collies were undoubtedly used by the Shetland farmers who established the breed, it is thought that Icelandic and Norwegian dogs may have been introduced along the way. There is also a belief that the King Charles Spaniel may be responsible for some of the Shetland Sheepdog's colouring characteristics.

When he appeared in the latter part of the nineteenth century, the "Sheltie" as he is affectionately known, was primarily a working dog. His luxurious warm coat and deceptive toughness made him a prized asset to a Shetland crofter. The breed was then known as the Shetland Collie, a name still used by Shetlanders, but Collie breeders of the time voiced strong objection and when he was registered officially in 1914, it was as the Shetland Sheepdog.

For people who may be fond of the "Lassie" type dog, but who are short on space, the "Sheltie" makes a manageable alternative to a Rough Collie. They are a highly intelligent breed, having given good accounts of themselves in the obedience ring and can therefore be easily trained. They respond well to a family environment and are renowned for their longevity. Although the "Sheltie" is used less as a working dog now, regular exercise is vital to his well being.

KEY TO CHARACTER	
INTELLIGENCE	*****
TEMPERAMENT	****
EASE OF COAT CARE	***
SUITABILITY FOR SMALL DWELLING	****
***** (5) = VERY GOOD	

BRITISH KENNEL CLUB STANDARD

SHETLAND SHEEPDOG

CHARACTERISTICS. — To enable the Shetland Sheepdog to fulfil its natural bent for sheepdog work, its physical structure should be on the lines of strength and activity, free from cloddiness and without any trace of coarseness. Although the desired type is similar to that of the Rough Collie there are marked differences that must be noted. The expression, being one of the most marked characteristics of the breed, is obtained by the perfect balance and combination of skull and foreface, size, shape, colour and placement of eyes, correct position and carriage of ears, all harmoniously blended to produce that almost indefinable look of sweet, alert, gentle intelligence.

The Shetland Sheepdog should show affection and response to his owner, he may show reserve to strangers but not to the point of nervousness.

GENERAL APPEARANCE. — The Shetland Sheepdog should instantly appeal as a dog of great beauty, intelligence and alertness. Action lithe and graceful with speed and jumping power great for its size. The outline should be symmetrical so that no part appears out of proportion to the whole. An abundance of coat, mane and frill, with shapeliness of head and sweetness of expression all combine to present the ideal Shetland Sheepdog that will inspire and secure admiration.

Head and Skull. — The head should be refined and its shape when viewed from the top or side is a long blunt wedge tapering from ear to nose. The width of skull necessarily depends upon the combined length of skull and muzzle and the whole must be considered in connection with the size of the dog. The skull should be flat, moderately wide between the ears, showing no prominence of the occipital bone. Cheeks should be flat and merge smoothly into a well rounded muzzle. Skull and muzzle to be of equal length, central point to be the inner corner of the eye. In profile the topline of the skull should be parallel to the topline of the muzzle, but on a higher plane due to a slight but definite stop. The jaws should be clean and stong and with a well developed underjaw. Lips should be tight. Teeth should be sound and level, with an evenly spaced scissor bite.

Eyes. — A very important feature giving expression to the dog. They should be of medium size obliquely set and of almond shape. Colour dark brown except in the case of merles, where blue is permissible.

Ears. — Should be small and moderately wide at the base, placed fairly close together on the top of the skull. When in repose they should be thrown back, but when on the alert brought forward and carried semi-erect with tips dropping forward.

Neck. — The neck should be muscular, well arched and of sufficient length to carry the head proudly.

Body and Quarters. — From the withers the shoulder blade should slope at a 45 degree angle, forward and downward to the shoulder joint. At the withers they are separated only by the vertebrae but they must slope outwards to accommodate the desired spring of ribs. The upper arm should join the shoulder blade at as nearly a right angle as possible. The elbow joint to be equi-distant from the ground and the withers. The forelegs should be straight when viewed from the front, muscular and clean, with strong bone. Pasterns strong and flexible. The body is slightly longer from the withers to the root of the tail than the height at the withers, but most of the length is due to the proper angulation of the shoulder and hind quarters. The chest should be deep reaching to the point of the elbow. The ribs well sprung but tapering at their lower half to allow free play of the forelegs and shoulders. The back should be level with a graceful sweep over the loins and the croup should slope gradually to the rear. The thigh should be broad and muscular, the thigh bones to be set into the pelvis at right angles, corresponding to the angle of the shoulder blade. The stifle joint where the femur bone joins the tibia bone must have a distinct angle, hock joint to be clean cut, angular and well let down with strong bone. The hock must be straight when viewed from behind.

Tail. — Set on low, tapering bone must reach at least to the hock joint, with abundant hair and slight upward sweep, raised when the dog is moving, but never over the level of the back.

Feet. — Oval in shape, soles well padded, toes arched and close together.

Gait. — The action of the Shetland Sheepdog should denote speed and smoothness. There should be no pacing, plaiting, rolling or stiff stilted up and down movement.

Coat. — Must be double, the outer coat of long hair of harsh texture and straight, the under coat soft (resembling fur) short and close. The mane and frill should be very abundant and forelegs well feathered. Hind legs above the hocks profusely covered with hair, but below the hocks fairly smooth. The mask or face smooth. What are commonly known as smooth coated specimens are barred.

Colour. — Tricolours should be an intense black on the body with no signs of ticking, rich tan markings on a tricolour to be preferred. Sables may be clear or shaded, any colour from gold to deep mahogany but in its shade the colour should be rich in tones. Wolf sable and grey colours undesirable. Blue Merles, clear silvery blue is desired, splashed and marbled with black. Rich tan markings to be preferred, but the absence not to be counted as a fault. Heavy black markings, slate coloured or rusty tinge in either top or under coat is highly undesirable. General effect should be blue. White markings may be shown in the blaze, collar, chest frill, legs, stifle and tip of tail. All or some tan markings may be shown on eyebrows, cheeks, legs, stifles and under tail. All or some of the white markings are to be preferred whatever the colour of the dog, but the absence of these markings shall not be considered a fault. Black and White and Black and Tan are also recognised colours. Over markings of patches of white on the body are highly undesirable. The nose black whatever the colour of the dog.

Size. — Ideal height measured at the withers 14 inches for Bitches, 14½ inches for Dogs, anything more than 1 inch above these heights to be considered a serious fault.

Faults. — Domed or receding skull, lack of stop, large drooping or pricked ears, over-developed cheeks, weak jaw, snipy muzzle, not full complement of teeth, crooked forelegs, cow hocks, tail kinked, short or carried over the back, white or white colour predominating. Pink or flesh coloured nose, blue eyes in any other colour than merles. Nervousness. Full or light eye. Under or overshot mouth.

Note. — Male animals should have two apparently normal testicles fully descended into the scrotum.

MAIN AMERICAN KENNEL CLUB VARIATION TO STANDARD FOR THE SHETLAND SHEEPDOG —

Size. — The Shetland Sheepdog should stand between 13 and 16 inches at the shoulder.

SHETLAND SHEEPDOG REGISTRATIONS 1981 — 87 INCLUSIVE

1981 — 4198
1982 — 3805
1983 — 3900
1984 — 3466
1985 — 3687
1986 — 3146
1987 — 3048

YET TO WIN CRUFTS BEST-IN-SHOW.

SIBERIAN HUSKY

The layman would probably attach the name 'Husky' to any of the Spitz-type dogs, so it is perhaps fitting that the dog who performs this arduous work best is the Siberian Husky.

For centuries he has been kept as worker and companion by the people of the Siberian wastes but his origins are thought to have been in north-east Asia. He was developed by tribes there into the ultimate pulling machine, having boundless stamina and strength coupled with speed.

Eventually the breed came to the attention of the people of the far north of the U.S.A. and they began to incorporate Siberian Huskies into their dog teams. Sled racing was and still is, popular in the U.S.A. and these eastern imports proved to be superior at this sport to the likes of the Alaskan Malamute. As well as this great strength and fitness the Siberian Husky has good resistance to disease and a generally uncomplaining disposition.

The quite fearsome appearance of these dogs and exaggerated tales of them fighting to the death with fellow pack-members, should not influence a decision to own one. Having lived amongst people so closely for so long, the Siberian Husky will blend very well into the right type of home. Although children should not torment him to excess he is very fond of human company and if exercised extensively will make a responsive and loyal companion. The Siberian Husky shows very well and the incredibly dense coat looks superb if brushed regularly.

KEY TO CHARACTER	
INTELLIGENCE	****
TEMPERAMENT	****
EASE OF COAT CARE	***
SUITABILITY FOR SMALL DWELLING	*
***** (5) = VERY GOOD	

BRITISH KENNEL CLUB STANDARD

SIBERIAN HUSKY

TEMPERAMENT. — Friendly and gentle, but also alert and out-going. Should not display traits of guard dog, nor be unduly suspicious of strangers or aggressive with other dogs. Some measure of reserve and dignity expected in mature dog. Intelligence, tractability and eager disposition make him an agreeable companion and willing worker.

CHARACTERISTICS. — Medium size, moderate bone, well balanced proportions, ease and freedom of movement, proper coat, correct tail and good disposition all most important.

GENERAL APPEARANCE. — A medium-sized working sledge dog, quick and light on his feet, free and graceful in action, with a well-furred body, erect ears and brush tail. His proportions reflect a basic balance of power, speed and endurance. Males appearing masculine but never coarse, the bitches feminine but without weakness of structure. Neither sex heavy or cobby. In proper condition, with muscle firm and well developed, should not carry excess weight.

Head and Skull. — Head presents a finely chiselled fox-like appearance, neither clumsy nor too fine. Slightly rounded on top, tapering gradually from widest point to eyes. Muzzle of medium length and width, neither snipy nor coarse, and tapering gradually to rounded nose. Distance from tip of nose to stop equal to distance from stop to occiput. Stop clearly defined but not excessive, and line of nose straight from stop to tip. Nose black in grey, tan or black dogs; liver in copper dogs; and may be flesh coloured in pure white dogs. In winter, a pink-streaked "snow nose" acceptable.

Eyes. — Almond shaped, moderately spaced and set somewhat obliquely. Expression keen but freindly, interested, and even mischievous. Eyes may be any shade of blue or brown; one of each colour, or parti-colours equally acceptable.

Ears. — Medium-size, relatively close together, triangular in shape, height slightly greater than width at base. Set high on head, strongly erect, and at attention carried practically parallel, inner edges quite close together at base. Slightly arched at the back. Thick, well furred outside and inside, with tips slightly rounded.

Mouth. — Lips well pigmented and close fitting. The jaws should be strong, with a perfect, regular and complete scissor bite, i.e. the upper teeth closely overlapping the lower teeth and set square to the jaws.

Neck. — Medium length, arched and carried proudly erect when standing. When moving at a trot, extended so that head carried slightly forward, not too long, nor too short and thick.

Forequarters. — The shoulder blade well-laid back at an approximate angle of 45 deg. to the ground. Upper arm angling slightly backward from point of shoulder to elbow, and never perpendicular to the ground. Muscles and ligaments holding shoulder to rib cage firm and well-developed. Straight or loose shoulders highly undesirable. When standing and viewed from the front forelegs modertely spaced, parallel and straight, with elbows close to body and turned neither in nor out. Viewed from the side, pasterns slightly sloping, with wrist strong but flexible. Length of leg from elbow to ground slightly more than distance from elbow to top of withers. Both proportionate to size. Dew claws may be removed.

Body. — Back straight and strong, with a level topline from withers to croup, of medium length, not cobby, nor slack from excessive length. In profile the body, from point of shoulder to rear point of croup slightly longer than the height from the ground to the top of the withers. Chest deep and strong but not too broad, deepest point just behind and level with elbows. Ribs well sprung from spine but flattened on sides to allow for freedom of action. Loin slightly arched, well muscled, taut and lean; viewed from above, narrower than rib cage. Slight tuck-up. Croup sloping away from spine at an angle, but never so steeply as to restrict rearward thrust of hind legs.

Hindquarters. — Viewed from the rear when standing, hind legs moderately spaced and parallel. Upper thighs well-muscled and powerful, stifles well-bent, and hock joint well-defined and set low to ground. Dew claws, if any should be removed.

Feet. — Oval in shape, but not long, and turning neither in nor out in natural stance. Medium in size, compact, well-furred and slightly webbed between toes. Pads tough and thickly cushioned. Trimming fur between toes and around the feet permissible.

Gait. — Smooth and seemingly effortless. Quick and light on his feet and when in the show ring, gaited on a loose lead at a moderately fast trot, exhibiting good reach in forequarters and good drive in hindquarters. When walking, the legs moving parallel but, as the speed increases, gradually angling inward to track close (single tracking). As the pad marks converge, the forelegs and hindlegs carried straight with neither elbows nor stifles turning in nor out, and each hindleg moving in the path of the foreleg on the same side. topline of back remaining firm and level during gaiting.

Tail. — Well-furred round fox-brush shape set on just below level of topline, and usually carried over the back in a graceful sickle curve when the dog at attention. When carried up, not curled too tightly, nor should it curl to either side of the body, or snap flat against the back. Hair of medium length, and approximately the same length all round. A trailing tail normal when working or in repose.

Coat. — Double and medium in length, giving a well-furred appearance, and never so long as to obscure the clean-cut outline. Undercoat soft, dense of sufficient length to support outer coat. Guard hairs of the outer coat straight and somewhat smooth-lying, never harsh, rough or shaggy, too silky, nor standing straight off from the body. Trimming on any part of dog, except on the feet, not allowed.

Colour. — All colours, including white, are allowed, and all markings. A variety of markings on the head common, including many striking patterns not found in other breeds.

Weight and Size. — Height: dogs 53 to 60 cm. (21 in. to 23½ in.) at the withrs; bitches 51 to 56 cm. (20 in. to 22 in.) at the withers. Weight: dogs 20 to 27 kg. (45 to 60 lbs.); bitches 16 to 23 kb. (35 to 50 lbs.).

Weight should be in proportion to height. These measurements represent the extremes in height and weight, with no preference given to either extreme. A dog should not exceed 60 cm. (23½ in.) or a bitch exceed 56 cm. (22 in.).

Faults. — Any departure from the foregoing points should be considered a fault and the seriousness with which the fault should be regarded should be in exact proportion to its degree.

Note. — Male animals should have two apparently normal testicles fully descended into the scrotum.

SIBERIAN HUSKY REGISTRATIONS 1981 — 87 INCLUSIVE

1981 — 52
1982 — 59
1983 — 92
1984 — 154
1985 — 170
1986 — 245
1987 — 316

YET TO WIN CRUFTS BEST-IN-SHOW.

CARDIGAN WELSH CORGI

Although probably from the same original stock as the Pembroke Welsh Corgi, the Cardigan differs in several ways. The most obvious are the rare blue merle colouring of some Cardigans, which is not to be found in the Pembroke, is thought to be attributable to the introduction of Welsh Collie blood in the late nineteenth century.

Both Welsh Corgis were exhibited in the showring under the same classification until 1934 when the Kennel Club granted each breed seperate status. It was some time, however, before the two became completely pure bred due to there having been much interbreeding prior to 1934.

The Cardigan Welsh Corgi is an amiable house dog with good guarding instincts and fondness for human company. He is slightly easier going than the Pembroke and might therefore be the more suitable of the two for a household where children are present. He was bred to work so exercise is a high priority.

KEY TO CHARACTER	
INTELLIGENCE	***
TEMPERAMENT	****
EASE OF COAT CARE	****
SUITABILITY FOR SMALL DWELLING	****
***** (5) = VERY GOOD	

BRITISH KENNEL CLUB STANDARD

WELSH CORGI (CARDIGAN)

CHARACTERISTICS. — Alert, active and intelligent, with steady temperament.

GENERAL APPEARANCE. — Sturdy, mobile and capable of endurance. Overall silhouette long in proportion to height, terminating in a fox like brush, set in line with the body. Alert expression.

Head and Skull. — Head foxy in shape and appearance, skull wide and flat between the ears tapering towards the eyes above which it should be slightly domed. Moderate amount of stop. Length of foreface in proportion to skull as 3 is to 5, tapering moderately towards the nose, which should be black, slightly projecting and in no sense blunt. Underjaw clean cut, strong but without prominence.

Eyes. — Medium size, clear, giving a kindly, alert but watchful expression. Rather widely set with corners clearly defined. Eyes preferably dark, or to blend with the coat, rims dark. One or both eyes pale blue,blue or blue flecked, permissible only in blue merles.

Ears. — Erect, proportinately rather large to the size of the dog. Tips slightly rounded, moderately wide at the base and set about 9 cm (3½ inches) apart. Carried so that the tips are slightly wide of a straight line drawn from the tip of the nose through the centre of the eyes, and set well back so that they can be laid flat along the neck.

Mouth. — Teeth strong, with a perfect regular and complete scissor bite, i.e. the upper teeth closely overlapping the lower teeth and set square to the jaw. Pincer bite permissible. The teeth should be evenly arranged and not crowded in relation to one another.

Neck. — Muscular, well developed and in proportion to the dog's build, fitting into well sloped shoulders.

Forequarters. — Shoulders well laid and angulated at approximately 90 degrees to the upper arm; muscular, elbows close to sides. Strong bone carried down to feet. Legs short but body well clear of the ground, forearms slightly bowed to mould round the chest. Feet turned only slightly outwards.

Body. — Chest moderately broad with prominent breast bone. Body fairly long and strong with deep brisket, well sprung ribs and clearly defined waist. Topline level.

Hindquarters. — Strong, well angulated and aligned with muscular thighs and second thighs, strong bone carried down to feet, legs short; when standing, hocks should be vertical viewed from the side and rear.

Feet. — Round, tight, rather large and well padded. All dewclaws should be removed.

Gait. — Free and active, elbows fitting closely to sides, neither loose nor tied. Forelegs should reach well forward without too much lift, in unison with thrusting action of hindlegs.

Tail. — Like a fox's brush set in line with the body and moderately long (to touch or nearly touch the ground). Carried low when standing but may be lifted a little above the body when moving, but not curled over the back.

Coat. — Short or medium of hard texture. Weatherproof with good undercoat. Preferably straight.

Colour. — Any colour, with or without white markings, but white should not predominate.

Weight and Size. — Height as near as possible 30 cm. (12 inches) at the shoulder. Weight in proportion to size, with overall balance as prime consideration.

Faults. — Any departure from the foregoing points should be considered a fault and the seriousness with which the fault is regarded should be in exact proportion to its degree.

Note. — Male animals should have two apparently normal testicles fully descended into the scrotum.

MAIN AMERICAN KENNEL CLUB VARIATION TO STANDARD FOR THE CARDIGAN WELSH CORGI —

Size. — Dogs and bitches should be from 10.5 to 12.5 inches at the withers when standing naturally. Ideally, dogs should be from 30 to 38 pounds; bitches from 25 to 34 pounds.

CARDIGAN WELSH CORGI REGISTRATIONS 1981 — 87 INCLUSIVE

1981 — 132
1982 — 100
1983 — 143
1984 — 98
1985 — 139
1986 — 122
1987 — 134

YET TO WIN CRUFTS BEST-IN-SHOW.

PEMBROKE WELSH CORGI

The Pembroke Welsh Corgi has been known in South Wales for many hundreds of years, although exactly when he first came about is unknown.

It is thought probable that dogs brought over to Wales by Swedish traders were used in his development and a strong resemblance to the Swedish Vallhund is plain to see.

In his early days he was an extremely efficient working dog. The cattle drovers of the time used him to assist with rounding up wayward herd members. The tactics employed by the Pembroke Welsh Corgi were to snap at the cow's legs and nimbly evade any retaliation, thus sending the offender back to the main herd. It was a job requiring hardiness, courage and intelligence, traits that are still evident in the Pembroke Welsh Corgi's character today.

Unlike the Cardigan Welsh Corgi, the Pembroke has a docked tail. In fact ideally they are born with no tail but such puppies are so rare that docking has long been common practice.

As a spirited small pet, the Pembroke Welsh Corgi has many good points. He is loyal and affectionate and is sturdy enough to offer some security in the home. His working past, though, has left him with a slight tendency to snap if teased or angered, so firm early training is recommended.

His dietary needs are not excessive and regular brisk exercise is important.

KEY TO CHARACTER	
INTELLIGENCE	***
TEMPERAMENT	***
EASE OF COAT CARE	****
SUITABILITY FOR SMALL DWELLING	****
***** (5) = VERY GOOD	

BRITISH KENNEL CLUB STANDARD

WELSH CORGI (PEMBROKE)

GENERAL APPEARANCE. — Low set, strong, sturdily built, alert and active, giving an impression of substance and stamina in a small space, outlook bold, expression intelligent and workmanlike. The movement should be free and active, elbows fitting closely to the sides, neither loose nor tied. Forelegs should move well forward, without too much lift, in unison with thrusting action of hind legs.

Head and Skull. — Head to be foxy in shape and appearance, with alert and intelligent expression, skull to be fairly wide and flat between the ears; moderate amount of stop. Length of foreface to be in proportion to the skull as three is to five. Muzzle slightly tapering. Nose black.

Eyes. — Well set, round, medium size, hazel in colour and blending with colour of coat.

Ears. — Pricked, medium sized, slightly pointed. A line drawn from the tip of the nose through the eye should, if extended, pass through, or close to, the tip of the ear.

Mouth. — Teeth level, or with the inner side of the upper front teeth resting closely on the front of the under ones.

Neck. — Fairly long.

Forequarters. — Legs short and as straight as possible. Ample bone carried right down to the feet. Elbows should fit closely to the sides, neither loose nor tied.

Body. — Of medium length, with well sprung ribs. Not short coupled or terrier like. Level top line. Chest broad and deep, well let down between the forelegs.

Hindquarters. — Strong and flexible, slightly tapering. Legs short. Ample bone carried right down to the feet. Hocks straight when viewed from behind.

Feet. — Oval, the two centre toes slightly in advance of two outer ones, pads strong and well arched. Nails short.

Tail. — Short, preferably natural.

Coat. — Of medium length and dense; not wiry.

Colour. — Self colours in Red, Sable, Fawn, Black and Tan, or with White markings on legs, chest and neck. Some white on head and foreface is permissible.

Weight and Size. — Dogs 20 to 24 lbs.; Bitches 18 to 22 lbs. Height from 10 to 12 inches at shoulder.

Faults. — The following are serious faults:
White on the body giving a piebald or skewbald effect, or hound like markings.
Long fluffy coat, accompanied with feathering on ears and feet.
Overshot or undershot mouth.

Note. — Male animals should have two apparently normal testicles fully descended into the scrotum.

PEMBROKE WELSH CORGI REGISTRATIONS 1981 — 87 INCLUSIVE

1981 — 1475
1982 — 1320
1983 — 1371
1984 — 1394
1985 — 1297
1986 — 1308
1987 — 1252

YET TO WIN CRUFTS BEST-IN-SHOW.

PEDIGREE DOGS IN COLOUR

BOOK SIX

TOY GROUP

This is Book Six in a volume consisting of six books each dealing with a main group of dogs. The page numbering follows that used in the main volume.

Affenpinscher

Bichon Frise

AFFENPINSCHER

The history of the tiny Affenpinscher stretches back several centuries and it is believed that the Griffon Bruxellois and the Miniature Schnauzer owe their ancestry to him. He was develolped in Germany and the unique monkey-like face is reflected in the name, Affenpinscher, which translates to 'Monkey Pinscher'. Until the end of the nineteenth century he had been confused with a similar dog, the short-haired Pinscher, both having been classed as the same breed. But after a major German show in 1888 the two breeds were separated.

Whilst he is now fundamentally a pet dog, the Affenpinscher does have a working past as a fine ratter and this has added a touch of spirit and hardiness to his disposition, making him a lively and interesting companion. Although never a big success in Britain, American dog fanciers have kept the Affenpinscher in fair numbers since his registration in the U.S.A. in 1936.

He is not a dog that requires pampering and as well as his manageable size, the easily kept coat makes for an easy life for his owner. He will show devotion to the family and is not afraid to assert himself if required to guard. Although he does not need a great deal of space, he is of an energetic nature and will enjoy frequent walks and play sessions.

KEY TO CHARACTER	
INTELLIGENCE	***
TEMPERAMENT	****
EASE OF COAT CARE	****
SUITABILITY FOR SMALL DWELLING	*****
***** (5) = VERY GOOD	

BRITISH KENNEL CLUB STANDARD

AFFENPINSCHER

CHARACTERISTICS. — The dog is lively and self-confident, carrying itself with a comic seriousness. A loyal and loving companion to family and friends and, though not given to yapping, watchful to strangers and fearless towards aggressors.

GENERAL APPEARANCE. — Wire haired, stout with an apish expression. Though small, the Affenpinscher is sturdy in build and not delicate in any way.

Head and Skull. — The head fairly small in proportion to the body; a domed forehead, broad brow and marked stop which, however, should not be indented. Muzzle blunt and short but not flattened as far as would cause difficulty in breathing or wrinkling of the skin. The chin prominent with good turn-up. The distance between the dark eyes and black nose forming an equally sided triangle.

Eyes. — Round, very dark and sparkling. Medium in size and not protruding.

Ears. — Ears set high, upright ears preferred, although a small, neat drop ear is permissibe.

Mouth. — The mouth should be slightly undershot with the lower incisors gripping scissor-like in front of the uppers. The teeth or tongue must not show when the mouth is closed.

Neck. — The neck short and straight. Skin of the throat tight and unwrinkled.

Forequarters. — The front legs should be straight, elbows close.

Body. — The back short and straight. Height at withers about equal to the length of the back. The barrel shaped ribs combined with only a slight tuck-up at the loin giving the back a sturdy appearance.

Hindquarters. — Hindlegs should be well set under the body without much angulation.

Feet. — The feet should be small, round and compact and turn neither in nor out. The pads and nails should be dark.

Gait. — A tripping, prancing movement.

Tail. — The tail set high and carried high; left a natural length or docked to the third joint.

Coat. — The coat should be rough and harsh in texture, short and dense on some parts of the body and shaggy and long on others. In particular, it should be long on the neck and shoulders. On the head a wreath-like circle should stand away from the skull framing the eyes, nose and chin giving the desired monkey-like appearance.

Colour. — The colour should be black, although dark grey and black with grey, rich tan or brown markings are permissible.

Weight and Size. — Height 24 to 28 cm (9½" to 11"). Weight 3 to 4 kg. (6½ to 9 lbs).

Faults. — Any departure from the foregoing points should be considered a fault and the seriousness of the fault should be in exact proportion to its degree.

Note. — Male animals should have two apparently normal testicles fully descended into the scrotum.

MAIN AMERICAN KENNEL CLUB VARIATION TO STANDARD FOR THE AFFENPINSCHER —

Tail. — Cut short, set and carried high.

Size. — The smaller dog, if of characteristic type, is more valuable, and the shoulder height should not exceed 10¼ inches in any case.

AFFENPINSCHER REGISTRATIONS 1981 — 87 INCLUSIVE

1981 — 25
1982 — 26
1983 — 23
1984 — 33
1985 — 23
1986 — 26
1987 — 38

YET TO WIN CRUFTS BEST-IN-SHOW.

BICHON FRISE

Formerly known as the Bichon Teneriffe, this breed descends from the Barbet, a French Water Spaniel. the Spanish are said to have introduced these dogs to the Canary Islands, where they thrived. The name Bichon Teneriffe was taken from the largest of the Canary Islands, Teneriffe.

The Breed became extremely popular with the French aristocracy of the sixteenth century and King Henry III was said to have kept several to which he was devoted to the point of obsession. Their glamourous appearance and portable size also made them favourites with ladies of the upper classes.

The name Bichon Teneriffe was changed in the 1930's to "Bichon a poil frise", (curly coated Bichon) and this has since been abbreviated to Bichon Frise.

This is definitely a pet dog first and foremost and one to be recommended for his cheerful disposition and lack of malice. Children are completely safe in his company, and he enjoys play with anyone who will oblige. He is a small eater and can live quite contentedly in a small home, providing he receives regular outings. The coat, especially if showing is contemplated, requires meticulous grooming to achieve the delicate "cotton wool" look.

KEY TO CHARACTER	
INTELLIGENCE	***
TEMPERAMENT	*****
EASE OF COAT CARE	*
SUITABILITY FOR SMALL DWELLING	*****
***** (5) = VERY GOOD	

BRITISH KENNEL CLUB STANDARD

BICHON FRISE

GENERAL APPEARANCE. — Gay, happy, lively little dog, the coat falling in soft, corkscrew curls. The head carriage is proud and high; the eyes alert and full of expression.

Head and Skull. — The skull longer than the muzzle, the whole head in balance with the body. The muzzle should not be thick or heavy; nor should it be snipy; the cheeks flat and not very strongly muscled; the stop should be slight and the hollow between the eyebrows just visible. Skull flat when touched, although the hair tends to make it look round. The nose should be round, black, soft and shiny.

Eyes. — Dark, with dark eye-rims, fairly round, never almond shaped nor obliquely set; not too big; never showing any white. Neither large nor prominent. The socket should not be pronounced.

Ears. — Narrow and delicate. Hanging close to the head and well covered with tightly curled, long hair. Carried forward when the dog is alert but in such manner that the forward edge touches the skull and not carried obliquely away from the head. The leather should reach halfway along the muzzle.

Mouth. — Scissor bite, that is to say, the incisors of the lower jaw should be placed immediately behind and in contact with those of the upper jaw. The lips should be fine, fairly tight and completely black, drooping just sufficient for the lower lips to be covered by the upper, but never heavy nor hanging. The lower lip should be neither heavy, protruding nor flabby and should never show the mucous membrane when the mouth is closed.

Neck. — Fairly long, carried high and proudly. Round and slim near the head, gradually broadening to fit smoothly into the shoulders. Length about one third the length of the body (proportions of 33 cm. (13″) - 11 cm. (4½″) for a dog of 27 cm. (10½″) high at the withers).

Forequarters. — Shoulders oblique, not prominent, and equal in length to the upper arm (approx 10 cm. (4″)). The upper arm should fit close to the body. Legs straight when seen from the front, perpendicular and finely boned. The pastern should be short and straight when viewed from the front, very slightly sloping when viewed from the side.

Body. — Chest well developed, with deep brisket. The floating ribs well rounded and not terminating abruptly. Loin broad, well-muscled, slightly arched and well tucked-up. The pelvis broad, the croup slightly rounded.

Hindquarters. — Thighs broad and well-rounded, oblique. Stifles well-bent and hocks well let down.

Feet. — Small, rounded and well knuckled-up. Nails preferably black.

Tail. — Normally carried raised and curled gracefully over the back but never tightly curled. It should not be docked and should not touch the backbone but the hair should always fall on to the back. Slightly low set.

Coat. — Fine, silky, with soft corkscrew curls. Neither flat nor corded, and measuring 7 to 10 cm. (2¾ to 4″) in length. The dog may be presented untrimmed or have muzzle and feet slightly tidied up.

Colour. — Pure white. Under the white coat dark pigment is preferred.Black, blue or beige markings are often found on the skin.

Height. — Less than 30 cm. (12″), smallness being highly desirable.

Faults. — Any departure from the foregoing points should be considered a fault and the seriousness of the fault should be in exact proportion to its degree.

Note. — Male animals should have two apparently normal testicles fully descended into the scrotum.

MAIN AMERICAN KENNEL CLUB VARIATION TO STANDARD FOR THE BICHON FRISE —

Size. — Dogs and Bitches 9½ to 11½ inches should be given primary preference.

BICHON FRISE REGISTRATIONS 1981 — 87 INCLUSIVE

1981 — 387
1982 — 520
1983 — 603
1984 — 738
1985 — 794
1986 — 864
1987 — 1055

YET TO WIN CRUFTS BEST-IN-SHOW.

CAVALIER KING CHARLES SPANIEL

The forerunners of this breed were undoubtedly the Toy Spaniels that were popular some five hundred years ago. For centuries these dogs, being adored by the aristocracy, were featured in tapesties and in oils and it can be seen from these old works that todays Cavalier King Charles is of very similar conformation and marking. It is believed that either imported Pekingese from the Royal Palace of China or Spanish toy dogs were the root stock of these dogs.

The man who lent the breed his name, King Charles II, was obsessed with them. So much so, in fact, that his aides became thoroughly aggravated by the constant presence around the King of a large group of the dogs. But Charles was not to be discouraged as he often put the comfort of his dogs ahead of all else.

Until 1923 there were four types of Toy Spaniel. These were the King Charles, the Red, the Prince Charles and the Blenheim. These categories were all determined by the colour and after the above date they all became collectively known as the King Charles Spaniel.

The need was felt by some breeders for a smaller version of the King Charles and after much careful, conscientious work the Cavalier King Charles became registered as a seperate breed in 1945.

There is no doubt that this breed owes much of his present popularity to his amiable, playful disposition and manageable size. He is fearless and totally without malice and is especially to be recommended as a companion for the elderly as exercise is not of paramount importance.

KEY TO CHARACTER	
INTELLIGENCE	***
TEMPERAMENT	****
EASE OF COAT CARE	***
SUITABILITY FOR SMALL DWELLING	*****
***** (5) = VERY GOOD	

BRITISH KENNEL CLUB STANDARD

CAVALIER KING CHARLES SPANIEL

GENERAL APPEARANCE. — An active, graceful and well-balanced dog. Absolutely fearless and sporting in character and very gay and free in action.

Head and Skull. — Head almost flat between the ears, without dome. Stop shallow. Length from base of stop to tip about 3.8 cm. (1½"). Nostrils should be well developed and the pigment black. Muzzle well tapered. Lips well-covering but not hound like. Face should be well filled out underneath the eyes. Any tendency to appear "snipy" is undesirable.

Eyes. — Large, dark and round but not prominent. The eyes should be spaced well apart.

Ears. — Long and set high with plenty of feather.

Mouth. — Level; scissor-bite preferred.

Neck. — Moderate length — slightly arched.

Forequarters. — Shoulders well laid back; legs moderate bone and straight.

Body. — Short-coupled with plenty of spring of rib. Back level. Chest moderate leaving ample heart room.

Hindquarters. — Legs with moderate bone; well-turned stifle — no tendency to cow or sickle hocks.

Feet. — Compact, cushioned and well-feathered.

Tail. — The docking of tails is optional. No more than one-third to be removed. The length of the tail should be in balance with the body.

Coat. — Long, silky and free from curl. A slight wave is permissible. There should be plenty of feather.

Colour. — The only recognised colours are:
Black and Tan: Raven black with tan markings above the eyes, on cheeks, inside ears, on chest and legs and underside of tail. The tan should be bright.
Ruby: whole coloured rich red.
Blenheim: Rich chestnut marking well broken up on a pearly white ground. The markings should be evenly divided on the head, leaving room between the ears for the much valued lozenge mark or spot (a unique characteristic of the breed).
Tricolour: Black and white well spaced and broken up, with tan markings over the eyes, on cheeks, inside ears, inside legs, and on underside of tail. Any other colour or combination of colours is most undesirable.

Weight and Size. — Weight — 5.4 to 8.2 kg. (12 to 18 lbs). A small well-balanced dog well within these weights is desirable.

Faults. — Light eyes. Undershot and crooked mouths and pig jaws. White marks on whole-coloured specimens. Coarseness of type. Putty noses. Flesh marks. Nervousness.

Note. — Male animals should have two apparently normal testicles fully descended into the scrotum.

CAVALIER KING CHARLES SPANIEL REGISTRATIONS 1981 — 87 INCLUSIVE

1981 — 8530
1982 — 9539
1983 — 9978
1984 — 9767
1985 — 10090
1986 — 9766
1987 — 9110

CRUFTS BEST-IN-SHOW WINNER

1973 ALANSMERE AQUARIUS — MESSRS. HALL AND EVANS.

CHIHUAHUA

This, the smallest breed of all, originated in Mexico in the days of the Aztecs and draws his name from the state of Chihuahua.

The Aztecs practised the bizarre custom of burying a dead man's dog alongside him and since the most popular domesticated dogs were of the Chihuahua type, countless thousands of these dogs were killed on the demise of their owners.

These early specimens were probably quite similar to today's. The main reason for this being that the Chihuahua is so minute that it is physically almost impossible for another breed to mate with it and thus a true bred ancestry is the outcome.

Less common than the smooth-coated Chihuahua is the long-coated variety. Apart from it's coat, which can be wavy or flat, it is identical to the smooth coated.

This breed is not necessarily as delicate as might be imagined but one or two precautions are recommended. The Chihuahua detests the cold and a coat should be used in the winter. Kennel living is not to be contemplated.

A unique feature of the breed is a small hole in the top of the skull known as the molera and naturally this is a weak spot so care should be taken to avoid heavy knocks to the head.

He is a house loving dog and his small exercise and feeding needs make him a good choice for a sedentary owner.

KEY TO CHARACTER		
INTELLIGENCE		***
TEMPERAMENT		****
EASE OF COAT CARE	SMOOTH	*****
	LONG	***
SUITABILITY FOR SMALL DWELLING		*****
***** (5) = VERY GOOD		

BRITISH KENNEL CLUB STANDARD
CHIHUAHUA (SMOOTH COAT)

CHARACTERISTICS. — An alert and swift moving little dog with a saucy expression.

GENERAL APPEARANCE. — Small, dainty and compact with a brisk forceful action.

Head and Skull. — A well rounded "Apple Dome" skull with or without Molerol cheeks and jaws lean, nose moderately short, slightly pointed. Definite stop.

Eyes. — Full, round but not protruding, set well apart, dark or ruby. (Light eyes in light colours permissible).

Ears. — Large, set on at an angle of about 45 degrees; this gives breadth between the ears.

Mouth. — Level, scissor bite.

Neck. — Slightly arched, of medium length.

Forequarters. — Shoulders should be well up, lean, sloping into a slightly broadening support above straight forelegs that are set well under, giving free play at the elbows.

Body. — Level back, slightly longer than the height at shoulder. Well sprung ribs with deep brisket.

Hindquarters. — Muscular with hocks well apart, neither out nor in, well let down.

Feet. — Small with toes well split up, but not spread, pads cushioned. Fine pasterns (neither "Hare" nor "Cat" foot). A dainty foot with nails moderately long.

Tail. — Medium length carried up or over the back. Preferred furry, flattish in appearance, broadening slightly in the centre and tapering to a point.

Coat. — Smooth, of soft texture, close and glossy.

Colour. — Any colour or mixture of colours.

Weight. — Up to 2.7 kg. (6 lbs.), with 0.9 to 1.8 kg. (2 to 4 lbs.) preferable. If two dogs are equally good in type, the more diminutive preferred.

Faults. — Cropped tail, brokendown ears.

Note. — Male animals should have two apparently normal testicles fully descended into the scrotum.

CHIHUAHUA (LONG COAT)

The Standard of the Chihuahua (Long Coat) is the same as the Standard of the Chihuahua (Smooth Coat) with the exception of the following:—

Coat. — Long, of soft texture (never coarse or harsh to the touch) either flat or slightly wavy. No tight curly coat. There should be feathering on the feet and legs, pants on the hind legs, a large ruff on the neck is desired and preferred, the tail should be long and full as a plume.

SMOOTH COAT CHIHUAHA REGISTRATIONS 1981 — 87 INCLUSIVE

1981 — 1071
1982 — 960
1983 — 1018
1984 — 820
1985 — 838
1986 — 755
1987 — 627

YET TO WIN CRUFTS BEST-IN-SHOW.

LONG COAT CHIHUAHUA REGISTRATIONS 1981 — 87 INCLUSIVE

1981 — 1938
1982 — 1857
1983 — 1636
1984 — 1679
1985 — 1758
1986 — 1433
1987 — 1322

YET TO WIN CRUFTS BEST-IN-SHOW.

CHINESE CRESTED DOG

This extraordinary breed is instantly recognisable by its's almost total lack of hair. There are several types of hairless dog throughout the world and China is known to have had such dogs for many centuries. The exact ancestry of the Chinese Crested that we see today is unclear, but it seems likely that the breed was developed in the U.S.A. from oriental imports. The feature which distinguishes this breed from his close relative the Mexican Hairless, is the crest of long hair on the head and the hair on the end of the tail and on the feet.

Since making a sensational Crufts debut in 1969, the Chinese Crested has risen steadily in numbers, this is due to a gradual build-up of public curiosity and, eventually, affection.

Despite the lack of coat, he manages to adapt well to our cool temperatures, partly due to the fact that he has a naturally high body temperature. Although never used as a working or sporting dog, the Chinese Crested displays a fair level of intelligence and is easily house-trained. He loves children and can become very strongly attached to the whole family. Although his size is hardly an advantage, he can act as quite a forceful guard. Exercise needs are not excessive.

KEY TO CHARACTER	
INTELLIGENCE	****
TEMPERAMENT	****
EASE OF COAT CARE	***
SUITABILITY FOR SMALL DWELLING	*****
***** (5) = VERY GOOD	

BRITISH KENNEL CLUB STANDARD

CHINESE CRESTED DOG

GENERAL APPEARANCE. — A small, active and graceful dog; medium to fine boned; smooth hairless body, with hair on feet, head and tail only.

Head and Skull. — Skull slightly rounded, moderate stop; fairly long muzzle; cheeks lean; head carried high. Crest flat, high or long flowing; full crest preferred; sparse crest acceptable.

Eyes. — Medium size, moderately dark in colour, round and set wide apart.

Ears. — Large upstanding ears, with or without ear fringe.

Teeth. — Pincer or scissor bite. Prominent canines. Absence of premolars should not be penalised.

Neck. — Long. Slightly arched. Sloping gracefully to shoulders.

Forequarters. — Straight, medium to fine boned. Furnishings not to extend above knee on foreleg.

Body. — Should be medium to long. Level back. Rump slightly rounded. Chest deep and fairly broad. Belly moderately tucked up. Skin smooth and soft.

Hindquarters. — Hocks well let down. Furnishings not to extend above hock on hind leg.

Tail. — Carried over back or looped, never curled. Plume on last two-thirds, of tail. Full plume preferred. Sparse plume on tail acceptable.

Colour. — Any colour, plain or spotted.

Weight. — Weight may vary between 3.2 to 5.4 kg. (7 to 12 lbs.) but overall balance is the essential requirement.

Faults. — Any departure from the foregoing points should be considered a fault and the seriousness of the fault should be in exact proportion to its degree.

Note. — Male animals should have two apparently normal testicles fully descended into the scrotum.

CHINESE CRESTED REGISTRATIONS 1981 — 87 INCLUSIVE

1981 — 75
1982 — 100
1983 — 98
1984 — 113
1985 — 149
1986 — 253
1987 — 242

YET TO WIN CRUFTS BEST-IN-SHOW.

Cavalier King Charles Spaniel
Chihuahua (Long-Coat)

Chihuahua (Smooth-Coat)

Chinese Crested Dog

ENGLISH TOY TERRIER (BLACK AND TAN)

The game little English Toy Terrier is a good choice for someone who wants a very small dog and the advantages that go with it, combined with the lively spirit of a hunting Terrier.

In the early days of the breed, his chief role was as a ratter. He was put to use for the everday extermination of rats and also for the entertainment of working class men who used him as a rat-pit dog. He was produced from the Black and Tan Terrier of the time by breeding from selected diminutive specimens. This Black and Tan Terrier is still to be seen in similar form today, as the Manchester Terrier.

The English Toy Terrier (Black and Tan) was originally known as the Toy Black and Tan Terrier and was given his present title officially when the Kennel Club recognised the breed in the early 1960's. In the U.S.A. he is called the Toy Manchester Terrier.

He is a dog known for a fair level of intelligence and shows boundless affection for his owner. Children will find him endearing and he will revel in their attentions. Being tiny does not discourage him from guarding well as he is far from cowardly. Maintenance will suit anybody with a tight budget and limited time to spare. A regular pattern of exercise will be appreciated by the English Toy Terrier as he does have an active past.

KEY TO CHARACTER	
INTELLIGENCE	****
TEMPERAMENT	****
EASE OF COAT CARE	*****
SUITABILITY FOR SMALL DWELLING	*****
***** (5) = VERY GOOD	

BRITISH KENNEL CLUB STANDARD

ENGLISH TOY TERRIER (BLACK AND TAN)

GENERAL APPEARANCE. — A well balanced, elegant and compact Toy with Terrier temperament and characteristics. It must be borne in mind that in the past the breed was required frequently to be able to acquit itself satisfactorily in the rat pit. Therefore present day specimens should be sleek and cleanly built giving an appearance of alertness combined with speed of movement but not of whippet type.

In realization of the fact that this is a Toy Dog with Terrier characteristics unduly nervous specimens cannot rank as wholly typical representatives of the breed. Judges, when officiating, should bear this in mind.

Head and Skull. — The head should be long and narrow with a flat skull, wedge-shaped without emphasis of cheek muscles and well filled up under the eyes. The top and bottom jaws should be held tightly together within compressed lips. Upon close inspection of the foreface one finds indications of a slight "stop". The foreface then tapers gently to provide a wedge-shaped impression in profile similarly corresponding to that given when it is viewed direct. Although an illusion of being "overshot" can result, any suggestions of a snipy appearance is undesirable. Nose — Black.

Eyes. — These should be very dark to black without light shading from the iris. They should be small, almond shaped, obliquely set and sparkling.

N.B. — Light, large and round, protruding or disproportionately wide or narrow set eyes should be regarded as faults.

Ears. — These should be of "candle-flame" shape, slightly pointed at the tips, placed high upon the back of the skull and proportionately close together. A guide to the size can be obtained by bending the ear forward. It should not reach the eye. From nine months of age the ear carriage must be erect. The entire inside of the ear should face the front. The leather of the ear should be thin. A cat ear appearance is wrong.

Italian Greyhound

Japanese Chin

English Toy Terrier (Black and Tan)
Griffon Bruxellois

N.B. — Large or "flapping" ears should be regarded as faults.

Mouth. — Teeth should be level and strong. The upper front teeth should close slightly over the lower front teeth, the latter to lean forward fractionally thus establishing the correct level bite.

Neck. — The neck should be long, graceful, and slightly arched. The shoulders should be well laid back not straight. The pattern of the neck line flowing into the shoulders, and sloping off elegantly. Throatiness is undesirable.

Forequarters. — The chest narrow and deep. Legs falling straight from the shoulders, with the elbows close to the chest providing a straight front. Loose elbows and wide fronts are faults. Fine bone is eminently desirable. The ideal fore-movement is that akin to the "extended trot", hackney action is not desirable; equally to be discouraged is a "shuffling" gait.

Body. — The body is compact, head and legs proportionate thus producing correct balance. The back very slightly curving from behind the shoulder to the loin falling again to the root of the tail. The chest should be narow and deep with the ribs well sprung to a well cut up loin. The buttocks should be gently rounded.

Faults. — A roached, dipped or dead flat back, hindquarters higher than the shoulders.

Hindquarters. — A well-rounded loin leading to a good turn of stifle is required, hocks well let down, a "tucked under" appearance is undesirable. Hind-action should be smooth and suggest ease and precision combined with drive. There should be a "flowing quality" to give true soundness.

Feet. — Dainty compact, split up between the toes, and well arched, with jet black nails; the two middle toes of the front feet rather longer than the others and the hind feet shaped like those of a cat. Hare feet are not desirable, and should be regarded as a fault.

Tail. — The tail should be thick at the root, tapering to a point. Set low and not reaching below the hock. A "gay" tail carriage is undesirable if displayed to excess.

Coat. — The texture should be thick, close, smooth and of glossy appearance. A density of short hair is required.

N.B. — Sparse, weak coats should be regarded as faults.

Colour. — Black and Tan. The black should be ebony and the tan can be likened to a new chestnut, deeply rich. These colours should not run, or blend into each other, but should meet abruptly, forming clear and well defined lines of colour division. Forelegs tanned to the knee in front. The tan then continuing inside and at the back of the foreleg to a point just below the elbow. A thin black line up each toe (Pencilling) and a clearly defined black mark "thumb mark" on the centre of each pastern, and under the chin. The hind legs should be well tanned in front and the inside, with a black "bar" dividing the tan at the centre of the lower thigh. Each toe "pencilled". Heavy tan on the outside of the hind-quarters, "breeching", is a fault. On the head the muzzle is well tanned, nose black, the black continuing along the top of the muzzle, curving below the eyes to the base of the throat. A tan spot above each eye and a small tan spot on each cheek. The under jaw and throat are tanned, the lip line black. The hair inside the ears tanned (tan behind the ears a fault). Each side of the chest is slightly tanned. The vent and under root of the tail tanned. White hairs forming a patch anywhere are a serious fault.

Weight and Size. — The ideal weight is between that of 2.7 to 3.6 kg. (6 to 8 lbs.) and a height of 25½ to 30½ cm. (10″ to 12″) at the shoulders is most desirable.
Judges are encouraged to use scales, as it is hoped this will help to establish uniformity.

Note. — Male animals should have two apparently normal testicles fully descended into the scrotum.

MAIN AMERICAN KENNEL CLUB VARIATION TO STANDARD FOR THE ENGLISH TOY TERRIER (BLACK AND TAN) —

Known as the Manchester Terrier (Toy) in the U.S.A.

The standard for this breed closely follows that of the Manchester Terrier except for — Ears — of moderate size; set well up on the skull and rather close together; thin, moderately narrow at base; with pointed tips; naturally erect carriage.

Weight. — Not exceeding 12 pounds.

ENGLISH TOY TERRIER (BLACK AND TAN) REGISTRATIONS 1981 — 87 INCLUSIVE

1981 — 50
1982 — 32
1983 — 36
1984 — 55
1985 — 52
1986 — 44
1987 — 73

YET TO WIN CRUFTS BEST-IN-SHOW.

King Charles Spaniel
Maltese

Miniature Pinscher

Papillon

GRIFFON BRUXELLOIS

This, one of the hardiest of the toy breeds, is a dog of Belgian origins, Brussels having been the main centre for his early development. It seems that the Affenpinscher was crossed with local Belgian terrier-type dogs in the latter half of the Nineteenth century. There are some who believe that Yorkshire Terrier and King Charles Spaniel blood was also introduced at the latter stage of the Griffon's development.

He was very much a working man's companion and was used for ratting and the pursuit of small game. A smooth-coated version of the breed known as the Petit Brabancon was produced by crossing the Bruxellois with the Pug. The Griffon Bruxellois and the Petit Brabancon are now identical save for the coat.

Although a dog of quite lowly origins, it is true to say that he moved up in public esteem when Belgian royalty began to show interest in him. The end result of this has meant that the Griffon is now something of a fashionable breed in some circles.

He is an independant type, something which many find attractive and he is easily cared for. A Griffon can become strongly attached to a family and displays a good level of intelligence. His terrier-like nature and constitution are unusual for such a small dog and he normally enjoys a long, healthy life.

KEY TO CHARACTER	
INTELLIGENCE	****
TEMPERAMENT	****
EASE OF COAT CARE	
BRUXELLOIS	****
PETIT BRABANCON	*****
SUITABILITY FOR SMALL DWELLING	*****

******* (5) = VERY GOOD**

BRITISH KENNEL CLUB STANDARD

GRIFFON BRUXELLOIS

CHARACTERISTICS. — The Griffon is a smart dog with the disposition of a terrier. There are two varieties, the rough coated, the Griffon Bruxellois and the smooth coated, the Petit Brabancon. Both with the pert monkey-like expression but heavy for their size.

GENERAL APPEARANCE. — A well-balanced square little dog, lively and alert, giving the appearance of measuring the same from withers to tail root as from withers to ground. Its action should be free, well bent hocks giving the correct drive from behind and moving true coming and going. High stepping front movement should be discouraged.

Head and Skull. — The head should be large and rounded but in no way domed and should be wide between the ears. Hair on the skull, in the rough variety, should be rather coarse. Nose always black, as short as possible, with large open nostrils, high set sloping back to the skull with a deep stop between nose and skull. Wide muzzle, neat lips and with good turn-up. Chin prominent and slightly undershot without showing teeth and (in the rough variety) furnished with a beard.

Eyes. — Black rimmed, very dark, large and round, clear and alert.

Ears. — Semi-erect, high set, the smaller the better.

Mouth. — Mouth slightly undershot with regular teeth.

Neck. — Of medium length, slightly arched, springing from well laid-back shoulders.

Forequarters. — Chest rather wide and deep, legs straight of medium length and bone.

Pekingese

Pomeranian

Pug

Yorkshire Terrier

Body. — Short back, level from withers to tail root, neither roaching nor dipping, deep well-sprung ribs, short strong loin.

Hindquarters. — Well muscled thighs of good length, short hocks, carried well bent and turning neither in nor out.

Feet. — Small, thick cat-like feet with black toenails.

Tail. — Short docked, carried high, emerging at right angles from a level top-line.

Coat. — Roughs: harsh wiry and free from curl, preferably with an undercoat. Smooths: short and tight.

Colour. — Clear red, black or black and rich tan. In the clear red, a darker shade on the mask and ears is desirable. Ideally each hair should be an even red from tip to root. Frosting on the muzzles of mature smooths should not be penalised.

Weight and Size. — From 2.3 to 5 kg. (5 to 11 lbs), most desirable 2.7 to 4.5 kg. (6 to 10 lbs).

Faults. — Showing teeth or tongue, overshot or wry mouths, light eyes, brown nose, eyerims or toenails, curly coat, white patches. Roaching or dipping the back should be penalised.

Note. — Male animals should have two apparently normal testicles fully descended into the scrotum.

MAIN AMERICAN KENNEL CLUB VARIATION TO STANDARD FOR THE GRIFFON BRUXELLOIS —

Known as the Brussels Griffon in the U.S.A.

Ears. — May be shown cropped or natural.

Weight. — Usually 8 to 10 pounds, and should not exceed 12 pounds.

GRIFFON BRUXELLOIS REGISTRATIONS 1981 — 87 INCLUSIVE

1981 — 247
1982 — 201
1983 — 283
1984 — 239
1985 — 274
1986 — 281
1987 — 230

YET TO WIN CRUFTS BEST-IN-SHOW.

ITALIAN GREYHOUND

There are mentions of small Greyhound-type dogs being kept as long ago as the days of the Roman Empire. These dogs had been developed by breeding from the smallest of the larger Greyhounds until a pet size dog was arrived at. This method was refined over many centuries resulting, quite naturally, in a more mild and sensitive natured dog than the larger version.

The Italian Greyhound has no great interest in work or extrovert behaviour, but his followers would contend that his gentleness and ease of management more than compensate. Although not the most robust of dogs, the Italian Greyhound is still equipped with good running speed and will enjoy lively play and frequent exercise. Children should not be allowed to be heavy handed with this breed as this could lead to nervousness, apart from the possibility of injury. He has an intense aversion to the cold and during the winter months a coat is often needed.

The Italian Greyhound is essentially an undemanding, graceful little dog who can be kept in a flat or small house and will prove an affectionate and obedient companion.

KEY TO CHARACTER	
INTELLIGENCE	****
TEMPERAMENT	*****
EASE OF COAT CARE	*****
SUITABILITY FOR SMALL DWELLING	*****
***** (5) = VERY GOOD	

BRITISH KENNEL CLUB STANDARD

ITALIAN GREYHOUND

CHARACTERISTICS. — High stepping and free action.

GENERAL APPEARANCE. — A miniature Greyhound, more slender in all proportions, and of ideal elegance and grace in shape, symmetry and action.

Head and Skull. — Skull long, flat and narrow. Muzzel very fine. Nose dark in colour.

Eyes. — Rather large, bright, and full of expression.

Ears. — Rose-shaped, placed well back, soft and delicate.

Mouth. — Teeth level.

Neck. — Should be long and gracefully arched.

Forequarters. — Shoulders long and sloping. Legs straight, well set under the shoulders; fine pasterns; small delicate bones.

Body. — Chest deep and narrow. Back curved, and drooping at the hindquarters.

Hindquarters. — Hocks well let down. Thighs muscular.

Feet. — Long, hare-feet.

Tail. — Rather long, fine, with low carriage.

Coat. — Skin fine and supple. Hair, thin and glossy, like satin.

Colour. — Recognised colours, all shades of fawn, white cream, blue, black and fawn and white pied.

Weight and Size. — The most desirable weight is from 2.7 to 3.6 kg. (6 to 8 lbs), and not exceeding 4.5 kg. (10 lbs).

Faults. — Black or blue with tan markings, brindle.

Note. — Male animals should have two apparently normal testicles fully descended into the scrotum.

MAIN AMERICAN KENNEL CLUB VARIATION TO STANDARD FOR THE ITALIAN GREYHOUND —

Size. — Height at withers ideally 13 inches to 15 inches.

ITALIAN GREYHOUND REGISTRATIONS 1981 — 87 INCLUSIVE

1981 — 133
1982 — 111
1983 — 114
1984 — 90
1985 — 78
1986 — 86
1987 — 63

YET TO WIN CRUFTS BEST-IN-SHOW.

JAPANESE CHIN

Like all small dogs of the Far East, the Japanese Chin has an ancient and unclear history. He undoubtedly shares ancestry with the Pekingese, but exactly where the paths of the two breeds crossed is not known. Indeed, it is not certain whether the Japanese Chin appeared in Japan first or China. For many centuries he was highly esteemed by the Japanese hierarchy and it was quite a frequent practice for a Japanese emperor to present these dogs as a gift to other heads of state. These very early specimens were a fair bit larger than the Japanese Chin of today, and it is thought that some of these dogs were brought to Europe by sailors who had been impressed with them on their Eastern travels. But it was centuries later when Queen Victoria acquired a pair of Chin that the breed began to grow in popularity outside Japan. Although not as popular as the Pekingese, for instance, the breed has gained a solid following in Britain, particularly as a striking show dog.

Although it would be wrong to call this breed rough and ready, he is not as puny as his light frame would suggest. He enjoys lively play sessions with children and is loyal and friendly if treated well. As long as an owner is prepared to devote some time to maintaining the beautiful coat, the Japanese Chin makes a very manageable companion. Exercise should be regular including some off-the lead runs.

KEY TO CHARACTER	
INTELLIGENCE	***
TEMPERAMENT	****
EASE OF COAT CARE	**
SUITABILITY FOR SMALL DWELLING	*****
******* (5) = VERY GOOD**	

BRITISH KENNEL CLUB STANDARD
JAPANESE CHIN

CHARACTERISTICS. — The Japanese Chin is a lively little dog of dainty appearance, smart compact carriage and profuse coat. These dogs should be essentially stylish in movement,lifting the feet high when in motion, carrying the tail, which is heavily feathered, closely curved or plumed over the back.

Head. — Large but in proportion to size of dog, broad skull rounded in front, rounded between ears but in no way domed.

Nostrils. — Should be large and black, except in the case of the red and white where the colour can be the same as the markings.

Eyes. — Should be large, dark, set far apart. It is desirable that the white shows in the inner corners, this gives the Japanese Chin that characteristic look of astonishment (wrongly called squint) which should on no account be lost.

Muzzle. — Muzzle very short and wide and well cushioned, i.e. upper lips rounded on each side of nostrils and mouth level.

Ears. — Small, set wide apart and high on the head, carried slightly forward, v-shaped and well feathered.

Neck. — Moderate length held up proudly.

Body. — Should be squarely and compactly built, wide in chest, "cobby" in shape. The length of the dog's body should be equal to its height at the withers.

Forequarters. — Legs straight, and bone fine, giving them a slender appearance, well feathered to the feet.

Hindquarters. — Straight viewed from behind, good turn of stifle, profusely feathered from the back of the thighs.

Feet. — Should be slender and hare shaped, feathered at tips.

Tail. — Set high on a straight back, profusely feathered, closely curved or plumed over the back.

Coat. — Profuse coat, long soft and straight of silky texture. Absolutely free from curl or wave, not too flat, having a tendency to stand out especially at the frill of the neck.

Colour. — Black and white or red and white. Red includes all shades, sable, brindle, lemon or orange. The brighter and clearer the red the better. Colour evenly distributed on the cheeks and ears, and as patches on the body. Not too heavily marked desirable. White should be clear, not flecked.

Size. — The daintier they are the better, providing type, quality and soundness are not sacrificed. As a guide suggested size 1.8 to 3.2 kg. (4 to 7 lbs).

Faults. — Flying ears, wry mouth, tongue showing, tri-colour.

Note. — Male animals should have two apparently normal testicles fully descended into the scrotum.

MAIN AMERICAN KENNEL CLUB VARIATIONTO STANDARD FOR THE JAPANESE CHIN —

General Apearance. — When divided by weight, classes should be under and over 7 pounds.

JAPANESE CHIN REGISTRATIONS 1981 — 87 INCLUSIVE

1981 — 166
1982 — 201
1983 — 181
1984 — 260
1985 — 280
1986 — 291
1987 — 264

YET TO WIN CRUFTS BEST-IN-SHOW.

KING CHARLES SPANIEL

Known as the English Toy Spaniel in the U.S.A., this breed takes it's name from King Charles II who was a great admirer of small Spaniels. He had several and would often exercise them in public places, much to the delight of onlookers.

The Cavalier King Charles and the King Charles Spaniels come from the same stock which some believe originated in the Far East some 4,000 years ago.

The very early specimens in Britain were all more of the Cavalier type than the King Charles. The flatter muzzle of the latter was introduced by selective breeding as this head shape became more fashionable. The ladies of the court of Charles II were very keen on these dogs, keeping them purely as pampered lap-dogs.

Nowadays it is the Cavalier which is by far the more popular although the King Charles still has much to offer as a pet. With animals and people alike he is totally without malice and revels in attention from his owner. He is sufficiently high spirited and energetic to be engaging and yet is small enough to be managed by even an elderly lady, for example. As with the Cavalier the choice of colours for the King Charles is varied and interesting. There is Blenheim, which is white and chestnut, Tri-colour, which is white, black and tan, Ruby, which is a whole coloured chestnut red and Black and Tan is the other variety.

He is a very clean dog who will exist happily in any size house. Exercise should be regular but need not be excessive. The slighly wavy coat looks far better for a daily brushing, which with a dog of this size is not great task.

KEY TO CHARACTER	
INTELLIGENCE	***
TEMPERAMENT	*****
EASE OF COAT CARE	***
SUITABILITY FOR SMALL DWELLING	*****
***** (5) = VERY GOOD	

BRITISH KENNEL CLUB STANDARD

KING CHARLES SPANIEL

GENERAL APPEARANCE. — Compact and cobby, on refined lines, chest wide and deep, legs short and straight, back short and level. Tail well flagged, and not carried over the level of the back. Movement free active and elegant.

Head and Skull. — Skull massive in comparison to size, well domed, and full over the eyes. Nose black with large wide open nostrils, very short and turned up to meet the skull. The stop between skull and nose should be well defined. Jaw; muzzle square, wide, and deep and well turned up, lower jaw wide, lips exactly meeting, giving a nice finish. The cheeks should not fall away under the eyes, but be well cushioned up. A protruding tongue is objectionable, but does not disqualify.

Eyes. — Very large and dark, set wide apart, with eyelids block square to face line, and with pleasing expression.

Ears. — Set on low, and to hang quite flat to cheeks, very long and well feathered.

Coat. — Long, silky and straight, a slight wave allowed, not curly. The legs, ears and tail should be profusely feathered.

Colour. — Black and Tan: A rich glossy black, with bright, mahogany tan markings, on muzzle, legs, chest, linings of ears, under tail, and spots over eyes. Tri-colour; Ground pearly white and well distributed black patches, brilliant tan markings on cheeks, linings of ears, under tail, and spots over the eyes. A wide white blaxe between the eyes, and up the forehead. Blenheim: A ground of pearly white with well distributed chestnut red patches. A wide clear blaze with the "spot" in centre of skull. The "spot" should be a clear chestnut red mark about the size of a sixpence in centre of skull. Ruby: Whole coloured, a rich chestnut red.

Weight and Size. — The most desirable size is 3.6 to 6.3 kg. (8 to 14 lbs).

Faults. — The presence of a few white hairs on the chest of a Black and Tan or Ruby is undesirable, but a white patch is a major fault.

Note. — Male animals should have two apparently normal testicles fully descended into the scotum.

MAIN AMERICAN KENNEL CLUB VARIATION TO STANDARD FOR THE KING CHARLES SPANIEL —

Known as the English Toy Spaniel in the U.S.A.

Size. — The most desirable size is from 9 pounds to 12 pounds.

KING CHARLES SPANIEL REGISTRATIONS 1981 — 87 INCLUSIVE

1981 — 205
1982 — 261
1983 — 282
1984 — 256
1985 — 286
1986 — 289
1987 — 248

YET TO WIN CRUFTS BEST-IN-SHOW.

MALTESE

This is a truly ancient breed and some even believe the Maltese to be the oldest of all the Toy Breeds of Europe. As with all dogs of such long history, there are differing views on his exact beginnings. Although Malta is perhaps the most widely accepted place of origin, ancient writings have told of similar dogs being known in and around Sicily. Whichever was his first home it is certain that this dog has been abundant on Malta for many centuries.

Dogs very similar to the modern Maltese have featured frequently in paintings of some of the old masters and, more recently, Landseer has depicted a Maltese. He had believed that the breed was on the verge of extinction and had painted what he thought was to be one of the last specimens. Fortunately he was proved wrong.

The Maltese has been very much associated with women, his small size and glamourous coat making him a natural companion for an elegant, well-heeled lady. But this image is a little misleading as he is not as frail and timid as this might suggest. In fact, he is quite sturdy and active and is known for his longevity.

He has made a fair impact on the show world and his temperament and appearance are well suited to this sphere. The coat requires much attention if the Maltese is to appear at his very best and the dazzling white can be difficult to maintain.

He is a disarmingly friendly dog and is ideal for a family with children. Exercise need not be excessive but a daily walk should always be provided.

KEY TO CHARACTER	
INTELLIGENCE	***
TEMPERAMENT	****
EASE OF COAT CARE	*
SUITABILITY FOR SMALL DWELLING	*****
***** (5) = VERY GOOD	

BRITISH KENNEL CLUB STANDARD

MALTESE

CHARACTERISTICS. — Sweet tempered and very intelligent.

GENERAL APPEARANCE. — Should be smart, lively and alert. The action must be free; without extended weaving.

Head and Skull. — From stop to centre of skull (centre between forepart of ears) and stop to tip of nose should be equally balanced. Stop should be defined. Nose should be pure black.

Eyes. — Oval, not bulging, dark brown, black eye-rims.

Ears. — Should be long and well feathered and hanging close to the side of the head, the hair to be mingled with the coat at the shoulders.

Mouth. — Level or scissor bite with teeth even.

Neck. — Of medium length — set on well sloped shoulders.

Forequarters. — Legs should be short and straight. Shoulders well sloped.

Body. — Should be in every way well balanced and essentially short and cobby with good rib spring and the back should be straight from the tip of the shoulders to the tail.

Hindquarters. — Legs should be short and nicely angulated.

Feet. — Should be round and the pads of the feet should be black.

Tail. — Should be well arched over the back and feathered.

Coat. — Should be good length, but not impeding action, of silky texture, not in any way woolly and should be straight. It should not be crimped and there should be no woolly undercoat.

Colour. — Pure white, but slight lemon markings should not penalise.

Size. — Not over 25½ cm (10″) from ground to top of shoulder.

Faults. — Bad mouth, over or undershot; gay tail; curly or woolly coat; brown nose; pink eye rims; unsound in any way.

Note. — Male animals should have two apparently normal testicles fully descended into the scrotum.

MAIN AMERICAN KENNEL CLUB VARIATION TO STANDARD FOR THE MALTESE —

Size. — Weight under 7 pounds, with from 4 to 6 pounds preferred.

MALTESE REGISTRATIONS 1981 — 87 INCLUSIVE

1981 — 436
1982 — 449
1983 — 471
1984 — 529
1985 — 458
1986 — 446
1987 — 487

YET TO WIN CRUFTS BEST-IN-SHOW.

MINIATURE PINSCHER

This fine little breed has many attributes both as a pet and show dog, in fact his faults are so few, he has been nicknamed the 'King of the Toys'.

Many people once believed that there was a direct link between the Miniature Pinscher and the Dobermann Pinscher, the theory being that the former was a scaled down version of the latter. This has since been shown to be not the case, the Miniature Pinscher having developed totally separately. His true ancestor is a very old breed, the German Smooth-haired Pinscher. It seems likely that Dachshund and Italian Greyhound blood was introduced before the breed was eventually standardised in 1895.

There is a fair size following for the Miniature Pinscher in Britain and the U.S.A., largely due to his aptitude for the showring. It is in this environment that he is in his element, displaying great smartness and self confidence.

In the home, too, he shows confidence as a guard and, if required, as a controller of vermin. House-training should be no great problem and he is as easily maintained as any dog imaginable. He has an appealing individual gait and is an amusing companion for all age groups. Being one of the sturdier Toys he will enjoy a good deal of exercise and it would be true to say that an owner would derive most pleasure from his Miniature Pinscher if he catered to his lively disposition.

KEY TO CHARACTER	
INTELLIGENCE	***
TEMPERAMENT	****
EASE OF COAT CARE	*****
SUITABILITY FOR SMALL DWELLING	*****
***** (5) = VERY GOOD	

BRITISH KENNEL CLUB STANDARD

MINIATURE PINSCHER

GENERAL APPEARANCE. — The Miniature Pinscher is structurally a well balanced, sturdy, compact, elegant, short-coupled, smooth-coated toy dog. He is naturally well groomed, proud, vigorous and alert. The natural characteristic traits which identify him from other toy dogs are his precise Hackney gait, his fearless animation, complete self-possession and his spirited presence.

Head and Skull. — Rather more elongated than short and round. Narrow and without conspicuous cheek formation. In correct proportion to the body. The skull should appear flat when viewed from the front. The muzzle must be rather strong and proportionate to the skull. The nose well formed, black only with the exception of livers and blues, which may have a self-coloured nose.

Eyes. — Fitting well into the face. Neither too full nor round, neither too little nor slanting. Black or nearly black.

Ears. — Must be set on high, as small as possible, erect or dropped.

Mouth. — Scissors bite.

Neck. — Strong yet graceful. Slightly arched. Well fitted into the shoulders. Free from throatiness.

Forequarters. — Forechest well developed and full, moderately broad, shoulders clean, sloping with moderate angulation. Co-ordinated to permit the true action of the Hackney pony.

Body. — To be square, back line straight, sloping slightly towards the rear. Belly moderately tucked up. Ribs well sprung, deep rather than barrelled. Viewed from the top slightly wedge shaped.

Hindquarters. — Should be parallel to each other and wide enough apart to fit in with a properly built body. The hindquarters should be well developed and muscular with a good sweep of stifle and their hocks turning neither in or out.

Feet. — Legs straight, medium bone. Feet cat-like, elbows close to body. Nails dark.

Tail. — A continuation of the top-line carried a little high and docked short.

Coat. — Smooth, hard and short. Straight and lustrous. Closely adhering to and uniformly covering the body.

Colour. — Black, blue, chocolate with sharply defined tan markings on cheeks, lips, lower jaw, throat, twin spots above eyes and chest, lower half of fore-legs, inside of hindlegs and vent region, lower portion of hocks and feet. All the above colours should have black pencilling on toes with no thumb marks. Solid red of various shades. Slight white on chest is permissible but undesirable.

Height. — The height is to range from 25½ to 30½ cm. (10″ to 12″) at the withers.

Note. — Male animals should have two apparently normal testicles fully descended into the scrotum.

MAIN AMERICAN KENNEL CLUB VARIATION TO STANDARD FOR THE MINIATURE PINSCHER —

Ears. — May be cropped or uncropped.

Size. — Ten inches to twelve and one-half inches in height allowed, with desired height eleven inches to eleven and one-half inches measured at highest point of the shoulder blades.

MINIATURE PINSCHER REGISTRATIONS 1981 — 87 INCLUSIVE

1981 — 181
1982 — 155
1983 — 245
1984 — 241
1985 — 221
1986 — 210
1987 — 217

YET TO WIN CRUFTS BEST-IN-SHOW.

PAPILLON

The origins of this attractive little breed are rather unclear. Some authorities believe that the Chihuahua has played a major part in it's history and think it possible that the Papillon was actually developed in America. Others favour the idea of Spanish descent, believing it to have evolved from a strain of dwarf Spaniel around the middle of the sixteenth century. There is a strong case, too, for the theory that a toy Spaniel from Italy was the forerunner of the Papillon. Support for this proposition can be found in the abundance of old Italian paintings featuring Papillon-type dogs, some of these dating back to the fourteenth century.

Wherever it originated, the breed achieved it's greatest popularity in France and it is the French who named it. "Papillon" is French for "butterfly" and the ears of these dogs could be said to resemble the wings of a butterfly. In Europe there can be found a drop-eared version of this breed which is called the Phalene (French for "moth").

Although frail in appearance, the Papillon is a confident, high spirited dog, which if handled considerately is surprisingly robust. Although not ideal with very small children who might be too demanding of him, the Papillon is good natured and intelligent, responding quickly to proper training. He will enjoy more exercise than might be expected of such a tiny dog and the coat, although not too difficult to maintain, does need a daily brushing.

KEY TO CHARACTER	
INTELLIGENCE	****
TEMPERAMENT	***
EASE OF COAT CARE	**
SUITABILITY FOR SMALL DWELLING	*****
***** (5) = VERY GOOD	

BRITISH KENNEL CLUB STANDARD

PAPILLON

GENERAL APPEARANCE. — This dainty, balanced little toy dog should have an attractive head, an alert bearing and an intelligent and lively expression. Movement should be sound, light and free and not cramped or restricted in any way.

Head and Skull. — The Skull slightly rounded between the ears, the muzzle finely pointed and abruptly thinner than the skull accentuating the stop which should be well defined. Length from tip of the nose to the stop approximately a third length of the head. Nose should be black.

Faults. — Muzzle over long or coarse. Skull flat or apple shaped. Nose other than black.

Eyes. — Of medium size, rounded, dark in colour, placed rather low in the head and should not bulge.

Faults. — Eyes light in colour, too small or too large or protruding.

Ears. — The ears should be large and mobile with rounded tips, heavily fringed, set towards the back of the head far enough apart to show the slightly rounded shape of the skull. The ears must be completely erect or dropped. When the ears are erect they must be carried obliquely like the spread wings of a butterfly, therefore the name, Papillon. When the ears are dropped they must be completely dropped, and this type is known as the Phalene (moth).

Faults. — Semi-erect or not fully dropped, small, sharply pointed or set too close together.

Mouth. — Scissor bite, upper teeth fitting close over lower. The lips thin and tight.

Faults. — Over or undershot to the extent that the incisors do not touch at all. Wry mouth.

Neck. — Of medium length.

Forequarters. — Shoulders well developed and sloping back. Chest rather deep. Forelegs straight and slender and fine boned.

Faults. — Shoulders straight. Out at elbow.

Body. — Level topline. The body should have plenty of length, well formed with well sprung ribs, good length of loin which must not be weak, with slightly arched belly.

Faults. — Topline roached, dipped or cobby. Legs malformed and crooked, cow-hocked, too long or too short. Stifles straight, coupled with weak hindquarters.

Hindquarters. — Well developed, good turn of stifle. Legs when viewed from behind, should be parallel. Dew claws on the hind legs must be removed.

Feet. — Fine and fairly long as in the hare. The tufts of hair between the toes extending far beyond them.

Tail. — Long and well fringed, set on high, arched over the back with the fringes falling to the side to form the plume.

Faults. — Tail unduly short, too low set.

Coat. — Should be abundant, (flowing) but without undercoat, long, fine, silky, falling flat on back and sides forming a profuse frill on the chest, short and close on the skull, muzzle and front part of the legs. Back part of the front legs to pasterns, tail and thighs covered with long hair.

Faults. — Harsh, curly or stand-off coat.

Colour. — White with patches which may be any colour except liver. A tricolour must be black and white with tan spots over the eyes, tan inside ears and under root of tail and on cheeks. The head marking should be symmetrical about a white, narrow, clearly defined blaze.

Size. — The ideal height at the withers from 20.3 to 28 cm. (8″ to 11″). The dog will appear to be slightly longer than high when properly furnished with ruff and hind fringes.

Faults. — Muzzle over long or coarse. Skull flat or apple shaped. Nose other than black. Eyes light in colour, too small or too large or protruding. Ears semi-erect or not fully dropped, small, sharply pointed or set too close together. Mouth over or undershot to the extent that the incisors do not touch at all. Wry mouth. Shoulders straight. Out at elbow. Topline roached, dipped or cobby. Legs malformed and crooked, cow hocked, too long or too short. Stifles straight, coupled with weak hindquarters. Tail unduly short, too low set. Harsh, curly or stand-off coat.

Note. — Male animals should have two apparently normal testicles fully descended into the scrotum.

PAPILLON REGISTRATIONS 1981 — 87 INCLUSIVE

1981 — 775
1982 — 840
1983 — 857
1984 — 782
1985 — 895
1986 — 683
1987 — 747

YET TO WIN CRUFTS BEST-IN-SHOW.

PEKINGESE

The only written account of the origin of the Pekingese is to be found in an ancient Chinese legend. It is a ludicrous yet quaint tale of how a Korean lion was besotted with a marmoset, of all things, and was given the opportunity to marry her if he were to forfeit his size and strength. This he agreed to and in his miniaturised state he duly married her and the offspring of the union were said to be the Pekingese Lion Dogs. The title "Lion Dog" is still used and some of the characteristics of this stalwart little dog are not without semblance to a lion's. An impressive shaggy mane and fearless disposition are common to all pure bred Pekingese.

For many hundreds of years, though sadly no longer, the breed was held in immense esteem in China although his true ancestry is far from clear. This is not surprising considering that the early version of the Pekingese is thought to be some twelve hundred years old.

The first of the breed to reach Britain were actually looted from the Royal Palace at Peking by marauding British troops in 1860. English royalty took a shine to these new imports and the Pekingese grew steadily in popularity until it's official Kennel Club registration in 1898.

He is by no means a puny or weak minded character, being sturdily built and able to move sharply to defend himself. The smaller of the breed are usually favoured but correct proportions and good musculature are essential.

He makes a faithful pet, not requiring large amounts of exercise or space, but plenty of regular grooming is necessary.

KEY TO CHARACTER	
INTELLIGENCE	***
TEMPERAMENT	****
EASE OF COAT CARE	*
SUITABILITY FOR SMALL DWELLING	*****
***** (5) = VERY GOOD	

BRITISH KENNEL CLUB STANDARD

PEKINGESE

GENERAL APPEARANCE. — Should be a small, well-balanced, thickset dog of great dignity and quality. He should carry himself fearlessly in the ring with an alert, intelligent expression.

Head and Skull. — Head massive, skull broad, wide and flat between the ears, not domed; wide between eyes. Nose very short and broad, nostrils large, open, and black; muzzle wide, well wrinkled, with firm underjaw. Profile should look quite flat with nose well up between the eyes. Deep stop.

Eyes. — Large, round, clear, dark and lustrous. Prominent but not bolting.

Ears. — Heart-shaped, set level with the skull and carried close to the head. Long profuse feathering on ears. Leather not to come below the muzzle.

Mouth. — Level lips, must not show teeth or tongue.

Neck. — Very short and thick.

Forequarters. — Short, thick, heavily-boned forelegs; bones of forelegs bowed but firm at shoulder. Absolute soundness essential.

Body. — Short but with broad chest and good spring of rib, falling away lighter behind; lion-like with distinct waist, level back; well slung between the legs, not on top of them.

Hindquarters. — Hind legs lighter but firm and well shaped. Close behind but now cow-hocked. Absolute soundness essential.

Feet. — Large and flat, not round. The dog should stand well up on feet, not on pasterns. Front feet turned slightly out. Absolute soundness essential.

Gait. — A slow dignified rolling gait in front, with a close gait behind, this typical movement not to be confused with a roll caused by slackness of shoulders.

Tail. — Set high, carried tightly,slightly curved over back to either side. Long feathering.

Coat. — Long and straight with profuse mane extending beyond the shoulders forming a cape or frill round the neck; top coat rather coarse, with thick undercoat. Profuse feathering on ears, legs, thighs, tail and toes.

Colour. — All colours and markings are permissible and equally good, except albino or liver. Parti-colours should be evenly broken.

Weight and Size. — The ideal weight of the Pekingese should not exceed 5 kg. (11 lbs) for dogs and 5½ kg (12 lbs) for bitches. The dog should look small but be surprisingly heavy when picked up; heavy bone and a sturdy well-built body are essentials of the breed.

Note. — Male animals should have two apparently normal testicles fully descended into the scrotum.

MAIN AMERICAN KENNEL CLUB VARIATION TO STANDARD FOR THE PEKINGESE —

Size. — Being a toy dog, medium size preferred, providing type and points are not sacrificed; extreme limit 14 pounds.

PEKINGESE REGISTRATIONS 1981 — 87 INCLUSIVE

1981 — 2650
1982 — 2277
1983 — 2164
1984 — 2049
1985 — 1987
1986 — 1727
1987 — 1733

YET TO WIN CRUFTS BEST-IN-SHOW.

POMERANIAN

The chirpy and attractive little Pomeranian is a scaled down version of his main ancestors, the powerful sledge dogs of the Arctic, the early specimens of which gave rise to all dogs of the Spitz type.

The province of Pomerania in Germany gave the breed it's name as it was there that it was developed into something like it's present form. The early dogs were often white, a colour rarely seen nowadays and much bigger, often weighting six times the weight of modern P'omeranians.

The breed has been popular in Europe for hundreds of years and it was only in 1890 that the Pomeranian took off in Britain. This was due to Queen Victoria's love for the breed and her aquisition of several specimens in that year. Such was the surge in popularity of the Pomeranian, that a breed standard was drawn up a year later and although the dogs of those days were larger, the major points of the standard are unchanged.

The Pomeranian makes a good companion for anyone who might prefer a less demanding breed. Space requirements are minimal and exercise need not be hectic or lengthy, although a daily walk is advised. Although they do revel in human attention, over pampering can result in neurotic nature. Grooming is very important as the double coat is extremely dense. This being said, the coat of the Pomeranian when properly presented is his biggest asset.

KEY TO CHARACTER	
INTELLIGENCE	***
TEMPERAMENT	****
EASE OF COAT CARE	*
SUITABILITY FOR SMALL DWELLING	*****
***** (5) = VERY GOOD	

BRITISH KENNEL CLUB STANDARD
POMERANIAN

GENERAL APPEARANCE. — The Pomeranian in build and appearance should be a compact, short-coupled dog, well knit in frame. He should exhibit great intelligence in his expression, activity and bouyancy in his deportment.

Head and Skull. — The head and nose should be foxy in outline, or wedge-shaped. The skull being slightly flat, large in proportion to the muzzle, which should finish rather fine and be free from lippiness. The hair on the head and face should be smooth and short-coated. The nose should be black in white, orange, and shaded sable dogs; brown in chocolate tipped sable dogs, but in other colours may be "self-coloured", but never parti-coloured or white.

Eyes. — Should be medium in size, slightly oval in shape, not full, not set too wide apart, bright and dark in colour, and showing great intelligence. In white, orange, shaded-sable and cream dogs the rims round the eyes should be black.

Ears. — Should be small, not set too far apart, nor too low down, but carried perfectly erect like those of a fox.

Mouth. — Teeth should be level, and should on no account be undershot, or overshot.

Neck. — Should be rather short and well set in.

Forequarters. — The shoulders should be clean and well laid back. The legs must be well feathered and perfectly straight, of medium length and not such as would be termed "leggy" or "low on leg", but in length and strength in due proportion to a well-balanced frame.

Body. — The back must be short and the body compact, being well ribbed up and the barrel well rounded. The chest must be fairly deep and not too wide but in proportion to the size of the dog.

Hindquarters. — The legs and thighs must be well feathered down to the hocks and must be neither cow-hocked nor wide behind. They must be fine in bone and free in action.

Feet. — The feet should be small and compact in shape.

Tail. — The tail is one of the characteristics of the breed, and should be turned over the back and carried flat and straight, being profusely covered with long, harsh, spreading hair.

Coat. — There should be two coats, an undercoat and an overcoat, the one a soft, fluffy undercoat, the other a long, perfectly straight coat, harsh in texture and covering the whole of the body, being very abundant round the neck and fore-part of the shoulders and chest, where it shall form a frill of profuse off-standing straight hair, extending over the shoulders. The hindquarters should be clad with long hair or feathering from the top of the rump to the hocks.

Colour. — All whole colours are admissible, but they should be free from black or white shadings. At present the whole-coloured dogs are:— white, black, brown, light or dark, blue, as pale as possible. Orange, which should be as self-coloured and bright as possible. Beaver. Cream dogs should have black noses and black rims around the eyes. Whites must be quite free from lemon or any other colour. A few white hairs, in any of the self-coloured dogs, shall not heavily penalise. Dogs (other than white) with white or tan markings, are decidedly objectionable and should be discouraged. They cannot compete as whole coloured specimens. In parti-coloured dogs, the colours should be evenly distributed on the body in patches; a dog with white or tan feet or chest would not be a parti-coloured dog. Shaded-sables should be shaded throughout with three or more colours, the hair to be as uniformly shaded as possible, and with no patches of self-colour. In mixed classes, where whole-coloured and parti-coloured Pomeranians compete together, the preference should, if in other points they are equal, be given to the whole-coloured specimens.

Weight and Size. — 1.8 to 2 kg. (4 to 4½ lbs) for a dog and 2 to 2.5 kg. (4½ to 5½ lbs) for bitches.

Faults. — Undershot or overshot mouths; double jointed; light eyes; off-coloured nose; a tail carried to the side; "hare" feet.

Note. — Male animals should have two apparently normal testicles fully descended into the scrotum.

MAIN AMERICAN KENNEL CLUB VARIATION TO STANDARD FOR THE POMERANIAN —

Size. — The weight of a Pomeranian for exhibition is 3 to 7 pounds. The ideal size for show specimens if from 4 to 5 pounds.

POMERANIAN REGISTRATIONS 1981 — 87 INCLUSIVE

1981 — 1057
1982 — 1078
1983 — 1188
1984 — 1076
1985 — 1099
1986 — 1013
1987 — 1004

YET TO WIN CRUFTS BEST-IN-SHOW.

PUG

There are two basic schools of thought as to the origin of this breed. One is that he has the same ancestry as the Mastiff and Bulldog, the other that he descends from the ancient Chinese stock which gave rise tothe Pekingese and other oriental flat-faced breeds. The latter is the more probable as there are some basic structural differences between Pugs and Mastiff types. Also there is evidence to suggest that Pug-like dogs were present in China many centuries ago and that they, like the Pekingese, were held in an esteem which verged on worship.

Their first introduction to Europe came via Russia and the first western country to initiate a surge in the Pug's popularity was Holland. In the 16th century they imported a great many from China and they became known to Europeans as Dutch Mastiffs.

It was William of Orange who introduced the breed to Britain in the late 17th century. He had visited Holland and become sufficiently fond of the Pug to import a fair number. The breed reached great heights of popularity with the English aristocracy and was definitely in vogue at the time.

The modern Pug owes much of it's current standard to two renowned Victorian breeders, a Lord Willoughby and a Mr. Morrison. The two distinct strains which they created were later merged but their work greatly helped to improve the breed.

The Pug is a friendly, manageable dog. He is naturally clean, adapts excellently to the home and will respond well to sound training. He is not a voracious eater, and can remain healthy without an enormous amount of exercise. Well suited to a sedentary owner.

KEY TO CHARACTER	
INTELLIGENCE	****
TEMPERAMENT	****
EASE OF COAT CARE	*****
SUITABILITY FOR SMALL DWELLING	*****
***** (5) = VERY GOOD	

BRITISH KENNEL CLUB STANDARD

PUG

GENERAL APPEARANCE. — A decidedly square and cobby dog. The Pug should be "multum in parvo", but this condensation should be shown be compactness of form, well-knit proportions, and hardness of developed muscle.

Head and Skull. — Head large, massive, round — not apple-headed, with no indentation of the skull. Muzzle short, blunt, square but not upfaced. Wrinkles large and deep.

Eyes. — Dark in colour, very large, bold and prominent, globular in shape, soft and solicitous in expression, very lustrous, and when excited, full of fire.

Ears. — Thin, small, soft, like black velvet. There are two kinds — the "rose" and the "button". Preference should be given to the latter.

Forequarters. — Legs very strong, straight, of moderate length, and well under the body.

Body. — Short and cobby, wide in chest and well-ribbed.

Hindquarters. — Legs very strong, straight, of moderate length, and well under.

Feet. — Neither so long as the foot of the hare, nor so round as that of the cat; well-split-up toes; the nails black.

Tail. — (Twist). Curled tightly as possible over the hip. The double curl is perfection.

Coat. — Fine, smooth, soft, short and glossy, neither hard nor woolly.

Colour. — Silver, apricot fawn or black. Each should be clearly decided, to make the contrast complete between the colour, the trace and the mask. Markings:— Clearly defined. The muzzle mask, ears, moles on cheeks, thumbmark or diamond on forehead and the trace should be as black as possible. Mask:— The mask should be black, the more intense and well defined, the better. Trace:— A black line extending from the occiput to the twist.

Weight and Size. — Desirable weight from 6.4 to 8.2 kg. (14 to 18 lbs) (dog or bitch).

Faults. — Lean, leggy. Short legs and long body.

Note. — Male animals should have two apparently normal testicles fully descended into the scrotum.

PUG REGISTRATIONS 1981 — 87 INCLUSIVE

1981 — 632
1982 — 512
1983 — 594
1984 — 649
1985 — 619
1986 — 713
1987 — 700

YET TO WIN CRUFTS BEST-IN-SHOW.

YORKSHIRE TERRIER

One of the most lively and appealing of the toy breeds, the "Yorkie" has remained extremely popular for many years. Their elegant, sometimes pampered appearance is rather deceptive as they were originally bred to control rats. They first came on the scene some 100 years ago in Yorkshire and were developed by working men probably around the Halifax region. The exact lineage of the Yorkshire Terrier is not clear but it seems fairly certain that the Skye, Old English and Scottish Terrier of the time were used, with possibly Cairn Terrier and Maltese, the latter having been frequently brought into Yorkshire by returning seamen. One reason for the "Yorkie's" uncertain origins is that the people who first bred him deliberately kept their breeding methods to themselves in order to create a more unique and therefore more saleable dog.

When first exhibited at shows they were sometimes referred to as Scotch Terriers or Broken-Haired Terriers, but the name was standardised to "Yorkshire Terrier" in 1886 and the breed was registered officially in 1898.

When choosing a "Yorkie", smaller puppies are favoured and they should be light in the bone, this being desirable as the breed has been consistently reduced in size so that the current mature weight limit is 7 lb.

The Yorkshire Terrier's most striking feature is undoubtedly his coat, and to be maintained correctly much care and attention is imperative. The layman, might believe that the tying of a ribbon on a "Yorkie's" head is merely unnecessary decoration, but in fact it serves to keep his long coat from his eyes.

KEY TO CHARACTER	
INTELLIGENCE	***
TEMPERAMENT	***
EASE OF COAT CARE	*
SUITABILITY FOR SMALL DWELLING	*****
***** (5) = VERY GOOD	

BRITISH KENNEL CLUB STANDARD

YORKSHIRE TERRIER

GENERAL APPEARANCE. — Should be that of a long-coated toy terrier, the coat hanging quite straight and evenly down each side, a parting extending from the nose to the end of the tail. The animal should be very compact and neat, the carriage being very upright and conveying an "important" air. The general outline should convey the impression of a vigorous and well-proportioned body.

Head and Skull. — Head should be rather small and flat, not too prominent or round in the skull, nor too long in the muzzle, with a perfect black nose. The fall on the head to be long, of a rich golden tan, deeper in colour at the sides of the head about the ear roots, and on the muzzle where it should be very long. On no account must the tan on the head extend on to the neck, nor must there be any sooty or dark hair intermingled with any of the tan.

Eyes. — Medium, dark and sparkling, having a sharp intelligent expression, and placed so as to look directly forward. They should not be prominent and the edge of the eyelids should be of a dark colour.

Ears. — Small V-shaped, and carried erect or semi-erect, and not far apart, covered with short hair, colour to be of a very deep rich tan.

Mouth. — Perfectly even, with teeth as sound as possible. An animal having lost any teeth through accident not to be faulted providing the jaws are even.

Forequarters. — Legs quite straight, well covered with hair of a rich golden tan a few shades lighter at the ends than at the roots, not extending higher on the forelegs than the elbow.

Body. — Very compact with a good loin. Level on the top of the back.

Hindquarters. — Legs quite straight, well covered with hair of a rich golden tan, a few shades lighter at the ends than at the roots, not extending higher on the hind legs than the stifle.

Feet. — As round as possible; the toe-nails black.

Tail. — Cut to medium length; with plenty of hair, darker blue in colour than the rest of the body, especially at the end of the tail, and carried a little higher than the level of the back.

Coat. — The hair on the body moderately long and perfectly straight (not wavy), glossy like silk, and of a fine silky texture.

Colour. — A dark steel blue (not silver blue), extending from the occiput (or back of skull) to the root of tail, and on no account mingled with fawn, bronze or dark hairs. The hair on the chest a rich bright tan. All tan hair should be darker at the roots than in the middle, shading to a still lighter tan at the tips.

Weight and Size. — Weight up to 3.2 kg. (7 lbs).

Note. — Male animals should have two apparently normal testicles fully descended into the scrotum.

YORKSHIRE TERRIER REGISTRATIONS 1981 — 87 INCLUSIVE

1981 — 14149
1982 — 12755
1983 — 12407
1984 — 11788
1985 — 12141
1986 — 10637
1987 — 10241

YET TO WIN CRUFTS BEST-IN-SHOW.